S0-BEZ-290

VOTE
FOR
WOMEN
THE
DIVISION
IN
THE
WOMENS
MOVEMENT
ONLY A FIGURE OF SPEECH.
Votes !

British Commemoratives

Commemoratives for W.G. Grace, the famous cricketer who scored 1016 runs in May 1895 (see page 97).

British Commemoratives

ROYALTY, POLITICS, WAR AND SPORT

Lincoln Hallinan

ANTIQUE COLLECTORS' CLUB

ISBN 1 85149 129 5

British Library CIP data
A catalogue record for this book is available from the British Library

Printed in England on Consort Royal Satin from Donside Mills, Aberdeen
by Antique Collectors' Club Limited, Woodbridge, Suffolk IP12 1DS

The Antique Collectors' Club

The Antique Collectors' Club was formed in 1966 and quickly grew to a five figure membership spread throughout the world. It publishes the only independently run monthly antiques magazine, *Antique Collecting*, which caters for those collectors who are interested in widening their knowledge of antiques, both by greater awareness of quality and by discussion of the factors which influence the price that is likely to be asked. The Antique Collectors' Club pioneered the provision of information on prices for collectors and the magazine still leads in the provision of detailed articles on a variety of subjects.

It was in response to the enormous demand for information on 'what to pay' that the price guide series was introduced in 1968 with the first edition of *The Price Guide to Antique Furniture* (completely revised 1978 and 1989), a book which broke new ground by illustrating the more common types of antique furniture, the sort that collectors could buy in shops and at auctions rather than the rare museum pieces which had previously been used (and still to a large extent are used) to make up the limited amount of illustrations in books published by commercial publishers. Many other price guides have followed, all copiously illustrated, and greatly appreciated by collectors for the valuable information they contain, quite apart from prices. The Price Guide Series heralded the publication of many standard works of reference on art and antiques. *The Dictionary of British Art* (now in six volumes), *The Pictorial Dictionary of British 19th Century Furniture Design, Oak Furniture* and *Early English Clocks* were followed by many deeply researched reference works such as *The Directory of Gold and Silversmiths,* providing new information. Many of these books are now accepted as the standard work of reference on their subject.

The Antique Collectors' Club has widened its list to include books on gardens and architecture. All the Club's publications are available through bookshops world wide and a full catalogue of all these titles is available free of charge from the addresses below.

Club membership, open to all collectors, costs little. Members receive free of charge *Antique Collecting*, the Club's magazine (published ten times a year), which contains well-illustrated articles dealing with the practical aspects of collecting not normally dealt with by magazines. Prices, features of value, investment potential, fakes and forgeries are all given prominence in the magazine.

Among other facilities available to members are private buying and selling facilities, the longest list of 'For Sales' of any antiques magazine, an annual ceramics conference and the opportunity to meet other collectors at their local antique collectors' clubs. There are over eighty in Britain and more than a dozen overseas. Members may also buy the Club's publications at special pre-publication prices.

As its motto implies, the Club is an organisation designed to help collectors get the most out of their hobby: it is informal and friendly and gives enormous enjoyment to all concerned.

For Collectors —By Collectors —About Collecting

ANTIQUE COLLECTORS' CLUB
5 Church Street, Woodbridge Suffolk IP12 1DS, UK
Tel: 01394 385501 Fax: 01394 384434
or
Market Street Industrial Park, Wappingers' Falls, NY 12590, USA
Tel: 914 297 0003 Fax: 914 297 0068

Dedicated By Her Gracious Permission To
Her Majesty Queen Elizabeth The Queen Mother

Contents

A selection of Boer War commemoratives (see page 103).

Foreword

Memorabilia is a contemporary record of national events and characters.

The ideal is a ceramic record in the form of a commemorative piece. But not every event or important person is the subject of a ceramic. Silver, glass and metal are also used, though not in such quantity. Biscuit, tea and chocolate tins produced by some of the well-known manufacturers have played a huge part since the beginning of the century and have provided us with an inexpensive means of taking part in national events. In addition, some of the better known confectioners have done the same thing with their chocolate boxes, all reflecting the period in which they were produced.

Perhaps the least appreciated and yet the most available commemorative is contemporary ephemera, such as magazines and postcards, cigarette cards and playing cards. Many an event not recorded ceramically has been rescued from oblivion by ephemeral items that have contributed to the interest the nation holds for memorabilia.

The field is vast and no book can hope to cover every item produced. From pre-Victorian times events not thought to have been recorded can suddenly turn up from the least expected source.

This book seeks to give a representative picture of the life of the nation in the form of memorabilia.

Selection of commemoratives for Lloyd George (see page 155).

Queen Elizabeth II coronation commemoratives (see page 254).

Acknowledgements

The author wishes to acknowledge the help given by John May, who allowed him to use his most valuable notes. To Steven Jackson, Secretary of the Commemorative Collectors' Society for supplying much information and photographs of recent commemorative pieces, and to his two daughters Julia and Teresa for transcribing the manuscript.

He also wishes to thank The Victoria & Albert Museum, The London Museum, The City of Birmingham Museum, Helen Davies of Cadbury's Limited, Narisa Chakra, James Blewitt, Eric Knowles of Bonham's and Peter Jones China, Wakefield for the loan of photographs. Eric Williams, Dr Margot Richards, Mrs Peter Halewood and Mrs Joanna Cory kindly loaned items to be photographed. Thanks also to Mike Woodward of Terence Soames Limited, Cardiff for taking all but a few of the photographs.

CHAPTER 1

The Stuarts, Georges and William IV

The people of England, bruised by Civil War and tired of the puritanical rule of Cromwell and the Commonwealth, wanted to have their King returned.

The restoration of Charles II was the cause of such public celebration that a permanent record was sought. The manufacture of commemorative pottery began and has continued ever since.

The purpose of a commemorative is to record, in permanent form, events and individuals who played an important part in the life of the nation. A true commemorative must be contemporaneous with the event, concluding with the death of important national figures. A strict adherence to this concept would exclude, for example, pieces which have been produced to commemorate the hundredth anniversary of the Battle of Trafalgar, the birth of Churchill, the productions for the 150th anniversary of the Coronation of Queen Victoria and the recent pieces to commemorate the Tercentenary of the Glorious Revolution of 1688. A commemorative record should end with the actual event itself, or the death of a national figure. To extend this concept for perhaps commercial rather than commemorative purpose would offend the principle, which is a contemporary record.

A case can be properly made for pieces specially commissioned for age-old centenaries of our cathedrals, churches or abbeys, as part of a means of providing funds for restoration purposes. Spode produced a number of fine quality pieces for this reason and though to be commended, they ought not to be regarded as strictly contemporary commemorative pieces. Commemoratives cover various aspects: royalty, militaria, politics and miscellaneous subjects, such as exhibitions.

The earliest commemoratives were either of delft or slipware and in some cases majolica. English delft started as a result of a petition by two Dutchmen to Queen Elizabeth for permission to set up a pottery in London. This later spread to Bristol, and once established was to continue until the end of the eighteenth century. Although there are some early English delft plates, those for Charles I were probably not manufactured during his reign and it was not until the coronation of Charles II that they became popular.

Slipware was the name given to an earthenware which was decorated with contrasting lines and dots, the most famous pottery being Thomas Toft. Commemoratives for the last Stuarts are very rare, although they occasionally appear in

***Plate 1.(left)** London majolica charger. 13in (33cm) diameter.*
Victoria and Albert Museum

***Plate 2.** Two London delft wine cups produced in 1660, the year of accession, and 1661, Coronation year.* The London Museum

Plate 3. *English delft bleeding bowl. 5in (14cm) diameter.* Birmingham City Museum

Plate 4. *Bristol delft plate with half-length portraits of William and Mary, 8¼in (22cm) diameter.*

Plate 5. *Bristol delft charger showing full-length portraits of William III in armour. 13in. (33cm) diameter.*

Victoria and Albert Museum

Plate 6. *Bristol delft plaque of Queen Anne. 9in (22.9cm) x 7in. (18.4cm).* Victoria and Albert Museum

Plate 7. *London delft plate commemorating the Act of Union with Scotland in 1707, monogram 'AR'. 9in. (22.9cm) diameter.*

Plate 8. *Delft plate for George I. 9in (22.9cm) diameter.*

Plate 9. *Worcester porcelain mug printed in black by Robert Hancock with profile bust of George II after Thomas Wolridge. 3in. (8.5cm) diameter.*

Plate 10. *Chinese export porcelain mug 'Victory at Culloden April 6th, 1746'. 6in. (15.9cm) high.*

auction houses. Some are in private collections and others in various museums. Those for Charles II vary between the handsome charger (Plate 1) which portrays the King in full robes wearing a crown, with the initials CR and the date 1660, to the smaller wine cup (Plate 2) which normally shows his head and shoulders, also wearing the crown, the royal monogram and the date. For his marriage to the Portuguese Princess, Catherine of Braganza, there is at least one known majolica charger, now in the Victoria and Albert Museum. Majolica was first produced in Italy, but later manufacture took place in Holland. The charger contains half-length portraits of Charles and Queen Catherine within a trophy of arms and a border of fantastic animals to commemorate their marriage in 1663.

The King's marriage to Catherine of Braganza was childless, but he made full use of mistresses, most of whom were made Duchesses and whose offspring were made Dukes. The most famous of his many natural children, born out of wedlock as a result of his liaisons, was the Duke of Monmouth, from whose marriage into the Buccleuch family are descended the present Duchess of York and also Alice, Duchess of Gloucester. On his death he was succeeded by his brother, the Duke of York, James II, for whom there is very little recorded ceramically, although there is known to be an English delft bleeding bowl (Plate 3), made either in Lambeth or Brislington, in the Birmingham City Museum. The bowl bears a half-length portrait of James II inscribed 'IR2' with a laurel wreath. The handle bears the initials PNM and the date 1686, the year following the Coronation.

Only four pieces for James II are known to have been recorded. There seems to be nothing to record either of his marriages, first to Anne Hyde, the mother of the last two Stuart Queens, Mary and Anne, or to his second wife, Mary of Modena who was the mother of the Old Pretender. Unhappily there also appears to be nothing to record the Glorious Revolution which resulted in the landing of William III at Torbay to claim the throne of England.

For William and Mary, who were first cousins, being grandchildren of King Charles I and both of whom had a claim to the English throne, there are some commemoratives, though not many. They are normally shown together, both wearing crowns and the initials WMR. There is an English delft plate (Plate 4) with half-length portraits of William and Mary wearing crowns with the initials WMR underneath probably made for the Coronation circa 1689. In the Victoria and Albert Museum is a Bristol delft charger (Plate 5) for the coronation of William III. This is a fine charger, showing the King in full coronation regalia, his robes over a suit of armour, wearing his crown and carrying the orb and sceptre with the initials WR. This was probably produced during the reign but after the Battle of the Boyne as the armour would suggest a soldier King. It is not known whether a similar charger was manufactured for Mary. After the death of Mary, William reigned alone until he was succeeded in 1702 by Mary's sister Anne, for whom there are few commemoratives.

The Victoria and Albert Museum is fortunate in having a very fine Bristol delft plaque (Plate 6) which shows a likeness of Queen Anne after a portrait by Sir Godfrey Kneller, the famous portrait-painter of the period, dated 1704 and initialled AR. But perhaps the most interesting commemorative piece for the reign of Queen Anne is a delft plate (Plate 7) commemorating the Act of Union with Scotland. This can probably be regarded as the first political commemorative. The plate features the English rose and the Scottish thistle, surmounted by the initials AR with the crown in between. It should be pointed out that although many of these delft plates had a somewhat primitive appearance, they are a most important part of commemorative history.

With the coming of the Hanoverian dynasty there is little to commemorate George I. The Elector of Hanover, directly descended from James I, brought with him a mistress, having disposed of his wife in Ahlden Castle and for whom there are a few commemoratives, also of delft. One is printed with the inscription 'God Save King George 1716' (Plate 8) decorated with a blue band and two thin blue bands.

With the accession of George II the commemorative field did improve. An early Worcester mug (Plate 9) bears the head and shoulders of the King, taken from an engraving and surmounted by a crown, and a child sitting on a cannon which displays various weapons of war and flags. Underneath is the word 'Liberty'.

The 1745 Jacobite Rebellion is featured on a Chinese export tankard (Plate 10) which bears the head and shoulders of the Duke of Cumberland, surrounded by the words 'Victory at Culloden, April 16th, 1746'. There are few, if any, other commemoratives recorded for the Duke of Cumberland. He was not so successful when, on the 11th May 1745, the pragmatic army of which he was officer in command led a 44,000 strong army in a frontal attack on 76,000 Frenchmen at Fontenoy. The British fought valiantly but were finally halted and were then repulsed by the emergence of the Jacobite Irish Brigade. Marshal Saxe, who commanded the French Army, proceeded to overrun most of Flanders and the British were put to shame. The French factory at Sèvres produced a very fine plate (Plate 11), depicting the meeting between the Duke of Cumberland and Marshal Saxe after the battle. It is highly decorated, the Marshal depicted on horseback and the Duke almost pleading in front of him. Around are soldiers in red and in blue coats, a highly colourful scene. It may well be that the actual painting was done later than the plate itself, but whether or not that is the case, it is a magnificent commemorative of a battle in which the British army took part. This Duke was the First Duke of Cumberland who died without an heir. The Second Duke, the brother of George III, also had no heir and the Third Duke was the son of George III, Ernest, who ultimately became King of Hanover. It would appear that the only Cumberland commemorated was the First.

Ministers of the Crown and Political Figures and Events

Few, if any, political items were produced for the late Stuarts and George I and none for Sir Robert Walpole or for the South Sea Bubble. The political field is rather better covered in the reign of George II. This is fortunate because it was during his reign that the Great Pitt, William the Elder, later Earl of Chatham, became one of England's greatest statesmen. Some commemoratives do exist for William Pitt.

Plate 11. *Plate of Sèvres porcelain portraying the meeting of the Duke of Cumberland and Marshal Saxe after the Battle of Fontenoy in 1745.*

There is a bell-shaped mug (Plate 12A), of creamware, probably Cockpit Hill, black-printed with a fine portrait of the Elder Pitt. The print is captioned in a scroll cartouche: 'The Right Honourable William Pitt Esquire'. This mug is very probably the earliest creamware political commemorative known. It is not certain when it was made, but it clearly must have been before 1766 when he received his title. The actual date of manufacture of this mug is uncertain, but various possibilities exist. It may in fact have been produced for the coronation of George III, on the other hand it may have been before but clearly, as Pitt was the greatest statesman in the reign of George II, it is right and proper that it should be included among commemoratives of that King's reign.

Another mug (Plate 12B) is for the first period Worcester, probably Doctor Wall, showing a print of William Pitt engraved by Hancock, flanked by Hancock's engravings of fame and war and this was probably made about 1758.

Various plaques (Plate 13) were also produced. These were presumably either shipped up from the Birmingham Wolverhampton area or they may have been made locally. No certainty exists as to the source of supply of the undecorated enamels, but as they have a distinctive character of their own, a cold tone in the enamel, it is quite possible that they were obtained locally.

Election plates, mostly of delft, were manufactured during

Plate 12A. *Creamware bell-shaped mug with bust of William Pitt the Elder. 4in. (10.2cm) high.* ***B.*** *1st period Worcester small cylindrical tankard, with bust of William Pitt after William Hancock, 1758. 3in. (8.5cm) high.*

this King's reign, perhaps the earliest being a delft, probably of Bristol, wine cup (Plate 14), painted in blue with a political inscription – 'Mansell for Ever'. Bussy Mansell first stood for Parliament in the by-election of January 1727, as a result of the death of the sitting member, Edward Stradling, who was the nominee of the Tory Windsors of Cardiff Castle. He contested the seat successfully in 1727 but in 1734 was ousted by the Windsor family, who acquired the seat for Herbert Windsor, who had by then come of age. Mansell transferred his political hopes to Glamorgan, which was in fact the traditional seat of the Mansell family, who had occupied it from 1670 to 1712. Bussy was unsuccessful in 1734, losing to the Whig, William Talbot, son of the Lord Chancellor, but when Talbot inherited his father's title later that year, Mansell acquired the seat, and then held it successfully until his own elevation to the peerage in 1745.

There is also a delft plate (Plate 15) bearing the words 'Rolle for Ever'. The Rolles were one of the leading families in Devon. They represented various Devon constituencies, almost in unbroken sequence from Elizabethan times. The Rolle mentioned on this plate is one of those from the first half of the eighteenth century. The father, John, and his son Henry stood unopposed most of the time and so it was unlikely that they bothered to electioneer, let alone issue plates. But on two occasions in the period this plate fits into, the father and son broke with this idle precedent. The first was in 1722. John Rolle had stood for Saltash in 1703-05, for the county seat from 1710-13, for Exeter in 1713-15 and for his local seat of Barnstaple from 1715-22. Then suddenly the stalwart Tory seat of Exeter came under attack from the Whigs and at the instigation of the City Corporation Rolle came back to Exeter for the 1722 election to defend it,

Plate 13. *Liverpool enamel oval plaque painted by Sadler and Green with three-quarter bust portrait of the Rt. Hon. William Pitt.*

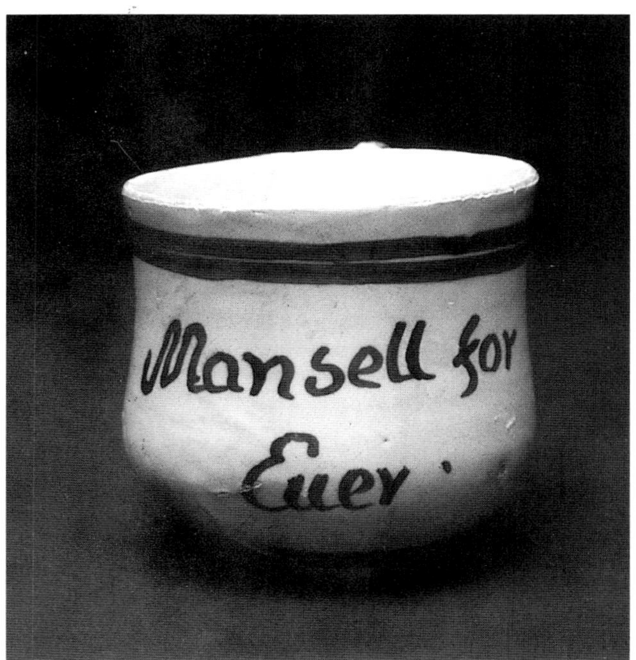

Plate 14. *Small English delft blue and white bell-shaped cup inscribed 'Mansell for Ever'.*

Plate 15. *Bristol delft blue and white plate inscribed 'Rolle for Ever'. 8in (20.3cm) diameter.*

Plate 16. Bristol delft blue and white woolsack pattern plate inscribed 'Sir John Pole for Ever 1754'. 9in (22.9cm) diameter.

Plate 17. English delft manganese woolsack plate inscribed below a heart 'Calvert and Martin for Tukesbury'. 9in (22.9cm) diameter.

successfully, against two local Whig candidates. The votes cast are interesting, and show the small electoral roll of that period: John Rolle and Francis Brown, both Conservative, polled 887 and 806 respectively, and Samuel Molineux and Charles Stewart – both Whigs – polled 665 and 664 respectively. In 1741 Rolle's son Henry stood for Barnstaple. He had, on the death of his father in 1730, adopted the County seat to which John had reverted after his five year stint at Exeter. But in the election of 1741 Henry switched his allegiance from the Tories to the Whigs, forfeited the safe county seat and now stood as a Whig for the family seat of Barnstaple. Because the family had the seat pretty much in their pockets he was unopposed, but it would be very understandable if in these circumstances he had decided to electioneer with verve and vigour and to have had campaign plates made. If this is when these plates were produced, then they equal the earliest recorded delft electioneering plates, 'Fortescue for Ever' issued to support the cause of Theophilius Fortescue, who, replacing Rolle, stood for the county seat in 1741. This plate might well fit either date. The decoration is what is called the Merriman cartouche. This is recorded as early as 1722 and as late as 1742.

A delft plate (Plate 16) exists for the election of Sir John Pole in 1754 inscribed 'Sir John Pole for Ever'. This was published for his election at Taunton. Another Bristol delft plate (Plate 17) like the Pole plate, painted in blue and sponged with manganese, is ornamented with the legend 'Calvert and Martin for Tukesbury', sold by Webb. The powder blue border is bedecked with four panels of oriental fishermen. This was published for the 1754 Election. John Martin and Nicholson Calvert were both Independent Whigs. Martin first stood for the seat in 1734 – unsuccessfully – but was a member from 1741-47. He did not contest the seat in 1747 but was re-elected in 1754. Calvert represented the constituency from 1754-68.

Election plates for the reign of George II are comparatively rare and are mostly found in private collections or in museums.

George III

During this reign matters improved. His coronation was commemorated in ceramic form. There is a creamware moulded tea caddy (Plate 18) decorated in Whieldon glazes of brown and green, of hexagonal sections with domes, shoulders and pointed cover, the side panels embossed and coloured with half-length portraits of George III and Queen Charlotte with beaded green and yellow frames, the ground painted with sprays of roses and other flowers, the neck collar with a chain. The King's portrait was inspired by Billing's engraving of Morland's painting of the King when Prince of Wales. The Queen's is from an engraving by Thomas Frye.

A creamware teapot (Plate 19) was produced for the capture of Cuba on 18th August, 1762, under the command of the Earl of Albemarle. Manufactured by Wedgwood, it was printed by John Sadler from plates engraved by William Billings in 1762. On one side is a portrait of the King and on the other, the Queen. The interesting feature lies in the small map of Cuba with the word 'Havana'.

The invention of creamware by Josiah Wedgwood considerably increased the amount of commemorative pottery. Creamware produced little wastage as it was far easier to decorate and transfers were much easier to apply.

The King's recovery from insanity was the subject of many commemorative pieces. The government of the day was anxious to ensure that the public realised that the King had recovered, in an attempt to foil the efforts by Fox and the Prince of Wales, later George IV, to proclaim a Regency. A

Plate 18. *Creamware tea canister and cover for Coronation.*

pearlware bowl (Plate 20), printed in underglazed blue, features a design of Britannia holding a medallion portrait of George III. The print is inscribed, 'Britons Rejoice in this Grand Thing, Protect Your Country and Your King'.

There is an attractive dish (Plate 21) with a small monogram bearing the King in a cartouche surmounted by a crown with the words 'Felicitas Publica'. This dish bears the impressed mark of Wedgwood Burslem. A ten inch diameter creamware plate, printed in red, with the royal coat of arms of George III, is inscribed below with: 'Long Live the King and Queen and Prosperity to the Nation'. This may well have been published in 1793 and pairs with a plate, only one of which is known, showing a man-of-war and the slogan 'Britannia rule the waves – Success to the British Fleet'. This plate may either be part of the Tory propaganda to record the King's recovery or it may be attributed to the propaganda for

Plate 19. *Creamware teapot for the capture of Cuba marking the acquisition in 1762.*

Plate 20. *Pearlware bowl recording the recovery of George III from madness.*

the war with France.

The marriage between King George and Queen Charlotte seemed a happy one. Prior to this there had been some suggestion that he had secretly married Hannah Lightfoot, who came from Wapping, and there had also been some talk of a liaison with Lady Sarah Lennox, but once he settled down, to all intents and purposes it was a successful marriage.

They had sixteen children, but very few have been ceramically recorded. His eldest son, later George IV, has been the subject of commemorative pieces. His second son, Frederick, Duke of York, who took a prominent part in the war with France, is also the subject of some military pieces. A very fine bust of the Duke (Plate 22), head and shoulders, in white, on a plinth embellished with gold, on a separate stand with gold embellishments, was manufactured by Samuel Alcock of Cobridge, bearing a mark which contains the words 'Improved Porcelain'.

Whereas there are no commemoratives of the extra-marital relationships between Charles II and his many mistresses, there is one for the association between the Duke of York and Mrs Clarke. It is a jug of creamware (Plate 23), trimmed with silver lustre, black printed, with, on one side, a fine portrait of Mrs Clarke captioned 'Mrs Clarke, the late favourite lady of HRH the Duke of York', set within a decorated and inscribed frame, and on the other side a long and laudatory inscription. This was probably published around 1810, at the time that Colonel Wardell inspired scandal in the House about the sale of commissions. It is a pity that similar pieces were not recorded for Mrs Jordan to record her long association with King William IV, when Duke of Clarence, who bore a large number of Fitzclarences, or for Madame de St Laurent, the mistress of the Duke of Kent, before he married the mother of Queen Victoria.

The Duke of York died at Arlington House on 5th January 1827. Some commemorative pieces exist, the most common

Plate 21. *Lozenge-shaped creamware dish, also for the King's recovery. 10¾in. (27.5cm) diameter.*

Plate 22. *Porcelain bust of Frederick, Duke of York. 8¾in. (22cm) high.*

Plate 23. *Creamware jug for Mrs Clarke, favourite lady of the Duke of York.*

Plate 24. *Engraving showing funeral procession of Frederick, Duke of York, at St. George's Chapel, Windsor, 20th January, 1827.*

Plate 25. *Porcelain vase bearing portrait of the Duke of Kent and on the reverse a portrait of Prince Leopold of Saxe-Coburg.*

showing a sorrowing soldier, bearing an inscription 'In Memory of HRH Frederick, Duke of York, KG'. There is also known to exist a black transfer plate with a bust portrait, captioned 'Frederick, Duke of York', with the date of his birth, August 16th 1763, and that of his death.

A coloured engraving (Plate 24) was printed and published showing the funeral procession of the Duke, his coffin, under black draped funereal canopy, being borne behind two divines wearing the wigs common at the time, and led by a herald, captioned 'Funeral Procession of His Late Royal Highness, the Duke of York in St George's Chapel, Windsor, January 20th, 1827'.

King George's third son, the Duke of Clarence, was the subject of several commemoratives after he became King William IV. The fourth son, the Duke of Kent, father of Queen Victoria, has not been the subject of much commemorative pottery. There is, however, one vase (Plate 25), probably produced for the death of King George III, because it carried a black rim around its lip. It bears on one side a purple head and shoulders portrait of the Duke and on the other, Prince Leopold of Saxe Coburg, the husband of Princess Charlotte. There is reputed to be a plaque of Ernest, Duke of Cumberland and his wife, although it is uncertain where this can be verified. Nothing appears to exist for any of his daughters, with the exception of poor Princess Amelia who was born on 7th August, 1783 and died on 2nd November 1810. There is a rather sad engraving (Plate 26) of the Princess which was engraved by H.S. Agar from a miniature painted by Anne Mees which is stated to be in the possession of the Duke of Sussex, to whom this print is most respectfully dedicated by his Royal Highness's most devoted and humble servant, R. Ackerman. It was published on 6th November 1810 at Ackerman's Repository of Arts in the Strand and shows the head and shoulders of the late Princess surmounted by a crown in a frame which was obviously the miniature of her tomb, bearing her name and the dates of her birth and death inscribed, supported by two weeping cherubs. This may not be a ceramic commemorative, but it is at least contemporary and some effort has been made to record something of this unhappy Princess.

The War with France

This war has been ceramically recorded in many forms, one of the objects being to draw the people's attention to the dangers of the French Revolution and the importance of maintaining the Constitution and the Monarchy. Several jugs were manufactured to record the Duke of York's part in the war and there are some interesting scenes by way of transfer, in particular to celebrate his success at Valenciennes,

Plate 26. *Engraving of Princess Amelia recording her death on 2nd November, 1810.*

Plate 27. *Pearlware bowl on shell foot, the interior printed in blue with a double portrait of George and Charlotte inscribed 'A King Revered, a Queen Beloved. Long May They Live'. 7½in (19cm) diameter.*

Plate 28. *Staffordshire pearlware blue and white bowl, the interior printed with an anti-Revolution verse, propaganda from the war with France. 11in (27.9cm) diameter.*

Plate 29. *Black printed tankard captioned: 'The Contrast 1793 – French or British Liberty'. 6in (15cm) high.*

including General O'Hara before he was taken prisoner by the French in 1793. Most of these are in creamware and include tankards bearing, in some cases, the inscription 'Success to the Duke of York'. There is a bowl (Plate 27), blue underglaze printed, with the classic inscription of King George II and Queen Charlotte and captioned 'A King revered, a Queen beloved, Long may they Live'; the whole contained within a cartouche of laurels and with the bold inscription 'King and Constitution' flanking all. A very fine punchbowl (Plate 28), blue decorated, bears in the centre the words 'God Grant Us Grace to Love the King and pray for his Long Life and keep from democratic wolves his children and his wife, a bumper now my verse shall end, here goes to Church and State and he that will not drink his health shall have it on his pate'.

A black printed tankard (Plate 29), captioned 'The Contrast 1793 – which is best', has on one side 'British Liberty' and the other 'French Liberty'. 'British Liberty' shows a seated Britannia holding the scales with a sleeping lion, the Magna Carta, and a man-of-war, all within a circle, with the motto 'Religion, Morality, Loyalty, obedience to the laws, Independence, personal security, Justice, inheritence, protection, property, industry, national prosperity and HAPPINESS'. 'French Liberty' shows a Medusa-headed woman holding the Gorgon's head and underneath are the words 'Atheism, perjury, rebellion, treason, anarchy, murder, inequality, madness, cruelty, injustice, treachery, ingratitude, idleness, famine, national and private ruin and MISERY'. It is a graphic description of the difference between the revolutionaries in France and the freedom of England.

An even more graphic commemorative is a creamware mug (Plate 30) portraying the actual execution of the King of France, entitled 'Massacre and Execution of Louis XVI, King of France, January 21st 1793 aged 32 years 4 months, an event most wonderful of the history of the world'. Four figures surround the guillotine, two executioners, one holding up the severed head of the King with the words 'Behold the head of a tyrant' and de Feimand, Confessor to the King, and the Commandant General de Santere. The name of the engraver appears to be S. Aynsley. It is a most

Plate 30. *Cylindrical creamware mug depicting the gruesome details of the guillotining of Louis XVI of France.*

Plate 31. *Staffordshire mug entitled 'A New Puzzle of Portraits'. 3¾in. (9.5cm) high.*

gruesome record of a melancholy event.

Another interesting mug (Plate 31) is entitled 'A New Puzzle of Portraits'. This shows the silhouetted heads of the King and Queen of England and the King and Queen of France. Above the English sovereigns is the British crown and the English rose and surmounting the French sovereigns is the fleur-de-lis. Beneath appear the words 'Striking Likenesses of the King and Queen of England and the late King and Queen of France'. This mug is attributed to Swansea.

A creamware jug (Plate 32), black printed, shows on one side a mounted portrait of King William III, Prince of Orange, in military dress. The portrait is surmounted by the crown and panoply of war. On the other side is a very fine portrait of King George III, also surmounted by the crown and by various war-like symbols, with the inscription 'George III King of Britain'. A particular feature of this print is a small lion befouling the French flag (Plate 32B). This was clearly published in 1793 at the outbreak of war. It is a rare print and, it would appear, has previously only been recorded on one creamware mug in a private collection.

There were many commemoratives produced for both Wellington and Nelson. These are mostly in the hands of private collectors and museums and are not easily obtained.

An interesting aspect of the commemoratives for the Duke

Plate 32. *Creamware ovoid jug with profile bust of George III. The reverse with the equestrian figure of King William III. 6¾in. (17cm) high.*

of Wellington is that each of his various stages in the peerage are commemorated. His viscountcy and dukedom are in fact commemorated on the same Liverpool jug, manufactured by the famous Herculanean factory. His earldom is also recorded on a jug and his marquisite is commemorated on a jug celebrating his victory at Salamanca (Plate 33). The creamware jug has a coloured painting of Wellington on his horse, called Copenhagen, facing a castle. On the left is Salamanca, with a painting of part of the town with cathedral, all captioned 'Marquis Wellington'. On the reverse is the same castle with a field gun and the inscription reads 'The greatest General of the age Marquis Wellington, Duke of Cuidad Rodrigo who defeated the French at every engagement and gained Honour to the British Arms at Talavera, Busaco, Albuera, Cuidad Rodrigo, Salamanca, who drove the French out of Portugal and was successful in rescuing Spain out of the Usurper's hands.' The rim, spout and handle are in a design of puce lustre.

In 1802 there was a break in hostilities culminating in the Peace of Amiens, commemorated by two very interesting and attractive tankards. One is from Bristol (Plate 34A), captioned 'Preliminaries of Peace signed October 1st 1810'. This portrays the Goddess of Peace, holding an olive branch, standing amongst sheaves of corn and a cornucopia, overlooking the sea and various warships. It is purple in colour and there is a gold design around the whole of the mug. A beaker (Plate 34B) commemorating the actual peace was manufactured by Worcester, of the Chamberlain period, and is even more attractive than the one for the preliminaries. It is highly decòrated and in the centre there is a plinth, upon which rests the head of the King, George III, the plinth carrying the word 'Peace' and supported on one side by a British admiral and on the other by a British general. Above the King are two angels bearing the crown. On the right, adjoining the admiral, are warships and on the left are the pyramids of the Nile. Beneath are two angels, the globe, a trident and various other items. The whole beaker is decorated with gold bands. This panel is highly coloured and the reverse, together with the gold embellishment, is in a shade of orange.

Napoleon Bonaparte is commemorated on several pieces. Of some interest is a pair of canary coloured jugs allegedly manufactured by Swansea Pottery. The first is entitled 'Peace and Plenty' and shows a British country yokel celebrating and drinking, presumably to peace; one man holding a large tankard of beer, and on the barrel are the words '200 gallons brewed by John Bull at the beginning of the war and to be drunk on the first day of peace'. The second (Plate 35) is captioned 'Bonaparte dethroned April 1st 1814', which shows that these two jugs were issued to record the banishment of Bonaparte to Elba. It shows Bonaparte and various British people with balloon cartoons. The one perhaps most appropriate to the jug itself is 'Where is he going to?' and the reply: 'To Elba'.

The final record of the end of this war is recorded on a mug (Plate 36) marked from Bristol pottery, decorated in polychrome with a design representing peace and plenty, backed by the flags of Britain and the restored Bourbon monarchy in France, flanking an ornate obelisk inscribed 'Peace in Europe signed at Paris, May 30th 1814', the last topped by a triumphant laurel surrounding the royal cipher.

The Grand National Jubilee. King George III – Fifty Years on the Throne

It was during one of the King's more lucid periods, but also during the war with France, that he celebrated his Golden Jubilee. Hitherto there had been only two monarchs to reach

Plate 33. *Salamanca jug.*

Plate 34A. *Porcelain mug for the preliminaries of peace signed 7th October, 1810. 4¼in (10.8cm) high.* **B.** *Chamberlain Worcester beaker inscribed 'Peace', probably commemorating the Battle of the Nile or the Peace of Amiens in 1802. Painted in the manner of John Wood.*

Plate 35. *Canary coloured jug, probably Swansea, entitled 'Bonaparte dethroned April 1st 1814'. 5in (12.7cm) high.*

Plate 36. *Bristol Pottery cylindrical mug inscribed 'G R Peace of Europe signed at Paris, May 30th 1814'. 3¼in (8.3cm) high.*

this period, Henry III and Edward III. Many commemoratives were produced for this event and although some are rare, it is not impossible to obtain some of them, even today. They include a plaque (Plate 37) moulded into the likeness of the young George III and decorated in polychrome palette under the glaze. The chances are that this was made at the Portobello factory in Edinburgh, the colouring and style much resembling various pieces made for the Coronation and/or the visit to Edinburgh of George IV. This is probably the only piece so far recorded to show George as a young man. It could be a pair to the portrayal of him in his fiftieth year, rather as Victoria is portrayed in two portraits, both young and old, on one of the octagonal plates for her Golden Jubilee.

A cup and saucer (Plate 38) printed and painted by Josiah Wedgwood were also issued to mark this event. The set is reckoned by some, though not by Wedgwood, to have been made for one of the royal palaces, possibly the Pavilion in Brighton. It is of a very attractive design based on orange with interweaving flowers, with the head of the King and the badge of the Garter. A most impressive commemorative is a massive urn (Plate 39), brown glazed and decorated in gilding with a remarkable profile portrait of King George III, together with the inscription 'Mercy and Truth preserve the King'. This, which originally had a pottery foot integral with

Plate 37. *Plaque portraying likeness of George III as a young King.*

Plate 38. *Cup and saucer recording the 50th Anniversary of the accession of George III, printed and painted by Josiah Wedgwood.*

the piece, now finds itself on a gilt metal foot. It is possible however that the original silhouette of the King was designed for pieces made to record his recovery from madness in 1789.

The Herculanean factory at Liverpool published several commemoratives for the Golden Jubilee, perhaps the most exciting being the Amnesty Jug (Plate 40). This consists of the spirit of history and of Britannia, supporting a scroll with the words 'Happy will England be could George but live to see another Jubilee', his cipher is also included. The scene is a prison or a castle, flying the Union Jack, and beside it is a statue of George III on horseback, dressed in a Roman toga and wearing on his head what appears to be a laurel wreath. A large number of people are portrayed and the print is captioned 'Let the prisoners go free. Give God Praise Jubilee 25th October 1809'. The date 1809, although it actually preceded the fiftieth year, was the beginning of a year's celebration.

The terms for the amnesty were apparently a pardon for naval deserters, but for the army they were required to enlist again. There was a further pardon for all offences committed by members of the armed forces and there was also an amnesty for all prisoners-of-war, excluding the French. A further condition of the amnesty was a subscription which was to be used for the relief of insolvent debtors. Ordinary criminals, however, were not pardoned under this amnesty.

The Monument was erected to record the Jubilee and still stands in Liverpool. It was erected by public subscription. The reverse has the Hanoverian escutcheon which was signed Dixon and dated 1803.

Plate 39. *Large brown glazed urn bearing profile of George III inscribed 'Mercy and Truth Preserve the King'. To record the Golden Jubilee. 8¾in (22.5cm) high.*

The King and his Ministers and National Events

Although the King was served throughout his long reign by no less than thirteen Prime Ministers, only three appear to have found themselves commemorated in one way or another.

At his accession the First Lord of the Treasury was the Elder Pitt, who has already been mentioned. He was succeeded by the Earl of Bute, a Knight of the most Noble Order of the Garter and somebody upon whom King George as a young man greatly relied. There is a very handsome engraving of the Earl wearing his robes of office and the collar of the Garter, but nothing ceramic.

For Lord North, who was First Lord at the time of the war with the American colonies, there is no ceramic record. Neither is there anything for either of the Grenvilles, Portland, Shelburne, Grafton or Liverpool.

Addington is included on a Peterloo plate together with others and the only two remaining, the Young Pitt and Perceval. Pitt the Younger is the subject of a very handsome seated figure (Plate 41), on a chair, holding a book on a plinth, probably of Minton. Apart from this figure there does not seem to be any specific record for William Pitt the Younger on either a mug or a jug. There are, however, two interesting jugs (Plate 42) which record an important piece of legislation which he engineered. Following the Irish uprisings of 1798 Pitt determined that the only safeguard to political stability in the face of the war with France was to abandon the Irish Parliament and to unite Ireland with the seat of the United Kingdom. The Bill of Union was passed and received the Royal Assent on 1st August. There are a number of rare transfers commemorating this event. A jug 19.5cm by 9cm in creamware (Plate 42B); the neck and spout trimmed with green enamel, the whole transfer-printed in black bears the words on one side: 'Peace and Plenty'. In the centre there are two *putti* at sport, and the donee's name, and on the other side a transfer symbolising the union of Great Britain and Ireland. The print is captioned within the body of the design 'Great Britain and Ireland United MDCCC'.

Another jug (Plate 42A) is pink lustre trimmed, brown printed and overglazed clobber decorated with a verse lauding the Act of Union of 1800. This is the first time this verse has been recorded. Like all Sunderland pieces the jug may be later than the verse, but it is certainly not made after the 1810 period when the style veered towards the broader based so-called Georgian design. On one side of the jug are the words:

'The United Kingdoms
May Scotland's thistle and England's rose
the Irish harp in one repose,
the threefold core which can't be broke,
tyranny's severest yoke.'

This is surmounted by the three national symbols, the rose in the centre, the thistle to the right, and the Irish harp to the left. On the other side is a different verse:

'This world is vain and full of pain,
with cares and troubles sore,
those are bliss that are at rest,
with Christ for evermore.'

Plate 40. *Amnesty jug for the Golden Jubilee, 25th October 1809. Liverpool Herculaneum Factory. 8in (20.5cm) high.*

Plate 41. *Minton figure of William Pitt the Younger seated in an armchair holding a scroll, moulded base. 5¼in. (13.3cm) high.*

Plate 42. *A creamware jug* ***(A)*** *and a Sunderland jug* ***(B)*** *recording the Act of Union with Ireland in 1800.*

William Pitt's chief protagonist was Charles James Fox, and unfortunately there is very little to commemorate him. There is, however, a pottery plaque (Plate 43) of brown and blue glazing representing inside an oval frame a moulded figure of Charles James Fox, apparently taken from the well-known Wedgwood medallion of about 1806. In a quite different field there is a glass picture (Plate 44) of Fox on the hustings. This shows Fox in the 1802 Westminster Election; his opponents were Admiral Lord Gardner – this was an Irish peerage – and John Graham Esq. On the panels behind the figures are noted the votes cast for each candidate. Glass paintings of political elections are not easily found. There is known to be a similar one for Burdett, also on the hustings.

The other First Lord of the Treasury commemorated is Spencer Perceval, shown on a melancholy tankard (Plate 45). Perceval was MP for Northampton and became Solicitor General in 1801 in the administration of Addington. He became Attorney General the following year and also served as Chancellor under the Duke of Portland, becoming Prime Minister on the death of Portland in 1809.

On the afternoon of the 11th May 1812, a little after five o'clock, he was shot dead in the lobby of the House of Commons by a madman called John Bellingham. Bellingham had been a Liverpool broker, but to quote *The Times*: '...in the year 1804 he went to Russia on some mercantile business, and having finished that business, was about to take his departure from Archangel for England.'

Plate 43. *Pottery plaque, brown and blue glazing, portraying the moulded figure of Charles James Fox, 1806.*

Plate 44. *Glass picture of Fox on the hustings at the Westminster Elections 1802.*

At that time a ship called the *Solure* was lost in the White Sea. She was insured at Lloyds Coffee House, but the underwriters refused to compensate the owners and as a result of circumstances connected with this refusal which were not his concern, Bellingham was seized from his carriage as he passed the Russian frontier and was thrown into prison.

Bellingham applied unsuccessfully for help to the British Ambassador, Lord Granville Leveson Gower. He was incarcerated for five years in various Russian gaols and treated with great ferocity and was often marched through the streets, together with other felons and criminals, even in front of the window of the British Ambassador. He was bankrupt on his release and, as it turned out, became quite deranged. He made constant applications to the Government for financial compensation, but nothing was done.

Finally, he approached a Mr James Taylor, a tailor by trade, of Grays Inn Lane and on 25th April 1812 had him make a breast pocket on the left side of a dark coloured body coat. He gave particular instructions to make this about nine inches deep and in it, on the afternoon of May 11th, he concealed a pistol. Having discovered the time when Perceval usually went to the House of Commons, he placed himself at the entrance of the lobby where he awaited his victim and, just as Perceval was passing, shot him. Perceval died instantly, the only British Prime Minister ever to be assassinated. Bellingham was apprehended, tried, convicted and hanged.

There is an unique mug recording the event, a very rare piece which can be seen in the Brighton Museum. There is, however, another mug (Plate 45), black printed, with some overglazed clobber, with a frog in it. This creamware mug does not show a portrait of Perceval, but of Bellingham. It reads, under a head and shoulders portrait, 'John Bellingham who on the 11th day of May 1812 assassinated Mr S Perceval, Prime Minister', and is black edged. Very often medals were struck to commemorate events and such a medal was struck to commemorate this assasination. It shows on the one side, the head and shoulders of Perceval, and around it the letters 'The Rt Honble Spencer Perceval, Chancellor of the Exchequer', strangely not Prime Minister. On the reverse side, around a suitable mourning figure over a tomb, are the words 'he lived beloved, and lamented fell, assasinated May 11th 1812'. It appears that the British Museum have seen such medals in bronze and metal, but not in silver. The maker's initials are shown, 'W T F', probably William Taylor as much of his work was done in this way.

There is not a great deal of pottery to commemorate Lord Cornwallis, the well-known general. However, there is a silver medal showing the head and shoulders of Cornwallis, wearing the military headgear of the time, around which are the words 'Charles Marquis Cornwallis', and on the reverse, around a winged angel and various weapons of war, the words *ab oriente ad occasum*.

It was during the latter part of the reign of George III that public agitation started and the various moves for reform were initiated. Perhaps John Wilkes, with his saga of the Middlesex Elections and the publication of the '45' was the first ceramic record of public concern and the need for

Plate 45. *Frog mug recording John Bellingham, who murdered Spencer Perceval, Prime Minister, in the House of Commons, 11th May, 1812. 4½in (11.4cm) high.*

Plates 46 and 47. *Two delft plates recording John Wilkes – Liberty and the 45. Both for the Middlesex Election, 1768. 9in (23cm) diameter.*

Plate 48. *Derby porcelain figure of John Wilkes as Lord Mayor of London 1775.*

Plate 49. *Liverpool jug for Tom Paine. 5½in (14cm) high.*

reform in the widest sense.

There are several plates, mainly of delft, that are extremely rare, and mostly in museums. One plate (Plate 46) is of Lambeth delft, decorated in blue and white with a fine portrait of John Wilkes with the legend 'No 45 Wilkes and Liberty'. The blue is particularly fine. A delft plate of similar diameter and in the same blue colour (Plate 47) bears the words 'Always for Liberty'. When Wilkes returned from France to contest the 1768 Middlesex Elections, amongst the many factories to make commemorative items was the one at Derby. The Derby Porcelain Works commissioned Stefan, the notable freelance modeller, to make them a full length figure of Wilkes and this they produced on a scroll base in fairly considerable quantities. When Wilkes was elected Lord Mayor of London in 1775, Derby alone recorded the event. They re-issued the figure but this time on a flat Greek key base (Plate 48) which they then used on most of their figures and to it added the Great Sword and the Mace of the City of London. It is a very handsome figure.

There is known to be both a jug and a mug for Thomas Paine and his campaign for the Rights of Man. The jug has a full length portrait of Thomas Paine. A further jug (Plate 49) with a red transfer of Paine has beneath it the following verses: 'Prithy Tom Paine, why wilt thou meddling be in others business which concerns not thee, for while thereon thou dost extend thy cares, thou dost at home neglect they own affairs, God Save The King', and underneath 'Observe the Wicked and Malicious Man projecting all the mischief

Plate 50. *Creamware cylindrical tankard, printed and coloured. 'Lord George Riot made a Jew' portraying the circumcision. 6in (15.2cm) high.*

Plate 51. *Two jugs, one in canary lustre, the other in white and blue, portraying Sir Francis Burdett, committed to the Tower, 6th April, 1810, by the Speaker for asserting the rights of the British people.*

that he can, when common policy will not prevail, he rather ventures sole and all then fails'. On the front is a kind of motto 'May Britons true their rights pursue and ere espouse the cause of Church and King and everything that constitutes their laws'. This is placed in the centre of a cartouche which bears the motto of the garter *Honi soit qui mal y pense* and underneath *Dieu et mon droit*, supported by the lion and the unicorn, and surmounted by a crown with a rampant lion wearing a crown as its crest.

The Gordon Riots do not escape ceramic record. A creamware tankard (Plate 50), brown printed and polychrome enamelled, shows in satirical style the circumcision of Lord George Gordon of Gordon Riots infamy. The print is captioned 'Lord George Riot made a Jew'. It is indeed a most unusual subject for ceramic record and is extremely colourful. On becoming a Jew he took the name Israel Abraham.

In 1810 Sir Francis Burdett, MP for Westminster and noted for his radical oratory, was arrested for breach of privilege and lodged in the Tower upon the orders of the Speaker of the House of Commons. This affair became a very celebrated event and some commemorative pieces were published. There is an unusual jug (Plate 51), printed in canary lustre with silver lustre embellishment. In the centre is a fine portrait of Burdett, underneath are the words 'the determined enemy of corruption and the constitutional friend of his Sovereign'. On the reverse, also in a circle of silver lustre, are the words 'Francis Burdett Bart MP committed to the Tower 6th April 1810 by the House of Commons for firmly and disinterestedly asserting the legal rights of the British people'. Another jug in white with blue embellishment has again, on the front, a side profile of Burdett with the same wording and a similar inscription on the back. Francis Burdett had many interests in the reform movement. He was very pro Catholic emancipation for prison reform and on his arrest by the Speaker he barricaded himself in his house. He was supported by the people, but was in fact saved from the Tower by prorogation of Parliament. However in 1820 he was given three months imprisonment because of the letter he had written about Peterloo and in the end this strong radical joined the Tory party.

The move to abolish the slave trade was pioneered by William Wilberforce. Although slavery was abolished in 1806 the trade continued and was not finally abolished until 1833. Wilberforce, who had pioneered this important reform, although he was alive when the slave trade was abolished, had died before the Act had received the Royal Assent. There is very little to record Wilberforce and there seems to be nothing bearing his name on any ceramic piece. There is however a very fine Minton figure (Plate 52A) similar to that for William Pitt the Younger and also for Hannah Moore (Plate 52B). They are both, as in the case of William Pitt, seated and are important commemoratives for these two protagonists in the Abolition of Slavery Movement.

Plate 52A (right). *Minton figure of William Wilberforce seated with a scroll in an armchair.* ***52B (left).*** *Similar figure of Hannah Moore. 7¾in (19.7cm) high.* ***52C.*** *Pearlware circular plate, black printed with vignette of kneeling black slave. 5½in (14cm) diameter.* ***52D.*** *English porcelain shell inkstand, black printed with similar vignette, biblical inscriptions. 5½in (14cm) high.* ***52E.*** *Small jug inscribed 'Liberty Given To The Slaves'. 5½in (14cm) high.*

***Plate 53A (right).** Jug, red printed with a bust of Hunt inscribed 'Hunt and Liberty'. 4¾in. (12cm) high.* ***Plate 53B (left).** Small Staffordshire beaker with bust of the real Hunt. 2¾in (7cm) high.*

Although slightly out of time it might be appropriate to make mention of some of the few commemorative pieces for the Abolition of Slavery. There is a plate with a child negro which is in the Liverpool Museum (Plate 52C) and a porcelain ink-stand (Plate 52D) bearing the transfer of the same negro with his chains still on, under a palm tree and a quotation from the scriptures:

'And the nation to whom they shall be in bondage will I judge.' (Act VII CV VII)

'Ye shall not oppress'. (Leviticus 25 CHV)

'The mighty are gathered against me not for my transgressions nor for my sins.' (Psalm 59)

'Hath not one God created us.' (Malacai CII)

There is also a small jug (Plate 52E) showing a minister speaking to two slaves with the words 'Liberty given to the slaves'.

There was a medal to commemorate the Abolition of Slavery. It shows on one side a negro standing, holding his shackles, with a background of palm trees and around it is a quotation from the Psalms: 'This is the Lord's doing, it is marvellous in my eyes'. And underneath the words 'Jubilee August 1834'. On the reverse are the words 'In commemoration of the extinction of colonial slavery throughout the British dominions in the reign of William IV, August 1st 1834'.

The massacre in the fields of Peterloo in 1819 has been ceramically recorded on several jugs and plates. There is a jug (Plate 53A) published the year after Peterloo at the time Henry Hunt was tried, convicted and sent to Ilchester Goal with a sentence of two years, with a bond of £2,000 for good behaviour. Although this is alleged to be a portrait of Hunt, it is in fact Bainbridge, one of the American heroes of the 1812-15 war.

Portraits of these naval American personalities were often used as stand-ins for Hunt, presumably the potters reckoned that as they had been previously used solely for export, no-one would know. Hunt himself does appear on a very small beaker. (Plate 53B).

Two most interesting octagonal plates (Plate 54) are formed from a pair of prints taken from a reformist pamphlet entitled *The political house that Jack built.* These are printed in mauve, one showing three battered victims with a hillock in the foreground, with the battle of Peterloo in the background and the caption 'What man seeing this and having human feeling does not blush and hang his head to think himself a man'. The other plate shows a group, including Sidmouth, Castlereagh and Canning, with the caption 'Dream after dream ensues and still they dream that they shall succeed and still are disappointed'. The original print is also labelled 'Guilty Trio'. The appearance of Sidmouth is perhaps the only recorded ceramic record of Addington, subsequently Viscount Sidmouth. Although Canning does appear on a few commemoratives, nothing seems to have been recorded specifically for Castlereagh. This plate, therefore, has that

Plate 54. *Pair of Staffordshire octagonal plates printed in puce with moulded floral borders recording the Battle of Peterloo. 7½in (19cm) diameter.*

Plate 55. *Hunt cock-fighting jug, black and white transfer printed. 4½in (11.5cm) high.*

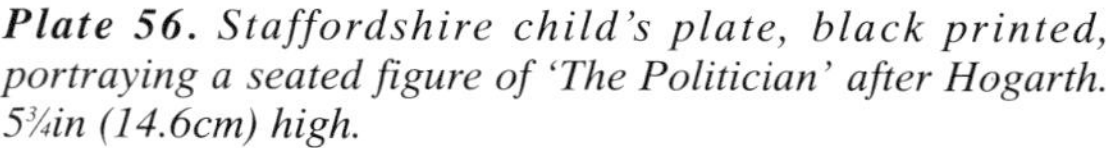

Plate 56. *Staffordshire child's plate, black printed, portraying a seated figure of 'The Politician' after Hogarth. 5¾in (14.6cm) high.*

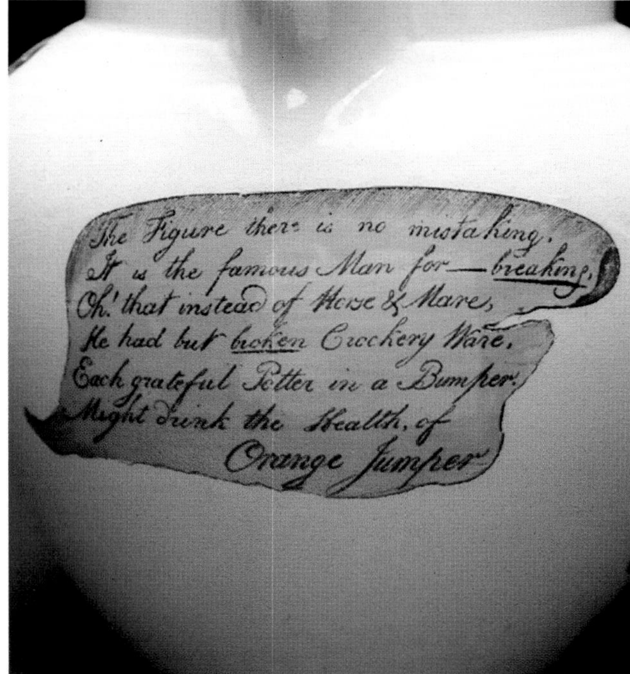

Plate 57. *Two views of a Don Pottery jug portraying the 'Orange Jumper' for the Yorkshire Election of 1807. 4¼in (11cm) high.*

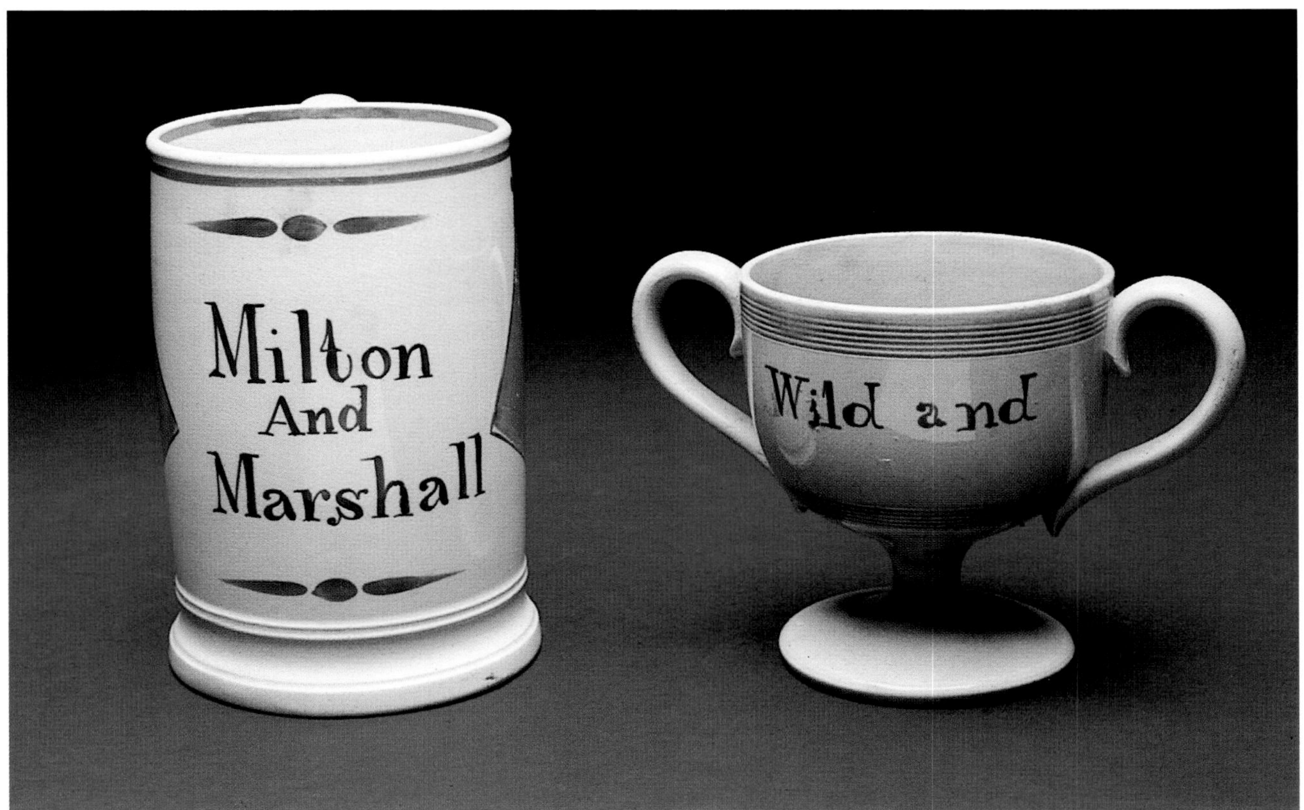

Plate 58A. *Creamware cylindrical mug inscribed 'Milton and Marshall'. 5¼in (13.5cm) high.* **Plate 58B.** *Pottery two-handled cup inscribed 'Wilde and Independence', for the 1831 Election. 3¼in (8.3cm) diameter.*

Plate 59. Staffordshire splash pink lustre soup plate inscribed 'Maule for Freedom'. 9½in (24cm) diameter.

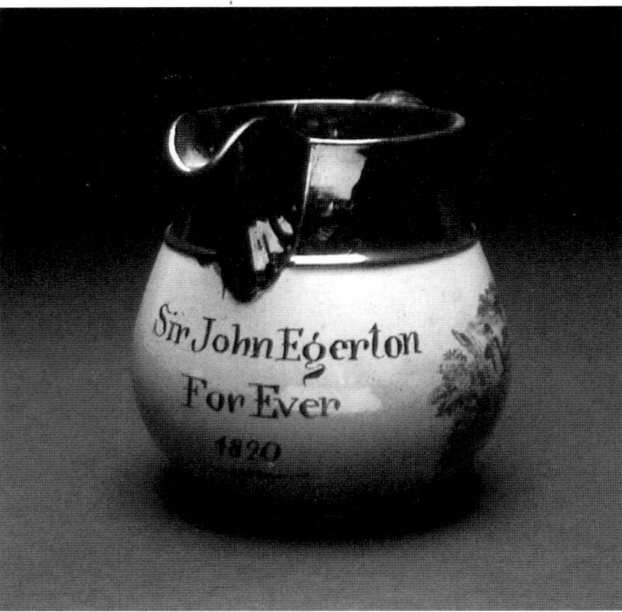

Plate 60. Copper lustre jug with wide blue band. Ground captioned: 'Sir John Egerton for Ever'.

added interest. Hunt is featured on a jug (Plate 55) in a caricature cock-fighting scene, the cock with the head of Henry Hunt, the pit surrounded by figures, one holding a script entitled 'Reform Bill', all of them with satirical verses inscribed by scene. It is black and white transfer printed with a floral decoration around the lip and top.

Politics and Elections in the Reign of George III

'A politician should as I have read be furnished in the first place with a head.'

This text forms part of a splendid Hogarth engraving called *The Politician*, which has been used in the centre of a small child's plate (Plate 56). He is shown at a desk reading a paper, wearing the clothes of the period. It may be that this plate was published rather later, but it embodies the political atttitudes of the time.

Elections at this time were full of corruption and it was not until the Reform Bill of 1834 that things became a bit more orderly. Politicians and candidates anxious to hold their seats employed the most dubious methods, one of which was to engage the services of thugs.

There is a very fine quality pottery jug (Plate 57), which has on it a painting of a very fat man holding a hat captioned 'Milton', and on the front in a scroll, an amusing verse commemorating the Orange Jumper. This jug is reputed to depict a Mr Mellish – a well-known pugilist – a Newmarket character, who plied his trade as a horse breaker at Wentworth and was one of the thugs employed by Earl Fitzwilliam, the father of Lord Milton, in the Yorkshire election of 1807, orange being the Fitzwilliam family's colours. The verse reads as follows:

'The figure there is no mistaking, it is the famous
man for breaking.
O that instead of horse and mare,
he had broken crockeryware.
Each grateful potter in a bumper
might drink the health of Orange Jumper.'

Milton was a candidate, together with Marshall, in a Yorkshire election, and a mug of creamware (Plate 58A), lustre decorated, and painted with a design of flags in orange, has the slogan 'Milton and Marshall' painted in red and brown. This election in fact took place in 1826 and gave birth to the notorious Alnwick election scandal.

A soup plate (Plate 59), lavishly decorated overall with splash pink lustre with, in the well, a freestyle painted display of flowers has the slogan 'Maule and Freedom'. William Ramsay Maule was the MP for Forfar in 1796 and again in 1805. He was a Whig and a close personal friend of Charles James Fox and was created Lord Panmure in 1831. An attractive jug depicts the Chester election in either 1818 or 1820. The Whig candidate was Lord Belgrave, together with Lieutenant General Grosvenor and the Tory candidates were Sir John Egerton and John Williams.

In 1820 the candidates were the same except that John Williams was replaced by Edgar Venables Townsend. The figures show that the Whigs polled 813 and 757 votes in 1818, and in 1820, 771 and 698 respectively. They were therefore the unsuccessful candidates. This seat was firmly in the gift of the Westminster family, although in these two years the Tories had made considerable inroads into this Whig stronghold and that is why Egerton bothered to have the jug (Plate 61) made the second time around. The jug is of lustre with a border of roses and primroses and there is

Plate 61. *Small Staffordshire jug printed with the names of the Whigs Lord Belgrave and the Hon Robert Grosvenor.*

Plate 62. *Silver lustre jug, black printed for John Jones of Yestrad. 5¾. (14.5cm) high.*

emblazoned on one side the coat of arms of the Grosvenor family. Underneath the names of Lord Belgrave and the Hon Robt. Grosvenor are the words 'And the house of Eaton for ever', Eaton being a reference to Eaton Hall, the seat of the Grosvenor family.

It was this family which was subsequently ennobled and was the last Dukedom created under the title of the Duke of Westminster. It was customary even for unsuccessful candidates to have commemorative jugs issued to their supporters, and in the election in which the Whigs succeeded in Chester, Sir John Egerton, although unsuccessful, had made a rather fine lustre jug (Plate 60), waisted in blue with a red transfer of a pastoral scene captioned 'Sir John Egerton for Ever 1820'. He polled 680 votes, eighteen less than Grosvenor, who succeeded together with Belgrave in the Whigs' cause.

Another jug (Plate 62), this time with silver lustre, records the election of John Jones of Yestrad. In a silver lustre circle on the reverse side are the words 'May the Independents of Carmarthen never want a supporter nor the Whigs of Liberty ever lose a feather'.

John Jones stood for Carmarthen in 1812 against the Whig, George Campbell, but did not win the seat. He tried again in 1818, also without success, but he won in a by-election, caused by the sitting MP succeeding to a title and becoming Lord Cawdor. Jones stood against Sir William Paxton and beat him by nine votes. The votes were very small, considering the size of the constituency: Jones 321, Paxton 312. He held the seat subsequently unopposed. Later in 1831 he held it on a disputed election.

Riots followed because of the Reform agitation in this constituency, but he lost the seat in the next year in the Reform Parliament to the Hon W. Yelverton, a Whig, the votes being 302 to the Whig and 185 to Jones. He then switched his seat to the county which he unsuccessfully contested in 1835, but won one of the two seats in 1837, was returned unopposed in 1841 and died as a sitting member in 1842. This is an interesting jug, because there are very few commemoratives for Welsh constituencies.

There is a silver jug (Plate 63), hallmarked for the year of 1807, in which Lushington and Farquhar were the unsuccessful Tory candidates for Canterbury. Lushington however, did succeed in winning Rye at a by-election. In the next election he resumed his attack on Canterbury and sat for that seat through the elections of 1812-26. He then retired and became Governor of Madras, but after his return from India, he again sat for the city in 1835. Lushington was a first cousin, once removed, to the Doctor Lushington who was one of the Caroline Protagonists and who appears on the green bag jugs which are mentioned in the reign of George IV.

Farquhar, who was also mentioned, abandoned politics and became Governor of Mauritius. However, he returned to England in the 1820s and entered Parliament as MP for Newton in Lancashire. He represented the seat for only one year and then switched to Hythe in 1826, which he held until his death.

In addition to the move for reforms there were also moves to relieve the exploitation of child labour, and there is a creamware jug (Plate 64), black printed, transferred with a print showing a scene at a loom with the workmen gesturing towards a small boy and the slogan 'Liberty to the sons of Britain'. This is positioned over a ribboned cartouche. The print is further ornamented with symbols of commerce and of cotton, and the clasped hands and sentiments variously expressing a desire for harmony within the cotton trade. This

Plate 63. *Silver jug hallmarked 1807 for Lushington and Farquhar.*

Plate 64. *Creamware jug with the slogan 'Liberty to the Sons of Britain', to draw attention to child labour. 9in. (22.9cm) high.*

Plate 66. *Dinner plate, part of a set, showing portrait of Queen Caroline.*

Plate 65.(left) *Blue printed dinner plate, recording the death of George III. 5¾in. (14.5cm) diameter.*

Plate 67. *Plate for the pupils of Lancaster Schools recording the death of George III. 5¾in. (14.5cm) high.*

Plate 68. *Dinner plate made for the Prince Regent, incorporating the Prince of Wales feathers.*

Plate 69. *Pair of porcelain plaques captioned: 'George IV and Queen Caroline'.*

jug is reputed to have been published in 1816 when Sir Robert Peel, father of the later Prime Minister, set up a committee to investigate child labour in the factories. It may, however, have been two years later, when in the face of considerable opposition, he forced through a Bill limiting both the age and the working hours of children in the cotton industry.

The Death of George III

The last few years of the King's reign were shrouded in mystery because of his insanity. He lived, in a sense, in seclusion in Windsor Castle, and was regarded as quite incapable of carrying out his normal duties as sovereign. There had been some recent deaths, including that of his wife, Queen Charlotte in 1818, and his fourth son, the Duke of Kent, died on 23rd January 1820. Only six days later the King died.

His reign was long and had seen many important developments, particularly with regard to the Constitution. It was during his reign that America became independent. There was the successful war against France and the great victories of Wellington and Nelson and the start of the Reform Movement in various ways had begun.

Despite his long reign and the many achievements, there is very little to commemorate his death. A very handsome plate (Plate 65), part of a set, shows a bust profile of the King, in uniform, with the inscription 'Sacred to the Memory of George III who died on 29th January 1820'. It is in blue and there is a moulded flower border on the child's plate, but on the dinner and soup plates the floral border is not moulded. It is a transfer border, boldly printed in blue and white Royal flowers. As part of the set there is a similar plate for Queen Caroline (Plate 66). This controversial lady will gain more prominence in the chapter on George IV.

Another plate (Plate 67) shows by way of transfer a child kneeling to receive a book from the King, and the caption reads 'I hope the time will come when every poor child in my dominions will be able to read the Bible'. It is associated with the work of the Lancastrian schools for the children of the poor, of which the King was patron. The movement got into financial difficulties and Lancaster was received by the King who is reported to have said to him what is quoted on this plate. It is likely that these plates may have been distributed to the schools and given to their pupils.

The Reign of George IV

All the Georges seemed to have had trouble with their eldest sons. George I could not stand George II and neither could George II stand his eldest son, Frederick, Prince of Wales, who died before he could become King.

George III, to put it mildly, had a great deal of trouble with his eldest son, George, Prince of Wales. Whereas George III had led a fairly blameless and chaste life, this cannot be said for his eldest son. He was extravagant, involved himself in various amorous liaisons, interfered with the political life of the Constitution by favouring Fox in an attempt to seize the Regency when his father went mad, and made a disastrous marriage.

To his credit, however, he was a great patron of the arts and whatever faults lay in his character, much of the interest in the arts can be attributed to George IV, both through his life as Prince of Wales and subsequently as King. He fell in love with Maria Fitzherbert, a woman of noble birth, and undoubtedly married her, probably under threat of committing suicide unless she agreed. However, he treated her extremely badly and cast her aside, because the only way of getting his debts paid by the State was by agreeing to marry his first cousin Caroline of Brunswick. It is said that, despite the way he treated Maria Fitzherbert, he loved her all his life, and on his death there was reputed to have been found around his neck a miniature of her.

A child's plate shows the Prince of Wales and Mrs Fitzherbert on a hobby horse and is captioned 'A Visit to Richmond from Carlton House'. Mrs Fitzherbert lived at No 1 Richmond Hill. This plate is regarded as an anti-George plate and may well have been produced during the anti-George campaign during the time of the Bill of Pains and Penalties.

There are one or two pieces to commemorate his life as Prince of Wales, one being an attractive dinner service. The dinner plate (Plate 68), has the Prince of Wales feathers in the centre, on an orange background. There is also a tea service, again with the Prince of Wales feathers, manufactured by Crown Derby; the mark is clearly seen on the base. It is a typical example of the Derby factory.

A black basalt teapot by Wedgwood has on the front, in relief, 'Prinny, George, Prince of Wales', and on the reverse his brother Frederick, Duke of York.

From almost the very moment that he succeeded to the throne problems began with his wife. Caroline had been separated from him since the birth of their only child Charlotte. She had the reputation of living an immoral life with an Italian at the Villa D'este on Lake Como, and George IV determined that she was never going to assume her rights as Queen. As a result of this attempt to exclude her from the throne ways and means had to be found to prevent her from becoming Queen. However, this did not stop commemoratives at the time of the King's accession from appearing showing them both.

There is a splendid pair of porcelain plaques (Plate 69), one having the head and shoulders of the King and the other, of Queen Caroline, with a fantastic hat, feathered and large. She had a reputation for wearing extraordinary headgear.

Caroline was determined to return to England and claim her rights as Queen and she undoubtedly had the support of the people. George IV was never popular as Prince of Wales and Caroline received a large number of loyal addresses. She was cheered in the streets and became so popular that the King retired to his pavilion in Brighton.

A commission had been set up in 1818 when George IV was Regent, entitled the Milan Commission, to try and obtain evidence for a divorce, and this resulted in a Bill being laid before Parliament entitled 'An Act for depriving Caroline Amelia Elizabeth, Queen of Great Britain, of and from style and title of Queen of these Realms and of and from the rights prerogatives and immunities now belonging to her as Queen Consort'. From this it is clear that until something happened she was still regarded as the Queen. The whole case rested

Plates 70 and 71. *Two satirical prints of Queen Caroline.*

upon adultery with Count Bartolomeo Bergami which is supposed to have taken place either at the Villa D'este or elsewhere. The Queen had two strong supporters in Henry Brougham and Denman, her solicitor and the Attorney General respectively. There was also Doctor Lushington. Another of her faithful supporters was an Alderman Wood who was in fact responsible for arranging the passage across the sea on the packet *Prince Leopold* to England, landing on the 5th January in Dover.

There is an amusing print (Plate 70) in the form of a cartoon entitled 'Queen Caroline's triumph over her enemies', published in 1821 by P. and P. Gulley of Clerkenwell. This shows the Queen, fully robed, again wearing one of her famous plumed hats, surmounted by a crown held by an angel, arriving in a carriage harnessed by two lions, and there is in an oval cartouche the head of Alderman Wood wearing a Roman toga. But the Queen was viciously satirised in various other prints. Perhaps the most astonishing (Plate 71) is entitled 'The Queen's Ars in a Bandbox', and this shows a very large buxom Caroline, again wearing masses of feathers on her head, in a box riding a striped hyena. The box is entitled 'Mother Woods' old hatbox', and the lid of the box has the words 'A present from Bar Bergami'. It was printed by G. Humphrey of St. James's

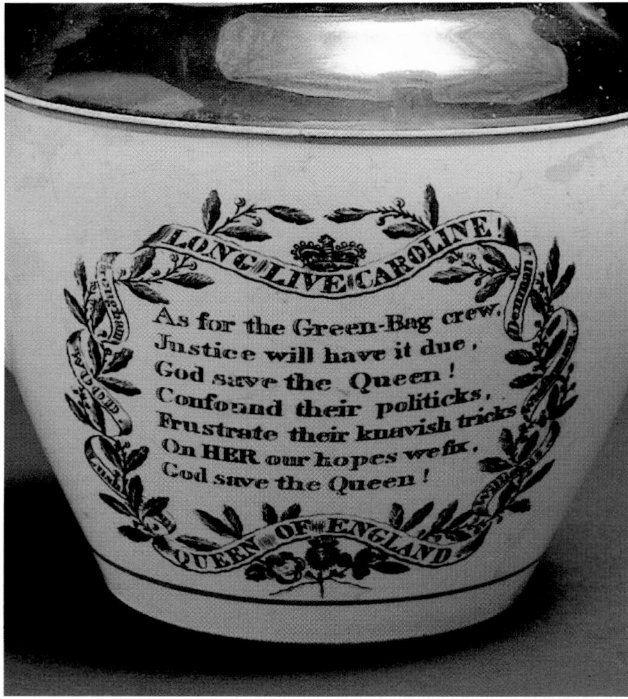

Plate 72. *Lustre jug, the ovoid body printed in black with a bust portrait of the Queen – on the reverse the 'Green Bag' verse. 4¾in. (12cm) high.*

Plate 73. *Nursery plate inscribed 'May the Diamonds in the British Crown glitter on the noble head of our Queen Caroline'. 9¾in. (25cm) diameter.*

Plate 74. *Large nursery plate entitled 'Caroline Regina'. 7¼in. (18.5cm) diameter.*

Plate 75A and C. *Staffordshire mask jug with busts of Brougham and Denman. 5in. (12.5cm) high.* ***B.*** *Prattware jug moulded and decorated in colour glaze with bust portraits of Queen Caroline with satyr mask tip. 6in. (15cm) high.*

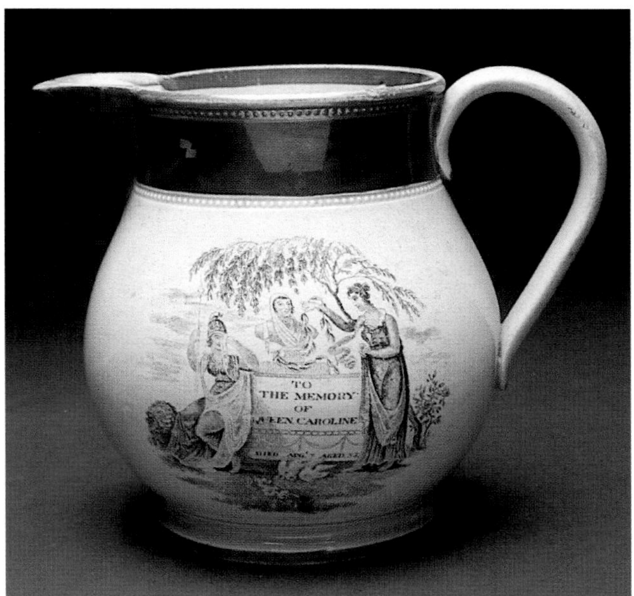

Plate 76. *Lustre jug commmorating the death of Queen Caroline. 5¾in. (14.5cm) high.*

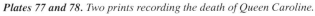

Plates 77 and 78. *Two prints recording the death of Queen Caroline.*

Street on 22nd January 1821. The proceedings in the House of Lords started on 17th August. The Queen attended but did not participate and there is a very famous oil painting by Sir George Hayter where she is portrayed wearing a lace mantilla. The trial continued with breaks until 10th November. There is an engraving of the House of Lords entitled 'The Trial of Queen Caroline'.

The trial involved the calling of various sordid witnesses and the most intimate details of the Queen's private life were unfolded, most unsavoury objects were produced giving alleged evidence of adultery and most of the evidence was brought in a green baize bag. This green baize bag has formed an interesting commemorative called the green bag jug (Plate 72). It is in lustre and again has on the front a portrait of the Queen wearing one of her feathered hats, with the words 'God Save Queen Caroline' and on the reverse, beneath the words 'Long Live Caroline Queen of England' the verse: 'As for the green bag crew justice will have it due, God Save the Queen, confound their politicks, frustrate their knavish tricks on HER hopes we fix, God Save the Queen'. This is surrounded by a wreath with the names of the Queen's supporters, Brougham Wood, Lushington, Denman, Williams and Whitman. The identity of the latter two is not known. The result of the trial went against the Queen, but the majority was only twenty-eight. The King, however, insisted that it went to Committee and on 9th November, Lord Liverpool recognised that the Bill would never be passed and the Lord Chancellor, who was then Eldon, was anxious not to have the Bill abandoned. When he realised at the Third Reading that the majority had dwindled even more – down to nine – it was clearly never going to be passed and was withdrawn. There was general rejoicing by the people, but of course it left the King in a very difficult position.

There was a large number of commemorative pieces for the Bill of Pains and Penalties. One plate (Plate 73) has the verse 'May the diamonds in the British Crown glitter on the head of our noble Queen Caroline'. The plates have other and different verses all praising the Queen. A particularly attractive child's plate (Plate 74) has a transfer of the head and shoulders of the Queen in blue, surrounded by a wreath of flowers, the border has a moulded floral pattern between two rings of orange. The words read 'Caroline Regina'. This portrait of the Queen makes her look rather more attractive than many of the others. She is not wearing one of her grotesque hats, but her hair is encrusted with flowers and a bandeau. There are two very fine jugs, one bearing the portrait of the Queen in profile wearing a flamboyant hat (Plate 75B). This is surrounded by encrusted and embossed royal flowers, the rose and the thistle. The rose in fact is yellow and the thistle is blue, probably because the colour scheme used in the preparation of this jug is basically blue. There is a masked spout and the edge of the jug is decor-edged. A smaller jug of a similar type (Plate 75A and C), with a masked spout, portrays, again in relief, the two great protagonists, Brougham in red and Denman in blue. This time, although surrounded by the royal flowers, the rose is red.

A loving cup, of Staffordshire pot, is decorated with a moulded rim, glazed in pale blue on the top and bottom of the bowl and with the words 'Wilde and Independence'

Plate 79. *Scottish moulded plate, the border embossed with basketweave to record the Coronation of King George IV. 8½in. (21.5cm) diameter.*

boldly hand lettered around the full body of the cup (Plate 58B). Thomas Sergeant Wilde, later Lord Truro, was one of Queen Caroline's attorneys during the Bill of Pains and Penalties. He is not mentioned as one of the protagonists on the green bag jug but he ought to be mentioned in this context. He contested the seat of Newark on a number of occasions, and in 1829 during the reign of George IV and in 1830 he was unsuccessful but in fact won the seat in 1831 when he then transferred to Worcester.

The King had not heard the end of Queen Caroline. At his coronation she sought to force an entry into Westminster Abbey claiming a right to be crowned Queen, but was prevented from so. It is quite clear that she really never recovered from this insult, and very shortly afterwards she died. There were some commemoratives produced for the death of the Queen. One is a Sunderland jug (Plate 76) with lustre which has on the front: 'To the memory of Queen Caroline, died April 7th aged 54'. The transfer shows a tomb bearing these words, on one side a weeping Britannia and on the other a goddess beneath a weeping willow. On the reverse is the following verse: 'Britons in sackcloth on their own shore lament Queen Caroline's no more. We trust in heaven we shall her see at God's right hand from guilt set free, and hear him say Daughter well done, thy fight is fought, thy battles won. Here take this crown in joy thou rest, removed from those who thee oppressed. On earth thou couldst not crowned be, but here thou are eternally'.

A very small cockle plate, black printed, with a daisy border, hexagonal in shape shows a tomb and the words 'To the memory of Queen Caroline' and on the tomb, 'of England'. Another plate actually depicts the cortege. This may have been inspired by a print (Plate 77) published by P. & J. Gulley, which shows the funeral procession passing

Plate 80. *Pear-shaped jug, possibly Scottish, for the Coronation. 5¾in. (14.5cm) high.*

Plate 81. *Jug bearing portraits of the King, with dates.*

Temple Bar. It is a graphic illustration of the scene; the black hearse, surmounted by the Royal Arms, and the horses bearing black saddlecloths, and it reads: 'The funeral procession of her most lamented Majesty Queen Caroline entering the City of Temple Bar, May 14th 1821, being the general wishes of the people'. A similar print (Plate 78), which may perhaps have inspired the transfer used on the jug in Plate 76A, shows a head and shoulders portrait of the Queen against a tomb, again wearing one of her grotesque hats. Underneath are the words 'Queen Caroline died at Brandenburg House, August 7th 1821, aged 54 years'. It is supported on the right by a weeping Britannia and another figure which cannot be identified on the left, the whole surmounted by a massive urn, against a weeping willow and reads: 'Britannia weeping at the monument of our beloved and universally regretted Queen Caroline, the wife of His Majesty George IV.

The King was crowned on 19th July 1821. He was a great showman and was anxious to have the most lavish coronation possible, spending what was then regarded as a vast fortune, over a quarter of a million pounds. It was an unpopular coronation and there are not a great number of commemoratives for it. There is a rather fine creamware plate (Plate 79). This has a basketweave border, and a moulded profile portrait of the King in the well. The King is shown head and shoulders and wearing the uniform of a Field Marshal, and underneath are the words 'King George IIII'. It is probably a Staffordshire piece. Around the border there are three separate cartouches of moulded flowers.

A jug (Plate 80) bears the portrait of the King wearing a very large crown, with the King's monogram GR in polychrome plate, surrounded by the embossed royal flowers, the rose and thistle, the rose in red and the thistle in a kind of claret as opposed to purple. The jug has around the top lip a further decoration of leaves in greens. There is an orange base and the top of the jug including the lip is also in orange, with orange decoration on the handle.

There are also a jug and basin from a washstand set (Plate 82), with moulded decorations of George IV. The pottery is late pearlware, very similar in style of painting to the George IV measure jugs that are occasionally seen. It may well be contemporary with the coronation, although there is nothing on it to indicate this. It is not sufficiently grand for a palace, and rather too grand to be sought after by the people as a souvenir. It may well be that was used in bedrooms and sold for this purpose.

There is a jug (Plate 81), black printed, either side bearing a fine portrait of King George IV captioned 'His Most Glorious Majesty George IV crowned July 19th 1821 in the fifty-ninth year of his life'.

The King had only one daughter, Charlotte, born following his marriage to Caroline. This daughter was the subject of great disagreement between them. Like her mother, Caroline, Charlotte was adored by the people and she was the heir to the throne. An unusual commemorative portraying the animosity between the then Prince of Wales, the Princess of Wales and Charlotte is shown, in what is termed the 'Regent Valentine Jug' (Plate 83).

The story is interesting: In 1813 the Princess of Wales, who was living apart from her husband, as she had done almost from the start of her marriage, handed to Lord Liverpool a letter to be sent to the Regent. It was returned unopened. It was then sent back to Lord Liverpool and again returned. It was then yet again sent back to the Lords. The Regent, George, Prince of Wales, was acquainted with the contents, but would not give any answer. So, the Princess of Wales

Plate 82. *Pearlware water jug and bowl, embossed 'GR IV'. 8¾in. (22cm) and 11¾in. (29.5cm).*

agreed to the publication of this letter, and in it was a plea to see her daughter, who had been removed to Windsor. But this letter had the very opposite effect, because Caroline was not allowed to see Charlotte when she came to London, and on St. Valentine's Day Lord Liverpool said that the reason for this was that she had allowed publication of the letter.

The jug is entitled 'The Regent Valentine' and shows the Regent wearing a plume of feathers entwined with two serpents, with Britannia and a lion behind him and Caroline kneeling in front of him holding out the letter. In the front can be seen another person, presumably Charlotte watching the whole procedure.

On 2nd May 1816, Charlotte, Princess of Wales, was married to Prince Leopold of Saxe-Coburg. There had been a previous betrothal to the Prince of Orange, but this did not last and the marriage between Charlotte and Leopold took place at Carlton House. There are several commemoratives for the event. The Princess wore a head-dress of rosebuds and leaves and these became something she was always remembered by. Leopold wore a British General's uniform. They are both portrayed on a moulded jug (Plate 84), which is decorated with lustre and has raised moulded portraits of Princess Charlotte on one side and Prince Leopold on the other. The handle of the jug is a simple scroll. Despite her unhappy childhood, the marriage seemed to be a happy one. They lived at Claremont, near Esher, and in the spring of 1817 she became pregnant.

There is a plate (Plate 85) published for the series of British Views, lavishly decorated in blue and white, with a flowered border, the well Claremont itself, and in the foreground a kneeling woman and child speaking to the Prince and Princess. There is also the Prince's horse and the Prince's pony chaise. However, tragedy was to follow. Princess Charlotte gave birth to a stillborn son and on 6th November 1817 she died.

Princess Charlotte was heir to the throne, after her father, and her death completely altered the succession of the English throne. The next in line was the Duke of York who, although married to a German princess, had no children. The

Plate 83. *The Regent Valentine jug.*

Plate 84. *Lustre jug recording the marriage of Princess Charlotte and Prince Leopold of Saxe-Coburg. 5¾in. (14.5cm).*

next in line was William, the Duke of Clarence, who was still maintaining his liaison with Mrs Jordon. After him came the Duke of Kent, who was also involved in an association with Madame de St. Laurent, and after him came Ernest, Duke of Cumberland. It would appear that no-one was very anxious for this son of George III to succeed.

Plate 85. *Blue printed plate from the British Views series depicting Princess Charlotte and Prince Leopold in the grounds of Claremont. 9¾in. (25cm) diameter.*

The Dukes of Clarence and Kent both recognised that they had a duty to their country to provide an heir and abandoned their mistresses. William married a German princess, Princess Adelaide of Saxe-Meinigen, but although he had two children, neither survived. The Duke of Kent married a widow who was the sister of Prince Leopold, the husband of the late Princess Charlotte, and as a result of this marriage Victoria, subsequently Queen of England, was born.

Charlotte was very popular and her death was regarded as a great loss to the nation and was commemorated in many ways. A tea-set, black edged, showed the head and shoulders of the Princess. There were also plates, rather similar to those commemorating her mother, Queen Caroline, showing Britannia weeping under a willow tree, and in many instances her head and shoulders wearing the famous wedding garland of rosebuds. These varied in size, and there is a small child's plate (Plate 86) with a moulded border with this engraving in the centre, and underneath are the words: 'The late and much lamented Princess Charlotte of Saxe-Coburg who departed this life November 6th 1817'.

The King and the Constitution

The moves for reform were still gathering momentum and Catholic emancipation occupied the mind of the King during his reign. Pitt the Younger had championed this cause but, coming up against George III's strong opposition, did not pursue the matter.

The King felt it was against his Coronation Oath to do anything to alleviate the rights of Catholics. The appearance of Daniel O'Connell, who was the founder of the Roman Catholic Association and who became the prime campaigner both in Ireland and in Great Britain, brought the matter to a

Plate 86. *Nursery plate recording the death of Princess Charlotte. 5⅜in. (13.7cm) diameter.*

Plate 87A. *Bournes Pottery spirit flask modelled as a figure of Daniel O'Connell. 7¾in. (20cm) high.* ***B.*** *Sunderland jug printed on both sides, inscribed Daniel O'Connell, Esq, MP for the County of Clare'. 4½in. (11.4cm) high.*

head. This was in 1826 in an Irish election. The Association first tried its hand in an election in Ireland in 1826 by putting up candidates against landlords. In 1828 the member for County Clare, Vesey Fitzgerald, was made a Minister. The custom was that on obtaining Office a Minister had to seek re-election. Normally this was a formality, because Fitzgerald was very popular and had a good record, but he was a Protestant and very much against Roman Catholic claims. O'Connell stood against him as a Catholic, realising that if elected he would not be able to take his seat. He was elected and was unable to sit in the House of Commons.

A number of commemoratives were made, particularly for the Irish market, to celebrate this important event. O'Connell appears on a salt-glazed gin flask (Plate 87A), marked Oldfield and Company featuring O'Connell holding in his hands, on a scroll, the words 'Irish Reform Cordial'. A Sunderland jug (Plate 87B) decorated with lustre has a fine portrait of O'Connell with the words 'Daniel O'Connel Esq MP for the County of Clare'. It is embellished and decorated with flowers around the handle and also under the lip.

This election pushed the question of Catholic emancipation to the forefront and finally on 13th April 1829 the Bill was passed by 213 votes to 109. The Royal Assent was given, very reluctantly, by George IV, on the same afternoon.

Canning, who had been Prime Minister for a very short time, following the death of Lord Liverpool, was a strong protagonist of Catholic emancipation. There is an interesting print (Plate 88), showing the ghost of Canning appearing before Wellington, who was Prime Minister at the time of the passing of the Catholic Emancipation Act saying: 'Now am I

Plate 88. *Print recording the ghost of Canning appearing to Wellington after the passing of the Catholic Emancipation Act 1829.*

Plate 89. *Minton figure of Wellington wearing a cloak. 11in. (28cm) high.*

avenged'. Wellington and the other Ministers of the Government are crouching in terror before this apparition.

Wellington as Prime Minister has very little, if anything, to commemorate him ceramically. However, there is a very fine bisque figure (Plate 89), full length, wearing a cloak. Wellington was not regarded as a great politician. He played his part in National Politics but was too reactionary in the days of Reform. He is featured dancing a polka with Peel on a Sunderland Pottery pink lustre jug, the larger reserves with prints of the Sailors Farewell and of the Mariners Compass.

For Canning also, very little is recorded. There is one very small coloured bust (Plate 90). It shows the head and shoulders of Canning on a multi-coloured plinth, wearing the clothes of the period. He has a bald head, his cheeks are very red, and on the back is impressed the word 'Canning'.

The other two Prime Ministers who served George IV were Lord Liverpool who was Prime Minister when he succeeded and for whom, as has already been indicated, nothing exists ceramically, and Frederick John Robinson, Viscount Goderich, who was Prime Minister for a short time and can perhaps be regarded, like so many of the Prime Ministers in the reign of George III, as contributing little to the nation's interests. He is not recorded in any form.

An interesting medal was struck to commemorate the Grand Musical Festival for the benefit of the Norfolk and Norwich Hospital in September 1824. The interest here lies in the fact that this seems to be one of the few mentions of anything commemorative for King George IV's brothers. There is a note included on the reverse:

Plate 90.(left) *Staffordshire bust of Canning. 5¼in. (13.5cm) high.*

Plate 91. *Cylindrical mug inscribed 'Lambton for Ever'. 4in. (10.5cm) high.*

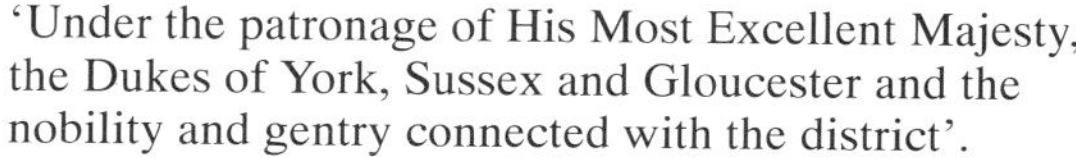

'Under the patronage of His Most Excellent Majesty, the Dukes of York, Sussex and Gloucester and the nobility and gentry connected with the district'.

The front of the medal bears a fine head portrait of King George IV, wearing a laurel wreath, and around him are the words: 'George IV, ascended the British Throne January 29th 1820 in the fifty eighth year of his age'. As far as it is known, little exists to commemorate the Dukes of Sussex and Gloucester.

So far as election pieces are concerned, an interesting mug (Plate 91) of fine pottery exists. This is decorated in rather a naïve style in pink lustre, with an impression of a house and trees, and at the base in black lettering the inscription 'Lambton for Ever'. John George Lambton was a noted Whig Member of Parliament, who stood for Durham. This mug was probably made for the 1826 General Election. He was created Lord Durham in 1828 and became Governor General of Canada.

The Alnwick Elections in Northumberland were famous because of the vast amounts of money spent by supporters of the Whigs and Tories. In the days when corruption was so prevalent, it is almost unbelievable that such very large sums of money were spent to ensure election. In the election held in July 1826 the two Tory candidates were Liddell and Bell. There were two Whig candidates, Beaumont and Lord Howick, the latter of whom withdrew. Bell and Liddell were successful and each of these candidates arranged for the production of mugs to celebrate their success and distributed them to their supporters. That for Liddell (Plate 92) shows, in a central cartouche, a head and shoulders figure of the candidate, around which are the words: 'The choice of the people and Northumberland's glory' with the votes obtained for each: Liddell 1562, Bell 1392, Beaumont 1335. Bell's mug shows a figure, again head and shoulders, of Bell, with the words: 'Bell and Northumberland, the great contest concluded at Alnwick July 6th 1826'. Both these pieces are from Sunderland and typical of the ware produced by those potteries, which of course were fairly close to Northumberland. Beaumont was unsuccessful, but there is a coming-of-age creamware jug for Thomas W. Beaumont Esq on the 3rd November 1813. It was not uncommon for wealthy families to have commemorative plates or mugs made for the coming-of-age of members of their family. Having been unsuccessful at Alnwick, Beaumont was offered the Stafford seat following the death of R. Ironmonger and, with his considerable Whig family interests, gained the seat in a by-election by sixty votes over his Tory opponent, Mr Spooner. Beamont polled 261 votes and Spooner, 191. Beaumont sat at Stafford until the next election in 1830. He then returned to contest Alnwick, this time successfully. Obviously having seen the pottery of successful candidates in Alnwick presented to their supporters he went to the same pottery and asked them to produce a similar piece for the elections at Stafford. This is a very attractive Sunderland jug (Plate 92), bearing in the centre the head and shoulders of Beaumont, around which are the words 'T W Beaumont MP for the County of Stafford, 1826'. On each side, in flags, are Beaumont for Ever' and 'Beaumont and Independency'. For the Alnwick Election Bell produced another, rather larger Sunderland mug, with a different portrait of himself, over which are the words 'Bell for Ever' and underneath 'True

Plate 92. *Two Staffordshire mugs recording the Alnwick Elections in 1826 for Bell and Liddell, and a jug for Beaumont at Stafford.*

Blue' (Plate 92).

There are few commemoratives in glass, but a rather handsome tumbler was produced for Sir Roger Gresley. He stood unsuccessfully for Lichfield in 1826, and was not successful until 1830 when he was returned in Durham, presumably after Lambton. The glass, which is engraved with vine leaves and grapes, is inscribed 'Sir Roger Gresley Bart for Ever'.

The Death of George IV

King George died on 26th June 1830. It cannot be said that his death aroused great public emotion. There are some commemoratives, the most common being a jug (Plate 93) in varying sizes, by the firm Goodwin, Bridgewood and Harris of Lane End, showing on one side the portrait of a young George and on the reverse the inscription 'To the memory of

Plate 93. *Goodwin Bridgewood and Harris jug recording the death of George IV. 5½in. (14cm) high.*

Plate 94. *Accession jug for King William IV and Queen Adelaide. 6¼in. (16cm) high.*

Plate 95. *Moulded accession plate for William and Adelaide.*

His late Majesty King George IV, born August 12th 1862, ascended the throne January 29th 1820, publically proclaimed January 31st 1820, departed this life June 26th 1830, aged 68 years'.

William IV

On the death of his brother, the Duke of Clarence succeeded as William IV and his wife, Adelaide, became Queen. The King was sixty-four at the date of his accession, and had previously served in the Royal Navy. Although he reigned for only seven years, this reign contained a very large number of important constitutional reforms, in particular the Reform Act, and perhaps King William IV is known more for ruling during the fruition of the Reform Movement than for anything else.

The accessions of some sovereigns were not commemorated, but William IV's was. There is a very handsome pottery jug (Plate 94) trimmed with pink lustre printed in black with the accession print, which shows the profiles of the King and Queen Adelaide together in the centre. Around it are the words 'William IIII and Queen Adelaide ascended the British throne 26th June 1830'. The same transfer appears on a child's plate. The actual coronation is commemorated with a similar child's plate to that of the accession (Plate 95). In the centre is the word 'coronation' over the crown and the letters 'W & A'. Underneath are the royal flowers, the thistle, the rose and the shamrock, and the words 'at Westminster September 8th 1831'. Both these plates had superb moulded borders featuring busts of the King and the Queen. A somewhat unusual pair of plates (Plate 96) depicts the King wearing a kind of Tudor ruff and captioned 'His Most Gracious Majesty King William IV, King of Great Britain', and in the case of the Queen, her full face, captioned 'Her Most Gracious Majesty, Adelaide, Queen of Great Britain'. These have again moulded borders with embossed flowers.

There is a very fine pair of Staffordshire busts (Plate 98) of both the King and Queen, decorated, in the King's case, in gold, with the letters 'WR IV', with no crown, and in the case of Adelaide, some gold decoration and the waist, beneath her belt, in a kind of claret red. The Queen wears a tiara bearing the word 'Adelaide'. These may have been made for the Coronation.

There is a Sunderland mug (Plate 97) bearing a portrait of William IV and described as 'the only royal reformer since Alfred'. On the reverse is a portrait of Queen Adelaide, head and shoulders, and wearing what could be her coronation mantle, but no crown in either case. There is a verse which reads:

'Success to all lovers
and may they prove true,
may their pleasures be many,
their sorrows be few.
Long may they live
and be happy together,
and never be parted
'til death doth them sever'.

It is doubtful whether this verse had anything whatsoever to do with the King and Queen who are portrayed on this mug, and it is more likely that this mug was produced during the Reform Bill because of the reference to the King being the Royal Reformer.

Many streets were decorated and festooned for the Coronation, and a particularly fine triumphal arch was erected adjoining the Royal Pavilion in Brighton. A print (Plate 99) of this arch is captioned: 'Erected in Honour of the

Plate 96. *Pair of nursery plates for the Coronation.*

arrival of their Most Glorious Majesties, King William IV and Queen Adelaide at Brighton on August 30th 1830'. The arch is very fine, with the word 'Welcome' and the initials of William and Adelaide thereon. It is festooned in swags and flags are flying from the top of it. It is a very colourful souvenir of the coronation.

The King and the Constitution

On 1st March 1831 Lord Grey, the new Prime Minister, introduced the Reform Bill. Lord John Russell, one of the protagonists of reform, presented the Bill, but it was carried by only one vote. This was not enough so the Government resigned, went to the country, was returned and a second attempt was made, passing on this occasion by fifty-four votes. When the Bill was taken to the Upper House by Lord Althorp, also a protagonist, Lord John Russell, Earl Grey, as Prime Minister, rose to present it, but the House of Lords threw it out. A new Bill was introduced and finally passed without a division on 23rd March 1832. It went to the Lords again, but the Duke of Wellington, a very strong opponent of the Bill, declared 'This is not reform, but revolution', and the

Plate 97. *Sunderland mug of William IV, 'the only royal reformer since Alfred'. 4¾in. (12cm) high.*

Plate 98. *Pair of Staffordshire portrait busts of William and Adelaide.*

Plate 99. *Print showing Coronation Arch at Brighton to record their visit, 30th August 1830.*

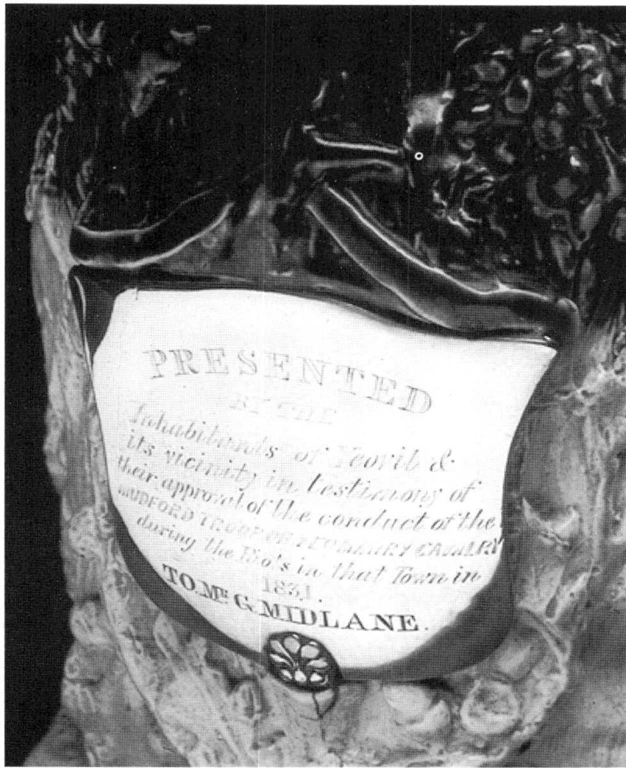

Plate 100A and B. *Brown salt-glaze jug, inscribed 'Presented by the inhabitants of Yeovil'. 9½in. (24cm) high.*

Bill was rejected. The Government found itself in a difficult position, approached the King and asked whether he would create sufficient peers to enable the House of Lords to pass it. The King was not very happy about this, but apparently he agreed. The Government, however, resigned. Wellington was sent for, was unable to form a Government and Grey was recalled. Whereas the King had originally shown much reluctance to create peers, this time he felt he had no alternative and being a constitutional monarch agreed to do so. The Bill was finally carried by a majority of eighty-four on 4th June 1832.

During the passage of the Bill and its rejection by the House of Lords, riots took place throughout the country. To commemorate these there is a jug (Plate 100), brown salt-glazed stoneware, moulded on one side with an impression of agricultural symbols and the other with the royal coat of arms surrounded by the panoply of war, topped by the helmet of a Yeoman volunteer. The jug is mounted with a silver rim and with a silver plaque (Plate 100B) and this is engraved with the passage: 'Presented by the inhabitants of Yeovil and its vicinity in testimony of their approval of the conduct of the Mudford troop of Yeomanry cavalry during the riots in that town in 1831 to Mr G Midlane'.

There were riots in Bristol, but there appears to be no commemorative pottery for them. However, there is an interesting postcard (Plate 101), showing the rifles and constable staves used in the Bristol riots in 1831 and placed in the hall of Knole Park, at Almondsbury in Gloucestershire. This house, now demolished, was the home of the Chester Masters and has been mentioned, only by a footnote, in the book on *English Eccentrics* by Dame Edith Sitwell and recently in a book entitled *Princess Cariboo* by John Wells.

For the Reform Bill itself there are a very large number of commemoratives, probably more than for any other political event in the nineteenth century. The main protagonists were Lord John Russell, Lord Brougham, Lord Grey and Lord

Plate 101. *Postcard showing rifles used at the British riots hanging in the hall of Knole Park, Almondsbury.*

Plate 102. *Set of four Bournes Pottery spirit flasks in the shape of the King, Lord Grey, Lord John Russell and Lord Brougham. 7in. (18cm) high. Lord Althorp is shaped in a flask of enamelled blue glaze. 6¼in. (15.9cm) high.*

Althorp. There is an interesting set of stoneware gin flasks (Plate 102) for the first three of these reform protagonists, with a fourth of the King himself, by Bournes Pottery of Derbyshire. This was probably used as propaganda, because although in the end the King had to agree, it is doubtful whether he really was in favour of reform. There is a much smaller flask for Lord Althorp. Lord John Russell's flask bears a scroll captioned 'The true spirit of Reform'. Brougham's scroll reads 'The Second Magna Carta' and Grey's reads 'The People's Rights'. Each contains the words 'Reform Cordial'. The potters were Belper and Denby. That for Lord Althorp is in enamelled glazing wearing a blue cloak, and on his scroll are the words 'The true spirit of Reform'. There are two amusing satirical Sunderland jugs, one with a coloured transfer of the King (Plate 103) wearing a crown rising from an elaborate copper lustre throne and in

Plate 103. *Baluster-shaped jug portrays in satirical form the King wearing his crown with balloon cartoons. 7in. (17.5cm) high.*

Plate 104. *Bowl, puce printed with figures, holding a scroll inscribed to Grey, Brougham, Russell, Althorp, Burdett, Norfolk and others. 7¼in. (18.5cm) high.*

the balloon cartoon: 'Begone ye Borough mongers I shall trust to my faithfull people' and on the other side three of the protagonists, and in a similar balloon cartoon: 'what shall we do now we are dismissed by our King, our Constitution will not have, we dare not face the people'. It is highly coloured. The second slightly smaller jug bears two of the protagonists with balloon cartoons, one stating 'The King and Reform Bill', the other 'Grey, Russell, Althorp and Reform'. These two figures are also brightly coloured.

A Sunderland jug bears two portraits, this time William IV and Lord John Russell, in typical lustre colours and under the lip in a wreath of shamrocks, roses and thistles the word 'Reform'. A small mug, also Sunderland, bears a fine head and shoulders portrait of Earl Grey with the words 'The choice of the people and England's glory' and the words 'Jane Addison born February 4th 1830'. This is obviously a christening mug. Another mug again bears the heads and shoulders of three of the protagonists, Earl Grey, Lord John Russell and Lord Brougham with the words 'The Champions of Reform'. The transfers are black and white. There are a number of jugs in various sizes, each bearing on either one side or the other portraits of the protagonists and under the lip, with a crown and the royal flowers the same words, 'Champions of Reform'; some are in purple, some in black. There are various commemoratives in either jugs or basins (Plate 104) in pink, one bears in the centre transfers of two of the protagonists, Brougham and Grey, carrying a scroll with the names of these who were in the forefront of this movement. It also includes the names of Burdett and Norfolk. Above the scroll are the words: 'We are for our King and the People, the Bill the whole Bill and nothing but the Bill'. Althorp, although a strong protagonist, does not seem to have been commemorated as much as the others and ceramic records for him are rarer. There is a purple printed pottery jug, 9.5cm high, on one side bearing the bold word 'Reform' surrounded by a cartouche of the royal flowers, and on the other a fine portrait of Lord Althorp and captioned: 'The Statesman flanked by the upright sprays of the national flowers'. The jug is marked on the base C & R, either for Chesworth and Robinson of Lane End or Chetham and Robinson of Longton.

A more unusual jug (Plate 106) shows Wellington and the Tory Cabinet propping up the Rotten Borough Tree while

Plate 105A and B. *Staffordshire puce printed jug with the Dissolution of Parliament. 5¾in (14.5cm) high.*

Plate 106. *Staffordshire jug, brown painted with a cartoon of Reformists chopping down the Rotten Borough Tree. 5¼in. (13.3cm) high.*

Grey, Althorp, Russell and Brougham lay an axe to its roots. This perhaps is the most desirable of all the reform transfers. It was published about 1832. Two other clearly indentifiable characters are William IV and Queen Adelaide. For Lord Brougham there is also a creamware mug (Plate 107), trimmed with a painted blue band, black printed with a most unusual portrait of Henry Brougham and a long verse lauding his various achievements. This was probably produced about 1832 for the Reform Movement but it must have been published before his elevation to the peerage in 1830 when he was returned for the York seat earlier that year. The laudatory words are as follows: 'The incorruptible patriot of the eloquent and the enlightened advocate of religions, the father of the fatherless, liberty, the friend of commerce, the undoubted supporter of the people's rights, the enemy of slavery, the champion of independence, the pride and glory of his country'.

A rare jug, blue printed, has on the front, within a design of the royal flowers, the bold words: 'Reform and Success to the National Union' and on the other side, in bold letters 'Victory' and the names on flags of each of the four protagonists.

A small creamware bowl (Plate 108) bears the head and shoulders of George Kinloch Esq MP. The inscription reads 'On the 22nd December 1819, forced to flee his country and proclaimed an outlaw for having advocated the cause of the people and the necessity of reform. On the 22nd December 1832 proclaimed the chosen representative of the town of Dundee in the reformed House of Commons'. The inscription is surrounded on each side by black and white flowers.

At long last a reformed Parliament met. Shropshire has maintained a strong reputation for commemorating its various elections and a magnificent blue glazed jug (Plate 109) was made by Coalport for the 1835 election which was the first for the reformed Parliament. It is decorated in gold and has around the lip the 'Lord Lieutenant of the County, the Earl of Powys, aged 82' and underneath the names of those elected, headed by The Rt Hon The Lord Hill of Hardwick Grange, Commander in Chief; underneath the date 1835 and the words 'In commemoration of the twelve

Plate 107. *Small creamware cylindrical mug, black printed with bust of Brougham and inscribed with an elaborate eulogy. 3½in. (9cm) high.*

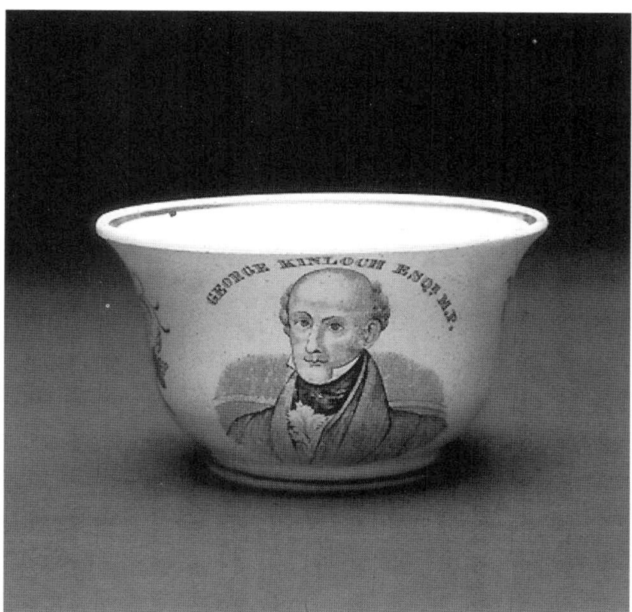

Plate 108. *Staffordshire pottery bowl printed with a bust of George Kinloch, the Scottish MP reformer. 4in. (10cm) diameter.*

Conservatives of Shropshire, representatives of a free and intelligent people'. There then follow the names of each of the successful candidates. Also in a gold decoration are the words, surmounted by a crown: 'Church, King and Constitution' and the coat of arms of the county. On the other side, again in a gold decorated band, the words: 'when bad men conspire, the good must unite – Eldon. Be just and fear not, let all the ends thou aimest at be thy Country's, thy God's and truths – Shakespeare'. Although not directly involved in this reign, it might be appropriate to mention that there is a similar jug for 1841, again with the names of the successful candidates in Shropshire, but in a gold band with the county's coat of arms are the words: 'Church, Queen and Constitution'. Around the lip are the words: 'All friends

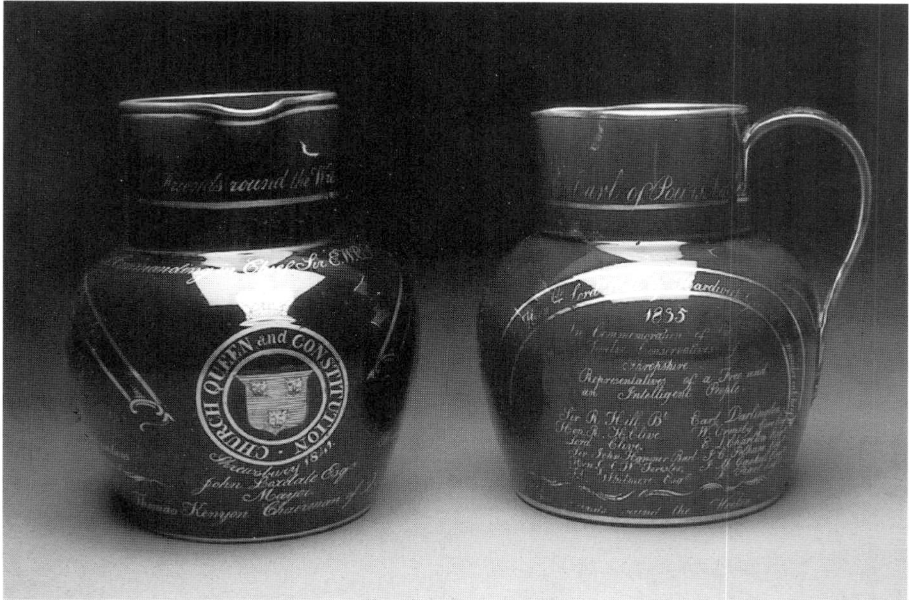

Plate 109. *Two solid blue stoneware jugs by Coalport recording the election of the 12 Members for the Shropshire Constituencies in 1835 and 1841. 9½in. (24cm) high.*

Plate 110. *Large jug with scrolled handles, black printed with busts of Brougham, Burdett and Joseph Hume. 17in. (43.2cm) high.*

Plate 111. *Octagonal child's plate printed with 'Confound the Bishoprics'. 6¼in. (16cm) diameter.*

round the Wrekin'.

A high jug (Plate 110), transfer printed in black, portrays three Whig politicians, Sir Francis Burdett, Baron Brougham and Vaux, Joseph Hume Esq FRCS. Mention has already been made of the part played in the Reform Movement of both Burdett and Brougham but so far, Hume has not been mentioned. Joseph Hume was one of the noted radicals in the House of Commons. He opposed the Orange Society's plot to disbar Victoria from the Crown at a later stage, and was a fervent abolitionist of flogging in the army. This jug was clearly published as part of the Reform Movement's propaganda.

There is an octagonal child's plate (Plate 111), with a moulded border, bearing the inscription in the well of the plate: 'Confound the Bishoprics, frustrate their knavish tricks, on BILL our hopes we fix, God Save the King'. This is a reference to the fact that the Bishops in the House of Lords all opposed the Reform Bill when it came for approval there. Plates for the Reform Movement are not so easily found. A blue and white printed plate (Plate 112), with a design of the royal flowers in garlands shows in the centre Britannia with her trident and her shield with the Union Jack before a kneeling woman with a cornucopia and in the background, two flags, one of which has on it the word Reform'. In the background are the masts of ships. The same motif of Britannia and flags is shown on a puce printed jug with, in addition to the word 'Reform', the word 'Union'. An added feature is the British Lion.

Several of the so-called H.B. cartoons were issued for the Reform, two of which are appropriate. There is an amusing cartoon (Plate 113) of King William riding in a carriage entitled 'The new State Carriage – if my new State Carriage cannot be got ready I will go in a hackney coach, for I will in person send out to the people for their decision'. Standing behind, as postillions, are Brougham and Grey and there is a comment above the coach which reads 'The Aristocracy have too long kept the Crown and the Government in subjection to the manifest injury of the people. The people shall have their rights', and then further comments: 'and nothing less than a knight of the whip for this' said by the coachman brandishing

Plate 112. *Rogers blue printed plate, printed with Britannia inscribed 'Reform'. 10¼in. (26cm) diameter.*

Plate 113. John Doyle cartoon, 'The New State Carriage', showing caricatures of the King driving to Parliament in a hackney carriage.

Plate 114. John Doyle cartoon showing the King holding a birch rod with the word 'Reform'.

Plate 115. Staffordshire pottery jug with a bust of General Scarlett. 3½in. (9cm) high.

Plate 116. Staffordshire pottery mug with a portrait of George Holyoake. 3¼in. (8.3cm) high.

his whip, and there is a large crowd of the populus shouting 'The Reform Bill for ever'. It is coloured and effectively portrays the intention of the King to go to Parliament himself to ensure that the Bill was passed. Another cartoon (Plate 114) shows William IV brandishing a birch with the word 'Reform'. Behind him are Brougham, in his robes, and Grey, and the King is saying: 'Get you gone and never let me see you again til you are reformed'. On the other side are the Opposition with Wellington looking very woebegone shouting 'O Bobby, Bobby, what shall we do now', together with other Members who are saying 'I'm afraid I shall never be admitted into the school again'. Another one: it's a shocking bad job' and a third: 'Who would have thought I should have been hunted out already'.

Plate 117. Staffordshire child's plate inscribed 'New Marriage Act', circa 1836. 6¼in. (16cm) diameter.

A jug (Plate 105A and B) portrays the King dissolving Parliament. There is a cartouche with the King standing beneath a throne, addressing members of the House of Lords, with the following words: 'My Lords, Gentlemen, I have been induced to resort to this measure for the purpose of ascertaining the sense of my people in the way in which I can be most constitutionally and authentically expressed'. The jug is purple printed and underneath the lip is a statue of a man holding a torch with the words 'Reform burning' and underneath the following quotation: 'Disenfranchise stone walls and parks, give members to the people' and underneath 'King and Constitution'. This jug was published by Imperial Filigree, on the base is the mark with a crown surmounted by a lion with the words 'No 10' and on each side of the words 'Imperial Filigree' are the initials 'GH' which presumably refer to the initials of the potter.

An interesting personality who was elected Member of Parliament at this time was General Scarlett. He represented the seat of Guildford in 1836 until 1841, at which time he was a Major in the army. He then seems to have dedicated himself to a wholly military career and it was he who led the heavy cavalry charge at Balaclava. After that war he returned to England and pursued a notable career in the Army. He did not regain a seat in Parliament, although he did contest Burnley in the 1868 election, the election of the Second Reform Parliament, but he did not succeed. There is a small jug (Plate 115), blue printed, bearing the head and shoulders of General Scarlett GCB. He has a fine mutton-chop moustache and on the other side is his wife Lady Scarlett, head and shoulders, in the dress of the period. She was, before she married, Charlotte Hargreaves, an heiress in Burnley. It may be that this jug was published for the Burnley election, although there is no mention of this.

The Chartist Movement was active during this period, although there is little to commemorate any of the protagonists. However, there is a mug for George Jacob Holyoake (Plate 116), a strong supporter of the Chartist Movement, who was, in fact, the last person to be tried for blasphemy. He was tried at the Gloucester Assizes on 15th August 1842. He defended himself with a nine hour speech, but was sentenced to six months imprisonment. The mug has a small sepia portrait of his head, sporting a fine beard, around which is a design of flowers and the facsimile of his signature. It was published by the C.W.S., Labour and Waite, Longton.

1836 saw another reform, the introduction of the New Marriage Act. A small child's plate (Plate 117) commemorates this, highly coloured and with a moulded border in bright oranges and greens, in the centre of which are the words: 'The New Marriage Act' with an eloped bride and groom standing before a blacksmith, this being a reference, of course, to Gretna Green.

The Death of the King

The King died on 20th June 1837. Very little commemorates this event. Apart from the interest in reform his reign was not very interesting from the aspect of the part he took in the life of the country. Having decided to abandon Mrs Jordan and settle down with Adelaide, his Queen, he led a reasonably quiet and sober life.

CHAPTER 2

Queen Victoria 1837-1901

Following the death of her father, the Duke of Kent, in 1820, the young Princess Victoria was brought up by her mother, also named Victoria, who was the sister of Prince Leopold of Saxe-Coburg, the widowed husband of Princess Charlotte, and who became in later years the mentor of Queen Victoria when she started her reign, and was known as Uncle Leopold. He subsequently became the first King of the Belgians.

Her accession to the throne had clearly been anticipated and there is a gin flask, marked for Bournes Potteries, modelled as the head and shoulders figure of the young Victoria, the reverse of the flask with the inscription 'Queen Alexandrina Victoria'.

Before her accession Victoria was often known as the Princess Alexandrina, and it was not known how she would sign herself as Queen until the first Privy Council, when she opted for Victoria. It is likely that this gin flask was made before the death of William IV, ready for publication as soon as the Queen's Accession has been announced.

Her proclamation as Queen is the subject of a ceramic jug (Plate 118) which carried the head and shoulders of the Queen wearing the 'crown bun' with which she was associated at the time of her accession. It is blue printed, the neck of the jug has a design of basketweave and royal flowers and underneath the lip is the crown surrounded by the words 'Victoria Regina', the date of her birth, '25th May 1819' and 'Proclaimed 20th June 1837'. In fact her birth date is an error. She was actually born on 24th May.

A glazed Staffordshire figure of the young Queen (Plate 119), probably a 'potter's trial' model for a figure which

Plate 118. *Proclamation jug of squat shape and high scroll handle. 7in. (18cm) high.*

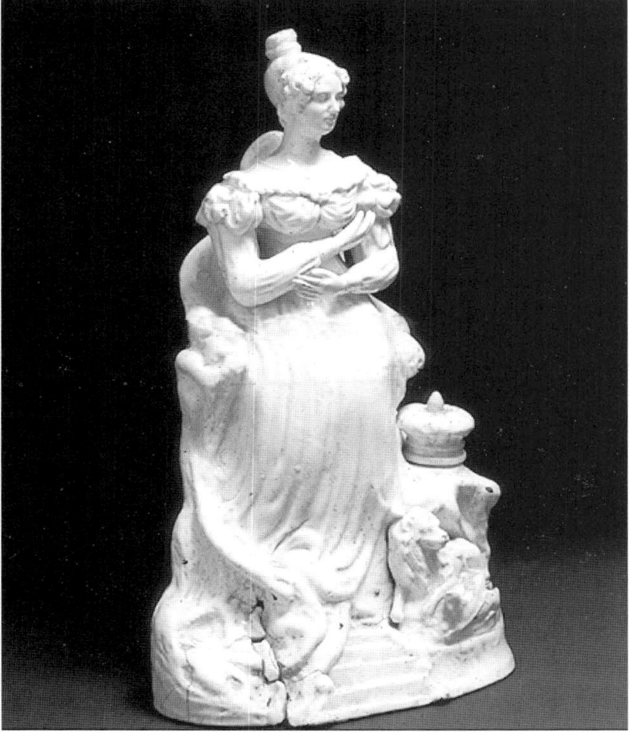

Plate 119. *Staffordshire porcelain figure of the Queen. 13½in. (34.5cm) high.*

Plate 120. *Small purple printed mug for the Coronation and Swansea nursery plate. 6¼in. (16cm) diameter.*

Plate 121(left). *Two Coronation mugs for the Coronation, pink and purple printed. 3¼in. (8.5cm) high.*
Plate 122(above). *Blue printed jug for the Review that did not take place.*

Plate 123A. *Marriage jug of squat shape with fluted shoulders and multiple spur handle printed in blue. 7in. (18cm) high.* **B.** *Small plate printed in green with the date of marriage. 6½in. (16.2cm) diameter.*

Plate 124. *Nursery plate for the marriage. 7in. (17.5cm) diameter.*

Plate 125. *Family tree of Victoria and Albert published for their Golden Jubilee, 1887.*

Plate 126A. *Bowl, brown printed with floral rim and showing the Queen and Prince Albert. 5¾in. (14.5cm) diameter.* **B.** *Salt-glazed stoneware spirit flask embossed with portraits of Victoria and Albert. 7¼in. (18.5cm) high.* **C.** *Cowrie shell to record the birth of Prince Alfred, carved in cameo – August 6th 1844. 2¾in. (7cm).* **D.** *Memorial saucer for the death of the Duke of Clarence 14.1.1892.*

Plate 127. *Nursery plate with daisy border with portrait of the Queen. 7¼in. (18.2cm) diameter.*

Plate 128. *'Mary mug' with Queen on horseback.*

proved to be too difficult and costly to be produced commerically, is extremely rare and may be a unique piece. It was probably produced for her accession in 1837. The crown to her side would be standard practice in indicating that she had not yet been crowned. The difficulties in potting such a complicated figure are obvious from the firing flaws. This figure is not recorded anywhere and it is safe to assume that production on a commercial scale was abandoned. Anthony Oliver, author of *The Victorian Staffordshire Figure* believes that this piece is of great rarity.

An interesting coronation souvenir is in the form of a parasol (Plate 183). The handle of the parasol is of porcelain, perhaps Crown Derby, bearing the head of the Queen in colour and underneath is a gold rim bearing the monogram 'VR' and the date, 1837.

Her coronation was recorded on plates and mugs (Plates 120 and 121) which are highly sought-after. They were made either in Staffordshire or in Wales, at Swansea. The distinction is a small one, those made in Staffordshire had a slight loop of the necklace, whereas those made in Swansea have a straighter necklace. They are all purple printed, have the dates, either of the birth, proclamation and accession, as well as coronation, some without the proclamation. The mugs come in two sizes, large and small.

Following her coronation there was to be military review. However, a dispute arose with Lord Melbourne, who refused to let her ride, though the Queen insisted upon riding. As a result the review was cancelled. A pottery jug (Plate 122) records the review that never was. It is blue printed.

Her marriage to Prince Albert of Saxe-Coburg has been recorded on several pieces. A jug (Plate 123A) shows both Albert and Victoria, but it is very difficult to recognise either of them from the portraits shown. A child's plate (Plate 123B) with a moulded border has in the centre a green printed portrait of the Queen and Prince Albert, captioned 'Married February 10th 1840'.

The Queen described her marriage as idyllic and they had nine children. The various marriages of her children and of her grandchildren resulted in her being described as the 'Grandmama of Europe'. A family tree (Plate 125) shows at the base the Queen and Prince Consort and on the various branches their children and the grandchildren who resulted.

There are several commemoratives recording their life together. A very rare bowl (Plate 126A) shows the Queen and Prince Albert in the centre, standing behind is a lady-in-waiting, the border is decorated with various escutcheons with the initials 'V' and 'A' surmounted by a crown and laurel leaves and the royal flowers.

An early plate of the Queen is a child's plate (Plate 127) with a daisy border showing in the centre the Queen wearing a tiara, black and white printed, head and shoulders, below which are the letters, 'VR'. A mug, black printed (Plate 128), shows the Queen, side-saddle on a horse, riding at Windsor Castle. It was clearly published for somebody called Mary because the mug bears the name 'Mary' within a wreath. A tall jug (Plate 129), blackberry printed, shows the Queen and Prince Albert with some of the royal children in front of Old Balmoral. This castle was subsequently altered drastically by Prince Albert and became the Highland home of the Queen.

Both the Queen and Prince Albert are the subject of a gin flask (Plate 126B). It shows in relief the head and shoulders of the Queen with the crown, the initials 'VR' and the name of the potter 'ST' in a kind of gothic arch. On the reverse is Prince Albert, head and shoulders, with the letters 'PA'. Prince Albert is the subject of a separate gin flask (Plate 164A), a standing portrait, salt-glazed, with his hand on the crown, captioned 'Albert'.

A figure in wax (Plate 130) shows the Prince and Queen

Victoria seated on a sofa, the Queen wearing a dress of lace with the order of the garter and a tiara, and Albert in court dress, wearing scarlet military uniform with gold epaulettes.

A bisque figure (Plate 131) of Queen Victoria was modelled by Cocker of Bedford Square, London, and shows the Queen seated in a chair.

The Children of Queen Victoria and Prince Albert

Their eldest child was Princess Victoria, the Princess Royal, who subsequently married the Crown Prince of Prussia and became the Empress Frederick of Germany. Her christening was allegedly recorded on a curious plate (Plate 132) showing a bishop christening a child while the parents kneel before him on a cushion, and is captioned 'The Bishop of Heliopolis'. The same transfer has been seen with the inscription 'Royal Christening', but quite who the bishop was is not clear. A coloured engraving (Plate 133) of the royal christening shows a clergyman holding the baby princess with Queen Victoria and Prince Albert looking on. Her marriage to the Crown Prince of Prussia was recorded in various cups and saucers (Plate 134), green, black and purple printed. They show the very tall Prince with the Princess surrounded by wreaths of flowers and on the reverse, Potsdam Palace.

Their second child, the Prince of Wales, became King Edward VII. His birth and christening have been commemorated on a pottery plate (Plate 135) with moulded border and the inscription 'Albert Edward the Prince of Wales born Nov. 9 1841'. The body of the plate is printed with a view of his mother on horseback.

There is a porcelain mug (Plate 136), gilded with a fine inscription, 'Marking the Christening of Albert Edward, Prince of Wales'. His birth is also the subject of several children's plates, having in the centre different motifs, one being the little jockey (Plate 137) showing a small child on the back of a large dog, and around are the moulded letters indicating the date of his birth, 'Nov 9 1841'. He features later on a daisy border plate (Plate 138) as a small boy aged about two, this time on a horse, surrounded by the words 'England's Hope, Prince of Wales'.

The next child, Princess Alice, was born on 25th April 1853. For her there is very little of any ceramic nature. She married Prince Louis of Hesse and it is from this marriage that the Mountbatten dynasty started. There is a set of pottery plates (Plate 139), pink printed, with wedding portraits of the Princess Royal, Prince of Wales and Princess Alice. Apart from these there is very little known to be commemorated for Princess Alice. Her death was commemorated by a book-marker (Plate 140), silk woven. They both also appear on a child's soup plate (Plate 141), daisy bordered, bearing in the centre, coloured portraits of the three elder children, the Prince of Wales on a horse, with Princess Victoria and presumably Princess Alice, captioned 'England's Future King'. It would appear to be Sunderland.

One of the daughters of Princess Alice of Hesse married the Tsar of Russia. The Tsar and Tsarina visited France in 1896 when a Treaty between the two countries was signed. A pair of plates (Plate 142) records this event. In the centre of one is Nicholas II, Emperor of Russia, in an oval surrounded by emblems of the two countries, portraits of scenes of previous friendly encounters, the visit of Alexander III to Admiral Gervais at Kronstat in 1891, the reception of Admiral Avallan by Admiral Boissoudie at Toulon, 1893 and the Grand Manoeuvres, in 1895. The plate for the Empress has a portrait of Alexandra surrounded by regal emblems and three scenes of ceremony; the clergy receiving the Tsar, the engagement ceremony of the Tsarevich, as he then was, and Princess Alexandra, and the coronation of the Tsar. These plates are transfer-printed in grey, blue and brown on earthenware and are marked with the name 'Sarreguenines' and the superimposed initials W & G. Tsar Nicholas was a son of Princess Dagmar, a sister of Queen Alexandra of Denmark, and was therefore a first cousin of King George V.

Prince Alfred, the Duke of Edinburgh, was born on 6th August, 1844. An interesting piece commemorating his birth is in the form of a shell (Plate 126C), carrying the words 'Prince Alfred', surmounted by the crown and the date of his birth. Prince Alfred and the Princess Alice appeared in a masque called *The Seasons* performed before the Queen in 1848, and a pottery jug (Plate 143) carries moulded pottery figures of both of these children taken from the life-size statues executed by the distinguished sculptress, Mary Thorneycroft. The seasons portrayed are alleged to be summer and autumn. Prince Alfred embarked on a naval career and married the Grand Duchess Marie in St. Petersburg. A plate for the wedding (Plate 144) carried in the

***Plate 129.** Octagonal jug printed in sepia with a view of Old Balmoral Castle. 8¼in. (21cm) high.*

Plate 130. *Victoria and Albert modelled in wax seated together on a gilt-edged sofa. 13¼in. (34cm) high overall.*

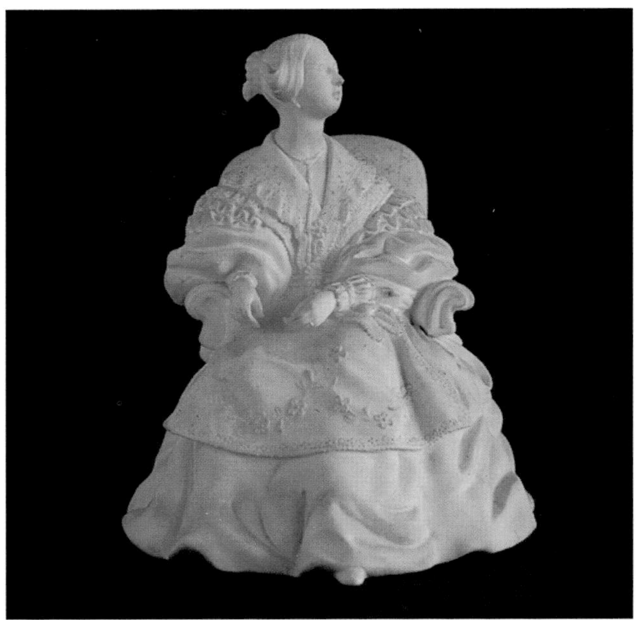

Plate 131. *Bisque porcelain figure of Victoria by George Cocker. 6¾in. (17cm) high.*

Plate 132. *Nursery plate with the 'Bishop of Heliopolis'.*

Plate 133(left). *Framed engraving of the royal christening.*

Plate 134(above). *Cup and saucer for the marriage of the Princess Royal and Prince Frederick of Prussia.*

Plate 135. *Plate recording the birth of the Prince of Wales with the Queen on horseback.*

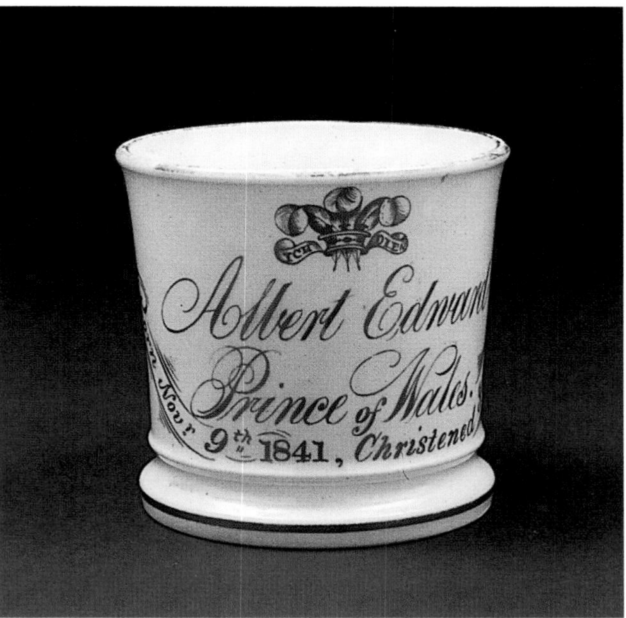

Plate 136. *Porcelain christening mug for the Prince of Wales.*

Plate 138. *Daisy border plate, 'England's Hope'.*

Plate 137. *Birth plate, 'The Little Jockey'.*

Plate 139. *Set of three pottery plates, pink printed, with wedding portraits of the Princess Royal and the Prince of Prussia, the Prince and Princess of Wales, Princess Alice and the Grand Duke of Hesse. 7in. (17.5cm) diameter.*

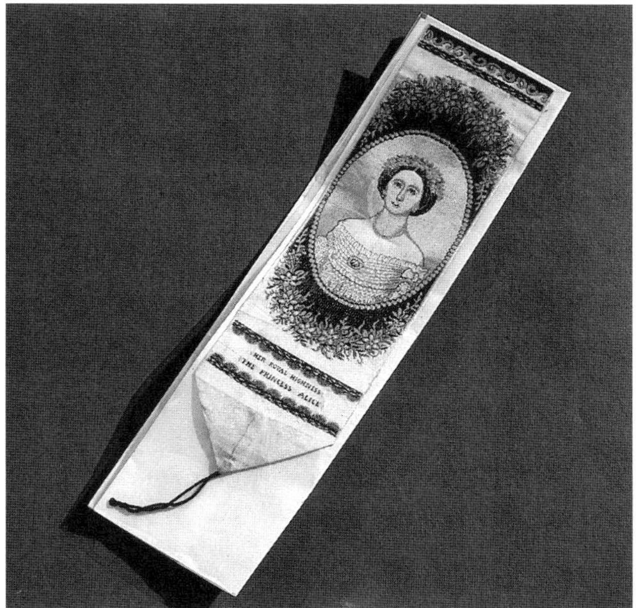

Plate 140. *Silk-woven bookmark recording the death of Princess Alice of Hesse.*

Plate 141. *An octagonal soup plate with daisy border edged in pink lustre printed in black and coloured 'England's Future King'. 8¾in. (22cm) diameter.*

centre portraits of the Duke and Duchess of Edinburgh. The plate has orange decorations.

Princess Helena was born on 26th May, 1846 and she married the Duke of Schleswig Holstein. There is practically nothing ceramically to record this rather private Princess although some photographs do exist (Plate 145). Her marriage was recorded on a bronze medal (Plate 146) and a small money-box (Plate 147) was published when she opened a hospital in Birmingham. It states that the hospital was opened by Princess Christian on behalf of the Queen on 7th July, 1897. The tin carries a full likeness of the hospital. She took a very active part in charities and in war work during the First World War. She was responsible for hospital trains and a feeding cup (Plate 409) bears the Red Cross surmounted by the words, 'Princess Christian's Hospital Train, 1915'. Both her daughters, Princess Marie Louise and Princess Helena Victoria also took an active part in work for charity and a key (Plate 148) was presented to Princess Helena Victoria when she opened the YMCA in Warrington on 26th November, 1931.

Princess Louise was born on 18th March, 1848. Nothing exists to commemorate her birth, but when she married the Marquis of Lorne, being the first British Princess to marry outside royalty, a tall jug (Plate 149) was published to record the event. It bears, in a heart-shaped centre on a purple background, portraits of the Princess and the Marquis with royal flowers, and it was published by Verriville Pottery. The Marquis of Lorne was appointed Governor General of Canada and a pressed glass white opaque bowl commemorates the event, when he landed with the Marchioness of Lorne at Halifax, Nova Scotia on 25th November, 1878. A fine pair of terracotta figures (Plate 150), head and shoulders on a plinth, probably to commemorate the marriage, was published by Watcombe Terracotta Clay Company, Torquay.

Prince Arthur, Duke of Connaught, was born on 1st May, 1850 and took up a career in the army. There are very few commemoratives for him. As part of his service in Egypt a plate (Plate 151) was published by a French pottery captioned, 'L'Egypte, 1882'. It shows the Duke together with other British soldiers with a field gun in the rear. The French caption reads 'Major General, the Duke of Connaught studying the positions of the Arabs before Ramleh'. Around the border in black and white are various features connected with Egypt, the pyramids and camels. Although he carried out several public duties, there is little in the way of commemorative records. However, his visit to Fairford in 1909 is recorded on a small bowl (Plate 152) which bears the coloured head and shoulders of the Duke in military uniform surrounded by flags, surmounted by a crown and captioned 'A Souvenir of the visit to Fairford, September 19th, 20th & 21st 1909'.

Prince Leopold, Duke of Albany (a child of anxiety), was born on 7th April 1853. His marriage to Princess Helena of Pyrmont Waldeck has been recorded on a bone china cup and saucer (Plate 153), black printed, which carries pictures of both the Duke and Duchess of Albany. There is also a silver medal to record the event. Prince Leopold was a haemophiliac, a sufferer of the royal condition, and there is little known to commemorate his life and activities.

The youngest daughter, Princess Beatrice, was born on 14th April 1857. She married Prince Henry of Battenburg, and by doing so created a situation whereby both a daughter and a grand-daughter of Queen Victoria married brothers.

Plate 142. *Pair of plates for the Tsar and Tsarina of Russia, a grand-daughter of Victoria.*

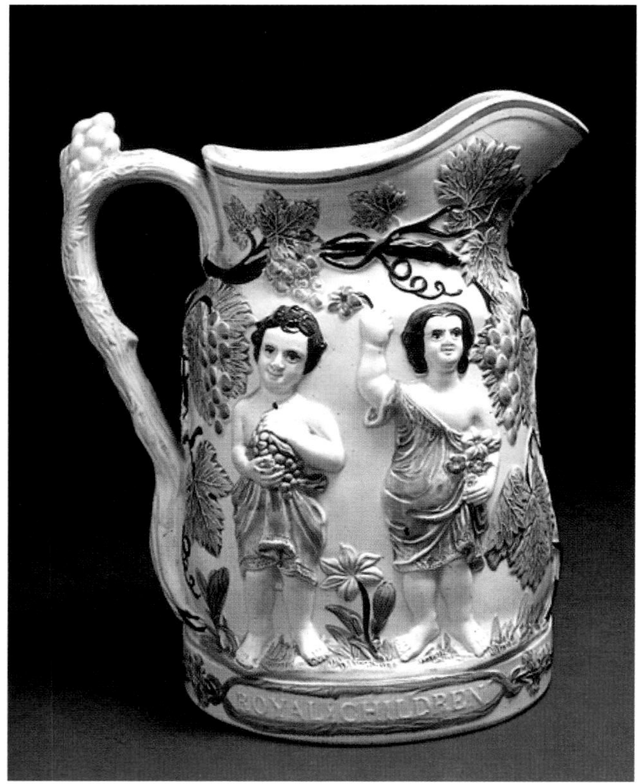

Plate 143(left). *Scottish relief-moulded jug, captioned 'The Seasons'.*

Plate 144. *Plate recording the marriage of Prince Alfred, Duke of Edinburgh and Grand Duchess Alice of Russia.*

Plate 145. *Photographs of Princess Helena.*

Plate 146. *Medal to commemorate the marriage of Princess Helena and Prince Schleswig Holstein.*

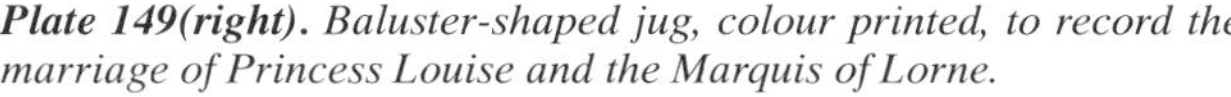

Plate 147(above centre). *Moneybox tin for the opening of the Birmingham Hospital in 1897.*
Plate 148(above). *Key presented to Princess Helena Victoria after the opening of the YMCA in Warrington – 26.11.1931.*

Plate 149(right). *Baluster-shaped jug, colour printed, to record the marriage of Princess Louise and the Marquis of Lorne.*

Plate 150. *Pair of terracotta busts depicting Princess Louise and the Marquis of Lorne – Watcombe Clay Co., Torquay.*

Plate 151. *Plate depicting the Duke of Connaught, black printed, at a military scene in 1882, entitled 'L'Egypte'.*

Plate 152. *Dish recording the Duke's visit to Fairford in 1909.*

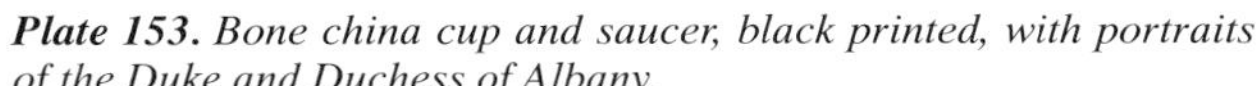

Plate 153. *Bone china cup and saucer, black printed, with portraits of the Duke and Duchess of Albany.*

Plate 154. Daily Graphic *wedding souvenir.*

Plate 155. *Mug recording the marriage of Princess Beatrice.*

The grand-daughter was Princess Victoria, daughter of Princess Alice, who married Prince Louis of Batterburg. Princess Beatrice lived with the Queen at Osborne, it being part of the agreement that when she married she should do so. Her marriage was recorded in a very dull mug which was manufactured on the Isle of Wight and states very baldly the details of the marriage (Plate 155).

The Great Exhibition of 1851 and Others

The greatest triumph of Victoria's reign was the Great Exhibition of 1851 which she attributed to Albert's initiative. At the opening she stated that this was Albert's day. Several commemoratives have been issued for this Great Exhibition,

A plate published in France (Plate 156), by the same pottery that published for the Duke of Connaught in Egypt, has in the centre the Queen and Prince Albert, together with the young Princess Royal and the Prince of Wales, entering the Exhibition to the accompaniment of trumpeters and Yeoman of the Guard. It is captioned 'Une Semaine à Londres. L'Ouverture de l'Exposition'. The border is decorated with various designs of swags and angels. A blue printed jug and a white loving cup (Plate 157) with gold trim portrays the Crystal Palace and an embossed chocolate box (Plate 158) of fine and coloured design provided a splendid souvenir of this momentous occasion.

Plate 156. *Plate recording the opening of the Great Exhibition 1851, captioned 'L'Ouverture de L'Exposition'.*

A pottery plate (Plate 160), black printed, shows the Crystal Palace in colour inscribed 'The Building for the Great Exhibition 1851. Proposed by HRH Prince Albert designed by Joseph Paxton, executed by Fox Henderson and Co', with detailed statistics of design. The success of the 1851 Great Exhibition gave the idea to other countries that exhibitions were a thing of the future and they started to take place in various other places.

In Dublin in 1853 there was a great industrial exhibition and a spill vase (Plate 161) has on it a sepia transfer of the buildings erected for the purpose. There was an exhibition at Madame Tussaud's, opened by the Prince and Princess of Wales, and there is a jug (Plate 161) showing two portraits, in ovals, of the Prince and Princess, and also of Madame Tussaud's building.

The Exhibition of 1862 was held on land now occupied by the Natural History Museum and the Imperial College of Science with the north part of the site of the present Albert

Plate 157A. *Blue printed jug showing the Crystal Palace.* ***B.*** *Porcelain loving cup with gilt lettering describing the Exhibition.*

Plate 158(left). *Decorated chocolate box embossed with the Crystal Palace.*

Plate 159. *Porcelain plate manufactured by Coalport and used on the royal table at the City of London Dinner to commemorate the Great Exhibition. 10in. (25.5cm) diameter.*

Plate 160(left). *Pottery plate, black printed with coloured view of the Crystal Palace. 6¼in. (16cm) diameter.*

Plate 161. Exhibitions. *Left to right: cup and saucer, mug, silk picture, 1882(centre), Cardiff medal, 1888, black and white spill vase and plate for Edinburgh, 1886. Ticket for Newcastle-upon-Tyne Mining Engineering 1887, brown transfer spill vase - Dublin 1853, cranberry handled glass for Indian Exhibition 1895, jug – Madame Tussauds – no date.*

Hall largely taken up by gardens of the Royal Horticultural Society. Prince Albert's Road is now called Queensgate.

The Exhibition was recorded in both ceramic and other forms. There is a silk picture (Plate 161) with a half-length portrait of the Queen, in an oval surround of roses, thistle and shamrocks. She wears a coronet and a décolletée dress with flounced sleeves and a double row of pearls. A diagonal sash and bracelet with a portrait of Albert captioned in gothic lettering 'International Exhibition London 1862'. The maker was J. Bauman. These were produced on a jacquard type mechanical loom using a pierced card system in black and white silk with brown used for the caption.

Portraits of this kind were being made by continental weavers for some years before. The idea was taken up by Stevens of Coventry and brought to a remarkable degree of perfection.

A small purple printed mug and a cup and saucer (Plate 161) bears the buildings of the 1862 Exhibition and is so captioned. A tall glazed jug (Plate 162) is highly decorated with the coats of arms of all the countries which took part in the 1862 Exhibition, including the Vatican. The handle is very ornate, surmounted by crowns. The other coats of arms shown are those of Denmark, Prussia, America, Austria. Greece, Brazil, Gibraltar, Portugal, Sardinia and Russia.

An Indian Exhibition was held in London in 1895 for which there is a small cranberry glass jug, inscribed in a white design (Plate 161).

There was an International Exhibition in Edinburgh in 1886. A plate (Plate 161) portrays, in the centre, a coloured painting of part of Edinburgh, headed 'Souvenir of Old Edinburgh'. There is also a spill vase, with a black and white transfer of the buildings erected for exhibition purposes and captioned 'International Exhibition Edinburgh 1886'.

A plate was published for the Bristol Industrial Exhibition in 1893.

An Exhibition was held in Glasgow in 1888 and a blue bowl, with a lid (Plate 163), shows a transfer of the exhibition buildings erected for the purpose and on the lid three transfers of the Bishop's Palace. A plate carries a full view of the Exhibition buildings.

On 27th June 1896 the Prince of Wales opened an industrial exhibition in Cardiff, for which there is an engraved glass portraying the details and the Prince of Wales feathers. Cardiff held another International Exhibition in

Plate 162. Tall glazed jug decorated with the coats of arms of the countries which took part in the 1862 Exhibition.

1888. A medal was struck to commemorate this. It is in metal alloy, bearing the shields of the Borough of Cardiff and the arms of the winner of the award 'The Cash Registering Machine Company', with its motto '*Avito verit honore*'. The name of the winner of the award is engraved on the reverse, with a wreath of laurel and oak leaves.

A medal was also struck for the International Inventions Exhibition, held in London in 1895. It shows on the other side an engraving of old London Bridge and with the words 'Ye Olde London Bridge'. An Exhibition was held at Douglas on the Isle of Man in 1892 for which there is a glass tumbler with engraved designs. On one side is the harbour at Douglas and on the other an old wooden man-of-war, surrounded by the royal flowers and inscribed 'M A Jenkins' – presumably made for this gentleman. There was also a Fine Art and Industrial Maritime Exhibition, again held in Cardiff in 1896.

In 1861 the Queen's world came to an end when Albert died. The death of Albert has been the subject of some commemorative pieces, although they tend to dwell rather more on his achievements than upon his death.

There is a very fine jug (Plate 164B), green transferred, which shows a portrait of Albert with the 1851 Exhibition in the background, and on the reverse the same portrait with the 1862 Exhibition with which he was very much involved, but died before it was opened.

There is a large tazza (Plate 165), either of cream and green, or orange and cream background with brown and black transferring in three panels. These show the three fields of Albert's achievements: Promoter of the Arts; President of

Plate 163. Bowl and plate for the Glasgow Exhibition, 1888.

Plate 164A. *A salt-glazed stoneware spirit flask in the form of Prince Albert. 10¼in. (26cm) high.* **B.** *Pear-shaped jug printed in green lamenting the death of the Prince Consort. 9½in. (24cm) high.*

Plate 165. *Copeland tazza made for the Art Union of London in memory of Prince Albert. 16¼in. (41.5cm).*

Plate 166. *Silk memorial picture of Albert.*

Plate 167. *Pair of continental porcelain vases of flower form supported by the Royal Arms in white biscuit with portrait medallions of Victoria and Albert. 8¼in. (21cm).*

Societies for Science; literature – Chancellor of a University. Between these winged figures are held the three symbols of his achievements, Osborne, the Island Palace Home, 1860, the Palace of Literature, 1855 and the Palace of Industry of All Nations, 1851; around the whole is an excerpt from his first speech on 18th May 1848. This was commissioned from Copeland by the Art Union of London and is so inscribed. It is a very handsome piece. There is also a porcelain plate (Plate 159) manufactured by Coalport which was actually used at the royal table at the City of London dinner to mark the Great Exhibition. Printed with flags on a turquoise and blue border.

The Queen liked to travel and she went to France in 1858. She also received the Emperor Napoleon III and the Empress in London. There is a rather fine pair of vases (Plate 167) bearing the head and shoulders of both the Queen and Albert, which were reputedly made for this visit. They are in bright green. There is also a pair of plaques (Plate 168), white bisque, one of Napoleon III and one of the Queen.

She also received the Shah of Persia and a miniature cup and saucer records this event. The cup bears in an oval gold frame the head of the Shah wearing an oriental kind of shako. The design is of blue flowers tinged with gilt decoration. This attractive commemorative piece has no manufacturer's mark. The Queen conferred the Order of the Garter on the Shah during the visit.

The Queen always took a great interest in her soldiers and when the volunteers were raised in 1860 and seven thousand men enrolled, the Queen decided to hold a review. One was held in London on 23rd June at Hyde Park and the second in Edinburgh on 7th August. An important moulded jug (Plate 169) was published by Sandford Pottery and comes in a

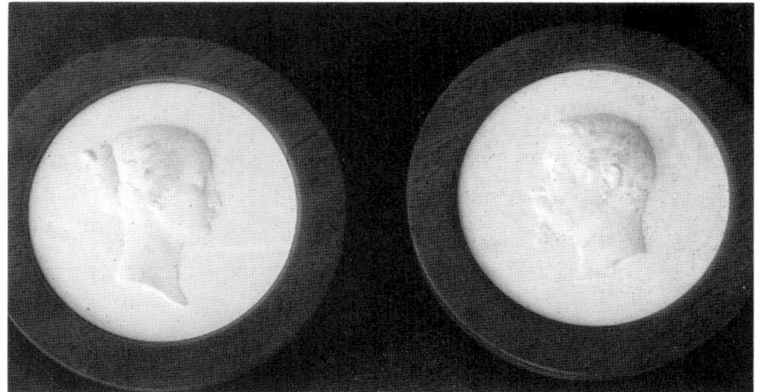

Plate 168. *Pair of continental white biscuit porcelain portrait medallions modelled with profile head of Victoria and Napoleon III. Both signed 'J. Beyre F. Nievwerkerke Dir'. 3in. (8cm) diameter.*

variety of sizes, the lip is moulded with the date 1860. In the centre is a finely modelled bust portrait of Queen Victoria with her hair plaited into the distinctive bun and loop style she favoured, the whole contained in a circular laurel wreath topped by the crown. Under this is a ribbon cartouche, inscribed 'Defenders of our Queen and Country'. Flanking this central motif as an overall frieze are figures of a soldier, a sailor, both holding hands, an English and a Scottish volunteer, and underneath them in a running caption is the wording: 'Our Army & Navy & Brave Volunteers'. These are either of dryware or rough-glazed light buff-coloured pot. The registration mark is for September which clearly indicates that it was inspired by these two royal reviews.

It was many years before the Queen was prepared to carry out public engagements.

When in 1877 she was proclaimed Empress of India, there was no ceramic to recall this event. However, there is a red silk banner (Plate 170), hand embroidered, bearing in the centre around an embroidered wreath the royal coat of arms, above which are the words, 'Victoria, Empress of India' and underneath the date, 1877.

Jubilees

The commemoratives that had been produced up until this time are not easily found, occasionally appearing in sales, but with the coming of the two jubilees in 1877 and 1897, the position changed dramatically. Both were heavily commemorated and many of the items made for both these occasions can still be readily obtained. The prices vary according to the quality, condition and what form they take. Mugs made for various cities and towns bearing the coats of arms and the names of the Mayor or Lord Mayor of the day

Plate 169. *Sandford Pottery white stoneware relief moulded jug representing 'Our Army & Navy & Brave Volunteers'. 10½in. (26.5cm) high.*

Plate 170. *Red silk embroidered banner proclaiming Victoria Empress of India, 1877.*

Plate 171. *Tapering mug inscribed 'Shipperies Exhibition'.*

can probably be obtained for a reasonable figure. Cups and saucers or full tea-sets can also be obtained, again at reasonable prices.

It was during the period of these jubilees that tinware became an important feature in the commemorative line. Various biscuit and tea manufacturers produced goods featuring members of the royal family or scenes concerned with royalty. This was a pattern which has continued right up until the present day. Many of the tins which were produced then are not easily found and are clearly collectors' pieces. If a collector of commemorative items is unable to find a ceramic piece, it is well worth giving consideration to a tin.

For the jubilee of 1877 the Queen visited Liverpool to open the Shipperies Exhibition and there is a mug (Plate 171) to recall this event. It has the head and shoulders of the Queen wearing a tiara and a lace veil and she wears her ribbons and orders. It is black and white printed.

In addition to this exhibition the Queen also opened the International Exhibition at Liverpool on 11th May, 1886. A jug (Plate 172) and a cup and saucer record this event, carrying a transfer in black and white of the buildings erected for the occasion.

The Queen laid the foundation stone of the Victoria Courts at Birmingham on 23rd March 1887, and an octagonal plate (Plate 173), black printed, records this event. Octagonal plates were common products during the latter part of the Victorian age.

The Jubilee Exhibition at Manchester, also opened by the Queen, is recorded on a plate (Plate 174), brown and white printed, carrying in the top centre the head of the Queen wearing a lace veil, on each side of her are two ships. The centre of the plate depicts the Exhibition Buildings and at the base are the Town Hall, the Exchange and the Infirmary. One

Plate 172. *Jug recording the opening by the Queen of the International Exhibition at Liverpool 11th May, 1886.*

Plate 173. *Octagonal plate, black printed, for the laying of the foundation stone of the Victoria Courts at Birmingham 23rd March, 1886.*

Plate 174. *Plate, brown and white printed recording the Queen opening the Jubilee Exhibition at Manchester, 1887.*

Plate 175. *Pottery ox roasting plate for Whittle-le-Woods.*

Plate 176. *Worcester Jubilee plate.*

ship is captioned 'Jamaica to Manchester' and the other is captioned 'Manchester to New York'. The plate has a fluted border.

The commemorative pieces for the 1887 exhibition take various forms and have some interesting features. A plate published by Hancock of Stoke-on-Trent (Plate 175) carries in the centre the large head of an ox, brown printed, around which are the words 'An ox was publicly roasted whole on the village green in commemoration of Her Most Gracious Majesty's Jubilee, June 21st 1887'. The place of the ox-roasting was Whittle-le-Woods.

A quality plate by Worcester (Plate 176) carries in the centre the head of the Queen in Grecian style captioned 'Victoria, Dei Gratia, Reg ad Imp. 1837-1887', it is headed

Plate 177. *Plate with sporting features.*

'Jubilee Year', with the name of the Mayor of Worcester, 'Walter Holland'. It is blue printed and has around the border a design of the royal flowers. There are various octagonal plates and other plates showing the royal palaces. One is of interest because it features sport (Plate 177). It is orange printed, and has in the centre the head of the Queen surrounded by flags and in a laurel wreath, and around are various sporting scenes: cricket, fishing, golf, shooting, yachting, cycling, racing, football. The plate is headed 'Victoria the Good. 1837-1887'; around are the dates of her birth, her accession, her marriage and her declaration as Empress of India.

Her Diamond Jubilee was perhaps even more ceramically recorded. A very attractive loving cup in slipware (Plate 178A) by Salopian, in greens and reds, has the words 'Victoria R I' surmounted by a crown and the dates 1837-1897'.

A plate by Coalport (Plate 179) has in the centre in a diamond-shaped frame the full-length portrait of the Queen, surrounded by the names of all the British dominions and colonies. It is blue printed.

Doulton produced several mugs, beakers and jugs (Plate 180) for this jubilee, typically portraying the heads in relief of the young and the old Queen in the usual Doulton colours

Plate 178A. *Pottery Loving cup, underglaze printed in colours with thistles, flowers and dates.* ***B.*** *Cardiff Jubilee mug.* ***C.*** *Parkinsons 'Royal Doncaster Butterscotch' tin.* ***D.*** *Queen Victoria Jubilee Year cup and saucer.* ***E.*** *Diamond Jubilee mug.*

Plate 179. *Coalport plate printed in blue with a statue and Commonwealth and Empire members.*

Plate 180. *Doulton Jubilee jug showing a young and the old Queen.*

of blue, green and brown, around the neck are the words 'Dei gratia Victoria, Queen and Empress, 1837-1897' and around the centre 'She wrought her people lasting good'.

Among the many mugs produced for school children by towns and cities is one from Cardiff District of the Independent Order of Oddfellows (Plate 178B), blue-printed, it states that it was presented to the juveniles in commemoration of the Queen's Diamond Jubilee in June 1897.

Of the many tins that were produced, Parkinsons provided a tin of butterscotch (Plate 178C) entitled 'Original Royal Doncaster Butterscotch price 1/-, as supplied to the Queen'. The hinged lid bears on each side, in red diamonds, the heads of the young and old Queen and around the side are the

Plate 181. *Colman's Mustard Jubilee tin.*

Plate 182. *Moss Rimington mustard Jubilee tin with portraits of leading statesmen and politicians.*

palaces she occupied – Balmoral, Windsor, Osborne and Kensington Palace, where she was born. The other side indicates 'As supplied to HRH the Late Duchess of Kent', referring to the Queen's mother.

Colmans Mustard produced a very fine decorative tin (Plate 181), on the hinged lid is a full portrait of the Queen in her coronation robes and the four panels contain a coloured likeness of the coronation itself, the Queen seated in St Edward's chair and the Queen seated in a carriage with two Scottish outriders at the back at the opening of the Imperial Institute on 10th May, 1896. The other sides have a train captioned 'Modern Express Train' above which is Stevenson's Rocket. The fourth side bears an Ironclad above which are two wooden sailing ships.

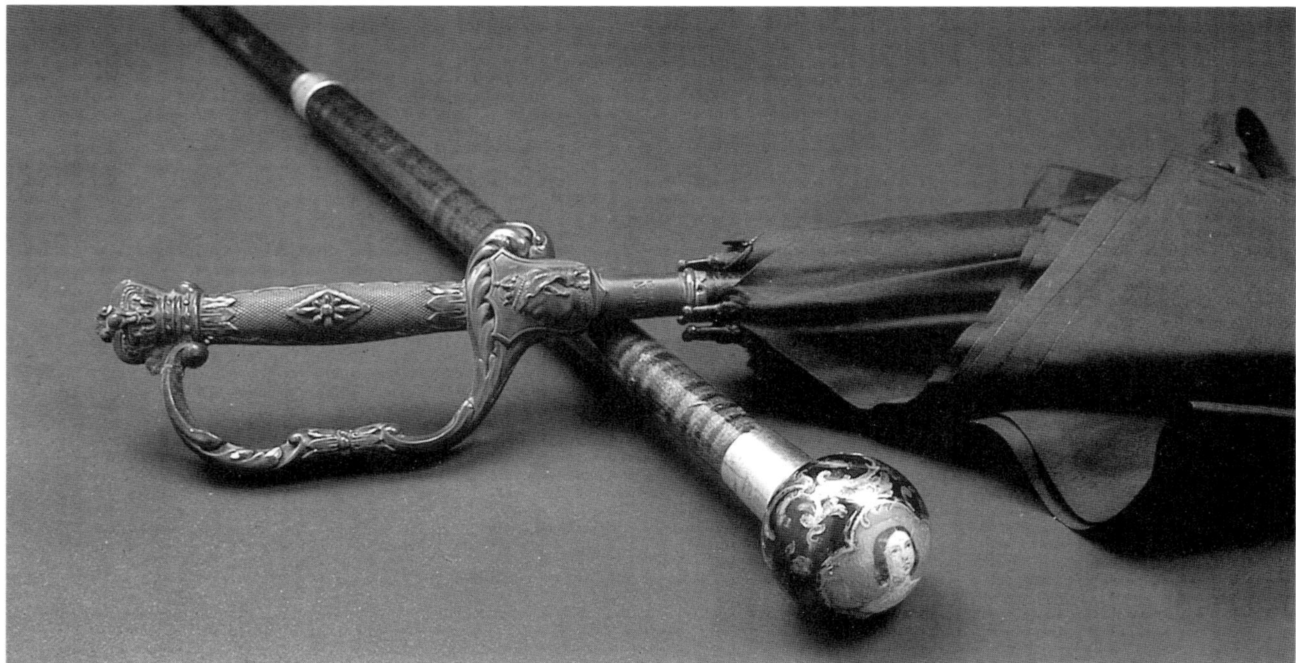

Plate 183. *Porcelain cane parasol handle of the young Queen. Umbrella with composition handle, shaped with the crown for the Jubilee.*

Plate 184. *Papier mâché plate showing the Queen holding Princess Alice.*

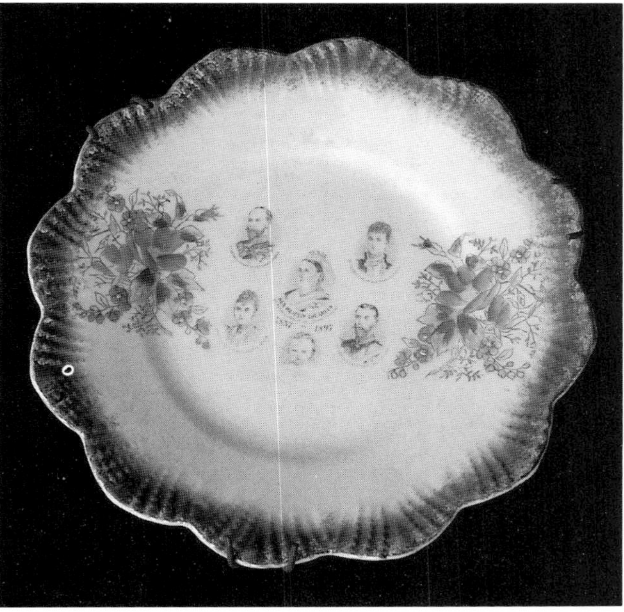

Plate 185. *Commemorative plate with blue border showing the Queen with the three next in order of succession.*

Another shaped tin has on the lift-off lid a central oval of the coronation ceremony and scenes in various panels. The Queen and Prince Albert with his greyhound Eos walking outside Windsor Castle, the Queen in later years accompanied no doubt by one of her daughters driving in a carriage outside Balmoral Castle, the Queen outside Holyrood House in Scotland and in deep mourning outside Osborne House. Alongside each of these panels are portraits of four of her Prime Ministers: Viscount Melbourne with whom she flirted, William Gladstone whom she thoroughly disliked. Benjamin Disraeli whom she greatly admired – 'we authors Ma'am', and the Duke of Wellington who was Prime Minister before she ascended the throne but upon whom she relied greatly for advice.

Another highly decorated tin for Moss Rimington mustard (Plate 182) has on the hinged lid the head and shoulders of the Queen wearing her small crown and her lace veil and her orders, looking rather severe. There are four panels, one for Gladstone, the other for Joseph Chamberlain, the third for the Marquis of Salisbury, the last Prime Minister to sit in the House of Lords, and the fourth is for Balfour who became Prime Minister after her death. Between each of these portraits are, in ovals, portraits of various well-known politicians, Rosebery, who was one of her Prime Ministers, La Bouchere, Harcourt, John Morley, Randolph Churchill, the Duke of Devonshire and two Irish Nationalists, William Davitt and William O'Brien. Although these tins are ninety years old, considering their age and use they are in extremely fine condition, and must be regarded as collectors' pieces.

There were other interesting commemoratives apart from tins and ceramics, including an umbrella handle (Plate 183) which is shaped, holding the crown at the top, the Queen's head on the rear and her Jubilee date of 1887. In spite of its age, this umbrella still keeps out the water and rain.

A papier mâché plate (Plate 184) shows the Queen seated, holding one of her great-grandchildren, Princess Alice, the mother of the Duke of Edinburgh, and Princess Beatrice is holding her own son, the Marquis of Carisbrooke.

An interesting plate, published in Germany (Plate 185), shows four generations: the Queen in the centre together with the Prince and Princess of Wales, the Duke and Duchess of York, later King George V and Queen Mary and young Prince Edward of York. It has a floral decoration.

On 24th May 1899 the Queen celebrated her eightieth birthday. Little exists to commemorate this event, other than a glass tumbler which has an engraving.

The year 1900 arrived and a pottery vase (Plate 186) commemorates this event. In the centre is an oval portrait of the Queen wearing her small crown and underneath it reads, 'Queen Victoria entered the 64th year of her illustrious and beneficent reign'. On one side appear the words 'Unification of the British Empire, Australian Federation and the Patriotic Support of our Colonial Brother in Arms during the Boer War'. On the other side, 'War in South Africa. The Orange River and Transvaal Colonies annexed by Lord Roberts, Commander in Chief, the Colonial Secretary, Mr J. Chamberlain', and around the lip of the vase reads 'To commemorate the last year of the 19th century'.

Queen Victoria's last visit abroad and almost her last public appearance was a visit to Ireland. A porcelain mug commemorates this event (Plate 187). It bears the portrait of the Queen, the one used for her Diamond Jubilee. On the other side is the Irish harp and the date of the visit. In addition, a brooch was made for this visit by Waterhouse and Co., the Queen's jewellers in Ireland (Plate 188). It shows in gold the letters 'VR' surmounting three sprigs of shamrock. The lid of the case reads 'The Queen's Visit in 1900. Children's Entertainment Executive'.

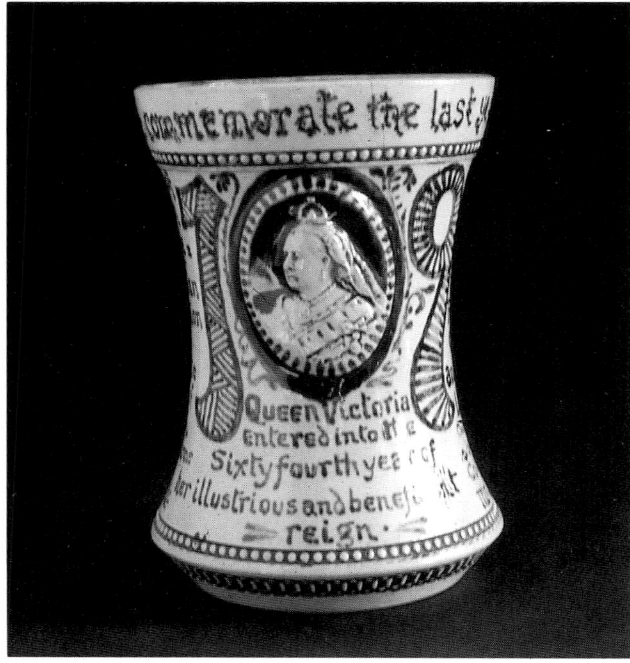

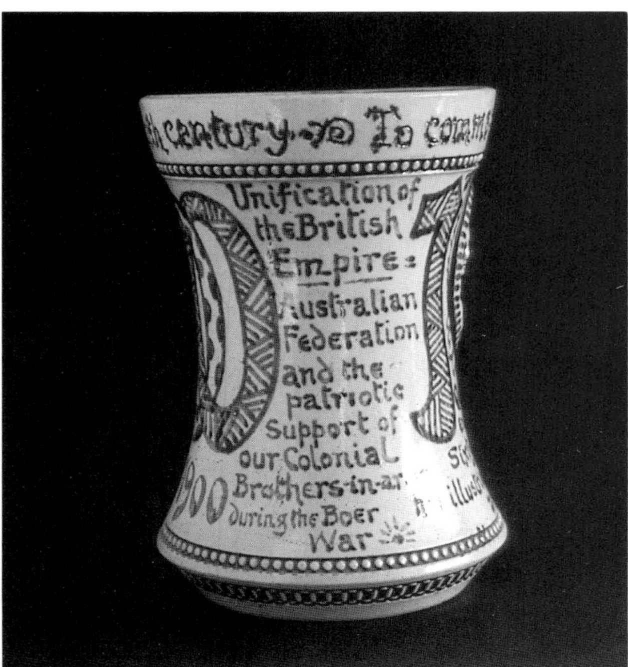

Plate 186. *Pottery vase boldly printed in blue on a grey base marking the end of the 19th century.*

The end of the era and the end of the life of the Queen came on the 23rd January 1901. Strangely there is not a great deal to commemorate this event. Three plaster figures of the Queen, King Edward VII and Queen Alexandra (Plate 189) commemorate the death of the Queen and the accession of the new King. On the rear of the Queen's figure are the words 'January 23rd 1901', but the date on the figures of King Edward and Queen Alexandra reads 'January 24th 1901'. Quite why a day passed before the Prince of Wales became King is not known.

A plate (Plate 190) shows the Queen wearing her bonnet and has her facsimile signature, 'Victoria RI', underneath are the words 'Queen and Mother' and the dates of her reign.

A tankard (Plate 191) shows the Queen wearing her

Plate 187. *Mug commemorating the royal visit to Ireland in April 1900.*

Plate 188. *Gold brooch, with three sprigs of shamrock, to record the visit to Ireland, 1900.*

Plate 189. *Three plaster busts of Victoria and the Prince and Princess of Wales recording the death of the Queen.*

Plate 190. *Small plate, printed in sepia, with head of the Queen wearing a bonnet, recording her death*

Plate 191. *Pottery tankard with a portrait of the Queen, recording her death.*

widow's cap with the words 'Victoria, the Good, Late Queen of England'. A plate (Plate 192) published by Ridgeway has in the centre a portrait of the Queen wearing her crown and her lace veil, with her orders in full colour above which is the crown and the inscription 'Victoria, Queen of Great Britain and Ireland, Empress of India' and underneath are the dates of her birth, her accession and death. The death date is given as 22nd January 1901, a mistake as it was in fact the 23rd. Around the border is a design of flowers.

A tin (Plate 193A), unmarked, in purple, has on its lift-off lid in ovals the head and shoulders of Queen Victoria and Prince Albert captioned 'HRH The Late Prince Consort and HM The Late Queen Victoria', indicating that it must have been produced to record her death. Around the side are panels of the new King, Edward VII, and HM The Queen Consort, and on the other side, the Duke and Duchess of York, captioned 'The Duke and Duchess of Cornwall and York', the royal coat of arms and its supporters are on the two other sides.

The death of the Queen and her funeral were the subject of lavish photographs and details of her life in various magazines, *The Sphere, The Illustrated London News* and *The Graphic*.

The Daily Graphic, priced 1d and dated London, Wednesday 23rd January 1901 (Plate 194), contains twenty pages of details of her death. The front cover contains a large oval, surrounded by black, with a central portrait of the Queen wearing a black bonnet and black cape and entitled 'The last photograph of Queen Victoria' photographed by La Fayette. Sandwiched between the advertisements, notices and public announcements are several pages devoted to pictures of the Queen's life.

Amongst the many funeral numbers published is one entitled *Black and White* (Plate 194) dated Saturday 9th

Plate 192. *Plate inscribed to record the Queen's death.*

Plate 193A. *Unmarked portrait tin in purple.* ***B.*** *Another tin, also probably to record her death, in the shape of a parcel with seals and red ribbon.*

Plate 194. *Funeral numbers from* The Daily Graphic, *and* Black and White.

Plate 195. *Funeral procession from* The Illustrated London News.

Plate 196(left). *Parian plaque moulded with a portrait of George Stephenson. 9½in. (24cm) diameter.*

Plate 197. *Pottery mug, black printed, with a portrait of Daniel Adamson and to wish success to the Manchester Ship Canal. 4⅛in. (10.5cm).*

February 1901. The front cover shows the head and shoulders of the late Queen, wearing a black bonnet and surrounded by a design incorporating the names of all previous female British sovereigns; 'Mary, Elizabeth, Mary II, Anne and Victoria'. The bottom right hand corner carries the British Lion, underneath which are the words 'Reg et imp'.

Among many drawings is one which has a poignant touch. It is entitled 'OUR FUTURE KING SALUTES THE SAD PROCESSION. This touching little incident was witnessed by our artist Mr Aldin on Saturday at Windsor. Prince Edward of York was accompanied by his sister and the young Eton Volunteers formed an appropriate background'. A supplement was included entitled 'THE NAVY'S TRIBUTE TO THE GREAT DEAD QUEEN'. Photographs of the *Alberta* passing the fleets, the torpedo boats leading

Plate 198 *Fenton Staffordshire plate printed with a bust of Daniel Adamson.*

Plate 199 *Black circular moulded plaque with head of Sir Roland Hill, inventor of The Penny Post.*

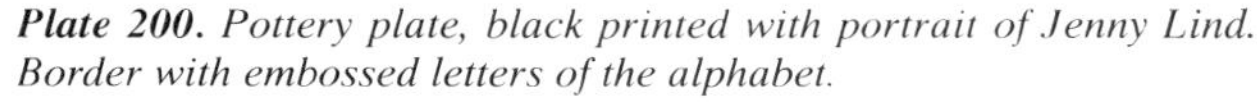

Plate 200. *Pottery plate, black printed with portrait of Jenny Lind. Border with embossed letters of the alphabet.*

Plate 201. *Octagonal plate, black printed with a portriat of Ellen Terry, floral decoration. 9½in. (24cm) diameter.*

the way in front of the Alberta and a double page drawing headed The sad passage through the fleets'. The *Alberta* was followed by the *Victoria and Albert* with the King on board, the *Osborne*, the *Hohenzollern*, and the *Enchantress*. On the left is seen the *Rattlesnake*, on the right the *Hood*, drawing by S M Lawrence our special artist'.

The Illustrated London News published a special number for the funeral procession (Plate 195) dated 7th February 1901 at the price of 2s and by post 2/0½d.

In addition individual people felt so deeply about the death of the Queen, who had seemed to be an institution, that they commissioned their own personal 'In Memoriam' cards. These were normally in silver, edged with black, having a portrait of the Queen and the years of her reign, and the details of her life, and with such words as 'Deeply Loved' and 'Deeply Mourned', or 'In Loving Memory'.

The Queen and Eminent People of Her Reign

During the Queen's long reign various celebrated people contributed in several ways to the prosperity of the nation. In the field of engineering there was George Stephenson, for whom there is a parian plaque (Plate 196) with a moulded

Plate 202(left centre). *Parian busts of Charles Dickens and John Ruskin.*

Plate 203A. *Pipe with head in the shape of W. G. Grace.* ***B.*** *Bisque figure of Grace holding a bat.* ***C.*** *Inkstand presented to Grace for scoring 1016 runs in May, 1895.*

Plate 204. *Octagonal plate, black printed and enhanced with colour. A memorial to Fred Archer, the famous jockey.*

Plate 205. *Plate for the Bishop of Manchester, black printed with floral decoration. 9½in. (24cm) diameter.*

profile portrait of him.

A pottery mug (Plate 197), black printed, has a portrait of Daniel Adamson who played a prominent part in the erection of the Manchester Ship Canal. A Fenton Staffordshire plate (Plate 198) carries a bust of Daniel Adamson and is inscribed: 'Royal Assent August 8th, 1885'. Around the centre are the words 'Eccles and Patricroft demonstration. Ox roasted, Aug. 31st'.

The two great Brunels, father and son, have been commemorated in several ways. Sir Isambard Kingdom Brunel's two great ships, *The Great Eastern* and *The Great Western*, which played such a large part in maritime history, have been recorded. A pottery plate exists for both depicting the two steamships.

Sir Roland Hill, who was responsible for the penny post, features on a black pottery plaque (Plate 199).

Plate 206(left). *Octagonal plate recording the life of the Rev. C. H. Spurgeon, enhanced with flowers in colour. 9½in. (24cm) diameter.*

Plate 207. *Parian busts of Cardinal Manning and Cardinal Newman. 8in. (20cm) high.*

Plate 208. *Bone china mug decorated in full colour and showing Sergeant Thomas defending the colours at Inkerman. 4in. (10cm) high.*

Plate 209. *Pottery plate printed with an impression of Hewett firing the Lancaster Gun at the advancing Russians.*

The two great explorers, David Livingstone and Henry Morton Stanley, have been commemorated in various ways. There is a moulded glass bust of Livingstone and a parian figure of Stanley. They also feature on other commemorative pieces.

In the field of arts, Jenny Lind, the great soprano, appears on a black-printed plate bearing her portrait (Plate 200). Ellen Terry, the actress, appears on an octagonal plate (Plate 201), with a black-printed portrait and some of the well-known novelists of the time appear in various commemorative pieces. There are busts for several of these literary figures including Charles Dickens and John Ruskin (Plate 202).

Among the many great sportsmen who lived during Victoria's reign was William Gilbert Grace (Plate 203). There is a tobacco pipe with a bowl portraying the head of Grace, the stem in the shape of a cricket bat, with a ball below. On the stem is the wording: 'W G G Aet 47 ad 1895' and the word centuplico' which refers to his hundredth century, in fact a double century of 288 against Somerset made in the second week of the 1895 season. There is a tall bisque full-length figure of Grace, with his black beard, wearing the MCC cricket cap and pads and wielding a bat. An inkstand, with Grace in the centre, in bronze, in full cricket clothing, under a tree and with a silver plate indicating that it was a gift to Grace reads: 'Presented to Dr W G Grace, who scored 1016 runs in May 1895'. W.G. Grace commemoratives are keenly collected and there are many pieces to honour his cricketing career.

The celebrated jockey Fred Archer appears on an octagonal plate (Plate 204) with a black printed portrait. This plate was a memorial to Archer.

A widening of the scope extends to Grace Darling who appears on a pottery mug during her famous epic rescue of a disaster at sea.

In the church several distinguished theologians played an active part in church affairs. In the Church of England there are two plates, one for the Bishop of Manchester (Plate 205) and the other for the Rev C H Spurgeon (Plate 206). In the Roman Catholic field both Cardinal Manning and Cardinal Newman were the subjects of parian busts (Plate 207).

The Queen and Her Wars

As the Victorian concept of industrial expansion and security at home prospered, there were constant troubles in parts of the Empire. Little wars sprang up, but matters reached danger point when the Turks refused to safeguard the interests of Christians in the Ottoman Empire.

The Crimean War that followed was bloody and wasteful, but it has been ceramically commemorated. The bone china mug (Plate 208) with full colour decoration shows Sergeant Thomas defending the colours at Inkerman and a naval lieutenant is shown on a pottery plate (Plate 209) firing a gun at the Russians, for which he was awarded the Victoria Cross.

A fine souvenir jug (Plate 210C) carries blue-printed transfers of 'The Charge of the Chasseurs D'Afrique at Balaclava' and on the reverse, 'The Charge of the Scots Greys at Balaclava'. The detail of the soldiers and horses is vividly portrayed. It bears the number 16 but no other potters' mark.

A French pottery plate (Plate 210D), blue-printed, depicts *Les Soeurs de Charité* administering to the wounded at the Siege of Sebastopol. The border carries the coats of arms of the allies, each surrounded by a design of flags, laurel and oak.

Plate 210A. *White parian figure of General Wolseley.* **B.** *Jug, pink, with black printed portrait of General Wolseley in battle uniform.* **C.** *Tall pottery jug with black printed detailed scene of the Charge of the Chasseurs D'Afrique and the Charge of the Scots Greys at Balaclava.* **D.** *Fairing entitled 'English Neutrality 1870 Tending The Sick And Wounded.'* **E.** *Cup and saucer featuring British Rifle Volunteers.* **F.** *French pottery plate, blue printed, graphically depicts Les Soeurs de Charité administering to the wounded at the Siege of Sebastopol.*

Plate 211. *Bone china mug decorated in full colour – 'A Present from the Crystal Palace – the Nightingale Jewel'. 3in. (7.5cm) high.*

Plate 212. *Porcelain mug, pink printed, of Sir Colin Campbell who led the Highland Brigade in the Indian Mutiny. 3¼in. (8cm) high.*

Plate 213. *Staffordshire figure of Sir Henry Havelock coloured blue.*

Plate 214. *Pottery jug, purple printed with a statue erected to General Outram.*

Plate 215. *Plate portraying a portrait of the head of the Duke of Cambridge with a decorated border, captioned 'Commander in Chief'. 8¾in. (22cm) diameter.*

Plate 216. *Blue printed tankard to record the opening of Preston Town Hall by the Duke of Cambridge.*

A bone china mug (Plate 211) shows the jewel specially designed for Florence Nightingale by Prince Albert and presented to her by the Queen.

When peace was proclaimed several commemoratives were published, the most impressive being the Royal Patriotic Jug by S. Alcock & Company on 1st January 1855. The slogan for most of these commemorative pieces features the Anglo-French Solidarity with the words 'May they ever be united'. A pottery plate, printed with overglazed clobber, features an example of this.

On the North West Frontier, a pottery loving cup carries a portrait of Sir Robert Napier who served in several of these 'little wars'.

The Indian Mutiny has not been forgotten in ceramic terms. A porcelain mug (Plate 212), pink printed, carries a portrait of Sir Colin Campbell who led the Highland Brigade. General Sir Henry Havelock, the other General most associated with the Mutiny, is featured in a Staffordshire figure (Plate 213). General Sir Thomas Outram, who was concerned with the siege of Lucknow is featured on a purple printed pottery jug (Plate 214).

The Queen's Commander-in-Chief was the Duke of Cambridge. He was a first cousin, his father being the brother of her father, the Duke of Kent. A transfer printed plate (Plate 215) with a border of birds and decorative swagging shows, printed in blue, a portrait of the head and shoulders of the Duke of Cambridge and is captioned 'Commander in Chief'.

As Commander-in-Chief he did occasionally attend

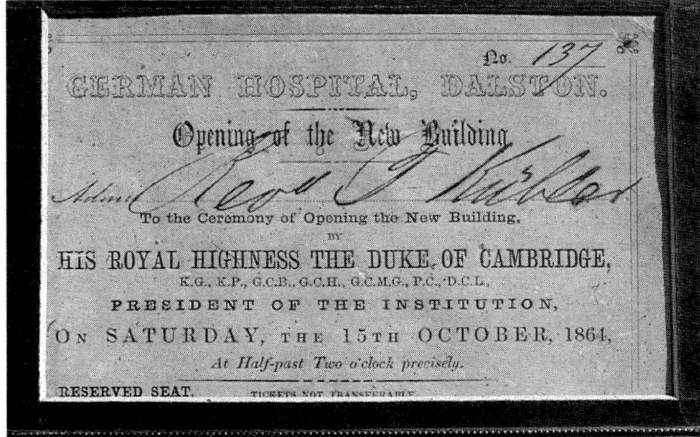

No. 137

GERMAN HOSPITAL, DALSTON.

Opening of the New Building

To the Ceremony of Opening the New Building,
BY
HIS ROYAL HIGHNESS THE DUKE OF CAMBRIDGE,
K.G., K.P., G.C.B., G.C.H., G.C.M.G., P.C., D.C.L.,
PRESIDENT OF THE INSTITUTION,
ON SATURDAY, THE 15TH OCTOBER, 1864,
At Half-past Two o'clock precisely.

RESERVED SEAT. TICKETS NOT TRANSFERABLE.

Plate 217. *Ticket for the opening of the German Hospital, Dalston, by the Duke of Cambridge.*

functions on behalf of the Queen. In 1887 he opened the Preston Town Hall and there is a barrel-shaped mug (Plate 216), featuring on the front a transfer of the Town Hall. There is an interesting ticket (Plate 217), allocating a reserved seat to a Rev B. Kuhler for the opening ceremony of the new building of the German Hospital, Dalston, by the Duke of Cambridge, on 15th October 1864.

The British Rifle Volunteers were commemorated in varying forms. Teasets were in common production (Plate 210). They have in the centre of the saucer an officer and a

Plate 218 A. *Doulton jug with portrait of General Gordon.* ***B.*** *Parian bust of the Prince Imperial.* ***C.*** *Doulton jug for Admiral Beatty, 1918.*

Plate 219. *Pottery plate, brown printed with a portrait of General Gordon.*

Plate 220. *Pottery plate, brown printed with a portrait of Dr. Jameson. 9¾in. (25cm) diameter.*

Plate 221A. *(centre right) Portrait head of President Kruger inscribed 'Oom Paul', the handle in the shape of a crown.* **B.** *Ribbon plate portraying the King's Royal Rifles storming the Heights, captioned: 'Battle of Glencoe'. 9in. (23cm) diameter.* **C.** *Biscuit tin, unmarked, showing Baden-Powell, Buller, White and McDonald.* **D.** *Commemorative gilt deckle edged ribbon plate with black and white portraits of Roberts, Kitchener, French, Buller, McDonald, White and Baden-Powell.* **E.** *Pair of plates portraying soldiers serving in the Boer War, the border in blue.* **F.** *Tobacco jar in the shape of the head of General Buller.* **G.** *Hair tidy portraying Lord Roberts.*

Plate 222. Ribbon plate with portrait of Lord Roberts in uniform.

Plate 223. Keen Robinson mustard tin portraying Lord Roberts with coloured scenes of his war experiences.

rifleman, in full uniform on the battlefield, around which is a laurel wreath captioned 'British Rifle Volunteers'. The cup shows a battleground with flags and colours and on the other side another scene on a battlefield with two riflemen. These were probably published for the Crimean War.

The Franco-Prussian War was a war in which Queen Victoria's soldiers were not involved. However, it was not forgotten by the English and an interesting fairing shows a wounded soldier being administered to by an Englishman with the caption 'English Neutrality 1870 – tending the sick and the wounded' (Plate 210D).

The disaster which culminated in the murder of General Gordon at Khartoum was recorded on a fine Doulton jug (Plate 218A), with the usual brown background, which has

Plate 224. British and Benningtons tea trading tin in the shape of a shell.

Plate 225. Victory Chlorodyne Lozenges tin.

***Plate 226** . Unmarked tin bearing a portrait of General McDonald on the lid.*

in the centre in a dark green cartouche the white head and shoulders portrait, wearing his fez, of the General, above which are the words 'General Gordon'. On the other side, in a scroll, is 'Governor General of Sudan 1874' with the quotation: 'by the help of God I will hold the balance level'. His date of birth, 'January 28th 1833', is also inscribed. On the other side, also in a cartouche: 'Hero of Heroes Khartoum' and a quotation: 'I decline to agree that your expedition is for me' and captioned 'Betrayed – January 26th 1885'. A plate (Plate 219) carries a brown printed bust of Gordon.

General Wolseley, Commander-in-Chief at the time in Egypt, is commemorated by a fine white parian bust (Plate 210A), and around his neck what would seem to be the Order of the Bath. There is no indication as to who the potter was. A jug (Plate 210B) was produced by James Miller & Company, potters of Glasgow. It is pink based with the half portrait of Sir Garnet Wolseley wearing the field uniform of the time on both sides.

The famous Zulu War does not appear to have been ceramically recorded. However, there is a fine parian bust by an unknown sculptor of the head and shoulders of the Prince Imperial (Plate 218B). Eugene Louis Jean Joseph was the only son of Emperor Napoleon III and Empress Eugenie of France. Known as the Prince Imperial and heir to the throne of the French Empire, he was killed whilst serving in the Zulu War on 1st June, 1879.

In 1895 Dr Jameson led the famous Jameson raid over the Transvaal Border which started off the Boer War, and there is a pottery plate (Plate 220), brown printed, showing a portrait of Dr Jameson.

The brains behind the Boers was Stephanus Johannes Paulus Kruger. This wily and clever Boer Statesman became President of the Transvaal in 1888. He is the subject of a portrait jug (Plate 221A) featuring his well-known face wearing a top hat, around which in a ribbon are the words 'OOM Paul', the name he was generally known by. The chief feature is a handle in the shape of a crown indicating the kind of sovereignty he exerted.

A vast number of commemoratives were issued to record the various personalities and battles of the Boer War. Collectors have specialised in Boer War memorabilia and a special book has been written giving a comprehensive list of what was produced. There follows here merely a selection of what was produced:

Lord Roberts, one of the most distinguished soldiers of the period, features on several pieces. A ribbon plate (Plate 222) bears in the centre his head and shoulders, wearing a scarlet tunic with his orders and decorations.

Keen Robinson & Co Limited produced a mustard tin (Plate 223). It is highly decorated and there are four panels bearing in a central cartouche surrounded by the Union Jack the royal emblems and the royal flowers, each surmounted by a crown depicting scenes from the Boer War. One panel depicts bringing up the guns – showing soldiers dragging a field gun, the next is captioned 'The Outpost', showing a soldier in khaki uniform keeping watch from a hill. Another panel portrays Lord Roberts riding his horse, accompanied by officers to the cheers of a family of passers-by entitled 'Lord Roberts entering Bloemfontein', and another shows a festive scene of Lord Roberts in scarlet uniform making a speech at a dinner consisting of officers underneath a decorated spray of flowers and flags, captioned 'Lord Robert's entertainment of the military attache at Pretoria'. The lid has a portrait of Roberts, head and shoulders in a central oval with a red background against the blue hills

Plate 227. *Unmarked tin captioned 'A Letter Home' in vivid colours portraying graphically the feelings of a soldier in action in the Boer War.*

within sprigs of laurel and captioned 'Field Marshal Lord Roberts'.

The British and Bennington's Tea Trading Association Limited of 118 Southwark Street, London manufactured a tin in the shape of a shell (Plate 224) captioned in a red shield facsimile of a shell 'Momento of the Transvaal War 1899-1900'. The tin is in khaki with gold bands and was manufactured by 'John Wilson Tin Printer, Shipley, sole maker'.

Another interesting tin was produced by Victory Chlorodyne Lozenges (Plate 225). The inside of the lid describes them as 'For chills and colds with the largest sales in the world'. The trademark is a soldier of the Royal Artillery in full uniform set to fire a field gun. The tin has an overall pattern of simulated basket work, in green and gold. On the centre of the lid is an oval bearing the head and shoulders of Queen Victoria wearing a lace head veil, held in position by a tiara and not the usual small crown. On each side are individual circular panels of four of the famous Boer War Generals – Lord Roberts, Sir Redvers Buller, Lord Kitchener and Field Marshal George White. Though perhaps less-known than the others, White was a very distinguished soldier who received the Victoria Cross for his part in the Afghan War and was a defender of Ladysmith. He subsequently became Governor of Gibraltar in 1900 and was awarded the Order of Merit in 1903.

Another tin (Plate 226), whose manufacturer is not marked, portrays on the lid, in a circle, the head of General Sir Hector McDonald. The General is wearing his uniform and it is backed with a Scottish tartan pattern. Around, on a similar tartan background, are four Scottish scenes – one tossing the caber, another curling, the third putting the shot, and the fourth a sword dance. The detail and the colours of these various four panels are vivid and colourful. The tartan has been captioned 'McKenzie Tartan'. Another tin (Plate 227), again of unknown manufacture, bears on the lid a soldier writing a letter captioned 'A Letter Home'. Around the side of the deep tin are four further panels, one captioned 'Home Again' showing the wife greeting her husband on his return from service; another shows victory, where a soldier bearing the standard is being held by a wounded soldier; another is entitled 'A Letter from Home', with the soldier

Plate 228. *Plate bearing portrait of Baden-Powell.*

Plate 229. Plate captioned 'War Declared in South Africa'.

Plate 230. Plate, black and white printed, captioned 'Our Boys'.

seated in an encampment of tents reading his letter; and the fourth one is the soldier going off to war, saying farewell to his wife with the word 'Goodbye'. These panels are vividly portrayed in colour and convey a clear and forthright message of the emotion felt by both the soldier and his wife during this period of service to his country.

A hair-tidy (Plate 221G) shows, as its central motif, Lord Roberts above a war medal, supported on the right by a volunteer and on the left by a colonial soldier and captioned 'Supporters of the Empire'. The reverse bears the names of the same Generals portrayed in the Victory Lozenges tin with the inclusion of General Baden-Powell and French within a pale blue cartouche surrounded by laurel and oak leaves and surmounted by a crown. It was published by Foley China.

Lord Baden-Powell, son of an Oxford Professor of Geometry, served in India and Afghanistan, was on the staff

***Plate 231A.** Queen's chocolate tin for the troop soldiers. **B.** Mug recording the end of the Boer War coinciding with the Coronation of Edward VII in 1902. **C.** Card produced for the declaration of peace in 1902.*

Plate 232. *Two music sheets containing marches composed for the Boer War.*

Plate 233A. *Plate for 'Cheddar Rejoicing'.* **B.** *Tin decorated with the Union Jack with portraits of Lord Methuen, Roberts, Baden-Powell, Kitchener and Buller.* **C.** *Tobacco tin presented to Scottish soldiers.*

at Ashanti and Matebeleland and was famous for his defence of Mafeking. Despite his success as a soldier, his fame lies more perhaps with his creation of the Boy Scout Movement, together with his sister Agnes who founded the Girl Guides. There are a large number of commemorative pieces for Baden-Powell, varying from mugs, jugs and plates and portrait figures. A typical plate (Plate 228) has within a green scallop border, the head and shoulders of the then Lieutenant Colonel Baden-Powell, wearing a khaki uniform and a bush-type hat. Another plate (Plate 229) has in the centre a cartouche with the words 'War declared in South Africa by President Kruger, Lord Roberts, Commander-in-Chief of Cape Colony, General Buller Commander-in-Chief of Natal'. The background is turquoise blue and around in gold are the words 'Ready Aye 1900', and beneath 'God Save The Queen'. Surmounting this is the Imperial Crown with the words 'Freedom, Liberty, Equality', on the right of which is a uniformed colonial soldier bearing the Union Jack Standard, and on the left a Highlander bearing a claymore, surmounting it is a field gun. The Royal Standard and the Union Jack, both bearing laurel leaves, are each side of the central cartouche and the words: 'England expects every man to do his duty'. Between sprays of the royal flowers are the words 'Britannia mourns her heroes now at rest'. The plate was published in England and had a registered number.

Sir Redvers Henry Buller served in the Chinese War, the Red River Expedition, the Ashanti and Kaffir Wars and won the VC in the Zulu War. He also took part in the Egyptian War and the Sudan Expedition. His Regiment was the Rifle Brigade and he became Commander-in-Chief in the Boer War and raised the siege of Ladysmith. Because he replied to criticism of British failures in South Africa he lost his command and was succeeded by Lord Roberts. Buller appears on an unmarked biscuit tin (Plate 221C) and his black and white portrait is on a plate (Plate 221D).

Another plate (Plate 230) has a black and white engraving of a scene portraying fighting troops. At the head are the words 'Our Boys' at the front and underneath 'For Queen and Country'. It is scallop edged. A porcelain plate (Plate 233A) was published by the small town of Cheddar in Somerset – around the rim are the names 'Kimberley, Ladysmith, Mafeking'. The centre has the initials VR surmounted by a crown within a wreath of the royal flowers and captioned 'Pretoria 1900'. The words are blue printed and also include 'Cheddar rejoices'. The impressed maker's mark is not identifiable.

Plate 234. *Salt glazed spirit flask in the shape of the figure of Lord Melbourne. 9½in. (24cm) high.*

Lord Metheun, one of the Commanders, is recorded on an unmarked tin (Plate 233B) coated with the Union Jack and a ribbon plate (Plate 221B) shows the Kings Royal Rifle Corps. storming The Heights.

The Queen herself had a specially prepared tin of chocolate made available for the troops of South Africa (Plate 231A). It bears a portrait of the Queen in the centre of a gold medallion. On the right are the words 'South Africa 1900' and on the left above her crown, her monogram 'VRI' and a facsimile message 'I wish you a Very Happy New Year VRI'. The history of this tin is interesting, as explained in the card which is inserted: 'QUEEN'S CHOCOLATE BOX WITH CHOCOLATES'. The recipient of this box (5940 Private Baker East Kent Regiment or Buffs) was wounded on 6 January at Waggonhill, Ladysmith. The box was sold by auction on 25th May 1900 by Debenhams & Company of London and the proceeds given to his parents. This tin contains the original chocolate in its original wrapping.

A tobacco tin (Plate 233C) was presented to the Scottish soldiers in South Africa. The inscription reads: 'Presented to the Scottish Soldiers in South Africa by the Scottish Regiment's Gift Fund William McDonald Sinclair DD, Archdeacon of London, Chairman Sir James RD McGregor Bart, Hon Treasurer.'

The lid has a yellow base with a central motif of the thistle, to the right of which are the words 'South Africa 1900' and to the left a shield bearing the Scottish Lion. Above are the words 'Frae Scots tae Scots' and beneath 'For Auld Lang Syne'. This tin contains the original tobacco in its original silver paper.

Of the many ephemeral items published for the Boer War, its marches (Plate 232) are of interest. The British Army was well-known for its marches and several were written for the Boer War. Some are composed by Henry Laski, one being the 'Scarlet Blue March' dedicated to Lord Kitchener. There was also the 'Kimberley March' by Ezra Read and the 'McDonald March' by Theo Bonheur. This is a tribute to General McDonald. Ezra Read composed a large number of marches for this war which were described by the London Music Publishing Stores as 'Easy and Pretty'. Their price was 2d and by post 3d. Some of the more famous were 'The Victoria Cross', a descriptive fantasy for Queen and Country, and a march dedicated to Lord Roberts, 'The relief of Mafeking March' with a photograph of Colonel Mahon and the famous 'Baden Powell March'. This title was dedicated to the 'Heroic Defender of Mafeking'.

A pair of plates (Plate 221E) showing soldiers of the Boer War, a calvary officer, a private in a Scottish regiment, a guardsman and a sailor, in one case firing a field gun, was published. It is marked 'Christmas 1900. A present from Williams Bros'.

There was a portrait jar (Plate 221F) of General Buller, wearing his service hat, which presumably held tobacco.

Plate 235A. *Octagonal Corn Laws plate.* ***B.*** *Jug to commemorate Peel's death. 5in. (12.7cm) high.* ***C.*** *Constitution Hill plate. 5¼in. (13.5cm) diameter.*

Plate 236A. *Salt glazed stoneware spirit flask modelled in the shape of Sir Robert Peel. 10in. (25.5cm) high.* ***B.*** *Cup and saucer featuring head of Sir Robert Peel.* ***C.*** *Staffordshire memorial jug, printed in blue with a bust of Sir Robert riding on Constitution Hill.*

Plate 237. *Porcelain cream jug inscribed 'Repeal of the Corn Laws 1866' and ribbon inscribed 'Emancipation'. 7in. (18cm) high.*

Plate 238. *Jug for the death of the Earl of Derby.*

The Queen and Her Ministers

During her long reign the Queen was served by ten Prime Ministers. At her succession the Prime Minister was Viscount Melbourne, upon whom she relied greatly, and for whom there is a very rare gin flask (Plate 234), produced by Bournes Potteries of Derbyshire, similar to those produced during the Reform Bill for William IV and the protagonists of reform.

He was succeeded by Sir Robert Peel for whom there are several commemoratives. Most noted perhaps for his reform of the Corn Laws, several ceramic records exist for this controversial matter. There is a jug (Plate 235B) covered overall with yellow glaze and black printed on one side with a waist-length portrait of Peel. The statesman is flanked by sheaves of corn and with two bound sheaves above his head. Under the print in ribbon cartouche is the inscription 'The Rt Honorable Sir R Peel', and on the other side an elaborate design of a tomb, a weeping willow and a weeping Britannia, the tomb having on its obelisk a curious poem mourning the loss of the great statesman. This was clearly manufactured at the time of Peel's death.

There is a pottery plate (Plate 235C), printed in black with a view of Constitution Hill, the place where Sir Robert Peel met with his fateful accident on 9th June 1850. This plate is part of a set of four showing different aspects of the tragedy.

There is a jug, together with a cup and saucer (Plate 236B), from a teaset of bone china, decorated with gilt and with black transfer prints. This cup and saucer are both decorated with prints of Sir Robert Peel and so captioned. The jug carries the slogan 'Emancipation 182 – and Repeal Corn Law 1846'.

Peel is also the subject of a very fine gin flask (Plate 236A), in the form of a full-length portrait, holding in his hand on a scroll 'Bread for the Millions', and in the other a sheaf of corn and captioned 'Sir R Peel'. There is a very fine jug (Plate 236C), blue-printed, showing Peel on his horse. Presumably this was again a reference to his death following a fall from his horse on Constitution Hill. On the other side, also blue-printed, with a laurel wreath, is a head and shoulders portrait of Peel. The base has the mark 'lamented by an Empire Sir Robert Peel'. The engraving of Peel on his horse is taken from *The London Illustrated News*.

An octagonal child's plate, with a daisy border, has in the well a coloured design of corn symbols, captioned 'Our Bread untaxed, Our Commerce free'. A further plate has a moulded border with coloured flowers and in the centre, again, a head and shoulders portrait of the late statesman, surrounded by sheaves of corn and captioned 'The Late Sir Robert Peel Bart'. A Staffordshire child's plate has a black and white transfer with a view of Constitution Hill.

Peel was succeeded by Lord John Russell who became Earl Russell. There are many commemoratives for the part he played in the Reform Act, but there appears to be nothing actually recorded for his period as Prime Minister.

Lord Derby succeeded Russell. There is little for him, although there is a jug (Plate 238), to commemorate his death. It shows the head and shoulders of Derby on a barrel-shaped jug with a handle and captioned 'The late Earl Derby'. Derby also appears on a small parian jug (Plate 386A) and on a mug (Plate 239) with a pink lustre rim, looking very fierce. The mug also has portrait heads of Disraeli and Hardy. Gathorne Hardy was a prominent Victorian Conservative politician who defeated Gladstone in

Plate 239. *Mug for Stanley, Earl of Derby.*

Plate 240(above right). *Mug for Gathorne Hardy, later Earl of Cranbrook.*

Plate 241(right). *'Arthur John Gilbert of the Aberdeen Cabinet deciding upon the expedition to the Crimea. Mixed method engineering by William Walker Private Plate, London 4th June 1857' published by the Engraver, 64 Margaret Street, Cavendish Square'. 19¼in. (49cm) by 26in. (66cm).*

Plate 242. *Parian bust of Palmerston. 8in. (20.5cm) high.*

Plate 243. *Bisque plaque of Viscount Palmerston. 4¾in. (12cm) high.*

Plate 244. *Pair of parian figures of Benjamin Disraeli and John Bright. 6in. (15.2cm) high.*

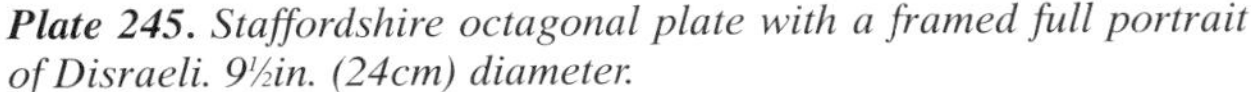

Plate 245. *Staffordshire octagonal plate with a framed full portrait of Disraeli. 9½in. (24cm) diameter.*

Plate 246. *Stoneware two-handled vase commemorating the death of Lord Beaconsfield. 5½in. (14cm) high.*

the famous Oxford University Election, 1878. He was ennobled as a Viscount and later became Earl of Cranbrook.

The next of the Queen's Prime Ministers was the Earl of Aberdeen, for whom there appears to be no ceramic record at all. This statesman has been much criticised for his alleged incompetence over the Crimean War. There is a very fine engraving (Plate 241) of the Aberdeen Cabinet deciding upon the expedition to the Crimea. This engraving hangs in the House of Commons.

Viscount Palmerston, who succeeded Aberdeen, is not much commemorated. However, there is a rather fine parian bust of the statesman (Plate 242), head and shoulders, sculpted by S.J. Camroux, July 1865, and captioned with bold letters 'Palmerston'. There is also a small bisque plaque (Plate 243) of the head of Palmerston captioned 'Viscount Palmerston'.

Benjamin Disraeli was more fortunate in his share of commemorative pieces; though more after his death than during his lifetime. There is a pressed glass jug and a bowl, translucent white with the words 'Earl Beaconsfield, the hero of the Congress of Berlin, July 1878'. The jug has a portrait of Disraeli and both jug and bowl are embellished with the royal flowers. There is a pair of parian figures (Plate 244), of Disraeli, and of John Bright. Disraeli is slightly stooping, wearing a top hat and sporting the inevitable beard. Bright is standing more upright, also with a top hat and his mutton-chop whiskers clearly visible.

Disraeli's death is commemorated on one of the octagonal plates popular in the period (Plate 245). It shows a black and white transfer of Disraeli sitting in a chair surmounted by the crown of an earl, with garlands of primroses (his favourite flower) and underneath the caption 'The Rt Hon Benjamin

Plate 247A and B. *Wedgwood pottery jug commemorating the death of Lord Beaconsfield, printed in black. 2½in. (6.5cm).*

Plate 248. *Framed tile of Gladstone.*

Plate 249A. *Staffordshire plate in memory of Gladstone with a portrait bust. 9½in. (24.5cm) diameter.* **B.** *Staffordshire plate with a portrait bust of Gladstone's wife. 9in. (23ccm) diameter.*

Disraeli of Beaconsfield KG', and the following verse: 'What practise howso'er expert in fitting, apt its words to things, or voiced the richest tone that sings, has power to give thee as thou wert', published by Wallace Gibson & Company. A rather fine pottery two-handled vase (Plate 246) records his death. On the front, in relief, in a dark blue against a grey-blue background, are the words 'Beaconsfield' surmounted by the Earl's coronet, primroses and 'April 19th 1881' and on the other side, below the British crown, a scroll containing the words 'Imperium et libertas', beneath which, surrounded by primroses, are the entwined letters 'PL' meaning the Primrose League. Perhaps the most impressive 'death jug' shows a very fine portrait of the head and shoulders of Disraeli surrounded by a laurel wreath. Around the neck of the jug are the titles of some of his novels: *The Young Duke*, *Venetia*, *Lothair*, *Endymion*, *Vivien Grey*, *Sybil*, *Tancred* and *Coningsby*. On the reverse are the words: 'Beaconsfield died April 19th 1881' and a fine engraving of Britannia in a kneeling position holding a wreath, with an excerpt from *Coningsby*.

Gladstone, whom the Queen so disliked, is commemorated perhaps more than any other Victorian Prime Minister. He appears on a rather splendid glazed tile (Plate 248), which was taken from a contemporary photograph; a very handsome charger in blue, showing the full head of Gladstone. It was made by Sherwin & Cotton at their works in Hanley in the County of Stafford 1898. A pair of plates (Plate 249A and B) was made specifically to commemorate his death. One is captioned 'In Memoriam The Rt Hon W E Gladstone' and it shows the famous man with his left hand against his ear. The other shows his wife, wearing the typical headdress of the period.

For his death there is a very fine Doulton tankard, barrel-shaped in the well-known two colours of brown, showing in

Plate 250. *Staffordshire pottery plate with waved rim, printed and coloured, with a bust of Gladstone.*

the centre a portrait of the statesman and on each side a tribute:

'Effort honest reflective action,
manful humble upon character,
effort succeeds better than by its success.'

At the base: 'William Ewart Gladstone' and around the neck of the jug 'England's great commoner'. There is also a very fine cotton napkin to record his death. In the centre,

Plate 251. *Unmarked tea tin portraying Gladstone on four sides and on the lid, as young, middle-aged and in old age. 4in. (10cm) x 6in. (15cm).*

Plate 252. Staffordshire pottery octagonal plate with portrait bust of Salisbury. 9in. (23cm) diameter.

Plate 253. Staffordshire pottery plate with a portrait of Salisbury. Similar to Plate 250 but with different flowers. 9in. (23cm) diameter.

above the words 'In Memoriam', is the well-known portrait in black and white, above is his wife captioned 'Mrs Gladstone' and beneath on the left is his father, Sir John Gladstone and on the right his mother, Lady Gladstone. Underneath are his date of birth – '29th December 1809'; the date of his death – '19th May 1898'; the date of his marriage to Miss Catherine Glyn – '25th July 1839', beneath which are details of the various offices he held and his various other activities. At the top on the right is a transfer of the Houses of Parliament, and on the left Haden Castle. The portrait itself is surrounded by sprigs of myrtle, laurel and oak leaves and the verse at the bottom reads:

'Leaves have their time to fall
and flowers to wither
at the north wind's breath
and stars to set
but thou has all seasons
for thine own death.'

A tin (Plate 251), of unknown manufacture, portrays in four panels the head and shoulders of Gladstone and his wife, she seated in a basket chair under a tree, Gladstone is holding a stick and wearing a frock coat and a black silk hat. Another panel is of the young Gladstone, and the final one is of Gladstone in the House of Commons at the Despatch Box with the Speaker in the background, captioned 'Mr Gladstone introducing the Home Rule Bill 1893'. The lid has a portrait of Gladstone seated at his desk.

The Marquis of Salisbury was ceramically recorded on plates. One (Plate 252), with a green and gold border, octagonal in shape, clearly shows him at a time when he was a young man. He is shown when he was older on one of a series of three plates (Plate 253), the other two being for Gladstone (Plate 250) and Joseph Chamberlain respectively. Each plate has a different border. That for Salisbury is in maroon, Gladstone's is black and Chamberlain's is blue. Each of them has his portrait at the top of the plate. Beneath Salisbury is what appears to be a design of pansies, beneath Gladstone what appear to be anemones and underneath Chamberlain, inevitably, orchids.

The last of the Queen's Prime Ministers, although not Prime Minister at her death, was Rosebery. There is a tall jug (Plate 254), in pale blue, black printed, showing the head and shoulders of Rosebery, in a cartouche surrounded by flowers, and on the other side, again in a cartouche, the coat of arms of the Rosebery and Primrose family surrounded again by flowers, the thistle being very prominent because of the Scottish origin and bearing the Earl's coronet. The jug was manufactured by Campbell Field potters in Glasgow and stamped 'Rosebery'.

The Queen and the Constitution

One of the controversial issues that arose during Queen Victoria's reign was the question of Home Rule for Ireland. The protagonist was Charles Stuart Parnell, for whom there is an octagonal plate (Plate 255) showing his head and shoulders, in a frame surrounded by flowers, and above, the words: 'Erin G O Bragh'. Underneath are the Irish harp and the Irish shamrock.

Brownfield and Sons manufactured a most interesting teaset (Plate 256) showing portraits of the well-known protagonists in the British Parliament of Irish Home Rule. The cups are in two sizes, small for tea and large for breakfast, and the design is shamrocks and harps. Those portrayed include T.P. O'Connor, Michael Davitt, John Dillon, Charles Stuart Parnell and William O'Brien.

There is a terracotta plaque (Plate 257) portraying Gladstone, seated, wearing a tam-o'-shanter, chiselling a

Plate 254. Scottish pottery blue ground jug with black printed portrait of Rosebery. 6¼in. (16cm) high.

Plate 255. Staffordshire octagonal pottery plate with a bust portrait of Charles Stuart Parnell. 9½in. (24cm) diameter.

Plate 256. *Brownfield teaset, each piece printed in brown with portraits of well-known Irish Nationalist members.*

Plate 257. *Terracotta plaque for Gladstone and Irish Home Rule, black and white, 13in. (33cm).*

Plate 258. *Staffordshire pottery plate with a titled portrait bust of Tom Ellis MP, Liberal Chief Whip. 9½in. (24cm) diameter.*

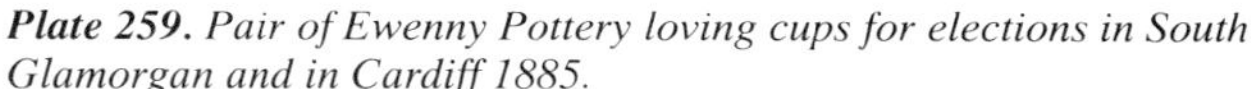

Plate 259. *Pair of Ewenny Pottery loving cups for elections in South Glamorgan and in Cardiff 1885.*

Plate 260(left). *Staffordshire memorial plate, with a bust of Lord George Bentinck. 7in. (17.5cm) diameter.*

Plate 261. Punch *cartoon captioned: 'Missed Again'.*

Plate 262. Punch *cartoon captioned: 'The Great Little Randolph'.*

gravestone, which reads: 'In Memoriam, Home Rule Bill for Ireland, murdered in the House of Lords September 1898 resurgam'. The base of the plaque is designed with shamrocks and there is a thistle at the very top. The whole plaque is surrounded by a laurel wreath in terracotta.

There is a plate portraying the head and shoulders of Tom Ellis MP (Plate 258), late Liberal Whip, presumably this was published for his death. The portrait is in colour, on a white background. Thomas Ellis was Liberal MP for Merionethshire and died in 1894 having served as Junior Lord of the Treasury. There is also a jug with a half-length black and white portrait of the politician.

A pair of loving cups (Plate 259), slip decorated, and marked for Ewenny Pottery commemorate the election of 1885. That for South Glamorgan shows that Wyndham Quinn had a majority of 825. The reverse of the cup carries in a cartouche a Welsh inscription 'Undeb dros byth'. The Cardiff cup was for the successful candidate J.M. McLean who had a majority of 824. The reverse of this cup carries the words 'Unionist Strength' in a cartouche.

Lord George Bentinck died in 1848. He was an English Tory politician and sportsman, son of the Fourth Duke of Portland. A plate (Plate 260) to record his death has a daisy border, in the centre of which is a black and white portrait of the head and shoulders of Bentinck, captioned 'Lord George Bentinck died 21st September 1848 aged 47'.

There are three most interesting political plaques painted onto stone china and fired which are direct translations of *Punch* cartoons by Sir John Tenniel. One, dated 1884, shows a shooting scene which is captioned 'Missed Again' (Plate 261). It shows Lord Randolph Churchill attempting to wrest the leadership of the Party from Sir Stafford Northcote, 'while Gladstone crows triumphantly on the farmyard fence'. The caption reads: 'Lord R as clown, out of the way you old un and let me come'.

Another dated 1886 shows a circus scene captioned 'The Great Little Randolph' (Plate 262). This records Churchill's resignation as Chancellor of the Exchequer, while Lord Salisbury continues to direct the 'horse' of government. The subsidiary caption reads 'I shan't play any more'. Lord Randolph resigned as Chancellor and Leader of the Conservative Party in the Lower House and never held Office in the Conservative Party again.

The third plaque, dated 1888, is taken again from *Punch*, and features the long-running scandal of the alleged involvement of Parnell in the Phoenix Park Murders (Plate 263).

The issue of free trade was also a movement which played a prominent part in the Queen's reign and there are some commemoratives for this including a large loving cup (Plate 264A), black and white printed, showing various aspects of trade, and captioned 'Free Trade with all the world' and on the reverse 'Manufactured in exchange for corn'. A plate with a moulded border (Plate 264B) has in the centre a transfer, again of a ship with the words 'free trade' and captioned 'Free trade with all the nations'.

The Queen took a great interest in all social reforms, one of which was the relief of hours of work. There is a pottery plate (Plate 265A), brown printed, with an elaborate design, featuring Burnett, the king of the 'Nine Hours Movement' and giving local retail support to the strike. On the 27th May 1871 the workmen of all the leading engineering firms of

Plate 263. Punch *cartoon captioned: 'Penance'.*

Plate 264A. *Large loving cup captioned: 'Free Trade with all the World'. 6in. (15cm) high.* ***B.*** *Staffordshire circular plate inscribed 'Free Trade with all the nations'. 7½in. (19cm) diameter.*

Gateshead in Newcastle came out on strike for a nine hour day under the leadership of the Nine Hour League – President, Mr Burnett. The strike lasted for nineteen weeks. Finally, as the plate claims, the men were victorious, although it was a limited victory, the employers settling for a fifty-four hour week, but with a clause that the men would contract to work virtually indefinite overtime. The border of the plate has some interesting comments. The plate was manufactured only by J. Wardell, North Street, Middlesex.

Riots broke out in Blackburn as part of the unrest over the 'Nine Hours Movement'. A pottery mug (Plates 266), black printed, shows on two sides chaotic views of the riots in progress in May 1878.

Two of the great reformers of the period during the Queen's reign were Cobden and Bright and there are some commemoratives for both these well-known radical politicians. There is a mug (Plate 267B), blue-printed, with on one side a portrait of John Bright M.P. and on the other a portrait of Richard Cobden M.P. and so captioned with the inscription on the front of the mug: 'By the Efforts of the League, the first approach to real freedom of trade obtained 1845'. They are all associated with the anti-Corn Law league. There is a very fine jug (Plate 267A), moulded and coloured under the glaze in a particularly fine palette, with on one side Peel and so captioned and on the other side, 'Cobden'. There is a pair of small children's plates (Plate 268), one for Cobden and one for Peel, each having colour portraits of the two statesmen. The borders are moulded.

The death of Bright was recorded on a small plate (Plate 267C), showing in the centre a head and shoulders portrait of

Plate 265A. *Staffordshire pottery plate to commemorate the 'Nine Hours Strike' of 1871. 8in. (20.5cm) diameter.* ***B and C.*** *Pottery jug printed with half-length portrait of Richard Oastler. 5½in. (14cm) high.*

Plate 266. *Mug for the Blackburn riots. 5¾in. (14.5cm) high.*

Plate 267A. *Staffordshire jug with busts of Cobden and Peel. 7¼in. (18.5cm) high.* ***B.*** *Staffordshire blue printed cylindrical mug with bust of John Bright and Richard Cobden. 4¾in. (12.2cm) high.* ***C.*** *Memorial plate, black printed, with a bust inscribed 'The Rt. Hon. John Bright MP' with dates of birth and death. 5½in. (14cm) diameter.*

Bright in black and white transfer, captioned 'The Rt Hon John Bright MP born November 16th 1811, died March 2nd 1889'. There is a barrel-shaped mug, similar to that for the late Earl Derby, which portrays on one side, the Rt Hon W.E. Gladstone MP and on the other the Rt Hon John Bright MP.

One of the great protagonists for social reform was Richard Oastler who was an enthusiast for Wilberforce and for the factory reformer, John Wood. He formed the notorious Fixby Hall Compact with the Huddersfield artisans to support Sadler's famous Bill to limit the working day of all children under nine to ten hours. He later organised a public meeting in York to support the Bill, persevered with the cause, but in 1838 his patrons, the Thornhills, felt that his radical views were too unpalatable for them and he was sacked. He became destitute and in December 1840 was committed to prison for debt. A fund was set up for him called 'The Oastler Liberation Fund' and rallies were held. In 1844 sufficient monies had been collected to free him from jail. He persisted in politics until the passing of the Ashley Act in 1847, retired from public life and died in Harrogate in 1861. A rather splendid jug (Plate 265B and C), presumably made in 1832, supports Sadler's campaign or perhaps it was made later, in 1842, to raise money for the fund. It was manufactured to record his interest in the social movement. It is black and white printed, has a head and shoulders portrait of Oastler holding a scroll of the 'Ten Hours Bill' and the words 'No Bastilles' captioned 'Richard Oastler, the friend of the poor'. There are two figures, with balloon cartoons: 'Oastler for Ever' and 'Quarter Loaf for 4'. They both stand near a pillar under which are the words 'Live and Let Live'.

There is a very small figure of Robert Lowe, Lord Sherbrooke, who first emigrated to Australia and practised in law, and then entered politics, returning to Britain in 1850. He entered Parliament and became Chancellor of the Exchequer in 1868, and Home Secretary in 1873.

A tall jug (Plate 269) commemorates the death of Earl Iddesleigh (formerly Stafford Northcote). It is captioned 'In Memoriam' and the words by way of tribute are 'He wore the white flower of a blameless life'. There is a similar portrait on one of the octagonal plates so prevalent at the time. The reverse of the jug carries the coat of arms of the Earl with the motto 'Christi crux est mea lux'.

Randolph Churchill, who was Chancellor of the Exchequer in 1886, is commemorated by another octagonal plate (Plate 270), showing the head and shoulders of Churchill in a frame surrounded by flowers and captioned 'Lord Randolph Churchill and his office'.

A jug (Plate 271) records Robert Ashcroft, who was a solicitor in Oldham. He had an outstanding record as an arbitrator in the cotton disputes which were bedevilling the

Plate 268. *Pair of child's plates featuring Peel on one and Cobden on the other, with pink lustre borders.*

Plate 269. *Staffordshire pottery jug with a titled portrait of Earl Iddlesleigh. 7in. (18cm) high.*

Plate 270. *Staffordshire octagonal plate with portrait of Lord Randolph Churchill. 9½in. (24cm) diameter.*

Plate 271. *Staffordshire pottery jug with a portrait bust of Robert Ashcroft MP. 4¼in. (11cm) high.*

Plate 272. *Staffordshire pottery plate 'Norfolk's Pride the Patriote Coke'. 10½in. (26.5cm) diameter.*

City's prosperity and entered Parliament as a Conservative for Oldham in 1895 with the largest vote ever polled. The jug records his election in 1895 showing the head and shoulders of the MP, headed 'Robert Ashcroft Esq MP' and underneath 'The Workers Friend'.

A handsome plate (Plate 272) was published for Thomas William, Earl of Leicester and Viscount Coke entitled 'Norfolk's pride the patriote Coke'. He was MP for Norfolk

Plate 273. *Small Staffordshire pottery plate with a portrait of Hugh Mason. 6¾in. (17cm) diameter.*

for most of his life, dying in 1842. He was one of the first to apply a scientific method to agriculture and revolutionise the whole practice and quality of farming in Norfolk. The plate is black and white printed, having in the centre a fine portrait of Coke surrounded by a design of flowers.

A terracotta bust (Plate 386C) was made of Spencer Compton Cavendish, Marquis of Hartington, the eldest son of the Duke of Devonshire who succeeded to the Dukedom in 1891. Hartington held many offices in the Liberal Party and was in Gladstone's Government. He was one of those responsible for sending Gordon to the Sudan and threatened to resign to force Gladstone to send a relief to Khartoum.

A jug to commemorate Henry William Ripley contains in the centre a sepia head and shoulders portrait, of Ripley. He was elected MP for Bradford but was tried for corrupt practices and the election was declared void. He was subsequently re-elected in 1874. He was known as the fighting cock and on his jug is a transfer of a cock.

Hugh Mason, who was MP for Manchester, was a friend of John Bright. He was a master spinner and Mayor of Ashton-Under-Lyme during the cotton famine riot of 1860 when he championed the riots. A plate with a moulded border (Plate 273) was issued to commemorate his death in 1866, in the centre of which is a head and shoulders portrait of Mason with his dates of birth and death, 1817-1866.

A great deal of election commemoratives were produced. Barnstaple features regularly in commemorative records. There is a very fine tall jug (Plate 274) for Thomas Cave Esq, MP for Barnstaple from 1865-1880, Queensbury House, Richmond, Surrey'. The reverse holds the words 'All hail to him who wins the prize thou fight and conquer if you can, but if ye fall or if ye rise be each pray God a gentleman'. There are various motifs, including daffodils and scrolls and presumably the family crest – a dog holding a cross

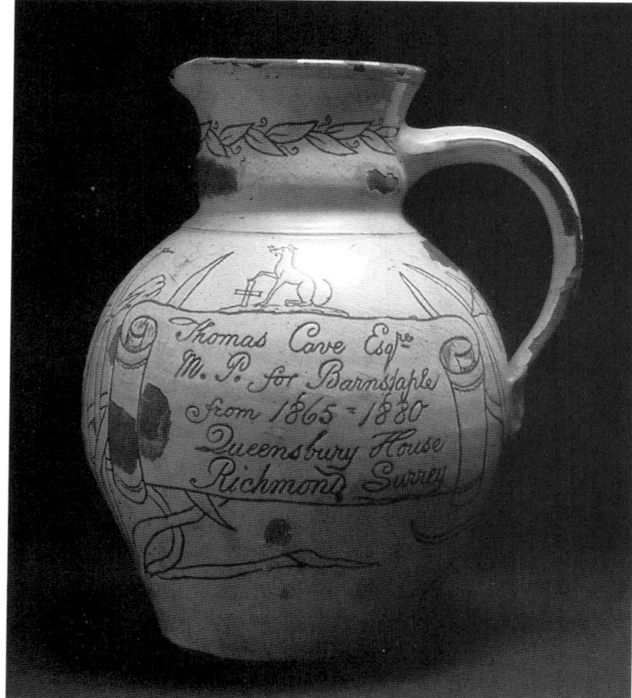

Plate 274. *Staffordshire slipware oviform jug for Thomas Cave MP. 10¼in. (26cm) high.*

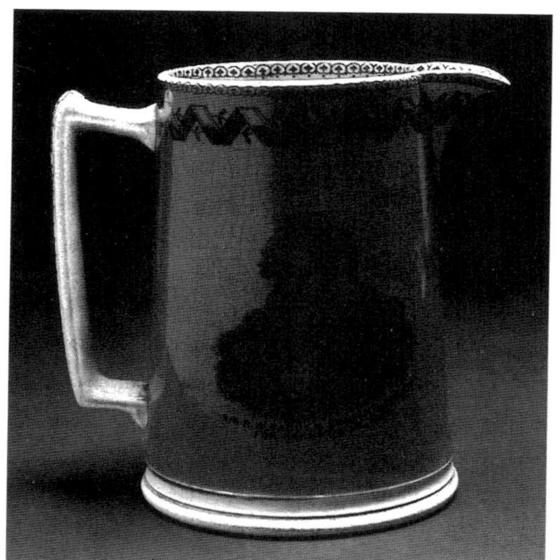

Plate 275. *Staffordshire pottery jug printed in black with titled bust portrait of R.W. Carden, Senior, Member for Barnstaple 1880. 6¼in. (16cm) high.*

Plate 276. *Pair of Doulton Lambeth stoneware vases with portrait busts of Herbert Gladstone and John Barrane for the Leeds election in 1880. 5½in. (14cm) high.*

surmounts the inscription. Another jug (Plate 275) for a Barnstaple election was that of R.W. Carden Senior, Member for Barnstaple in 1880. This is in a vivid blue with a black and white transfer portrait of the Member sporting a prolific beard.

A pair of barrel-shaped Doulton vases (Plate 276) in the two tone Doulton colour bears on one the portrait in relief of Herbert J. Gladstone, returned unopposed and on the other John Barrane with his portrait in relief '2,364 votes'. These were both for the Leeds election in 1880.

A fine Doulton three-handled tyg (Plate 277) commemorates the General Election of 1880 describing when, for the first time in its history, the West Riding of Yorkshire returned six Liberal Representatives to Parliament. Their names are given as Fitzwilliam, Letham, Cavendish, Wilson, Ramsden and Fairbourne. The High Sheriff was Sir

Plate 277. *Doulton Lambeth three-handled loving cup by Frank Butler with an inscription commemorating the success of the Liberal candidates in the West Riding in the General Election, 1880. 6¼in. (16cm) high.*

Plate 278. *Pear-shaped Staffordshire coffee pot and cover with a portrait of Lord Edmund Talbot, son of the Earl of Shrewsbury, who unsuccessfully contested Burnley. 7in. (18cm) high.*

Charles W. Strickland, Bart, who presumably conducted the return of the poll and the date is given as April 1880. There is a very fine design of the Yorkshire Rose in white on the other side.

Mortlock and Co. of Oxford Street, London, manufactured several similar interestingly shaped election jugs for the elections in July 1895. That for Buckinghamshire was manufactured to commemorate the Union of Success with the words 'Liberty, Loyalty and Prosperity' in a shield, the candidates being Rothschild, Curzon and Carlisle. The Unionist successes in Herefordshire were similarly recorded with the shield 'Union is Strength', the names being Biddulph, Radcliffe, Cooke and Rankin. Wiltshire, similarly, was commemorated by the single Union of Success in the same year. The candidates were Dixon, Poynder, Folkestone, Houlse, Challoner, Goulding and Hopkinson. The success of

Thomas Mellor who was elected for the Borough of Ashton-Under-Lyme on 18th November 1868 has also been commemorated.

Even unsuccessful candidates produced commemorative records of their attempts to enter Parliament. There is a coffee jug (Plate 278), black and white printed, for Lord Edmond Talbot. He is shown in a head and shoulders portrait and it reads 'Lord Edmond Talbot, the Conservative candidate who gallantly came forward to contest the good old cause in the Borough of Burnley, but was unsuccessful'.

Many *Punch* cartoons depict elections during the reign of Victoria. A very interesting one is entitled 'A Lord Mare's Nest' (Plate 279) showing the candidate, presumably somebody connected with the City of London, climbing a tree, under the branches is the word 'Andover' and in the top right hand corner is a bird, holding in its beak the words 'City Election Liberal Majority 506'. In the background is St Paul's Cathedral. This is dated 'August 10th 1861' and the Shropshire coat of arms and flags and the crowd.

An interesting teapot, shaped in the form of a tree-trunk (Plate 280), records the Liberal victory at Cockermouth on 18th November 1868. It was given and presented by his 'warm supporter' John Bairn. It was made at Broughton Moor. The MP elected was Isaac Fletcher.

The eightieth birthday of William Rathbone, MP for Liverpool and later for Caernarvonshire up to 1895, is commemorated in a handsome jug (Plate 281) bearing, on the front in a cartouche, the head and shoulders of William Rathbone of Greenbank dated 'February 11th 1899'. There is a design of interwoven orange flowers around the lip, handle and the neck of the jug and in the centre in a laurel wreath below the monogram 'WR' is a quotation which reads 'A man of deeds, not words, the steadfast friend of all that weak or ailing or distrest. For others good his days he loves to spend and find in strenuous toil his nobler rest. Britain's true wheel – not in these Isles alone, he saw and seeing her shunned the ways of creeping craft. For insolence o'er blown by honest labour in running bloodless bathes'. Underneath are the initials 'HFW' – presumably the author of the verse.

Plate 279. Punch *cartoon captioned 'A Lord Mare's Nest'.*

The death of Colonel North on 5th May 1896 is

Plate 280A and B. *A Broughton Moore commemorative teapot with an inscription on the base commemorating the Liberal Victory at the Cockermouth Election, 1868. 5in. (12.5cm) high.*

Plate 281. *Staffordshire pottery oviform jug with a portrait of William Rathbone. 5½in. (14cm) high.*

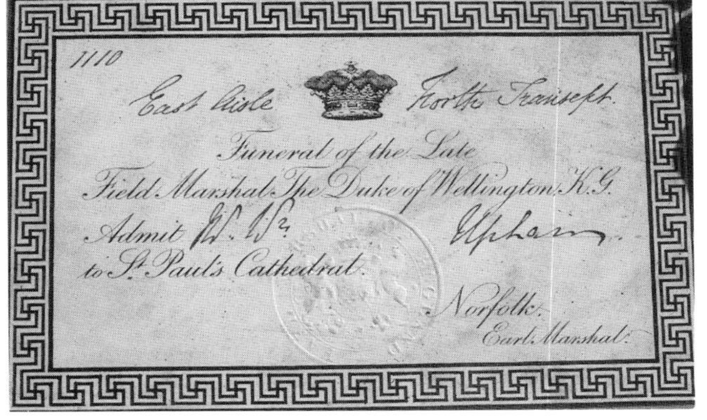

Plate 282. *Staffordshire Pottery mug commemorating Colonel John North of Kirkstall, Leeds. 4in. (10.5cm) high.*

Plate 283(above right). *Official ticket issued on the occasion of the funeral of the Duke of Wellington at St. Paul's Cathedral. 4½in. (11.5cm) x 7in. (18cm).*

Plate 284(right). *Small Staffordshire plate commemorating the death of the Duke of Wellington. 6in. (15.5cm) diameter.*

Plate 285. *Jug commemorating the death of Wellington. 5in. (12.5cm) high.*

Plate 286. *Selected photographs from Queen Victoria's Baveno Album.*

H:R:H: Princess Helena.

Leopold
1876.

H:R:H: The Princess Alice.

H:M: Queen Victoria.

Arthur
1876

Louise Margaret
1878.

Plate 287. *Linen cloth portraying the Queen with her Prime Ministers for the Jubilee 1887. Rosebery is not included since he had not yet claimed that position.*

commemorated on a mug (Plate 282) which shows an engraving of Kirkstall Abbey underneath which is recorded 'the gift of Colonel North to the Borough of Leeds January 1889' and alongside, the words: 'built in 1147, destroyed by Oliver Cromwell in 1539. He was known as the knight-trait King'.

The death of the Duke of Wellington was not only a great loss to the nation, but also to the Queen, who was devoted to this great soldier and statesman. She named her third son Arthur after the Duke, who stood as godparent. His funeral was a great and sad state occasion and invitation to St. Paul's was by ticket. These tickets (Plate 283) bore the Ducal Coronet and were signed by the Earl of Norfolk. A small Staffordshire plate (Plate 284) bears his dates. A jug (Plate 285) commemorating his death bears the same portrait but also a full-length portrait of him as a soldier in his great military days and a view of Walmer Castle in Kent, indicating he was held Warden of the Cinque Ports, where he died.

Italy

The Queen frequently visited Italy and stayed at the Villa Clara, Baveno, which is on Lake Maggiore. She had a special leather-bound album prepared for a Mr and Mrs Henfrey and it contains portraits of members of the Royal Family (Plate 286), the Queen of the first page, Prince Albert on the second and followed on each successive page by portraits of her nine children. There are also portraits of the Princess of Wales and the Duchess of Connaught. Most of these have been signed. On the cover, in gold letters, are the words of presentation, surmounted by, also in gold, the royal coat of arms. The album has its own locking device.

Plate 288. *Photograph of the Royal Family taken for the Queen's Diamond Jubilee.*

CHAPTER 3

Edward and Alexandra 1901-1910

The reign of Edward VII and Queen Alexandra, although it lasted only nine years, was splendid and glittering. The King introduced sparkle and liveliness to his courts. The strait-laced atmosphere of the latter part of the Victorian era came to an abrupt halt with the accession of the new King.

Commemoratives for his birth have been mentioned in the previous chapter. A rare souvenir is a porcelain head of the baby prince in its original mount and frame (Plate 289). The reverse bears the label 'To commemorate the birth of H.R.H. Prince Albert, Prince of Wales, 9th November 1841'. This was published by C.A. Martin of St Martin's Court.

Ceramic records exist for several events during the King's life. The early ones are not easily found. When he obtained his commission in the army some commemoratives were produced to record this event, usually carrying a purple-printed portrait of the Prince on horseback and the Prince of Wales feathers. These appear on a tall jug, and on a punch bowl (Plate 293).

During his life he made several visits to Canada, the first in 1860. The trip was commemorated by a rare moulded dry-ware jug (Plate 290) which has a portrait of Victoria on one side, Albert on the other, and the young Prince of Wales on the front. The lip is fashioned around the plume of feathers and it is dated 1860. A subsequent visit to Canada to open the University of Toronto is commemorated on an octagonal plate (Plate 291) showing a portrait of the Prince of Wales together with the university buildings at Toronto. His visit to the tomb of George Washington at Mount Vernon is featured on a Pratt pottery lid (Plate 292).

His marriage to the beautiful Princess Alexandra of Denmark is commemorated in several forms. A tall pear-shaped jug (Plate 293B) bears the head and shoulders portraits of both the Prince and Princess. Alexandra is portrayed as a bronze bust (Plate 294) on a tall fluted column. The mark of the sculptor is not obvious. A set of three loving cups (Plate 295) in different sizes has the Prince of Wales with his feathers on one side and Princess Alexandra on the other. A typical plate for the marriage

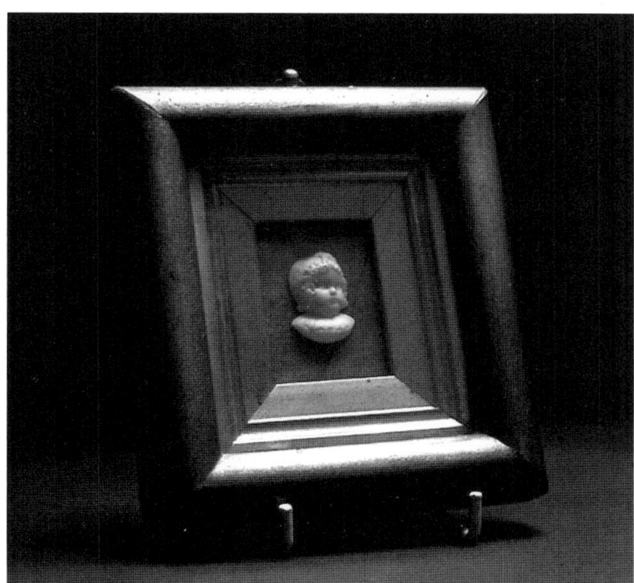

Plate 289. *Porcelain head of the Prince to commemorate his birth – 9th November 1841.*

Plate 290. *Sandford Pottery white stoneware relief moulded jug embossed to commemorate the visit to Canada. 11in. (28cm) high.*

Plate 291. Octagonal plate for the opening of Toronto University. 9½in. (24.1cm) diameter.

Plate 292. Pratt pottery lid depicting the Prince of Wales visiting Washington's tomb.

Plate 293A. Footed bowl by Crown Pottery to commemorate the commission, 9¾in. (25cm) diameter. B. Jug to commemorate the marriage to Princess Alexandra, 8½in. (21.5cm) high.

Plate 294. *Bronze head of Princess Alexandra.*

Plate 295. *Set of three loving cups for Edward and Alexandra's marriage.*

Plate 296. *Marriage plate for the Prince of Wales.*

Plate 297. *Plate for the Guildhall Freedom of the City.*

Plate 298. *Charger for the Paris Exhibition.*

(Plate 296) has portraits of the Prince and Princess beneath the Prince's feathers and the Welsh motto *Ich Dien* and the date of the marriage.

Shortly after their marriage they received the Freedom of the City of London at the Guildhall. Both the Prince and Princess of Wales attended in the supper room to celebrate the occasion and a special dinner service was made for the royal table by Daniell of London. The plates (Plate 297) had a maroon border scalloped with a decoration of gold leaves. The centre of the bowl contains the City of London's coat of arms, surmounted by the Prince of Wales' feathers.

He attended the Paris Exhibition in 1878 and by fixing the Union Jack alongside the French tricolour blazed the trail for the *Entente Cordiale*. A handsome porcelain charger published by Bretin Tissier features in colour the Exhibition buildings, including two balloons (Plate 298).

As President of the Annual Exhibition of all fine arts industries and inventions a special medallion was struck in 1873 by George Morgan bearing on the side the head of the Prince of Wales in relief with his feathers on the obverse showing the buildings in which the exhibition was held.

On the occasion of the Prince's thirty-eighth birthday Mortlock published a splendid jug (Plate 299). Tall and in brown glaze it has the embossed Prince of Wales feathers, captioned above and below 'Completed on the 38th birthday of the Prince of Wales, November 9th, 1879'. On each side are two advertising slogans, on the right:

'For right good ale
Is nectar fit for
Peasant, Prince or King'

on the left:

'the nut-brown draft
This pitcher holds
It's praises
Let me sing'

Around the neck and lip are the words 'Mortlock, established 1746, rebuilt 1879'. The potter's name is incised, F.S. Lee.

Barringer and Co., the mustard manufacturers of Mansfield, produced a tin (Plate 300) in 1880. The hinged lid bears the head and shoulders portrait of Alexandra, the Princess of Wales, wearing the cap and gown of a university of which she was presumably chancellor. Around her neck and placed over the white collar is a choker of spotted silk, in the centre of which is a heart-shaped gold brooch. On each side of the tin are large portraits of girls representing England with a rose, Ireland with the scarf of a colleen and the shamrock, Scotland with the glengarry and the plaid sash held by a cairngorm and Wales by the Welsh tall hat.

On 10th March, 1888 they celebrated their silver wedding and some commemoratives were produced for this occasion. A splendid Doulton tyg (Plate 301), a three-handled brown pottery mug, has the words around it 'It makes our hearts glad and the world rejoice with you, March 10th 1888'. There are portraits of both Alexandra and Edward on each side, and the words are surmounted by the Prince of Wales feathers and the royal standard for Princess Alexandra. A pressed glass jug and footed bowl can sometimes be found to commemorate the Silver Wedding. Pressed glass was a fairly common method of recording important events and people and items such as these can sometimes by obtained. There are similar ones for the relief of Pretoria, the relief of Mafeking and various other national events.

Plate 299A and B. *Doulton jug for the Prince of Wales' 38th birthday.*

Plate 300. *Barringer & Co. mustard tin for the Princess of Wales.*

Plate 301. *Doulton loving cup for the Silver Wedding of the Prince and Princess of Wales, 10th March, 1888.*

The Illustrated London News and *The Graphic* (Plate 302) published colourful and detailed issues to celebrate the Silver Wedding. *The Graphic* has three separate Prince of Wales feathers carried by a cherub. *The Illustrated London News* shows the Prince and Princess in a Grand Barge.

There were six children from this marriage. The eldest son was the Duke of Clarence, Prince Albert Victor. Prince Albert Victor and Prince George went on a world tour and they are both shown by *The Graphic* (Plate 303) at a reception, captioned 'The Young Princes at the Antipodes'.

Prince Albert Victor's celebration of his coming of age at a Ball at Sandringham is also shown in *The Graphic*. He

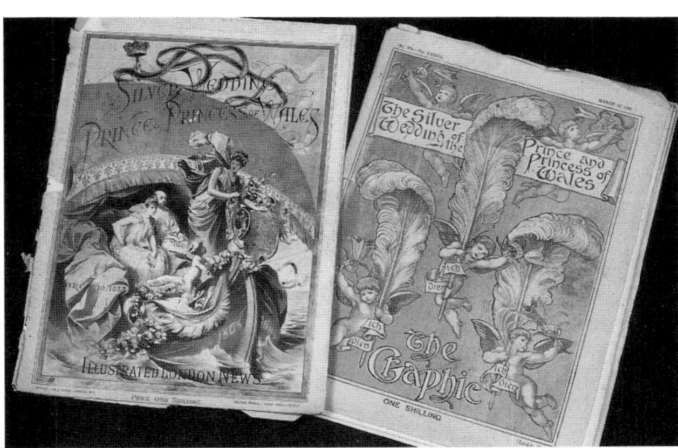

Plate 302. *Magazines to celebrate the Silver Wedding.*

Plate 303. *Two illustrations from* The Graphic *commemorating Prince Albert Victor and Prince George's world tour and Prince Albert Victor's coming of age, 1871.*

Plate 304. *Pair of Doulton jugs to commemorate the deaths of the Duke of Clarence and Cardinal Manning.*

Plate 305. *Octagonal plate for the Duke of Clarence's visit to Burnley.*

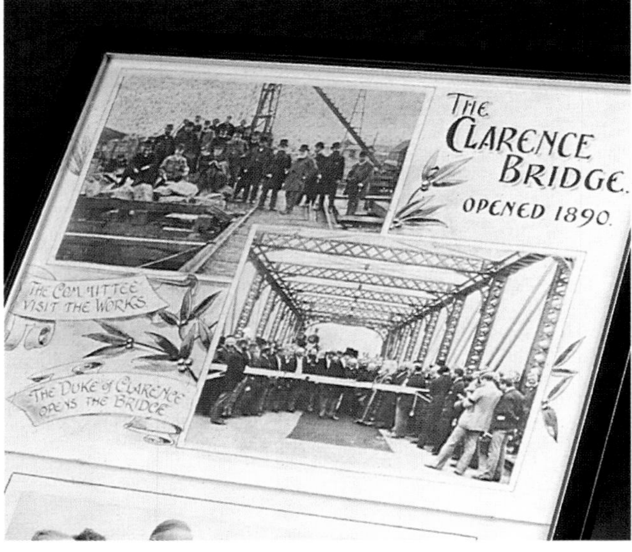

Plate 306. *Photograph of the opening of Clarence Bridge, Cardiff, 1890.*

Plate 307. *Parian bust of the Duke of Clarence.*

Plate 308. *Magazines to record the death of the Duke of Clarence.*

Plate 309. *Signed photograph of Princess Louise, Duchess of Fife.*

Plate 310. *Copenhagen Porcelain plate commemorating the marriage of Princess Maud and Prince Charles of Denmark.*

Plate 311. *Magazines to record the wedding.*

Plate 312. *Tankard to record the accession of the King and Queen of Norway, 1905.*

Plate 313. *Minton beaker for the opening of the Imperial Yeomanry Hospital.*

would have succeeded to the throne, but on 14th January 1892, he died. A Doulton jug (Plate 304), commemorates this sad event. It so happened that Cardinal Manning, the Cardinal Archbishop of Westminster, died on the same day and a similar jug was published by Doulton for the Cardinal's death. They make an interesting pair.

During his short life the Duke of Clarence had several public engagements. He made a visit to Burnley to open the Victoria Hospital on 13th October 1886. An octagonal plate (Plate 305), records this event. It has in the centre a head and shoulders portrait of the Duke in military uniform, around which are the royal flowers in colour and above, the Prince of Wales feathers.

The Duke of Clarence opened a Bridge over the River Taff in the Docks area of Cardiff on 17th September 1890 (Plate 306). He was later presented with the Freedom of the City, the fourth the Borough had created, the previous one being for William Gladstone in July, 1889. This famous bridge was a landmark and was removed in 1980.

A white parian bust (Plate 307) of the Duke shows him, in military uniform. The initials of the modeller are on the reverse 'A.L.'. His death is also recorded on a saucer (Plate 126D) which has an engraving in the centre of the Gordon Boys Chapel. The reverse carries the inscription: 'Dedicated to the Glory of God, in memory of HRH the Duke of Clarence and Avondale, KG. Presented to the Gordon Boys Home for uses of the Church of England, 1884'. Newspapers and magazines (Plate 308), gave full coverage to the death of the Duke of Clarence. *The Illustrated London News* shows a weeping Britannia, *The Daily Graphic* gave much detail and *Punch* carried a cartoon of a shrouded figure holding a crown by Swain, dated 14th January 1892.

Edward and Alexandra's second son, George, subsequently became King George V and commemoratives for his life and reign will be mentioned in the next chapter.

Of the three daughters, the eldest was Princess Louise, who married the Duke of Fife. She is hardly commemorated at all and there appears to be no ceramic piece in existence. However, there is a tin for her marriage which took place in 1889. On the hinged lid are coloured portraits of the Princess and her husband. On the sides are scenes of Sheen Lodge, Duff House and Mar Lodge, and of Queen Victoria and relatives waving goodbye as they depart in a coach after the wedding. This tin has rarely been seen in recent years.

The King's daughters were called Their Royal Shynesses' since they rarely carried out public engagements. Princess Louise was created Princess Royal and photographs of her are rare. There were two daughters from her marriage to the Duke of Fife, Alexandra who married Prince Arthur of Connaught and Maud, who married Lord Carnegie, later Earl of Southesk. A signed photograph (Plate 309), shows the Princess Royal with the young Alexandra.

Another daughter, Princess Maud, married Prince Charles of Denmark, in 1896, in the presence of Queen Victoria. A plate was published by the Royal Copenhagen factory for this event, it is simple in design and of fine quality (Plate 310).

Most national magazines covered the marriage. *The Graphic* (Plate 311), has a colourful cover with the bride and groom in a cartouche-shaped heart surmounted by a crown on a blue background entwined with garlands of roses, by Percy MacQuoid. Another magazine, entitled *Christian Herald*, has a black and white photograph of the wedding ceremony. Inside is a homily about the sanctity of marriage.

A plebiscite was held to decide whether Norway should have its own King. The people of Norway voted for an independent kingdom and Prince Charles of Denmark accepted the monarchy of Norway, becoming King Haakon

VII. To record the accession of the King and Queen of Norway a tankard (Plate 312) was issued in buff-coloured dryware, the lid bearing the date, 1905. In relief and in a wreath in the centre are profiles of the King and Queen and on either side, also in a wreath, the names of Norwegian statesmen. Beneath, in relief, are the royal palace and the Cathedral of Trondheim. The inscription is in Norwegian and translated means, 'We hope to have a country which is saved and free, not to have to compromise for its freedom'.

The third daughter, Princess Victoria, never married.

The sixth child, born in 1871, was Alexander John Charles Albert but he died within twenty-four hours of his birth. He is buried in Sandringham Churchyard.

In 1900 the Prince opened the Imperial Yeomanry Hospital for which Minton produced a beaker (Plate 313) on a cream background, the Prince of Wales feathers are in blue over a twisted ribbon.

The Coronation

If the reputed last word spoken by Queen Victoria was 'Bertie', it was a hint to her eldest son that he should call himself King Albert I. This was not to be because at the first accession council the King announced that he would henceforth be called King Edward VII.

On 9th November 1901 the King reached the age of sixty and a mug (Plate 314) commemorated that event, showing the King's monogram 'ERVII' surmounted by the crown, the rose of England, the thistle of Scotland and the shamrock of Ireland, published by Minton in two shades of blue and green.

One of the earliest orders made by the King was to add the arms of Wales to the royal insignia on 10th September, 1901. A cup and saucer (Plate 315) published for M.F. Sparks of Queen Street, Cardiff commemorates this important event for Wales. The inscription on the saucer is 'Freedom, Justice, Love' and inscribed on the cup is: 'The Red Dragon will lead the way to remember times past'. Both inscriptions are in Welsh.

The King had planned the grandest of coronations. He intended all foreign royalty to be present and wished it to be the most glittering occasion. Unfortunately things went wrong, he was operated upon for appendicitis and the original date of 26th June 1902 was postponed. It was subsequently held on 9th August.

The King's accession was commemorated by a plate (Plate 316A). It has two portraits of the King in full uniform with all his stars and medals and the ribbon of the garter on the right and Queen Alexandra on the left wearing a magnificently jewelled collar. Underneath the two portraits is the date 1901 and 'God Save our Queen and God Save our King'. Above is the crown, below is the English rose. The other royal flowers, the shamrock and the thistle, are also portrayed though only the rose is in colour. Prior to the coronation and probably for the first time on record, a plate was published by Wedgwood (Plate 317), which on the reverse reads '1902. A souvenir of the first year of the reign of the King'. The reverse bears the names of his possessions together with the orders and decorations appertaining to the realm and a list of sixty-four distinguished men of the day who added 'Lustre thereto. Politics, Army and Navy, Religion, Art, Science and Commerce, By his loyal subjects'. It was made in Bristol. There follow the words: 'To be crowned on August 9th with the naval review on August 16th'. This clearly must have been made after the new date had been agreed.

All members of the royal family wore robes with long trains of velvet trimmed with ermine. The Duchess of Albany, widow of Prince Leopold and mother of Princess Alice, Countess of Athlone, the last surviving grand-daughter of Queen Victoria, is shown in a photograph (Plate 318), taken in Berlin, signed 'Helen 1902' and dated 2nd August 1902.

Plate 314. *Minton mug to celebrate the King's 60th birthday.*

Plate 315. *Cup and saucer for the adding of the Arms of Wales to the Royal Insignia.*

Plate 316A. *Plate to commemorate the Accession of the King.* ***B.*** *Plate for the Coronation with portraits of the Viceroy, Governor Generals of India and the Dominions.*

Plate 317. *Both sides of a plate to record the first year of the King's reign.*

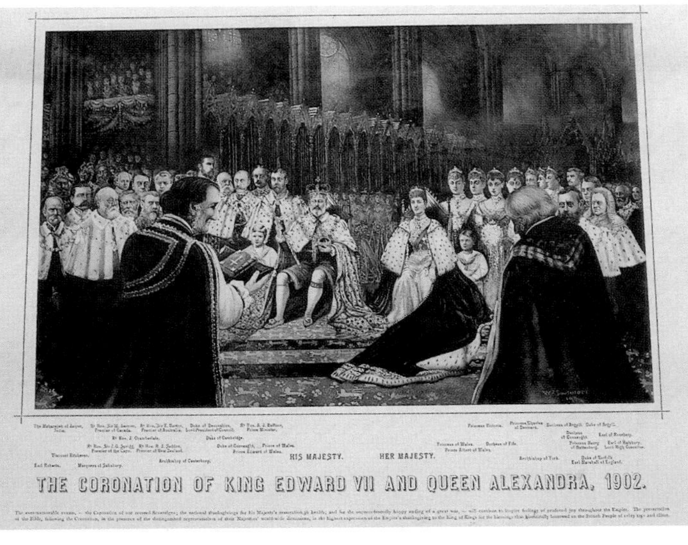

Plate 318. *Signed photograph of the Duchess of Albany in her Coronation Robes.*

Plate 319. *Engraving of the Coronation ceremony.*

Plate 320. *Mug to celebrate the end of the Boer War and, on the other side, the Coronation.*

Plate 321. *Pair of Doulton plaques of the King and Queen for the Coronation.*

Plate 322A and B. *City of Leeds plaque and Wedgwood plate for the Coronation.*

There is also a detailed engraving (Plate 319), of the actual coronation showing the Archbishop of Canterbury, the Marquis of Salisbury and Earl Halsbury together with the King and Queen's three daughters, the Prince of Wales and young Prince Edward, subsequently Edward VIII. In the far corner are Earl Roberts and Lord Kitchener together with various representatives from the Dominions and Colonies and the Prime Minister, Mr Balfour.

The coronation was lavishly commemorated in various forms, cups and saucers, tea and coffee sets, plates, beakers, mugs and jugs. Some had only the original date, and others the postponed date. One of the mugs for the coronation (Plate 320) has on the reverse the commemoration of the conclusion of the Boer War, showing a British soldier and a South African shaking hands overlooked by the angel and dove of peace. 'Peace and Prosperity, Unity is strength – Peace proclaimed June 11th 1902'. On the other side is the actual coronation portrait of the King and Queen in colour, stating 'God Bless Them Enthroned in the Hearts of Their People'. The conclusion of the Boer War was a great relief to the nation and enabled the King to start his reign in peace.

Doulton published a large number of commemorative pieces for both the original and the postponed date. The most elegant is a pair of plaques (Plate 321) showing the King in the scarlet jacket of a Field Marshal together with his orders and the Queen with a pearl choker and a magnificent necklace wearing stars, her shoulder covered with an ermine mantle and the ribbon of the garter. Above each is a crown and beneath each, their monograms, 'AR' for the Queen, 'EVIIR' for the King.

Wedgwood produced a plate in bright blue and white (Plate 322B), in the centre the King in an oval surrounded by the order of the garter and the garter motto. Again, around it are the various colonies and dominions. The rear bears the inscription 'Edward VII by the grace of God and Great Britain and Ireland and all the British Dominions beyond the seas, King, Defender of the Faith, and Emperor of India'. The Wedgwood mark is incised and it is dated '26th June, 1902'.

An unusual plate has, in addition to the King and Queen surrounded by flags of the Empire, the Prince and Princess of Wales, the young Prince Edward and also the Governor Generals of Canada, Lord Minto; South Africa, Lord Milner; Australia, Lord Hopetoun and the Viceroy of India, Lord Curzon. This appears to be the only recorded mention in a ceramic form of Lord Curzon.

An interesting beaker (Plate 323) published for the coronation shows on one side portraits of the King and Queen but on the other the Prince and Princess of Wales with, between them, in ovals, the Prince of Wales feathers, with the caption, 'Marlborough House'. Ceramic records seldom mentioned Marlborough House, so this is therefore somewhat rare. This beaker was published by Harrods Ltd., Brompton Road, London. A Doulton pottery jug (Plate 324) carries the typical two colours of brown showing the portraits of the King and Queen surmounted by the royal arms.

The City of Leeds commissioned a plaque (Plate 322A) and had the foresight to do one for both the 26th June and 9th August. The King and Queen are in the centre, surmounted by their crowns with the original date, 26th June, indicating that these plaques were presented as a memento of the coronation to the 80,000 children of the city by the Lord Mayor of Leeds. Published by J.W. Almack, on the rear are the words, 'The Coronation Postponed owing to the sudden illness of the King until August, 1902'. Various other memorabilia was published for the coronation, including a

Plate 323. *Beaker with portraits of the Prince and Princess of Wales at Marlborough House.*

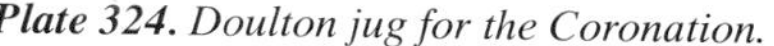

Plate 324. *Doulton jug for the Coronation.*

Plate 325. *Cigar case and miniature bible for the Coronation.*

Plate 326. *RAC badge bearing the King's head.*

miniature bible, a cigar case (Plate 325), and a special RAC car badge (Plate 326) bearing a portrait of the King's head.

A particular commemorative would have pleased the King. It was made in France, which always fascinated him. He loved Paris and it would appear that Paris loved him. The Carlton Hotel in Paris had a dinner in honour of the coronation in which a fan (Plate 327) was given to those who attended. On the reverse, in each section of the fan, are the signatures of those French people who were present.

Several tins were produced. An unusual casket-shaped tin (Plate 328) captioned 'Coronation Souvenir' bearing the head and shoulders of the King and Queen wearing their state crowns, has the unusual feature of having the base also captioned in colour. Although it is unmarked, there are in the centre, in a heart, the letters 'T. Ltd'. It is not quite clear what this signifies.

Mazawattee Tea provided a ceremonial tin, the hinged lid bearing the shields of the British royal arms and those of Denmark, surmounted by a crown and both held by the Lion and the Unicorn. Around the sides are part of the coronation regalia – St Edward's crown lying on the sword of state – the Archibishop's mitre resting on the order of ceremony and a crozier. The sceptre and orb and the cap of maintenance lie on a cushion with a gauntlet. It is highly decorated and in vivid colours. The base bears the words 'Mazawattee Tea, One 2/- Pound'.

W.D. & H.O. Wills produced a tobacco tin (Plate 329) on a pale purple background with portraits and the royal flowers.

Plate 327. *Fan from the Carlton Hotel, Paris for the coronation.*

Plate 328. *Casket tin for the Coronation.*

Plate 329. *Coronation mugs for Cardiff – Chamber of Commerce, Llandaff, Ely and Fairwater. Mug to record the visit by the King and Queen to Cardiff in 1907. Bristol tin. Wills tin.*

Plate 330. *Cup and saucer for the Coronation bearing the June date.*

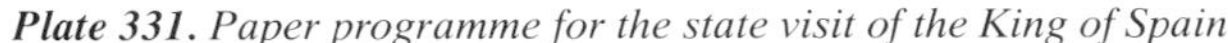

Plate 331. *Paper programme for the state visit of the King of Spain.*

PROGRAMME & SOUVENIR
OF THE
VISIT of the KING OF SPAIN

THE ROUTE TO GUILDHALL

ELABORATE DECORATIONS

Procession from Buckingham Palace to the Guildhall and back

Coronation pieces for Edward VII are still available. They normally take the form of mugs, probably those commissioned by various cities and towns. Cups and saucers (Plate 330) and plates can also be obtained. Those by Doulton are of a particular good quality. Cardiff was one of the towns that produced mugs (Plate 329) to celebrate the coronation. Three are known to exist, one in black and white which was presented by the President of the Cardiff Chamber of Commerce and was presumably given to those who attended a dinner given by the President, a Mr H. Wood Davey. Two districts of Cardiff, Ely and Fairwater, and also the City of Llandaff, produced mugs for the coronation, these are both in colour and indicate that they were commissioned for these two districts and for Llandaff. They were published by the Empire Porcelain Co., Stoke-on-Trent.

Following the coronation, several crowned heads of Europe made state visits to London, the first was Alfonso, the King of Spain. The young King had made up his mind that he wanted to marry an English Princess and first cast his eyes on Princess Patricia, daughter of the Duke of Connaught. However, she had made up her mind that she would marry a naval commander, which she subsequently did. Finally he was able to attract the attention of the daughter of Princess Beatrice of Battenburg, Princess Ena.

Plate 332. *Wemyss tankard for the marriage of the King of Spain and Princess Ena of Battenburg.*

Plates 333A and B. *Reverse of the Wemyss mug and a small plaque for the King and Queen of Spain.*

Plate 334. *Paper programme for the unveiling of the Duke of Cambridge's statue.*

Plate 335. *Copenhagen porcelain memorial column for the death of King Charles Christian IX of Denmark, the father of Queen Alexandra. 8in. (20.3cm) high.*

Little exists to record this visit other than a souvenir paper programme (Plate 331) which covered the event.

The marriage between the King of Spain and Princess Ena took place in Madrid on 31st May at the ancient church of Los Geronimos. The glittering occasion was to start with a blaze of heraldic uniforms and much pageantry. But it ended in tragedy because a bomb was thrown by an anarchist at the royal carriage as they were returning to the palace after their wedding; both narrowly escaped death. Several people were killed and the bride's gown was splattered with blood. Wemyss published a tankard (Plates 332 and 333A) to record this marriage. It has in the centre the crown and underneath, 'ER 1906'. There are the royal flowers, the thistle on the top surrounded by two shamrocks and two further thistles beneath, the shamrock in between. On each side there are two hearts pierced by an arrow and the words 'Praise God, Honour the King'. The thistles are significant because the young Princess was born at Balmoral.

There is also a small plaque (Plate 333B) of the King and Queen, it bears their heads and shoulders in pale green surmounted by a gold crown.

In March 1904 the Duke of Cambridge died. He was Commander in Chief for many years during the reign of Queen Victoria. The King unveiled a statue of the Duke of Cambridge on 5th June, 1907. A paper souvenir programme (Plate 334), which was a common method of telling the public how royal events took place, covers this occasion. It shows the Duke of Cambridge on his horse and carries the words 'Unveiled by the King, 15th June, 1907. The King and the Duke'.

In 1906 the Queen's father, King Christian IX, died. He may well be regarded as the grandfather of Europe. His daughter became Queen of England, another daughter became the Empress Dagmar of Russia, and his son became King George of Greece. A memorial column (Plate 335) was made by Copenhagen Porcelain to record the death of King Christian. It has a wreath around the top and on the base of the plinth are the dates 1863-1906. The King's monogram 'CIX' is on the reverse with the words, 'In Memoriam'.

Kaiser Wilhelm II made a state visit to London in 1907. He was a nephew of the King and the son of the King's eldest sister, the Empress Frederick. The details of this visit were also shown on a paper souvenir programme (Plate 336). During this visit the marriage took place between Prince Charles of Bourbon and Princess Louise of Orleans in November, 1907. A famous photograph (Plate 337) was taken at Windsor Castle by W.N.D. Downey, showing eight sovereigns, King Edward VII, Queen Alexandra, King Alfonso and Queen Ena of Spain, the Kaiser and Kaiserin, Queen Maud of Norway and the Queen of Portugal. Also included are other members of the royal family and other foreign duchesses and grand duchesses.

A plaque (Plate 338) was manufactured by Rosenthal in fine quality porcelain depicting the Kaiser in profile. It is in saxe blue against a white background, the prominently moustached head wears a military collar and his hair is neatly parted. The rim bears in German the Kaiser's titles.

The last of the state visits was that made by the King and Queen of Portugal, again commemorated by a souvenir programme (Plate 339), giving the details of the route and

Plate 336. *Paper programme for the state visit of Kaiser Wilhelm of Germany, 1907.*

Plate 337. *Photograph by W.N.D. Downey of eight sovereigns at Windsor Castle.*

Plate 338. *Rosenthal plaque of Kaiser Wilhelm.*

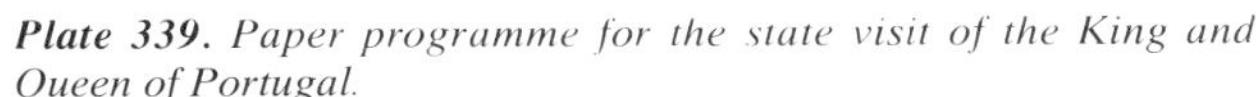

Plate 339. *Paper programme for the state visit of the King and Queen of Portugal.*

Plate 340. *Paper programme for the state visit of the King and Queen of Greece.*

what took place in London. A similar programme (Plate 340) was published for the visit to London of King George of Greece.

The King as a Diplomat

King Edward was interested in diplomacy. As by birth he was related to various royal families of Europe, he conceived the idea of making a European tour, starting in 1903, and far-reaching in its scope.

The King had always enjoyed visiting France, but at that particular time relations between France and Great Britain were far from happy, due to resentment by the French about the Boer War. However, the King insisted on visiting France, he won over the French with his charm and tact, and the visit became a resounding success. As a result of this visit the *Entente Cordiale* was instituted and formed the foundation of the relationship between France and Great Britain.

The Worshipful Company produced a pack of cards in 1908 to record the *Entente Cordiale*. The design is of Britannia and a French emblematic figure shaking hands, beneath which is the Company's coat of arms. A pack of cards issued for 1909 portrays England's naval supremacy. The central figure is Britannia, the British Lion lying at her feet and figures of a Naval rating and an Admiral at her side. Above are the twin coats of arms of the City of London and the Worshipful Company, with the inscription: 'Defence – not Defiance'.

When the President of France visited London there was a gala performance at Covent Garden. A silk programme (Plate 341), has the royal coat of arms at the top, the motto 'RF' on the tricolour and the cross of the Légion d'honneur and the ER VII monogram. Luisa Tettrazzini, the great soprano, took part in an aria from Faust and she is seen as Aida on a tin

Plate 341. *Silk programme from Covent Garden.*

(Plate 342).

The King visited his distant relative, King Carlos I of Portugal. He also visited Italy and became the first British sovereign to visit the Pope since relations broke with Rome

Plate 342(left). *Tea tin showing Tettrazzini as Aida.*

Plate 343. *Plate for Pope Leo XIII.*

Plate 344. *Tile for Pope Pius X.*

Plate 345. *Plate for the visit to Liverpool, 1904.*

four and a half centuries ago. He was met by the King of Italy, Victor Emmanuel III, with a very large retinue. The Pope, well into his ninetieth year, was anxious to meet the King, and after a great deal of argument it was agreed that this meeting should take place. The half hour meeting was cordial.

Some Papal commemorative items were manufactured including a plate of Pope Leo XIII (Plate 343). His portrait is in the centre, beneath the Papal coat of arms, embellished in blue. He died shortly after the visit and was succeeded by Pope Pius X. Although the King did not meet this pontiff a commemorative tile (Plate 344) exists for him.

He also visited Emperor Franz Joseph of Austria in 1906, and made an official tour of the Scandanavian States in 1908.

The King among his People

The King and Queen made several visits to cities and towns in England, Wales and Scotland. They both went to Liverpool on 19th July, 1904 to lay the foundation stone of a new cathedral and a plate (Plate 345) was published for this with a registered number on it. On the rear, showing the King on a central circle surmounted by a crown, the royal flags and the royal flowers, are the words 'Long Live the King'.

On 9th July, 1908 he went to the city of Bristol to open the new docks. A cup and saucer (Plate 346) commemorate this event. On the cup are portraits of the King and Queen with details of the occasion in between. The saucer has the national flags, the royal flowers and again, the purpose of the visit.

The King was anxious to visit Ireland, recalling that it was the last place Queen Victoria, his mother, had visited before her death. In 1905 the King and Queen visited Ireland and there is a silver plated spoon (Plate 347) made by Mappin and Webb to commemorate this event. On the spoon are their heads in profile.

On 13th July, 1907 the King and Queen, accompanied by Princess Victoria, visited Cardiff to open the Queen Alexandra Docks. The main interest on this occasion was that in 1905 Cardiff had been created a city with its own Lord Mayor, and the Lord Mayor, Sir William Crossman, was knighted publicly outside the City Hall by the King. A painting in the City Hall portrays this, the Queen looking on in her carriage. There is no commemorative item for the actual knighting of the Lord Mayor, though there is a postcard (Plate 348) taken from the painting. The visit is commemorated by a tin of chocolates (Plate 349B) from Fry's of Bristol bearing two oval portraits of the King and Queen. In the centre is the old Cardiff coat of arms and the words: 'Chamber of Commerce. Souvenir of the visit to Cardiff of the King and Queen presented by the Cardiff Chamber of Commerce'. A paper programme (Plate 350) was also published to record the details, not only of the visit to Cardiff but of the visit to South Wales. A mug (Plate 351) was produced by Primavesi of Cardiff with a blue border and portraits of the King and Queen.

In 1909 he presented the Royal Maundy at Westminster Abbey and presented the four silver coins in a leather box (Plate 349A) to those selected for the washing of the feet.

The King's Death

The King spent much of his time at Biarritz staying at the Hotel de Palais. In 1910, during one of these visits, he started to feel unwell. Ignoring advice, he continued to smoke cigars, which clearly had a serious effect upon his health. He died at Buckingham Palace on 6th May, 1910. He was a popular King and during his short reign added much dignity

Plate 346. *Cup and saucer for the visit to Bristol, 1908.*

Plate 347(Left). *Mappin & Webb spoon for the visit to Ireland, 1905.*

Plate 348(above). *Postcard of the King knighting the Lord Mayor of Cardiff.*

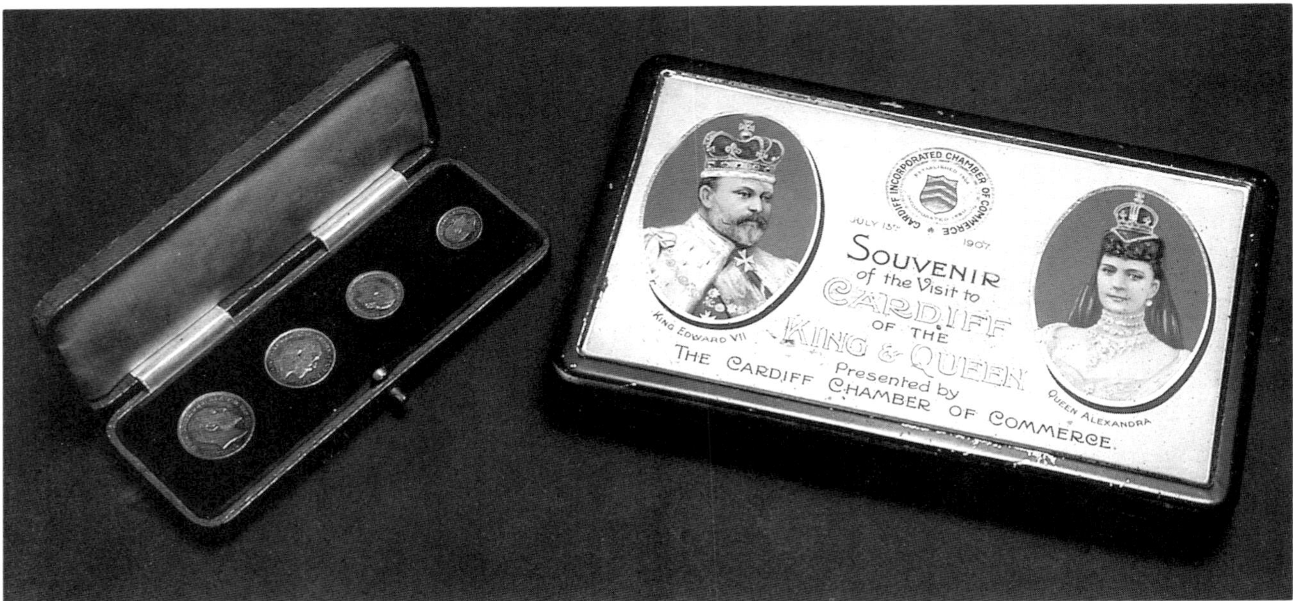

Plate 349A. *Set of Maundy money in a case.* **B.** *Fry's chocolate tin for the visit to Cardiff, 1907.*

SOUVENIR,
JULY 12 & 13.

In Commemoration of
KING EDWARD'S VISIT TO CARDIFF,
SOUTH WALES.

PROGRAMME.

FRIDAY, JULY 12th.

SATURDAY, JULY 13th.

God Save the King.

Plate 350. *Paper programme for the visit to Cardiff.*

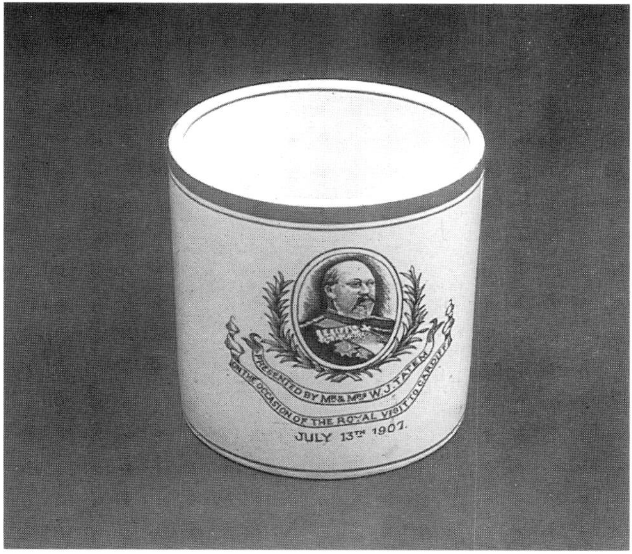

Plate 351. *Mug for the visit to Cardiff.*

and colour as well as splendour and glamour to the throne. This was certainly shown at the funeral, attended by the largest number of crowned heads at any British sovereign's funeral. Despite this popularity there were very few ceramic records made for his death. A plaque (Plate 352) shows a very large portrait of the late King in dark blue with his medals and stars and the words, 'King Edward VII, Peacemaker' and his dates of birth and death.

A fine stone-coloured bust (Plate 353) of the King on a blue plinth commissioned by Doulton of Lambeth was modelled by Harradine. It has in the centre 'Edward VII, 1910' and the crown.

A jug (Plate 352) shows the King in formal dress, with the words 'Edward, the Peacemaker' underneath and on the reverse are the dates of his birth, accession and death.

A tin (Plate 354) in mourning purple, of unknown manufacture, carries on one side a portrait of the King, captioned 'His Late Majesty' and on the other, 'Her Majesty

Plate 352. *Plaque and jug recording the death of the King.*

Plate 353. *Doulton statuette for the King's death. 6in. (15.2cm) high.*

Plate 354A. *Tin to commemorate the death of the King.* ***B.*** *The reverse of the tin with a portrait of the Queen Mother.*

the Queen Mother', showing Queen Alexandra in a circlet of laurel wreaths. The hinged lid bears the royal coat of arms. This must be one of the few commemoratives which actually mentions the 'Queen Mother'.

According to custom, a paper programme (Plate 355) was published for use by the public, indicating the details of the funeral, with a black border surrounded by coloured flags and flowers. An interesting inclusion is that the Earl Marshal authorised an announcement that admission to Westminster Hall would be without distinction of class and with no restriction to morning dress. This was in fact the first public lying-in-state of a sovereign.

National publications (Plate 356) gave full coverage to the death of the King and his funeral, and perhaps the most poignant illustration of all was a photograph (Plate 357) showing Queen Alexandra and the King's dog Caesar, the dog obviously confused and wondering what had happened to his master. He can be seen in many photographs of the procession and in a sense it could be said that he almost stole the show.

The King and his Ministers

Political figures from the aristocratic ruling classes of the Tories, or the industrial magnates of the Liberals fitted the sense of grandeur which was dictated by the Court. The importance of male dress was reflected in the silk hat, frock coat, white slipped waistcoats, spats, buttonholes and canes. There was an elegance about the statesman of the day who followed the standards which were formed by the great political figures of the late Victorian period.

The Prime Minister at the time of the accession was the aristocratic white-bearded Salisbury; the last peer to hold this position and a member of the Cecil family with his seat at Hatfield. The Marquis has been ceramically recorded on several items specified in Chapter 2 and is also on one of the panels of the 1897 Moss Rimington Mustard tin (Plate 182), where he is shown head and shoulders wearing cabinet uniform and the Garter. He was succeeded by his nephew, Arthur James Balfour. This tall, slim, distinguished statesman personified the Edwardianism of the day. He has few commemoratives but he also appears on the Moss Rimington tin together with his uncle and forms part of a series of gin flasks (Plate 358A) made by Bournes Pottery. There is also a copper plaque portraying his head and shoulders.

The great Liberal victory of 1905 was headed by Sir Henry Campbell-Bannerman (Plate 358B) for whom there is practially nothing of a commemorative nature. The only item known to the author is on a glass tumbler, where he is shown with Balfour, presumably produced for that election. The profiles are faint and between them are the words 'Before they Begin'. He resigned because of illness in 1908 and died on 20th April that same year.

Campbell-Bannerman was succeeded as Prime Minister by Herbert Henry Asquith. After being called to the Bar, he entered Parliament as Member for East Fife in 1886. He served in Gladstone's last government as Home Secretary in 1892 and continued as Prime Minister until 1916, when there was a Cabinet upheaval and he was succeeded by Lloyd George. He was defeated in the 1918 Election but later was returned as Member of Parliament for Paisley in 1920. He was defeated in 1924 and then accepted the customary earldom bestowed upon former Prime Ministers and became the Earl of Oxford and Asquith, a Knight of the Garter and died on 15 February 1928.

For the 1910 Election there is a plate (Plate 359) which can be seen in two ways. It shows Balfour and Asquith. If

In Beloved Memory
of
H. M. KING EDWARD VII.
PEACEMAKER
LYING IN STATE
BORN NOV. 9th, 1841
DIED MAY 6th, 1910
AGED 68 YEARS.
INTERRED MAY 20th
EVENTS IN THE LIFE OF THE KING

Plate 355. Paper programme for the King's death.

turned up one way they both face each other; Asquith wearing a helmet and with the words 'Rule Britannia'; and if turned upside-down it shows the same two politicians, in this case Balfour wearing the helmet, weeping through defeat and Asquith looking very pleased with himself because of victory and the words 'Britannia Rues'. The plate was published by J. & G. Meakin of Hanley in the Potteries of England. For Asquith there is also a gin flask (Plate 358A) made by Bournes Potteries.

Other well-known statesmen of the day have been

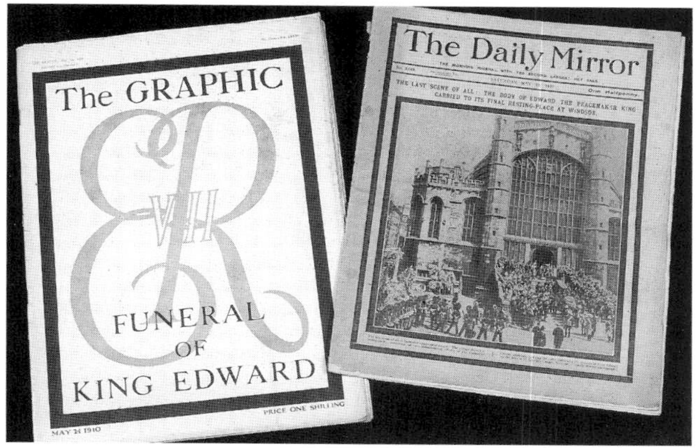

Plate 356. *Two publications recording the death and funeral of the King.*

commemorated in gin flasks, similar to that for Asquith. John Burns (Plate 358A) was a British Labour politician elected for Battersea in 1892. He became President of the Local Government Board in 1895 and the Board of Trade in 1914, but resigned at the beginning of the First World War. He was the first working man cabinet member in Great Britain.

Joseph Chamberlain, born in 1836, was a highly successful businessman and retired in 1874 with great wealth. Radical in outlook, he became Mayor of Birmingham, which he subsequently represented in Parliament. A controversial politician, in 1891 he was leader of the Liberal Unionists and in the Coalition Government of 1895 he took office as Secretary to the Colonies. He was serving in this capacity at the outbreak of the Boer War and is featured on the 1900 turn of the century mug. In 1903 he resigned office. He wished to be free to advocate tariff reform which was one of his main interests. He suffered from

Plate 357. *A touching scene showing the Queen and Caesar, the King's dog.*

Plate 358A. *Spirit flasks for Asquith, Haldane, John Burns, each 7¼in. (20cm) high.* ***B.*** *Postcard of Campbell-Bannerman.* ***C.*** *Postcard of the Liberal Cabinet – 1906.*

Plate 359. *Plate showing Balfour and Asquith. 'Rule Britannia, Britannia Rues', 1910 Election, 9in. (23cm) diameter.*

ill health from 1906 and withdrew from public life, but still took an active interest in the affairs of Birmingham and became the first chancellor of Birmingham University. A large 'treacle' plate (so called because of its treacly effect) has a fine portrait of Joseph Chamberlain, in the centre, in black. His death is recorded in a brass plaque.

Richard Burden Haldane, subsequently Lord Haldane, was a British Liberal statesman/philosopher and a lawyer, entering Parliament in 1879. He supported the Boer War, being Secretary of State for War. He remodelled the Army and founded the Territorials, perhaps his most lasting achievement. He became Lord Chancellor in 1912 but was sacked by Asquith for allegedly pro-German sympathies and later flirted with the Labour Party. In 1915 he was awarded the Order of Merit, and there is also a gin flask for him by Bournes Potteries (Plate 358A).

Austen Chamberlain is also featured on a Bourne's gin flask. The eldest son of Joseph Chamberlain, he became Chancellor of the Exchequer in 1903 and again in 1919. He held various other Government offices and was Foreign Secretary between 1924 and 1930, becoming a Knight of the Garter in 1925. He received the Nobel Peace Prize in 1925 for negotiating the Locarno Pact.

Archibald Phillip Primrose was the fifth Earl of Rosebery. He served in various capacities in Liberal Goverments and was a member of the first London County Council and its Chairman in 1899. He became a Knight of the Garter in 1892, and in the same year became Foreign Secretary, staying for two years, and became Prime Minister in 1894. There is little to record Rosebery apart from a jug (Plate 254).

David Lloyd George became Prime Minister in 1916. Known as the 'Welsh Wizard', he was a North Wales solicitor, a prominent member of the Liberal Party and Chancellor of the Exchequer. He was a very fiery character, and there is a plethora of commemoratives for him, some very amusing. There is a fine pair of tiles for both Asquith and Lloyd George (Plate 360). They are both modelled by George Cartlidge and made by J.H. Barratt & Company, Stoke-on-Trent, after photographs, in the case of Asquith by Reginald Haines, and in the case of Lloyd George by Ernest H. Mills. A brass figure of Lloyd George (Plate 361) holding money bags and two cartoons taken from *Punch* (Plate 362) indicate the manner in which *Punch* portrayed Lloyd George as Chancellor of the Exchequer. An amusing bust of Lloyd George with a large hand (Plate 361) is captioned 'Hand it over'.

A plate commemorating the passing of the National Health Insurance Act in 1912 is dedicated to the Rt. Hon. David Lloyd George by special permission. Lloyd George was a radical reformer and introduced the first National Health Insurance Act. A plate was published with a blue border bearing the names of twenty-four members of the Liberal Government including the interesting Augustine Birrell, perhaps better known as a wit and an essayist than as a politician. Although he was greatly interested in education, his name has been used in such a way that to 'Birrell' is to comment on life gently and elusively together with good nature and some irony. In the centre of the plate is an oval medallion of Lloyd George, with his name underneath it, and the words 'National Health Insurance Act 1912' and above it in a cartouche the initials 'NIA'. There is also a parian figurine of Lloyd George and a spirit flask from Bournes (Plate 361).

Wales recorded their great patriot in a fine portrait of Lloyd George in the black and gold ceremonial robes of Chancellor of the University of Wales, on a jug in English and in Welsh (Plate 361). The reverse has the Prince of

Plate 360. *Pair of Cartlidge tiles – Lloyd George and Asquith, 8½in. x 5½in. (21cm x 14cm).*

Plate 361. *Various commemoratives for Lloyd George: Jug, Lloyd George as Chancellor of the University of Wales, 4½in. (11cm) high. Plate for the National Insurance Act, caricature of Lloyd George, 'Hand it Over', 3¾in. (9.5cm) high. Spirit flask, 8in. (20cm) high. Parian figure. 5¼in. (13cm) high. Brass figure, 8in. (20cm) high.*

Plate 362. *Pair of* Punch *cartoons.*

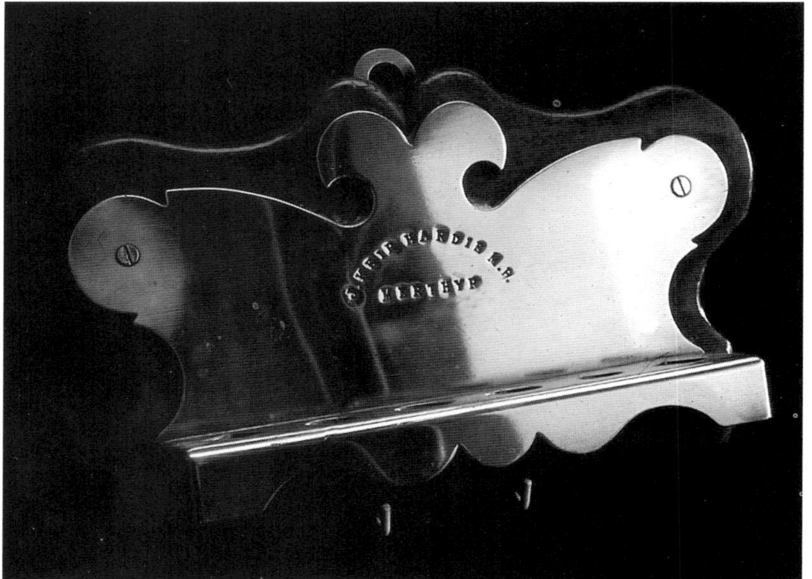

Plate 363. *Pipe-rack, Keir Hardie, 11in. (20cm) wide.*

Plate 364. *Photograph of Keir Hardie.*

Wales feathers and the Prince of Wales' motto *Ich Dien* in a cartouche made up of two leeks.

The Labour Movement had just started during the reign of King Edward VII. There is little of a commemorative nature, although there is a brass pipe rack (Plate 363), probably a gift to Keir Hardie, who was the MP for Merthyr Tydfil. Keir Hardie (Plate 364) was the Scottish Labour leader and one of the founders of the Labour Party. He was born in Scotland and at an early age worked in a coal pit. He was a champion of the miners and the first Labour candidate, but was defeated in 1888 at Mid Lanark. He was elected for West Ham South in 1892 and subsequently for Merthyr Tydfil in 1900, where he remained a member until 1915. He worked strenuously for socialism and founded the Independent Labour Party. This pipe rack is some acknowledgement in a permanent commemorative form of the important part that Keir Hardie, termed 'the man with the cloth cap' played in the history of the Labour movement.

The Co-operative Movement was beginning to play an important part in political life and there were several items made for various Co-operative stores throughout the country. There is a rather fine teapot (Plate 365) with, on the front, an engraving of the Abersychan British Co-operative Stores 1911. Among many mugs (Plate 365) is one for the Nantymoel

Plate 365. *Co-operative Movement teapot, 3in. (7.5cm) high.* ***(Top)****Mugs for Aberdare, 3in. (7.5cm) high, Abertridwr, 3½in. (9cm) high and Ammandford, 3in. (7.5cm) high. Blaenavon 3in (7.5cm) high, Working Men's Institute and Nantymoel, Children's Gala, 3in. (7.5cm) high.*

Industrial Co-operative Society Children's Gala June 18th 1907, and another for the Aberdare Working Men's Industrial Co-operative Society Limited captioned 'A Memento of the opening of the new Gadlys Branch September 1912', bearing a brown and white transfer of the new building. A tapering mug shows the Blaenavon Working Men's Institute Hall and the words 'Freed from debt'. Mugs from Abertridwr and Ammanford are for Working Men's Clubs.

Plate 366. *Jug for Beville Stanier, MP for Shropshire 1908, 6¼in. (16cm) high.*

Of the commemorative ceramics published for elections during the King's reign, Shropshire led the field. Their early records are of fine quality commemoratives, from Coalport, Caughley and Staffordshire Potteries. Shropshire tended to adhere to families of the county; the first being produced for the 1896 Election in which William Hill of Attingham Park was elected for Shrewsbury in a bitter and corrupt campaign. For the 1906 election, Coalport produced a handsome jug in porcelain. The body bears the arms of Shrewsbury and those of William Hill. In 1908 Beville Stanier was elected to succeed Hill. Trenthall Potteries published a tall straight-sided jug (Plate 366) bearing on one side a sepia portrait. On the other side crossed Union Jacks surmount the result giving Stanier a majority of 951 and dated 'May 15th 1908'. Both these ceramic records of Shropshire Elections together with a total of thirty-five other commemorative pieces from 1896 to 1970 are exhibited at the Clive Museum in Shrewsbury.

Exhibitions

Exhibitions were held for several events during the King's reign. The Imperial Exhibition in London 1909 has an art

Plate 367B. *Oval vase for Golden West Exhibition, 1909.* ***A and C.*** *Cup and saucer and bisque figure and plaque for the Imperial Exhibition, 1909.*

nouveau figure (Plate 367A), of a woman with a swathe of flags. Behind her head is an embossed view of the Exhibition buildings entitled: 'The Court of Honour'. Empire China produced a small cup and saucer (Plate 367C) for the same Exhibition. The centre of the footed cup has the buildings and the decoration is in yellow with rosebuds and a green border embellished with gold. The Golden West Exhibition was also held in London in 1909 for American Industries. A small two handled vase (Plate 367B), has as its central feature the American Eagle surmounting a shield of the stars and stripes, by English Souvenir China. The Franco-British Exhibition held in London in 1905 was a large affair and the subject of many postcards. A cup and saucer (Plate 368), similar in shape to the one made for the 1909 Imperial Exhibition, is embellished with orange and gold and carries the buildings in the centre of the cup. Adams of Tunstall published a plate (Plate 368). In the centre are the Union Jack and the French Tricolour surmounted by the words 'Entente Cordiale London 1908 – Franco-British Exhibition'. The border is a decoration of red, white and blue leaves in the form of a symbol.

Plate 368. *Cup, saucer and plate for the Franco-British Exhibition 1905.*

During his short reign the King observed the rules that do not allow a sovereign into the controversy of public life. He made known his views about the Parliament Bill and the row over the two Houses of Parliament and the creation of peers, but he was a constitutional monarch and never did anything to detract from his position. This is interesting in view of the well-known cartoon published during Queen Victoria's reign, showing a rather stout Queen with the Prince of Wales standing in the corner, indicating that he was not up to the standard required by his mother for participation in public life. When he did become King he was able to put this right. It is a great pity that there is nothing ceramic known to have been recorded for the passing of the Parliament Bill and for the constitutional crisis which preceded it. Fortunately, there are at least some ceramic records for those celebrated politicians and statesmen who took an active part in the political life of the Edwardian period.

CHAPTER 4

George and Mary 1910-1936

Until his marriage in 1893 there seems to be no ceramic record for Prince George, the second son of Edward VII who succeeded him as King George V.

Several royal princesses had been suggested as a bride, but none seemed suitable, until the selection of Princess Mary of Teck who was the daughter of a morganatic marriage between the Duke of Teck and Princess Adelaide of Cambridge on 12 June 1866. They were married at the parish church at Kew. *The Graphic* published an engraving of the wedding (Plate 369). Princess May had all the regal qualities of a future Queen of England.

There are few commemoratives for the marriage, which took place on 6 July 1893. A small tea plate (Plate 370) has in the centre two oval medallions, head and shoulders portraits of the Duke of York and Princess May, with sprigs of flowers on either side. The stamp on the reverse indicates it was made in Germany.

A fairly plain mug (Plate 371A) contains, within a horseshoe, the words 'The Marriage of the Duke of York to Princess May', and the date. The horseshoe is surmounted by the Prince of Wales feathers.

A cup and saucer (Plate 371B) with a registered number on the base shows, on both, the words 'George and May' and the royal standard. Underneath: 'Royal Wedding, 1893', the whole surmounted by a ship in full sail, presumably indicating the naval interest of the Duke of York.

A highly decorated tin, manufacturer unknown, shows the bride and groom surrounded by flowers in colour and Queen Victoria in a laurel wreath surrounded by flags on the lid. The Duke of Teck is shown, wearing uniform and a foreign order and decoration accompanied by his ample wife; the Prince of Wales wears a Field Marshal's uniform with stars and decoration and is with the Princess of Wales in a blue spotted gown and headdress of flowers. All are from photographs taken by Russell and Son of London.

Another colourful tin (Plate 372) records this wedding. The lid contains the head of Queen Victoria wearing her small crown and her veil and around her are portraits of the Duke of York and, as she then was, HSH Princess May, the head and shoulders of the Duke and Duchess of Teck and also of the Prince and Princess of Wales. More interesting are two portraits of Princess Maud of Wales and Princess Victoria of Wales, both of whom were bridesmaids and are shown, head and shoulders, wearing their bridesmaids' headdresses. This must be one of the very few records of Princess Victoria. The tin is in a design of royal flowers and

Plate 369. Graphic *engraving of the marriage of the Princess Mary Adelaide of Cambridge and the Duke of Teck.*

Plate 370. *Plate for the marriage of Prince George and Princess May.*

Plate 371A. *Mug to commemorate the wedding.* **B.** *Cup and saucer: Royal Wedding 1893.*

of the British royal standards, England, Scotland and Ireland. It is unmarked but has the outward appearance of being either Moss Rimington or Colman's.

On the death of Queen Victoria, the Duke of York also became Duke of Cornwall. He had not yet been created Prince of Wales.

He visited Canada in 1901 and there is a plate (Plate 373A) to commemorate this event showing portraits of the Duke and Duchess of York and Cornwall and the words: '1901. In Commemoration of the Royal visit to Canada'. On his return to Portsmouth the King made him Prince of Wales. There was no formal investiture.

During his time as Prince of Wales little was recorded ceramically for his various public duties. A colourful slipware beaker (Plate 374B) indicates that the Duke and Duchess of York visited an unknown town in July, 1899. On the beaker are the coat of arms of this place, with its motto, 'Semper fidelis'.

The King's Coronation

This took place on 22nd June, 1911 in the traditional style. A

Plate 372. *Mustard tin for the wedding.*

Plate 373A. *Plate to record the visit to Canada of the Duke and Duchess of York, 1901.* ***B.*** *Wedgwood plate for the Coronation.*

large number of commemoratives were produced for the occasion. They take the usual form of jugs, cups and saucers, plates, beakers and mugs. Many of these are readily available, normally at reasonable prices.

Some commemoratives are, however, unusual. A bottle (Plate 375) provided by Copeland in the shape of a flask was published on behalf of Andrew Usher and Co., Distillers, Edinburgh, with the crown forming a stopper. The royal flowers are in relief around the neck together with the King and Queen between two flags.

A plate by Wedgwood (Plate 373B) has exactly the same design as that produced by the firm for King Edward VII. Printed in blue, it shows the King in naval uniform in the central medallion surrounded by a crown with the order of the garter and its motto, surrounded by flags of the colonies and dominions. The reverse bears his titles and the date of his coronation: 'June 22nd, 1911'.

Plate 374A. *Slipware beaker for the Coronation.* ***B.*** *Slipware beaker for a visit to an unknown town.*

A highly decorative mug (Plate 376A) depicts the King and Queen in their coronation robes in colour, the Queen seated wearing the order of the garter, the King in his coronation mantle with the crown on the table.

Worcester produced a fine porcelain plate (Plate 376B) with profiles of the King and Queen in the centre of a laurel wreath, with the words 'Crowned June 22nd, 1911' and their names and that of the Mayor of Worcester, with the Worcester coat of arms surrounded by the royal flowers and oak leaves.

A slipware beaker (Plate 374A) with a green background has portraits of the King and Queen in yellow with the royal flowers, it reads 'Long to Reign Over Us, God Save Them Both', published by Lyndhurst Pottery.

Several cities and towns provided not only mugs but also tins of chocolates and tea (Plate 377). The Parish of Radyr near Cardiff produced a tin bearing their portraits on a background of ermine. The name of the manufacturer is not shown.

Cadbury's of Bourneville produced a small tin from the Mayor and Mayoress of Kensington. Rowntree's produced a tin of chocolate entitled: 'Bristol Souvenir of the Coronation', which carried portraits of the King and Queen, wearing their crowns, in oval cartouches with a red

Plate 375. *Copeland flask from Usher's for the Coronation, 1911.*

Plate 376A and B. *Worcester Coronation plate and mug.*

Plate 377. *A selection of Coronation tins and two minature cachou boxes portraying the Queen on one, the King on the other.*

Plate 378. *A Thorne's tin portraying the Prince of Wales, Prince George and Prince Henry; a Rowntree's casket and a pack of cards to record the King's recovery from illness, 1929.*

Plate 379. *Paper programme for the Coronation.*

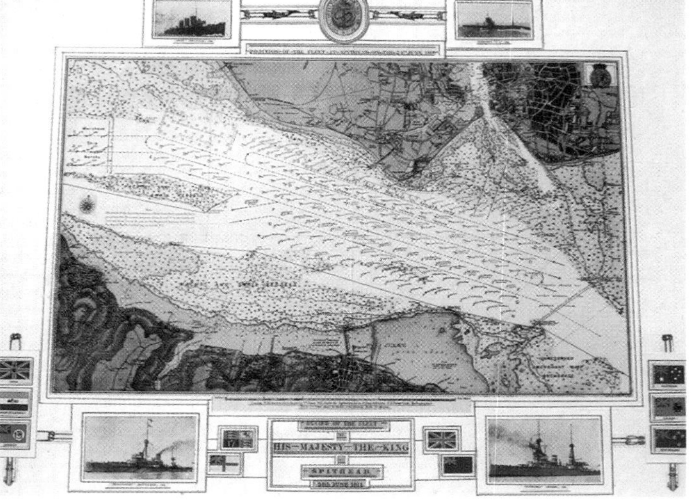

Plate 380. *Plan of Coronation Naval Review, 24th June 1911.*

SOUVENIR AND HISTORY OF THE
OPENING of PARLIAMENT
BY THE
KING AND QUEEN
On Wednesday, Feb. 14th 1912

Rd No 567332

Plate 381. *Paper programme for the Opening of Parliament, 1912.*

background surrounded by the royal flowers. Fry's produced a miniature tin in the shape of a crown bearing portraits of the King and Queen in cartouches surrounded by a design in gold with crown, sceptre and orb. J. Phillips and Co., chocolate manufacturers, provided a tin bearing portraits of both the King and Queen in a design of flags surrounded by crowns with the arms of the City of Newcastle-upon-Tyne and captioned 'A Souvenir'.

Rowntree's of York produced a tin in the shape of a casket (Plate 378). The King and Queen are shown on the lid in fine colour portraits with the date of the coronation and around them are the dependencies of the Empire: Canada depicted by three horses, Africa by a two-funnelled liner, India by elephants with the Taj Mahal in the background, and Australia by a river with a paddle steamer and a landing stage. The interesting feature is that the tin shows all six children, the Prince of Wales in midshipman's uniform, Princess Mary and the four sons Prince Henry, Prince Albert, who subsequently became King George VI, Prince George, who became Duke of Kent and the young Prince John who died at an early age. There are not many commemoratives which portray all six of the King and Queen's children. On one side, in a medallion, is the King as a midshipman and the King as an Admiral, between a British warship and, probably, HMS *Victory*. On another side is the King's birthplace, Marlborough House, together with the King at the age of about two years and also at the age of five years. On the opposite side is a two-funnelled liner with oval portraits of the King and Queen as Prince and Princess of Wales.

Two miniature cachou boxes of different shapes (Plate 377) have the Queen in colour on one and the King on another. As was customary, a paper programme (Plate 379) was provided for use by the people as a souvenir commemorating the coronation at Westminster Abbey at 1.40 pm on June 22nd, 1911. It contains details of the number of troops taking part and the processional route with details of the bearers of the King and Queen's regalia and the Standard Bearers in Westminster Abbey.

On 24th June 1911, the King reviewed the fleet at Spithead. A plan (Plate 380) of the positions of the vast fleet that took part was published at the Admiralty on 1st June 1911, under the superintendence of Rear Admiral H.E. Purey Cust, Hydrographer and was sold by J.D. Potter, Agent for the sale of the Admiralty Charts, 145 Minories.

Throughout their reign the King and Queen attended State Openings of Parliament. A paper programme (Plate 381) was issued for use by the public headed 'Souvenir and History of the Opening of Parliament by the King and Queen on Wednesday February 14th 1912'.

On 12th December 1912, King George and Queen Mary attended a Durbar in Delhi to celebrate their accession as Emperor and Empress of India. The occasion was full of oriental splendour, but nothing of a ceramic nature seems to have been published for this extravagant and almost bizarre event. The Worshipful Company of Playing Cards have come to the aid of those who wish to have some souvenir of this Imperial occasion. The design shows the Taj Mahal surrounded by a tiger's head, an elephant's head, an Indian lady in a sari and an Indian soldier wearing a turban. Two children are sitting beneath the arch and the whole picture is surmounted by the imperial crown. Packs were presented to the King and Queen at Buckingham Palace.

The King and the Constitution

The new King was plunged into political controversy at the very start of his reign. The struggle between the House of Commons and the House of Lords and the right of the House of Lords to block any legislation was still unconcluded.

There were two other political difficulties in the early part of the King's reign. The first was the suffragette movement. This was continuing with ugly incidents including forced feeding of suffragettes in prison. Physical assaults were made on Cabinet Ministers and a bomb exploded in a house being built for David Lloyd George. Perhaps the most graphic incident was in 1913 at the Derby when Emily Davidson threw herself under the King's horse and was killed. Despite this long struggle by the suffragettes there is little ceramic record. Three quacking ducks (Plate 382) have the inscription: 'We want your votes', and the same caption appears on a cat. Fortunately a very large number of postcards were available at that time showing the strength of the movement and some of these are very amusing.

The second problem was with Ireland, always a source of controversy, and in the early part of the reign the Irish Home Rule Bill was being debated. The new Asquith Government elected in 1910 relied heavily upon the Irish Nationalist Members of Parliament, led by John Redmond. A Bill for Home Rule was introduced in 1912. This was hotly contested by those who were against Irish Home Rule – particularly in the North. Sir Edward Carson was the very strong-minded protagonist against the Irish Home Rule Bill. To commemorate this bitterly fought measure there is a pair of plates (Plate 383), one with a green border, with a head and

Plate 382. *Two picture postcards and (centre) three ducks and a cat, commemorate the Suffragette Movement.*

shoulders portrait of Mr John Redmond MP with the words: 'Home Rule for Ireland', and a companion plate with a pale blue border with the head and shoulders of Sir Edward Carson and the words 'We want no Home Rule'. There is also a silk portrait of Carson (Plate 384A).

The Bill was introduced, making provision for an Irish Parliament in Dublin, although reserving certain matters to the Imperial Parliament at Westminster. It was passed in the House of Commons, due to the union of the Irish Nationalists and the Liberal Party, but the House of Lords rejected it. Although it was represented in 1912 and 1913 it never received the Royal Assent.

The Worshipful Company of Playing Cards issued two special packs to commemorate the establishment of the Irish Free State by Treaty with England. The design is Celtic and has in the centre the harp, the national emblem of Ireland,

Plate 383. *Pair of plates for Home Rule for Ireland: John Redmond and Sir Edward Carson.*

with the words: 'Ireland for Ever'. The design is by Edward Cunningham of Goodall and Sons. The Celtic border portrays features of Ireland together with the coat of arms of the four provinces, the whole surmounted in the centre by the Imperial Crown.

The King was served by five Prime Ministers. At the time of his accession Herbert Henry Asquith was Prime Minister. It was he who had to advise the King on constitutional matters dealing with the powers of the House of Lords and the ultimate Parliament Act, for which there appears to be no actual ceramic record. Asquith himself has not been much commemorated but he appears on a whisky decanter (Plate 385A), which commemorates the centenary of Watson Whisky, published for James Watson at Dundee in 1915. It has a bright blue background with portraits in sepia. On one side is the King in naval uniform and on the other side the Prime Minister, Asquith. It has its own stopper.

He was succeeded after a Cabinet upheaval during the War by David Lloyd George who has already been mentioned in the chapter on Edward VII. At a famous 1922 meeting of the Carlton Club, Bonar Law, as Leader of the Conservative Party, decided that the time had come to break from the Coalition and to continue party politics in the normal way. Lloyd George had to resign and Bonar Law briefly became Prime Minister in 1922 but he was not to hold that position for long. He suffered from cancer and had to retire. He died in 1923. There is one small parian figure of Andrew Bonar Law (Plate 386B), head and shoulders. Notes for a speech and a letter signed by Bonar Law (Plate 387), were given to the author by his son, Richard Law, who was created Lord Coleraine.

The successor to Bonar Law presented the King with a problem. There were some suitable candidates, among them Austen Chamberlain. F.E. Smith, later Earl of Birkenhead, was brilliant but was thought perhaps too volatile, so the

Plate 384A. *Silk portrait of Carson.* ***B.*** *Mug for the Act of Union in South Africa.* ***C.*** *National Strike paper boy.*

Plate 385A. *Watson whisky decanter for Asquith.* ***B.*** *Portrait jug of Stanley Baldwin.* ***C.*** *Spirit flask of Austen Chamberlain.* ***D.*** *Mug for election of Esmond Harmsworth.* ***E.*** *Reverse side of mug for Baldwin, receiving the Freedom of Bewdley.*

Plate 386A. *Jug for Lord Derby.* ***B and C.*** *Bust figures for Bonar Law and Hartington.*

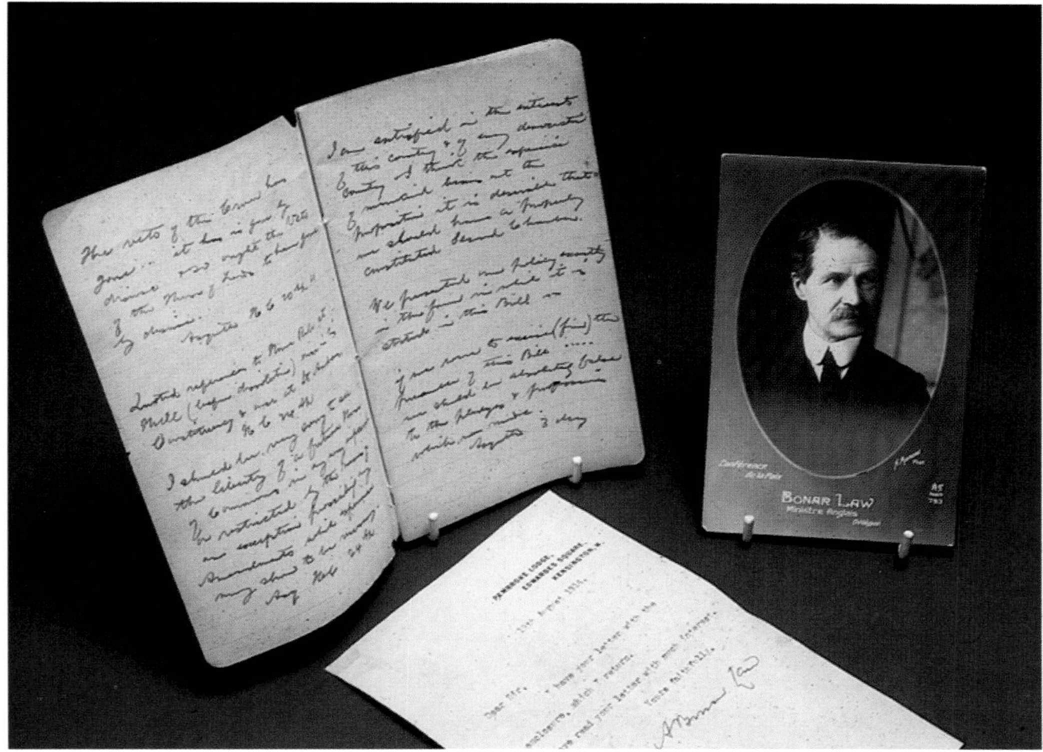

Plate 387. *Photographic postcard of Bonar Law, a letter signed by him, and notes for a speech written by him.*

choice seemed to be between Lord Curzon and Stanley Baldwin. There could hardly have been two more different characters.

Lord Curzon, an aristocrat, former Viceroy and now a Marquis, once descibed himself: 'My name is George Nathaniel Curzon and I am a most superior person'. Baldwin was an iron master from the Midlands, a typical English squire. He was fond of his pigs and his pipe and could be regarded as safe, more the people's choice.

The King received the advice of his Private Secretary, Sir Arthur Bigge, later Lord Stamfordham, that it would be imprudent to have a Prime Minister in the House of Lords. It was important that the Prime Minister should be in the House of Commons, so Stanley Baldwin became Prime Minister leaving Curzon utterly devastated and deeply hurt.

There is not a great deal ceramically recorded for Stanley Baldwin. Ashton Potters published a limited edition of portrait jugs in two sizes showing in cream the head of Baldwin with his pipe (Plate 385B). There is also a mug (Plates 385E and 388B) showing a portrait of Baldwin with his coat of arms and the inscription reads: 'Borough of Bewdley, a momento of the presentation of the Freedom of the Borough to the Rt Honorable Stanley Baldwin MP PM, a native of Bewdley, 8th August 1925'. Bewdley was a constituency in the centre of Worcestershire and he had represented it all his life. His personal gold pen-knife inscribed with his name and Astley Hall is shown (Plate 388A).

His premiership lasted only seven months. A General Election was held in December 1923 upon the issue of tariff reform. The result was that the Labour Party held the largest number of seats for the first time in its history and Baldwin's immediate reaction was to offer his resignation. However King George advised him to test the position in the House of

Plate 388A. *Baldwin's personal gold pen-knife.* ***B.*** *Baldwin Mug for the Freedom of Bewdley. See Plate 285E for reverse.*

Plate 389A. *Toby jug for Ramsay MacDonald.* ***B.*** *Booth's plate for Neville Chamberlain.* ***C.*** *Jug for Graham Pole, first Labour MP for South Derbyshire.*

Plate 390.(left) *Winston Churchill as Chancellor of the Exchequer.*
Plate 391.(centre) *Winston Churchill – Oxford Doctorate.*
Plate 392.(above) *Winston Churchill and Clemmie electioneering at Epping 1929.*

Commons first, which he did and he was defeated by 72 votes. In these circumstances the King sent for Ramsay MacDonald, the Leader of the Labour Party, who formed the first ever Labour Government. It was, however, a minority Government, reliant for support on the Liberals.

Ramsay MacDonald was born in Losiemouth, Scotland, the illegimate son of a Scottish ploughman. He joined the Labour Party in 1900, became Chairman of the Independent Labour Party in 1906 and Leader of the Labour Party in 1911. In 1935, as Prime Minister, he was defeated at Seaham, County Durham, by the redoubtable and turbulent Emmanuel Shinwell. MacDonald's final Parliamentary seat was as Member of the Scottish Universities between 1936 and 1937. There is very little of a commemorative nature for Ramsay MacDonald. A toby jug (Plate 389A) exists showing him wearing a red rosette on his hat and carrying the Union Jack in one hand and the Red Flag in the other.

On the defeat of the Labour Government Stanley Baldwin became Prime Minister again and in 1926 the most important event in this second administration took place, the General Strike. This Strike grew out of trouble in the Coal Industry, largely due to foreign competition which had undercut the price of British coal, causing the mines to run at a loss. It ended in defeat for the miners and there is little to commemorate or to record the General Strike. There is one small souvenir, a paper delivery boy (Plate 384C) with the words over his delivery bag 'Stop Strike' and on the print is the date, 1926. The registered number of the manufacturer is also shown.

The Government ran its full term and an election took

Plate 393. *Portrait jug for Douglas Hogg, First Viscount Hailsham.*

Plate 394. *Esmond Harmsworth mug, reverse side of Plate 385D.*

Plate 395. *Carruthers Gould toby jugs for (left to right): President Wilson, Beatty, Foch and Jellicoe.*

Plate 396. *Cartlidge tiles for Haig and Beatty.*

Plate 397. *Pair of vases. The three sovereigns and the President of France as the Allies. Lloyd George as Prime Minister.*

Plate 398. (Left to right) *Bachelor jug; small jug and basin with Allied flags; cup and saucer, French and Jellicoe; brass plaque with three Allied soldiers; small basin with message from Lloyd George about food consumption; figure of a soldier; King Albert soap-drainer; figure of a sailor, Bristol; candlestick with field gun and Copeland cup and saucer with bulldog motif.*

Plate 399. (Clockwise) *Beaded pin cushion; Kitchener jug; teapot with flags of the Allies; Goss cup and saucer; mug, French and Kitchener; cup and saucer with Allied flags, Goss plate.*

place in May 1929. This was the first time that women between the ages of twenty-one and thirty-five were entitled to vote and it was called the 'Flapper Vote'. The result was another Conservative defeat by the Labour Party who, although having a large number of seats, still had to rely upon Liberal support. Once again Ramsay MacDonald became Prime Minister.

There was a General Election in 1931 following an economic crisis. Ramsay MacDonald became Prime Minister under a national government supported by the Conservative Party. On his resignation Baldwin became Prime Minister yet again and remained so for the rest of the King's reign.

Of the many politicians and ministers during the King's reign few have been ceramically recorded. Winston Churchill was Chancellor of the Exchequer under Baldwin but went into the wilderness because of his opposition to the India Bill. He remained out of office until his recall by Chamberlain on the outbreak of war in September 1939. There is little to commemorate Churchill during these years. A series of cards was printed by Mirrorpic showing various stages of Churchill's life: leaving No.11 Downing Street to present the Budget in 1924 (Plate 390); receiving the Honorary Degree on the occasion of the 4th Centenary of Christ College, Oxford in 1925 (Plate 391) and acknowledging the cheers of his supporters as he and his wife Clemmie toured the Epping Constituency which he successfully fought in 1929 (Plate 392).

Neville Chamberlain, who became Prime Minister after Baldwin retired, is the subject of a fine plate (Plate 389B) published by Booth's. It shows his head and shoulders and, typically for him, winged collar and dark tie, surrounded by an embossed border. He became Prime Minister after the Coronation of King George VI.

The first Viscount Hailsham, Douglas Hogg, is the subject of the same kind of portrait jug (Plate 393) as that for Stanley Baldwin. The artist was Percy Metcalf.

Among the election commemoratives produced during the King's reign, two should be mentioned. In the 1924 Election Esmond Harmsworth, later Viscount Rothermere, stood for the Isle of Thanet for the Tories. He was returned as the House's youngest member with a majority of 14,351. The mug (Plates 385D and 394) shows a portrait of Mr Harmsworth and also of his wife. This mug was published by the Broadstairs Conservative Association. Harmsworth was a nephew of Lord Northcliffe. He played a prominent part in the abdication crisis in 1936 and was strongly in support of a morganatic marriage.

The other election item, for the 1929 Election, is a brightly coloured orange jug (Plate 389C) which reads: 'Major Graham Pole, first Labour Member for South Derbyshire, elected 1929'. It bears the portrait of the successful candidate and the words 'Victory Souvenir 1929'.

King George and the Great War

The murder of the Archduke Francis Ferdinand of Austria, heir to the Austro-Hungarian imperial throne, at Sarajevo on 28th July 1914, resulted in an Austro-Hungarian ultimatum being sent to Serbia. The whole European situation changed. War was inevitable and Sir Edward Grey, who was then Foreign Secretary, said: 'The lights are going out all over Europe'. There is little to commemorate him, apart from postcards and the inclusion of his name on the National Insurance plate of Lloyd George (see page 154).

The Declaration of War put an end to the controversial Irish Home Rule question and also quietened down the Suffragette Movement for the time being.

This terrible war resulted in the decimation of the flower of British youth. The Prime Minister's only son, Raymond Asquith, was one of the many casualties. The carnage at Passchendaele, the Somme, Mons and Ypres and throughout the whole of Flanders was on an unprecedented scale and this war completely changed the outlook of society and the future pattern of the country.

The great commanders of the war have been commemorated in various forms. Perhaps the most impressive are a series of toby jugs (Plate 395) produced by Wilkinson Limited of Royal Staffordshire Pottery in 1917 by Carruthers Gould. They were reserved for Soane and Smith of 462 Oxford Street. There were eleven in all, including King George V, President Wilson, Marshal Foch and Joffre for France, Sir John French, Earl Haig, Kitchener, Jellicoe, Beatty and Botha of South Africa.

Sir Francis Carruthers Gould was a well known modeller. The jug for French bears the words 'French pour les Francais'. That for Beatty shows the great naval chief seated, holding a shell and on either side of his seat are a submarine and torpedoes. That for Jellicoe shows the naval chief, also seated, holding a jug, captioned 'Hell fire back'. That for President Wilson shows the seated President holding a bi-plane with twin propellers. He sits on a plinth with the stars and stripes on one side and the American eagle on the other, and it is captioned: 'A Welcome Uncle Sam'. That for Foch is taller than the others. He is wearing his French Marshal's hat, and in one hand is a bottle captioned 'Au Diable le Kaiser' and in the other hand is a glass. He sits on a plinth with the French flag and the fleur de lis and around the base are various symbols of those who took part in the war; the American eagle, the French *coq* and the British lion. They are all highly decorative and highly coloured and are fine examples of the potter's craft.

Both Beatty and Haig are the subjects of tiles similar to those produced for Asquith and Lloyd George, modelled by George Cartlidge and made by J.H. Barratt & Company of Stoke-on-Trent. Beatty's is from a photograph by Speaight Limited, Haig's by Elliot and Fry (Plate 396).

Several other figures were produced for these war commanders. One for French has his head and shoulders, in red uniform and is captioned 'Sir J French'. Beatty appears on a Doulton tankard in the usual dark and light brown colours. It has in the centre the head of Beatty with, as always, his hat at a jaunty angle, in a cartouche with swags of laurel leaves, and under the lip the caption 'Admiral Beatty' and at the base 'Peace and Victory' (Plate 218C).

Lloyd George appears on a vase (Plate 397), in the centre are his head and shoulders and above, the caption: 'My object is to win the war' surrounded by the national flags and flowers and underneath the caption: 'D Lloyd George and Premier' between the Welsh leeks and the British lions. A pair to this vase has, in the centre, the four leaders of the

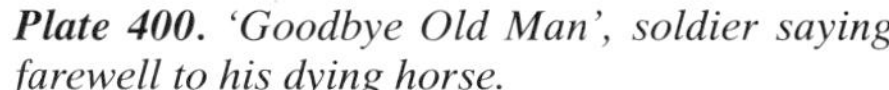

Plate 400. *'Goodbye Old Man', soldier saying farewell to his dying horse.*

Plate 401. *Recruiting posters, Wills cigarette cards.*

countries concerned, King George V, President Poincaré of France, The Tsar of Russia and the King of the Belgians, placed in circular cartouches of laurel leaves and the national flags, surmounted by the British crown and the caption is: 'Great Britain and France Unity is Strength, Belgium and Russia'.

The King of the Belgians appears on a soap drainer (Plate 398) produced by Booths Silicone China Limited entitled 'The Albert soap drainer – Order of Great Merit – Brussels Exhibition – July 1914'. In the centre is a head and shoulders portrait of King Albert, surrounded by the Belgian flags and the years 1914-15.

Various mugs, teasets and plates were produced during this war. One mug (Plate 399) has, in the centre, Kitchener and French in oval cartouches with the British flags on either side and the caption: 'Conquer or Die'. A cup and saucer (Plate 398) has, on the saucer, Admiral Jellicoe, wearing his admiral's hat. The cup shows Field Marshal Sir John French. There are other war-time features, a battle-ship and a field gun in sepia.

Special messages from the Prime Minister, Lloyd George, were included on various ceramic items, reading: 'Special Message from the Rt Hon D Lloyd George Prime Minister', and 'I have no hesitation in saying that economy and the consumption and use of food in this country is a matter of the greatest possible importance to the Empire at the present time'. A base reads 'The War-Time Sugar Basin for a family of ten, made by the girls of Staffordshire during the winter of 1917 when the boys were in the trenches fighting for liberty and civilisation'. These took various forms on plates and teapots and one small jug entitled 'The Bachelor's Milk Jug' (Plate 398).

Several artists were commissioned to depict various scenes of the war. Perhaps one of the most touching (Plate 400) shows a British 'tommy' saying farewell to his horse which lies dying on the roadside as a result of being wounded. A little further on, outside a bomb-struck cottage is another tommy, beyond which are the guns and a soldier driving the horses in retreat with the caption 'An Incident on the road to a battery position in Southern Flanders'.

Various cigarette cards were produced during the War. Wills produced a set of twelve cards (Plate 401) entitled 'A Series of Recruiting Posters'.

One of the most well-known characters of the Great War was 'Old Bill', created by William Bairnsfather. He epitomised the character of the British Army. Bairnsfather was born in 1885 in India, served in France during the Great War and became famous for these cartoons featuring Old Bill. He was an official war cartoonist attached to the US Army and he died in 1959. These cartoons took various forms: plates, plaques, dishes, mugs and beakers (Plate 402). A plaque shows Old Bill sitting in a dugout with the caption 'What time do they feed the sealions Alf?' Another shows Old Bill outside a bombed house in Flanders with the caption 'At present we are staying at a farm'.

Various teasets were produced by firms such as Carlton, Grafton, Shelley and Goss. Goss had an attractive shaped cup with a turquoise handle (Plate 399), the rim bearing in colour the flags of the Allies and two hands shaking in friendship. Another has a different design of flags entitled 'The Triple Entente, the Allied Armies United We Stand'. In the centre is the Union Jack in the form of a shield surmounted by the crown. A small jug and basin has the coloured flags of the nations captioned 'Allied Flags of Our Allies' and underneath the design the caption 'United We Stand'.

A brass ashtray in the form of a plaque bears the words: 'Ypres Porte de Menin Memorial des Heros Britanniques'. The English translation is beneath. In the centre is an

Plate 402. *Plates, mug and dishes of 'Old Bill' by William Bairnsfather.*

Plate 403. *Plate for the Welsh National War Memorial, Cardiff; plate for the Scottish National War Memorial, Edinburgh; three matchbox holders, two for Regiments, one for Robinson V.C.; Cowes Zeppelin model. Crested Ware: Field gun (Barry); dugout (Penrhiwceiber); submarine E boat (Cork); naval war memorial (Southsea); head and shoulders territorial (Aberayron).*

Plate 404. *Metal head plaque of Hindenburg; plate for Hindenburg; mug for the Kaiser; plate, Alsace-Lorraine; two-headed Kaiser; Kaiser jug: 'A Harder Nut to Crack'.*

Plate 405. *Cardiff Zeppelin, peace mug and hearth;* Lusitania *medal; lead battleship.*

Plate 406. *Crested Ware: Cenotaph (Woolwich); ambulance (Tenby); warship (Barry); plane (Cirencester); tank bank (Brighton); field gun (Lincoln).*

embossed engraving of the Menin gate with its pillars and archway surmounted by the British lion. On each side of the two cigarette holders is an English rose.

Various matchbox holders (Plate 403) were produced by regiments for their soldiers. They had on one side the name of the regiment, with its motto, and on the other side, either the badge of the regiment or the allied flags. A particularly interesting matchbox holder has on the front 'Lieutenant William Leefe Robinson VC, born 14th July 1895, destroyed Zeppelin L21 3rd September 1916', and on the other side the badges of the two regiments to which he belonged – the Worcestershire Regiment and the Royal Flying Corps. A brass plaque (Plate 398) portays three allied soldiers, British, French and Belgian.

Cowes, in the Isle of Wight, produced a model of a Zeppelin (Plate 403) bearing the words 'Zeppelin destroyed by Lieutenant Robinson VC at Cuffley, Essex. September 3rd 1916'.

Copeland produced teasets. The cup (Plate 398) has the British bulldog in the centre in fighting stance surmounted by the Enfield rifle and around it are a warship, the English and the French flags, the British tommy in a firing position, a British naval rating looking through a telescope, and a sword. On the saucer is the British bulldog standing alert on the Union Jack and around the side the two national flags of France and England, a field gun, a bugle, a Royal Flying Corps plane and what would appear to be a boy scout. All the decoration of these items is in blue.

An interesting plate (Plate 404) produced in France captioned 'Le Poilu en Alsace et Lorraine' shows on the front in colour a French soldier being greeted by two girls in Alsace-Lorraine national costume. He is carrying 'chocolat et sucre' and the caption is 'Voici des Vivres, mais Je demande a être croquet en premier lieu'. The top of the plate bears the coats of arms of Alsace-Lorraine in a laurel wreath, underneath is the date, 1918.

The Kaiser is commemorated in various forms. A mug by a unknown potter has in the centre the Kaiser in a laurel wreath, in colour, head and shoulders, wearing his uniform with his medals and the words 'Kaiser Wilhelm II'. Perhaps the most interesting item for the Kaiser shows two portrayals of him, one looking like Mephistopheles and the other as his normal self. Underneath are the words 'Which'll?' and the caption: 'Which'll he be you shall decree'. The following caption appears on the rear:

'5% of all Which'll articles sold goes to the leading funds for disabled heroes. The Kaiser caused the war, so make use of him to provide comforts for our wounded soldiers and sailors.'

It was made by Crown Staffordshire. Another caption reads as follows:

'This is the fiend with two faces. Thinks he's God's chosen one from all races. Thought he'd push, shove and blow and boss the whole show and put all the world in their places. But our soldiers and sailors gave chase and have altered the look on his face. We are proud of their pluck, so for victory and luck let us all give this mascot a place'.

Most of the commemorative items for the German commanders were manufactured in Germany. Paul von Beneckendorff und von Hindenburg was a German soldier of the old Prussian school coming from a well-known *Junker* family. He and Ludendorff were the most prominent German generals in the Great War. Hindenburg is the subject of a fine metal plaque (Plate 404) portraying his head and shoulders with prominent eyebrows and moustache. The foundry that produced this figure was Concordiahutte. After the abdication of the Kaiser, Hindenburg became President of the German Empire in 1925 and his firm opposition to Hitler prevented the establishment of the Third Reich until after his death.

Various towns and cities produced items for the war. Cardiff produced a field ambulance bearing its coat of arms. Cardiff also had a hearth with a black kettle (Plate 405) with the caption: 'Keep the Home Fire Burning'. The connection is that those words came from a well-known song by Ivor Novello who was born in Cardiff. Cardiff also produced a Zeppelin bearing the coat of arms and on the rear the German Cross. Tenby also produced an ambulance (Plate 406). Blaenau of Monmouthshire also produced an airship, though this time on a special plinth. For Lincoln there was a field gun. From Barry Island there was a warship and also a fieldgun. Merthyr Tydfil had an army car (Plate 409) bearing the town's coat of arms. Penrhiwceiber, a small Glamorgan valley coal-mining town, has an intriguing dug-out shelter (Plate 403) entitled 'Shrapnel Villa' showing the head of a tommy inside with the caption 'Tommy's dug out somewhere in France'. Produced by Carlton China, it bears the town's coat of arms. Southsea has a model of the naval war memorial. Cork, as an Irish souvenir, has an E9 boat. Aberayon has the head of a territorial soldier (Plate 403). The inscription on the back reads:

'Its the soldiers of the King my lads
Who fight for Englands Glory lads
And when we say we've always won
And when they ask us how its done

Plate 407. *Round framed silk embroidered panel.*

Plate 408. *Large 'Good Luck' tin. Princess Mary's brass cigarette tin for the troops.*

We proudly point to everyone
Of Englands soldiers of the King.'

A plate by Taylor of Longton, similar to that of the Welsh National War Memorial, shows the Scottish American War Memorial at Edinburgh (Plate 404). The plate carries the inscription:

'If it be life that waits I shall live forever unconquered
If death, I shall die at last strong in my pride and free'.

This is a very moving commemorative.

From Cirencester there was a warplane. The City of Bristol had a sailor (Plate 398). Paignton had a soldier with the caption: 'Our Great Defender'. Shelley produced a model tank (Plate 406) for Brighton which is in the form of a money box entitled 'Tank Bank'.

Many embroidered items were made during the War, some of them in great detail and highly colourful. One example (Plate 407) is round and has in the centre the years of the war embroidered with the words 'Souvenir of the Great War'. In a circle around the words are flags of some of the nations that took part. All these have been finely executed.

Pin cushions in the shape of hearts were made for various regiments. The centre sometimes includes beads and needlework and the head and shoulders of the war's commanders, or some of the regiments. Various other motifs were also included such as flags and 'Think of Me' and other slogans. The one shown (Plate 399) is for the Suffolk Regiment.

Various aspects of the war and commanders were commemorated upon tins of chocolate, tea, toffees, etc. One tin (Plate 408) has a coloured portrait of Princess Mary wearing the nurse's uniform of the Royal Red Cross within a horseshoe, with the words 'Good Luck' over it.

Princess Mary also sent a brass tin containing packets of cigarettes with the inscription 'H R H The Princess Mary's Christmas Fund 1914 – Cigarettes'. There are two packets, one has the monogram 'M' on each cigarette, the other has the cipher 'Honi soit qui mal y pense, the Royal Fusiliers'. Inside each tin is a card bearing a seated photograph of the Princess Mary with her signature, 'Mary'. On the other side is her monogram 'M' beneath the crown and the year 1914, and inside, flanked by a sprig of holly, 'Best Wishes for a

Plate 409. (Left to right) *Queen Alexandra's Christmas tin; St. Dunstan's match holder; Princess Christian's hospital feeding cup; King George's Christmas tin; Kitchener 'In Memoriam' matchbox-holder; tea tin showing Churchill as First Lord of the Admiralty; match strike chocolate and cigarette tin; oval tin from the British Grocers and army car, Merthyr Tydfil.*

Plate 410. (Left to right) *Tin with Kitchener on the lid; Dardenelles tin; long oblong tin with French, Kitchener and Jellicoe; peace mug from Ebbw Vale; Goss peace plate; brass tray, Menin Gate; Doulton peace mug; deep tin with motifs 'From the Empire'; tin with French, Kitchener and Jellicoe on the curved lid.*

Happy Christmas and a Victorious New Year from the Princess Mary and friends at home'. The front of the tin bears the embossed head of the Princess within a laurel circlet with the letter 'M' on each side, and on the left are the words 'France' among flags, on the right 'Russia' among flags and on each corner in a circlet: 'Belgium', 'Japan', 'Montenegro' and 'Serbia' and in between are the words, again embossed, 'Christmas 1914' and above the portrait of the Princess Mary are the words 'Imperium Britannicum'.

Mazawattee Tea produced a one pound tin with, on the cover, the fluttering flags of the nations which took part in the war and the heads of five soldiers of participating countries in circles on the front and the head of a sailor in a circle backed against a British dreadnought.

An unmarked tin, probably for biscuits, bears on its hinged lid a central head and shoulders portrait of King George V captioned 'Our Sailor King' within oak and laurel leaves. Queen Mary is portrayed in an oval cartouche surrounded by roses and the Prince of Wales similarly is shown on the reverse side.

A chocolate tin (Plate 409) has, on the hinged lid, an embossed raised portrait of the head and shoulders of King George V in a decorative cartouche on a mock ermine base. Inside on the cover of a card: 'Christmas 1914 with Hearty Christmas Greetings to the wounded soldiers and sailors and with best wishes for their speedy recovery from Cadbury Bros Limited Bournville'.

An oval tin (Plate 409) has in the centre the head of the King captioned 'His Majesty King George V' in a laurel wreath surrounded by the crown against the Union Jack, and on the other side within a laurel wreath surmounted by the crown: 'To our fighting heroes with Best Wishes from British Grocers' Federation Christmas 1914'.

A deep oblong tin has on its hinged lid the head and shoulders of the King wearing his crown surrounded by soldiers of the Empire with, in the background, a field gun and a battle scene and a warship on the high seas, all highly coloured. On the tin is a scene depicting India entitled 'Juma Musjid Delhi'. There is also a view to record the part played by South Africa, with a South African soldier overlooking Cape Town and Table Mountain with the harbour in front. Australia and New Zealand appear in two separate oval cartouches on the same panel. Australia features Sydney Harbour and New Zealand the Harbour at Wellington and in between is an Australian soldier. Canada is portrayed by the Government buildings of Ottawa and a Canadian soldier. There is no indication as to who produced this tin.

A long oblong tin (Plate 409), probably for both cigarettes and chocolate, has a match strike on the base. In the centre is the head and shoulders portrait of the King in an oval cartouche with flags of the Empire around it and dated 1915.

Another unmarked tin (Plate 410), probably for tea, has on the hinged lid two warships captioned 'The Dardenelles'. On one panel around the side: 'Suleman Mosque Constantinople', on the next one: 'Sultan's Palace Constantinople', on another: 'Landing at Gaba Tepe' showing the soldiers attacking the beach head with the mountains in the rear and the fourth panel, a warship captioned 'The Lizzie at Work'. This tin was clearly for the Gallipoli Campaign. Each of the panels is in an Eastern design.

A tall narrow tea tin (Plate 409) has on its hinged lid the head of the King wearing his Admiral's hat fully bemedalled, and around the panels, in shields or ovals, are Lord Kitchener and Sir John French in one, the Tsar of Russia and the Grand Duke Nicholas of Russia on another, the Rt. Hon. Winston Churchill and Sir John Jellicoe on another. Winston Churchill was at that time First Lord of the Admiralty. On the fourth panel are the King of the Belgians and General Joffre. Each panel contains various war scenes. There are not many other commemorative items for Joffre, apart from the Carruthers Gould toby jug (Plate 395).

The first of the three war commanders, French, Jellicoe and Kitchener appear on several tins in varying forms. One (Plate 410) has their heads in oval cartouches on a shaped lid and on the four panels are the Northern Mounted Rifles of South Africa, 'What orders from His Majesty for me and my men' from an Indian Maharaja, and underneath: 'All I possess for Britain the Rajah of Pudukote'. On the other panels are a battle scene of soldiers drawing a field gun and

Plate 411. Lusitania *mug.*

Plate 412. *'The Alliance Souvenir'.*

Plate 413. *Bust of Lenin.*

Plate 414. *Grimwades victory plate.*

Plate 415. *Paper programme for the victory parade.*

British warships in action on the high seas.

Another unmarked tin with a hinged lid bearing the head and shoulders of Lord Kitchener of Khartoum is captioned 'Secretary of State for War' and in different panels are Sir John French with a battle scene, two nurses in a hospital surrounded by flags and Admiral Sir John Jellicoe in an oval backed by warships and boy scouts, surrounded by flags.

A long oblong tin (Plate 410), probably for chocolate, although there is no manufacturer's mark, has the heads of Jellicoe, French and Kitchener in laurel wreaths surrounded by flags.

A small tobacco tin again has the heads of the three. This was made for B. Morris & Sons Limited, London.

Beef tea cubes were the subject of a tin entitled 'Allies brand'. It bears the Union Jack, the contents: 'twelve cubes, Gordon MacDonald & Company, 13 Northumberland Alley, London EC'.

It was not only in Flanders that the war progressed. Great danger to British shipping occurred as a result of the U Boat submarine warfare. One of the most tragic events was the sinking in 1915 of the Cunard liner *Lusitania* by *U20* off the Irish coast, with the loss of 1,198 people. A medal in German (Plate 405) was struck for this disaster depicting the great liner sinking into the waves. A green printed mug (Plate 411) shows the great four-funnelled liner leaving Fishguard Harbour.

The entry of the United States of America into the war has

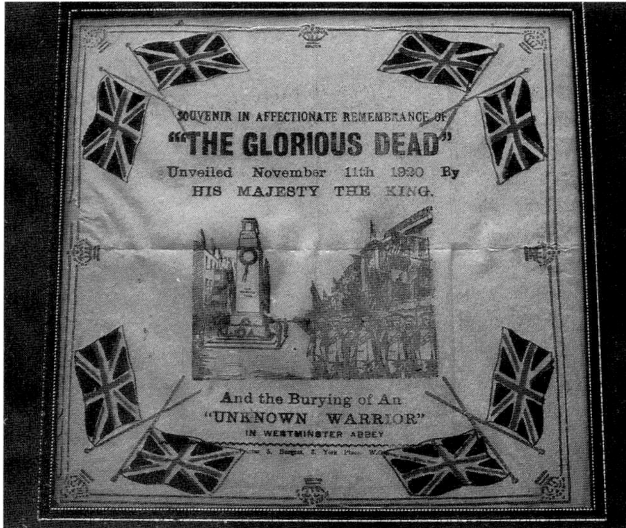

Plate 416. *Paper programme for the unveiling of the Cenotaph.*

Daily Mail

THEIR MAJESTIES THE KING AND THE QUEEN.

The Victorious Dead.

HOW THE PEACE TREATY WAS SIGNED AT VERSAILLES.

Plate 417. Daily Mail *victory edition.*

fortunately been commemorated by a pack of cards from the Worshipful Company. This important and decisive event has not been ceramically recorded, so far as is known, and the pack of cards, dated 1917, shows Colombia standing proudly facing the sea and bearing the stars and stripes of America. The head of the design portrays the Company's coat of arms.

A touching item was published by Scotes Limited, Newgate Street, London entitled 'The Alliance Souvenir' (Plate 412). A coloured cardboard poster captioned 'Faithful to the Empire' has King George in the uniform of an Admiral placed in a central circle, surmounted by a crown, supported by the lion and the unicorn, and surrounded by a swathe of British flags. An aeroplane is flying on either side. There is a space for the insertion of a photograph of a member of the armed forces, on each side of which are shields representing dominions and colonies, with the French flag on the left and the Russian flag on the right. Beneath are the embossed heads and shoulders of Admiral Jellicoe and General French, and in the centre base in a circle are two hands shaking in friendship. British warships are shown together with a rifle and anchor. The rose, thistle and shamrock form part of the design. Many a family used this to frame a photograph of a loved one away fighting for his country.

The Russian Revolution, which resulted in the defeat of Russia and its withdrawal from the war, has not, it would appear, been commemorated in this country. However, there are many busts of Lenin (Plate 413), who was the instigator of the Communist Revolution in 1917.

Peace

Various cities and towns produced mugs and other commemoratives to record peace. They all normally feature the same central motif of a seated Britannia below the globe with the word 'Peace' and the dove, surrounded by the Allied flags and the caption 'World War 1914-18', and underneath 'Liberty, Justice, Truth and Honour'. The one shown was produced for Ebbw Vale (Plate 410). On the rear of the mug is: 'Peace Celebrations 1919 Ebbw Vale' and the town's coat of arms, and underneath: 'War declared against Germany August 4th 1914, General Armistice signed November 11th 1918, Peace signed June 28th 1919'. Various plates and plaques were produced. Grimwades of Stoke-on-Trent produced a plate (Plate 414) with, in the centre in laurel wreaths, the Prime Minister, Lloyd George, Admiral Beatty and Field Marshal Haig captioned: 'To commemorate the triumph of right over might. Victory 1918'. The national flags form part of the design.

W.H. Goss produced a plate (Plate 410) which is very colourful, having in the centre the winged goddess of peace captioned 'Peace 1919', around which are the flags of the nations, a British warship and a field gun. Around the scalloped rim in a laurel wreath are the names of all the commanders who took part during the war. Many of those named have not been specifically commemorated in any way. For example Generals Plumer, Cavan, Allenby, Robertson, Pershing from America, Joffre, Birdwood and Rawlinson.

The establishment of the League of Nations was commemorated by a mug published by the Star China Company Paragon. Children in national costume dance with joined hands around the main part of the jug – China, Spain, Japan, Britain and Italy are those depicted. Inside are the words 'United We Stand'. 'The League of Nations' surrounds the Union Jack and the Red Ensign.

The Worshipful Company of Playing Cards published a pack of cards dated 1921 and captioned 'The League of Nations'. The spirit of world comradeship is symbolised by a woman opening wide the golden gate of happiness and prosperity to the various nations.

Most cities and towns had victory celebrations. London had a special ceremony to commemorate the Declaration of Peace. There is a souvenir in the form of a paper programme (Plate 415) for this event, which took place on 19 July 1919. It has portraits of the King and Queen and Lloyd George, the Prime Minister and Beatty. Details of the procession and the troops participating are set out. It is printed by Burgess of York Place in The Strand.

On 11 November 1920 the King went to Whitehall to unveil the Cenotaph. A paper programme (Plate 416) surrounded by the Union Jack reads:

'Souvenir in Affectionate Remembrance of the Glorious Dead and Unveiled November 11th 1920 by His Majesty the King and the burial of an Unknown Warrior" in Westminster Abbey.'

In the centre is a picture of the Cenotaph in Whitehall with soldiers marching past it.

Following the official opening of the Cenotaph various cities and towns commissioned models of the Cenotaph. They were produced either by Shelley, Grafton, Carlton or Goss. The one shown (Plate 406) is for Woolwich.

All the national newspapers and magazines carried victory editions. Perhaps the most comprehensive is that published by the *Daily Mail* (Plate 417) entitled 'A Golden Peace Number' dated June 30th 1919. The photographs and text are printed in gold. The front page carries a large head and shoulders portrait of the King in Field Marshal's uniform and the Queen wearing a tiara and a magnificent jewelled collar. Various articles were included, and a poem by Alfred Noyes called 'The Victorious Dead'. The leading article was written by Viscount Northcliffe.

Among the many cigarette card sets that were produced, W.D. & H.O. Wills of Bristol and London issued a set of fifty cards entitled 'Allied Army Leaders'. This is a comprehensive list showing the names of the many allies whose generals took a commanding part in the Great War. They contain fifteen from Britain, nine from France, and nine from Russia. This set forms an historical record, each card carrying on the reverse a potted biography of those whose portraits are shown, head and shoulders, in colour. Fifteen are wearing military headdress and the two Indian representatives are wearing turbans.

Postcards played a prominent part during the War. Many were of the King and his generals, as well as scenes at the front (Plate 418).

Two matchbox holders for Kitchener (Plate 409) are shown, giving the date of his drowning on 5th June 1916: 'In Memoriam'. Another in the same Plate is in aid of St. Dunstan's Hospital for soldiers and sailors blinded in the Great War.

One of the well-known songs for the war was 'It's a long

Plate 418. *War postcards.*

Plate 419. *'Tipperary' linen cloth.*

way to Tipperary'. A linen cloth (Plate 419) features this with a map of England, Wales, Scotland and Ireland, each showing a young girl. A British tommy stands on the Flanders part of France waving his hat. The title of the song is on the left and on the right: 'My Heart's Right There'.

Queen Alexandra

In November, 1925 Queen Alexandra died at the age of eighty. On 17th March, 1920 she had unveiled a memorial to Nurse Cavell in St Martin's Place, near Trafalgar Square. Although there is no ceramic to record this unveiling, many cities and towns produced a figure to commemorate Nurse Cavell (Plate 420). They are all of similar design, showing the standing figure of Nurse Cavell in uniform on a plinth captioned, 'Edith Cavell, Brussells, Dawn, October 12th, 1915'. They were published by Willow Art China of Longton and the words 'Humanity and Sacrifice' are on each side of the plinth.

Queen Alexandra will be remembered for her Rose Day, a summer street festival of rose sellers to raise money for hospitals and charities, started in 1912. Her drive around London became an annual event, the last being in 1923. Paragon produced a tea service, which is not easily found, the plate (Plate 421) has a design of roses on a pale primrose ground, the back carries the words: 'To commemorate

Plate 420. (left) *Crested statuette of Nurse Cavell.*

Plate 421. *Paragon Rose Day plate.*

Plate 422.(left) *Royal Copenhagen plate for the 70th birthday of Queen Alexandra.*

Plate 423.(above) *Pair of Devon vases for the death of the Queen.*

Plate 424.(below left) Illustrated London News, *death of Queen Alexandra.*

Plate 425. *Paper programme for the wedding of the Princess Royal and Viscount Lascelles, 1922.*

Alexandra's Rose Day, June 26th'.

As part of her contribution to the war effort a special tin of cigarettes was sent to troops, in the centre on a grey background in an oval cartouche is a head and shoulders portrait of Queen Alexandra and inside the lid is her fascimile signature and greetings with 'Best Wishes from Alexandra' (Plate 409).

In 1914 Queen Alexandra reached the age of seventy years and there is a Copenhagen Porcelain plate (Plate 422) with a silhouette portrait of the Queen in dark blue and in the centre are the words, along the top 'Alexandra' and on each side, '1844-1914'.

Little is known to exist ceramically to commemorate the Queen's death. One of the Devon Potteries produced a pair of vases (Plate 423), not in the usual cream but on a mauve background indicating mourning and included in the design are the Queen's favourite pink roses depicted in her Alexandra Rose Day.

The Illustrated London News (Plate 424) and other national magazines gave full coverage of her death.

The King's serious illness in 1929 has not been ceramically recorded, but fortunately The Worshipful Company of Cardmakers issued a pack of cards (Plate 378) to record his recovery. Each card has in the centre a portrait of the King in military uniform with his orders and stars

Plate 426. Two tins for the wedding of the Princess Royal.

Plate 427. *Cotton wedding handkerchief.*

Plate 428. Graphic *wedding edition.*

Plate 429. *Postcard for the wedding group.*

Plate 430. *Postcard of the wedding of Princess Patricia of Connaught and Commander Ramsay.*

surmounted with the crown and the date, 1929, and underneath, 'Our King Restored To Us', and beneath that, the Worshipful Company's motto.

Royal Weddings

Several members of the royal family were married during the reign of King George V, but few have been ceramically recorded. The Princess Royal was married on 28th February, 1922 at Westminster Abbey to Viscount Lascelles, son of the Earl of Harewood. A paper programme (Plate 425) has souvenir details and portraits of both the bride and the groom. Fortunately some tins were manufactured to record the event. A biscuit tin (Plate 426) shows on one side the Princess Royal in an oval cartouche surrounded by turquoise. On the reverse the bridegroom is shown. He is also in a cartouche and on another side are Harewood House and Chesterfield House in London and Goldsborough Hall in Yorkshire, on the other side is Westminster Abbey and the lid shows Buckingham Palace.

A tea tin again shows the Princess Royal and Viscount Lascelles on each side in oval medallions surrounded by orange blossom. The lid has wedding bells and on either side are sprigs of orange blossom tied with white ribbons.

Sharp's Super Kreem Toffee produced an attractive tin on an orange base, bearing on each side in an oval gold frame the head and shoulders of Princess Mary and Viscount Lascelles and captioned 'A Right Royal Favourite' (Plate 446A). A small cotton handkerchief (Plate 427) was produced for the wedding. In the top left-hand corner are portraits of the Princess Royal and Viscount Lascelles. *The Graphic* (Plate 428), covered the marriage in an edition entitled 'Wedding Number' with full-length portraits of the Princess and Viscount Lascelles within an oval cartouche surrounded by a wreath of orange blossom surmounted by the Princess's coronet and a Viscount's coronet. A postcard (Plate 429), shows the wedding group with bridesmaids including the future Queen Elizabeth, the Duchess of York, to the left of the bridegroom.

When Princess Patricia of Connaught married Commander Ramsay, no commemoratives were made for this event. However, there is souvenir programme which carries the portraits of both the bride and the groom and a postcard (Plate 430). After her marriage Princess Patricia renounced her royal title and was henceforth known as Lady Patricia Ramsay.

The Princess's sister, Princess Margaret, had married the Crown Prince of Sweden in 1905, but she died before becoming Queen. The Crown Prince subsequently married Lady Louise Mountbatten, a sister of Earl Mountbatten of Burma. There were hardly any commemoratives for Lady Louise, but a plate was published (Plate 431) much later as one of a series manufactured by Barrett's of Staffordshire for a Swedish firm anxious to promote interest in Sweden's monarchy. The series covers all Swedish Kings since Carl

Plate 431. *Plate showing Queen Louise of Sweden.*

***Plate 432.** Collage of newspaper photographs of the Duchess of Kent and her hats.*

Joachim and concludes with the present King, Carl XVI. Queen Louise carries a pekinese in her arms, the inscription on this plate bears the dates of the King's reign, 1950-1973.

The marriage of the King's second son, the Duke of York, will be described in more detail in Chapter 6.

In November 1934 the Duke of Kent married Princess Marina of Greece. Princess Marina was a classic beauty with a sense of fashion that has rarely been equalled. A selection of her marvellous hats is shown in a collage (Plate 432) taken from contemporary newspapers. Although this was the most glamorous wedding to take place for many years, there is little ceramically to record it. However, there are other commemorative items which have come to the rescue, such as a jigsaw puzzle by Chad Valley (Plate 433), being a composition of the royal family with the King and Queen in their coronation robes and Princess Marina in her wedding dress.

The Duke of Kent had not played a great part in public life and there is little to record what he did and where he visited. However a small tin (Plate 434A) was produced to commemorate the occasion of his visit to present the Royal Charter to the Borough of Goole in October 1933. It contains a portrait of the Duke in an oval and underneath are the

***Plate 433.** Chad Valley jigsaw puzzle of the wedding of the Duke and Duchess of Kent.*

Plate 434A. *Tin for the visit of the Duke of Kent to Goole.* ***B.*** *Plaque of the Duke and Duchess of Kent.* ***C.*** *Pair of gold Dux heads.* ***D.*** *Tin for their wedding.*

Plate 435. *Jigsaw puzzle of the Duke and Duchess at London Airport.*

Plate 436. *Fretwork framed wedding souvenir.*

Plate 437. *Postcard of the wedding.*

Plate 438. *Postcard for the wedding of Prince Henry, Duke of Gloucester and a box, which contained wedding cake.*

Plate 439. Illustrated London News *wedding souvenir for Prince Arthur of Connaught and the Duchess of Fife.*

words 'Presented to the Children'. It carries the Goole coat of arms with its motto 'Advance'. This tin was made by Rowntree's, as was a similar tin for the Duke's visit to the city of Peterborough in the civic week 1929 and it is so captioned.

A pair of small gold Dux plaques portray both the Duke and the Duchess (Plate 434C). Another jigsaw puzzle (Plate 435) shows the Duchess in her famous marina blue and her pill box hat together with Prince George waving from London airport. There is also a plaque (Plate 434B) showing a profile portrait of the Duke and Duchess taken by a well-known court photographer. A fretwork frame carries a head and shoulders portrait (Plate 436) of the Duke and Duchess entitled 'The Royal Wedding – the Duke of Kent and Princess Marina'. A postcard (Plate 437), shows the full wedding group.

The last marriage during this reign was that of Prince Henry, Duke of Gloucester, who married Lady Alice Montagu Douglas Scott, the daughter of the Duke and Duchess of Buccleuch. This wedding was to some extent less publicised and less formal because the bride's father died shortly before the wedding, which took place privately at Buckingham Palace. There is nothing ceramic to record this event. A small record is a box which contained the original wedding cake (Plate 438) with the initials 'AH' in silver and the crown above it and underneath the words 'Buckingham Palace 18th November, 1935'.

Prince Arthur, only son of the Duke of Connaught, married the Duchess of Fife, daughter of the Princess Royal, at the Chapel Royal of St. James's Palace on 15th October, 1913. *The Illustrated London News* produced a Royal Wedding souvenir (Plate 439).

Another fashionable society wedding was that of Edwina Ashley, the daughter of Lord Mount Temple and heiress to Broadlands, the former home of Lord Palmerston, to Lord Louis Mountbatten. This was covered by a postcard (Plate 440) which shows the bridal group with the bride wearing a 'nightcap' headdress of orange blossom. This has been preserved and can be seen, together with the sequin-edged train, at the Mountbatten Exhibition Room at Broadlands. With a sheaf of madonna lilies the whole effect is pure Twenties. There is nothing of a ceramic nature known to record this wedding.

A postcard (Plate 441) covers the wedding of Princess Maud, the youngest daughter of Princess Louise, who married Lord Carnegie. The postcard shows the full wedding group.

There were very well-known boxes of chocolates in circulation during the King's reign, manufactured by Cadbury's of Bourneville and entitled 'King George V chocolates' (Plate 442). The one-pound box bears the head of the King in a circular gold wreath surmounted by a crown, adjoining which are four golden sovereigns in different sizes of the four previous Kings who bore the name George. Each of their heads bears a laurel crown. A wide red sash runs from top right to bottom left which holds a red ribbon tied in

Plate 440. *Postcard for the wedding of Lord Louis Mountbatten and Edwina Ashley.*

Plate 441. *Postcard for the wedding of Princess Maud and Lord Carnegie.*

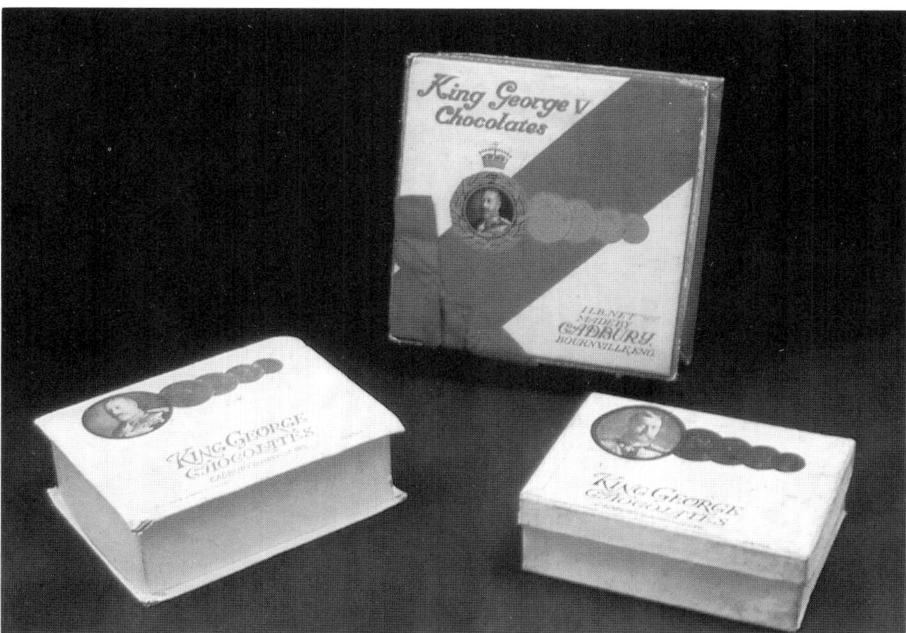

Plate 442. *King George V chocolate boxes.*

a bow. The colour is an overall cream edged with gold.

The half pound boxes are plainer and were packed in different shapes, one is clearly older in date as the King's head shows a younger man. The coins have the appearance of copper. The other box has gold coins and is a little more elaborate, both are on a white background.

Payne's also produced a box of chocolates entitled 'King George', bearing his portrait (Plate 446B). Although no special chocolate boxes were made for Queen Mary, Cadbury's of Bourneville produced a variety of tins on the base of which are three British Queens (Plate 443). Queen Mary occupies the central oval surmounted by a crown, on either side are pictures of Queen Victoria and Queen Alexandra. The design is of elaborate scrolls and the caption reads: 'Cadbury Bros. Ltd., have been honoured with the appointment as cocoa and chocolate manufacturers to Her Majesty Queen Mary'. They were similarly honoured by Her Majesty Queen Alexandra and Her late Majesty Queen Victoria. The hinged lid carries various well-known eighteenth and nineteenth century portraits, including the Gainsborough *Blue Boy* (Plate 444).

Three of the King's sons, the Prince of Wales in the centre in naval uniform, the Duke of York on the left in RAF uniform and the Duke of Gloucester on the right in army uniform, appear on a red tin produced by Thorne's Extra Super Cream Toffee (Plate 378).

The Princess Royal

The Princess Royal carried out many public engagements on behalf of the King and Queen. She was particularly interested in the work of nurses and in animals. There are a few

Plate 443. *The 'Three British Queens' tin.*

Plate 444. *The Gainsborough Blue Boy, the lid of the tin in Plate 443.*

Plate 445A. *Ashtray for the Royal Veterinary Society.* **B.** *Mug for the Princess Royal, opening a hospital.*

Plate 447. *Photograph of the Princess Royal and three of the King's sons for the Silver Wedding.*

Plate 446A. *Sharp's toffee tin for the Princess Royal.* **B.** *Payne's King George V chocolate box.* **C.** *Wedgwood cup and saucer for the visit to the Royal Scots as Colonel-in-Chief.* **D.** *Tin for christening of HMS* Rodney.

Plate 448A. *Mug for the visit to Shirebrook.* ***B.*** *Mug for the visit to Stoke-on-Trent.* ***C.*** *Jug for the opening of Stockport Town Hall.* ***D.*** *Mug for the opening of the Tyne Bridge.* ***E.*** *Mug for the visit to Padiham.*

commemorative pieces to record some of her activities. A mug (Plate 445B) commemorates her visit as Viscountess Lascelles to the opening of the War Memorial Maternity Home at Castleford, Normanton and District Cottage Hospital and the Castleford Public Market on 23rd August, 1929. Her interest in animals can be seen on an ashtray (Plate 445A) for the Royal Veterinary College Championship Dog Show held in 1927. The centre holds an embossed head of the Princess with her signature.

Wedgwood manufactured a teaset commemorating her visit as Colonel-in-Chief of the Royal Scots, the Royal Regiment in London on 13th December, 1930. The plain white cup (Plate 446C) carries the inscription and the badge of the regiment.

In 1925 Princess Mary christened Britain's latest warship, HMS *Rodney*. Lyon's Assorted Toffees produced a tin (Plate 446D) in the shape of a book entitled 'British Battleships'. The front cover shows the battleship bearing the new design and postion of its towering structure replacing the previous tripod foremast. The reverse gives the history of its building by Cammell Laird in Birkenhead, and its enormous cost, seven million pounds.

The Silver Wedding

The King and Queen celebrated their Silver Wedding in 1918. There are no known ceramic items although the national magazines covered the event. A photograph (Plate 447) was taken for the occasion, of four of their children – the Duke of York, the Duke of Gloucester (not yet with his moustache), the Duke of Kent and the Princess Royal.

The King and His People

The King made many visits to towns and cities throughout the country.

A mug (Plate 448B) for a visit to the County Borough of Stoke-on-Trent on 22nd and 23rd April, 1913 has the coat of arms of the borough in the centre and the front carries colour portraits of the King and Queen, clearly those commissioned for their coronations.

The visit to Padiham on 9th July, 1913 is also recorded on a mug (Plate 448E), again with a clear coronation set of portraits.

On 23rd April, 1913 they both made a visit to Leek. A porcelain beaker (Plate 449A) was published by Bishop of England. Fine portraits of the King and Queen wearing their crowns flank a design of laurel leaves bearing 'Souvenir of the Royal Visit' around the top.

A pottery mug (Plate 448A), buff-coloured with a darker brown border, commemorates the royal visit to Shirebrook

Plate 449A. *Beaker for the visit to Leek.* ***B.*** *Tin for the visit to Blackpool.*

on 23rd June, 1914. The portraits in this case are not coronation portraits.

On 10th July, 1912 Queen Mary made a solo visit to Rylands Factory in Barnsley. A glass jar of sweets bears the inscription 'Made to Commemorate the Visit of the Queen' with the date and place. The other side has the words 'God Bless the Queen' over a crown, the base with the words 'Rylands, Barnsley'.

The King and Queen visited Coatbridge on 9th July, 1914. A tin manufactured by Pettigrew's of Glasgow shows coloured portraits on a blue background and is captioned: 'As a Souvenir'.

Their visit to Blackpool was commemorated by a small tin (Plate 449B) produced by Cadbury's. The lid bears in oval cartouches portraits of the heads of the King and Queen on a red background and flanked by a large rose, captioned 'Visit of Their Majesties to Blackpool, 8th July, 1913. A souvenir presented to school children by the Mayor and Mayoress'.

Just before his illness in October 1928 the King opened the new Tyne Bridge. A tall mug (Plate 448D) with a coloured likeness of the bridge spanning the river Tyne is featured on it.

On 23rd April 1927 he attended the Cup Final which was won by Cardiff City for the first and only time. Ten thousand Welshmen, largely miners, attended, some of whom had walked there. A badge and a ticket to the North Grandstand of the Empire Stadium are shown (Plate 450), together with a miniature vase of the cup made by Carlton China carrying the city's coat of arms and the date of victory. An enlarged

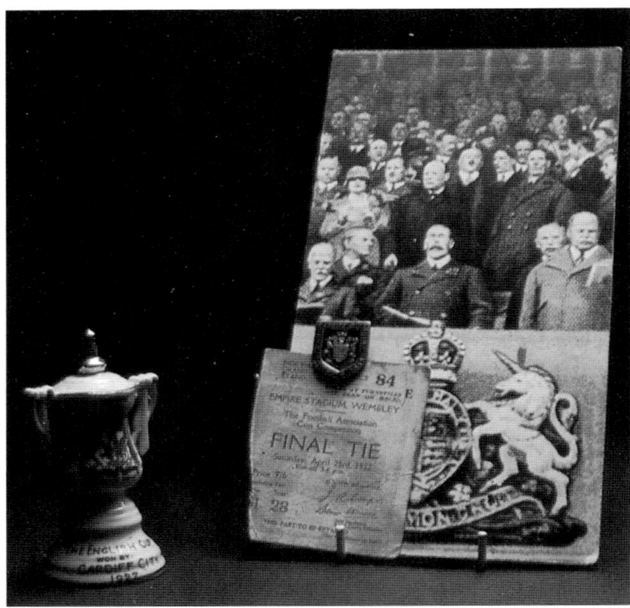

Plate 450. *King George at the Cup Final at Wembley when Cardiff won.*

Plate 451. (Left to right) A. *Beaker for the Anglo-American Exposition.* ***B.*** *Small vase for the Imperial Services Exhibition.* ***C.*** *Vase for the Festival of the Empire.* ***D.*** *Heart-dish for the Latin Exhibition.* ***E.*** *Vase for the Latin Exhibition.*

black and white photograph of a cigarette card which formed part of a set of fifty to commemorate the King's Silver Jubilee shows the King at the match in the royal box with the Earl of Derby on his right and Winston Churchill behind.

The Empire Exhibition of 1924 and others

The cult for exhibitions, which started in 1851 and continued in the reign of Edward VII, progressed during King George's reign.

The Festival of the Empire was held at Crystal Palace in 1911. Shelley produced a two-handled vase (Plate 451C), with a motif consisting of Britannia surrounded by symbols for India, Canada, Australia, South Africa and Newfoundland. The reverse bears a view of the Crystal Palace.

The Latin British Exhibition was held at the Great White City in 1912. Grafton China produced a heart-shaped dish (Plate 351D), and a vase with swan handles. The motif is a head of Mercury within a cartouche of flags of the nations taking part.

The Anglo-American Exposition held in London in 1914 is featured in a beaker (Plate 351A) by Grafton China, black and white printed with the two national flags and three scenes of the exhibition buildings, each within its own scrolled frame.

The Imperial Services Exhibition held at Earls Court in 1916 is recorded on a small vase (Plate 351B), also by Grafton China.

The cotton trade held an exhibition in London in 1913, entitled the British Cotton Textile Exhibition. A linen cloth (Plate 352) carries a head and shoulders portrait of Queen Mary wearing a splendid coronet in maroon surrounded by the names of the thirty-two cotton towns exhibiting, such as Rochdale, Preston and Nelson and Colne from the north-west of England.

The highly successful Empire Exhibition of 1924 was a vast affair and was opened by the King. It had as its mascot

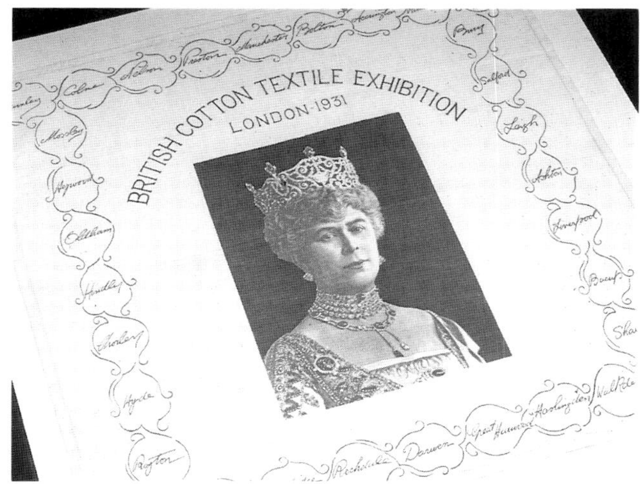

***Plate 452.** Linen cloth for the Textile Exhibition of 1931.*

***Plate 453.** **(Left to right) A.** Pin holder. **B.** Cup and saucer with Wembley Lion. **C.** Blue and white plate of Imperial Government Building. **D.** Cup and saucer with Prince of Wales and Duke of York. **E.** Brass tobacco jar. **F.** Hand and foot with Empire motif.*

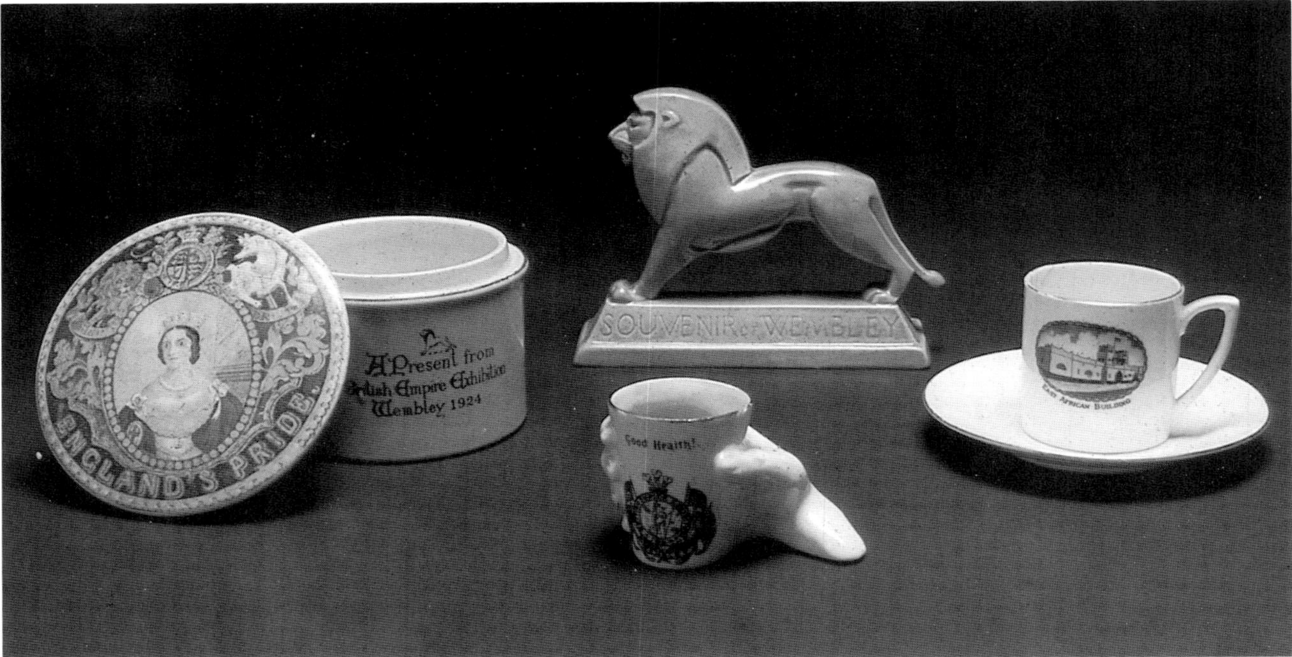

Plate 454A. *Pot with lid of Queen Victoria: 'England's Pride'.* ***B.*** *Wembley lion.* ***C.*** *Hand holding a small vase.* ***D.*** *Cup and saucer of South African Pavilion.*

the 'Wembley Lion'. Various commemorative items were produced bearing either the lion or another of the exhibition's motifs, Britannia, in an oval surrounded by the flags of the Empire, captioned: 'Wembley 1924, April to October, British Empire Exhibition'. There are various commemoratives in the shape of vases, cups and saucers, mugs, beakers a brass tobacco jar (Plate 453E), a pin holder (Plate 453A), and hand and foot ornament (Plate 453F) and meat pots, one with a head of Queen Victoria captioned 'England's Pride' and 'A present from British Empire Exhibition Wembley'. The opening of the Exhibition has not been ceramically recorded although there is an art deco teaset, the cup handle (Plate 453B) being in the shape of the lion, featuring the Presidents of the British Empire Exhibition, the Prince of Wales and the Duke of York.

Various pavilions were erected and these form separate ceramic records. For example the East African Pavilion was commemorated by a cup and saucer (Plate 454D). A plate (Plate 453D) by Cauldon of England has in blue a design of the Imperial Government Buildings as part of the series 'Views of the British Empire Exhibition Wembley 1924'. Paragon china produced a teaset portraying the British lion on the side of the cup with the Union Jack on the inside of the lip (Plate 453B).

The Silver Jubilee

No jubilee celebrations had taken place since Victoria's Diamond Jubilee in 1897. This was an occasion greatly looked forward to and has been lavishly commemorated in various forms. Cups and saucers, plates, mugs, beakers, jugs, all kinds of commemoratives were produced. Many of these are still easily available.

Royal Worcester produced an important pair of Silver Jubilee statuettes (Plate 455). They are beautifully modelled in china by Miss Gwendoline Parnell and decorated in colour. The King is in naval uniform, the Queen in Garter Robes, each standing on a pedestal. The edition is limited to 250 pairs and each statuette is numbered. In fact only

Plate 455. *Pair of Royal Worcester statuettes for the Silver Jubilee, 1935.*

Plate 456. (Left to right) A. *Mason's jug.* ***B.*** *Pair of statuettes.* ***C.*** *Plate with art deco silver design.* ***D.*** *Small Doulton art deco cottage.* ***E.*** *Burleighware mug with flag handle.* ***F.*** *Doulton mug.*

seventy-two were made because on the death of the King in January the following year, publication ceased. The first number went to the Queen, number two to the Princess Royal and number three to the Duchess of York.

Although the art deco period was drawing to its close there are some items in this style. Mason's produced a tankard jug (Plate 456A) with the head of the King in relief,

Plate 457. *Paragon Jubilee plate.*

the handle, lip and base with rings of silver on a deep cream background. An unmarked plate (Plate 456C) contains a central portrait of the King and Queen in a design of flags and shields, captioned 'Silver Jubilee'. The shape is basically octagonal with typical art deco moulding design in silver on a cream base.

A mug (Plate 456F) published by Royal Doulton is elegantly plain, on a white background is a small panel with art deco lines, bearing sepia head and shoulders portraits of the King and Queen without crowns. Burleighware published a mug (Plate 456E), silver rimmed bearing the head and shoulders of the King and Queen in laurel wreathed cartouches with the handle in the shape of the Union Jack. A small pair of bronze statuettes (Plate 456B) of the King and Queen, head and shoulders, are stamped 'G & M' on the plinth. A small Doulton cottage with a lid (Plate 456D), in art deco design has an orange chimney and the monogram 'GM' with a crown in between and the dates 1910-1935.

Paragon China, which specialised in commemorative pieces, published a colourful plate (Plate 457), in the centre of which, in cartouches of laurel, are the King and Queen surmounted by the crown and the royal flowers in their proper colours surrounded by the arms and the royal standard. The lion of Scotland, the harp of Ireland, but alas no Welsh dragon, are shown. Underneath the portrait are the words: 'His Majesty King George, Her Majesty Queen Mary 1910-1935'. The border is edged with silver and it states that it is to commemorate the Silver Jubilee. Paragon also published a two-handled loving cup (Plate 460A) in various sizes containing the same portraits of the King and Queen in colour with the same inscription. The handles are interesting in that they are modelled in the shape of the royal flowers.

Plate 458. (Left to right) A. *Cardiff mug.* **B.** *Mug with transfer of HMS* Queen Elizabeth. **C.** *Unmarked tin.* **D.** *Cup, saucer and plate.*

Plate 459. *Jubilee tins: McVitie and Price, Cadbury's, Rington and Mazawatee.*

the rose and the shamrock, in colour.

Most cities and towns produced mugs for presentation to their school children. The Cardiff mug (Plate 458A) bears on the reverse the coat of arms and the front portrays portraits of the King and Queen.

In addition to ceramics, several chocolate, biscuit and tea manufacturers produced commemorative tins. Mazawatee had a colourful tin (Plate 459) with, on each of its four sides,

Plate 460A. *Silver Jubilee Paragon loving cup.* **B.** *Wedgwood jug.* **C.** *Joshua Tetley tankard.*

Plate 461. *Jubilee tins: Arnott of Australia, two unmarked and George Barratt.*

portraits of the King, Queen, Buckingham Palace and Windsor Castle, each surrounded by an attractive red scroll and on each of the four corners swathed pillars of laurels. The hinged lid contains a dove of peace fluttering over the globe with the red of the British territories standing out and again surrounded by a red design of scrolls on a gold background. Inside are the words 'Delicious Mazawatee Tea' and on the base the price label. Cadbury's (Plate 459) produced a long narrow tin containing a bar of chocolate in the contemporary wrapper. The design is in silver with portraits of both the sovereigns and the dates of the Jubilee.

The London Co-operative Society produced an oval-shaped biscuit tin with a hinged lid bearing on a blue background portraits of the King and Queen in round cartouches surmounted by the crown and captioned '25 years Co-operation' – not the happiest of wordings.

Ringtons 'Royal Casket' (Plate 459) has portraits of the sovereigns surrounded by flags in oval cartouches within laurel leaves. The design is on a blue background with a decoration of roses. The central part of the hinged lid is not in silver but in gold.

McVitie and Price gave a free sample in a tin with a hinged lid (Plate 459). The design is in cobalt blue and silver and has two head and shoulders portraits of King George and Queen Mary, the King in Admiral's uniform and the Queen wearing the Garter ribbon and a tiara.

A colourful tin (Plate 459), probably for toffees, carries on a royal blue background, with a design of fleur-de-lis, portraits of the King and Queen in oval cartouches with the royal standard wreathed on the left, and captioned 'Silver Jubilee – Long May They Reign'.

George Barratt of Sheffield, manufacturing confections, produced an elegant tin (Plate 461) featuring portraits taken from photographs of the King and Queen, the Prince of Wales and the Duke of York. The hinged lid carries a portrait of the Duchess of York holding Princess Elizabeth. The cream background is bordered by a design of blue and green floral motifs.

Arnott Limited of Australia, with premises at Holmbush, New South Wales, produced a tin of lacto-malted milk for the Silver Jubilee. The tin (Plate 461) carries portraits, head and shoulders, of the King and Queen and the design is in blue and silver.

An unmarked tin (Plate 461), on a silver base, carries in the centre the head and shoulders of the King and Queen in profile, the Queen wearing a toque, surmounted by both their crowns and the dates, with the caption 'Long Live Their Majesties'. On each side is Windsor Castle, captioned 'Royal Windsor'. The hinged lid displays Buckingham Palace.

Plate 462. The Illustrated London News *and* The Sphere *Jubilee edition covers.*

A tankard (Plate 460C), presented by Joshua Tetley and Son Ltd., is captioned 'Beer is Best' with the royal crown and the royal standard. Underneath it states that it is for the Silver Jubilee. On either side in blue is a portrait of the King and Queen and part of the royal regalia on the other side. The mug is buff-coloured and is published by Clauston of London.

Among the many mugs, plates, beakers, tygs (three handled mugs) and loving cups published for the Silver Jubilee, was a teaset manufactured by Alma Ware of England. The central theme is the position of Great Britain in the world. The King and Queen are shown in oval cartouches surrounded by the royal flowers and the Union Jack and

Plate 463.(Left) *Linen souvenir Jubilee napkin.*

Plate 464. *Paragon cup and saucer to record 'Bluebird'.*

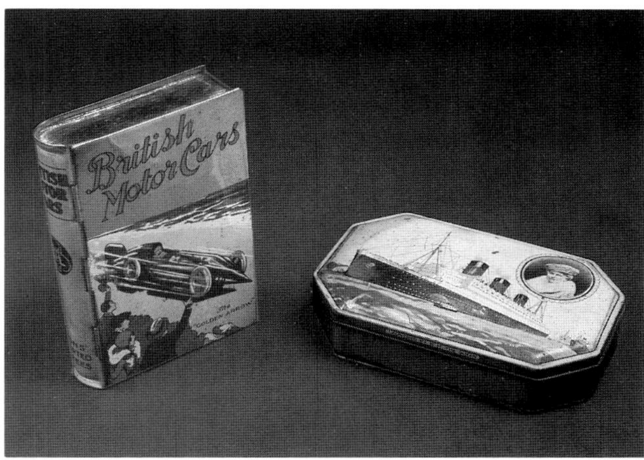

Plate 465A. *Lyon's Toffee tin in the shape of a book, for the 'Golden Arrow'.* ***B.*** *Toffee tin for the launching of the* Queen Mary.

royal standard above both sides of the globe in which the British dominions, colonies and possessions are coloured in red.

A mug carries a transfer of HMS *Queen Elizabeth* (Plate 458B). The royal coat of arms surmounted by a crown and the British flags is featured with the royal motto, each item has a thin blue rim.

The Illustrated London News and *The Sphere* (Plate 462) gave full and detailed coverage of the Jubilee. The cover for *The Sphere* has a coloured photograph of the King in Garter Robes and the Queen in a silver gown with the Garter ribbon. That for *The Illustrated London News* has soldiers of the Empire in full uniform.

Following custom, a souvenir programme was produced for use by the public, this time not in paper but on linen (Plate 463). The background is the Union Jack and in the centre are the King and Queen in circle medallions surmounted by a crown. In each corner there are details of the dominions, Canada, India, South Africa and New Zealand. Alongside the portrait of the Queen on the right is the 'Bluebird', the fastest car in the world, and the winner of the England to Melbourne race: 'the D.H. Comet 113,050 miles, 2 days 23 hours, arrived Melbourne 23rd October, 1934'. Underneath is the *Queen Mary* liner launched in Glasgow by the Queen in September, 1934.

'Bluebird' is also commemorated by Paragon in a tea and coffee set (Plate 464). The design shows bluebirds flying over a pastoral scene with hand-coloured flowers. The back stamp reads 'Malcolm Campbell, Bluebird. Copyright 1932'. This was published to commemorate his breaking of the world speed record.

The 'Golden Arrow', another great British racing car, is featured on a tin (Plate 465A) produced by Lyon's Assorted Toffees and in the shape of a book. The front cover bears a colourful picture of this famous car racing along Daytona Beach. It also carries the following: 'Daytona Beach, on 11th March, 1929, Sir Henry Seagrave drove the wonderful car, the Golden Arrow over a flying mile over a mean speed of 231.36 miles per hour', thereby beating the world speed record held by Captain Malcolm Campbell in the same year in the Bluebird.

Although nothing ceramic has been recorded for the launching of the *Queen Mary*, an unknown confectioner produced a tin, probably for toffees (Plate 465B). The lift-off lid bears a handsome picture of the splendid liner with its three funnels in colour. In the right hand corner is a head and shoulders portrait of Queen Mary in a circlet and shown wearing one of her famous toques. The side of the lid is captioned 'Launched by Queen Mary'.

Wedgwood published a jug (Plate 460B) with, on the front, a portrait of the King surrounded by a wreath of the royal flowers and the jubilee dates, and on the reverse between the royal flowers: 'To commemorate the silver jubilee of King George V and Queen Mary. Long May They

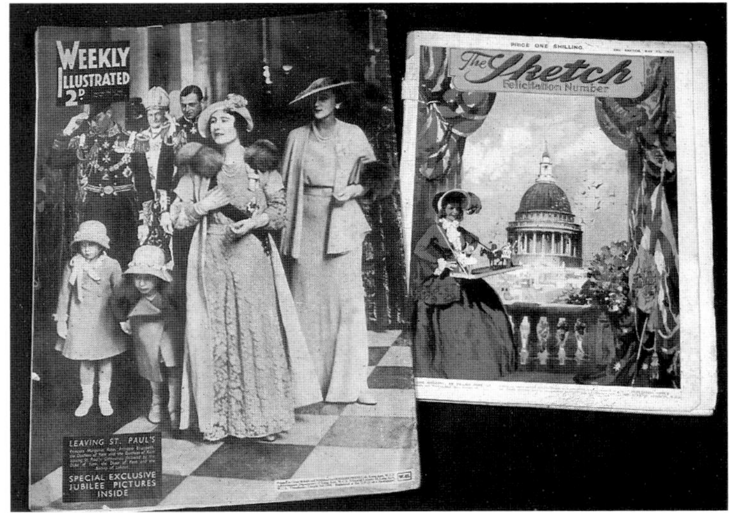

Plate 466. Weekly Illustrated *and* The Sketch *Jubilee number covers.*

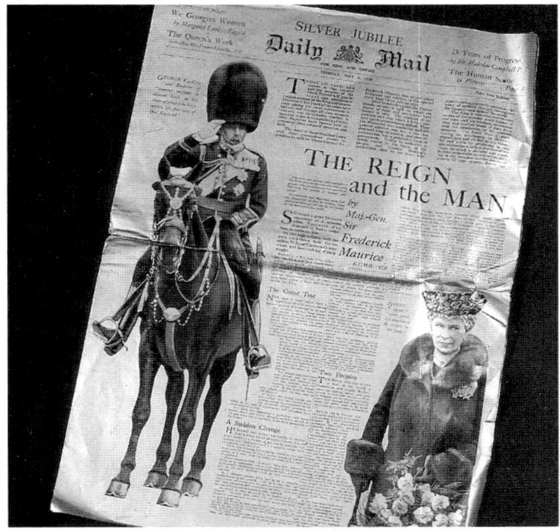

Plate 467. *Silver* Daily Mail *Jubilee edition.*

Plate 468. *Cigarette cards from Wills.*

Plate 469. *Twelve cigarette cards of the Royal Family.*

Reign.`

Weekly Illustrated (Plate 466), shows the Duke and Duchess of York and the Duke and Duchess of Kent leaving St. Paul's after the service, accompanied by the Princesses Elizabeth and Margaret Rose. *The Sketch* has a colourful front cover of St. Paul's with a young lady selling toys on a tray. The *Daily Mail* (Plate 467) printed their Jubilee Issue in silver showing the King on horseback and the Queen wearing a toque.

Cigarette cards played an important part in the life of the nation and several packs covered the Jubilee. Wills provided cards for the King's reign and shown are three from their album – The King and Queen in a state carriage going to open South Africa House in June 1933; the King meeting those playing cricket at a Test Match at Lords in June 1934, and the Opening of the Mersey Tunnel in July 1934 (Plate 468).

The International Tobacco Overseas Co. Limited of London issued a set of one hundred cigarette cards. Shown in Plate 469 are the King and Queen riding in the miniature railway at the Empire Exhibition 1924, the King laying a wreath at the Cenotaph, the King decorating soldiers, the

Plate 470. *Six cigarette cards from the Ardath set.*

Plate 471. *Four cigarette cards of the Royal Family.*

Plate 472. *Portrait of Princess Victoria of Wales by John Ernest Breuen.*

Plate 473. *Royal Doulton loving cup to record the death of the King.*

QUEEN ADORN THE COFFIN

KING EDWARD FOLLOWED BY HIS BR

Plate 474. *Pages from the* Daily Telegraph *of the King's funeral.*

Plate 475. *Linen 'In Memoriam' cloth.*

King visiting a child in Great Ormond Street Hospital, the King's four sons in full uniform, the King recuperating after his illness with the Queen at Bognor, the King and Queen at a Maundy Service, the King and Queen at the Delhi Durbar, the Queen inspecting troops, the King making his Christmas Broadcast, the King and Queen at the Garter ceremony, Queen Victoria, King Edward VII, King George V and Prince Edward of Wales.

Ardath issued a set of cigarette cards showing members of the Royal Family seldom recorded. Plate 470 shows the Duke and Duchess of Kent, three photographs of the Princess Royal and the Earl of Harewood.

A different set (Plate 471) shows the Earl of Athlone, brother of Queen Mary and Princess Alice of Albany, his wife, Lady May Abel Smith, a daughter of the Marquis of Cambridge, another brother of Queen Mary, and her children.

The Death of the King

The King was greatly upset by the death of his unmarried sister, Princess Victoria, who died on 3rd December, 1935. There is practically nothing of a commemorative nature for Princess Victoria, although her name does appear on a medal struck for the King and Queen's visit to Cardiff in 1907 and there is an original painting (Plate 472) by John Ernest Breuen, of the Princess in which she is described as 'HRH Victoria of Wales, Daughter of Albert Edward, Prince of Wales and Alexandra'.

The history of this portrait is that it was commissioned by Queen Victoria in 1900, completed in 1901, hung in Windsor Castle until 1911 and was then removed to Marlborough House. It was given to one of the Ladies-in-Waiting of the Court in 1937, on whose death it was given to her maid and sold on her death to a dealer in North Wales.

The famous bulletin, 'The King's life is drawing peacefully to its close', was composed by Queen Mary with the assistance of Viscount Dawson of Penn, the King's doctor. The King died quietly on 20th January 1936, in the presence of Queen Mary and their children.

Very little has been recorded for his death. One cream-coloured loving cup (Plate 473) is entitled 'A Royal Exemplar' and the title could hardly be more fitting. It was published by Royal Doulton and has on the front a portrait of the King surrounded by green laurel wreaths, surmounted by the words: 'King George V, a Royal Exemplar'. On the reverse are the words: 'The Friend of his People, so long as the history of the British Empire is written, his name will be recorded with gratitude' and the dates, '1910-1936'. It is edged with silver around the top, inside the lid and also around the base, this may be to acknowledge the silver jubilee which he had just celebrated.

National Magazine gave full coverage of the death of the King and of the state funeral which followed. Three pictures from the *Daily Telegraph* (Plate 474) show, on the right, the new King Edward VIII and his three brothers, the Dukes of York, Gloucester and Kent, walking behind the coffin. On the left is the coffin on the gun carriage and below this, foreign royalty and dignitaries following behind. A framed linen cloth (Plate 475) carries a portrait of the late King with the dates of his birth and death, his titles and the inscription 'In Memoriam'.

CHAPTER 5

'Prince Charming'

The eldest son of the Duke of York was born at York Cottage, Sandringham, on 23rd June 1894. He received the names of Edward, from his grandfather, Albert after his great-grandfather and Christian, after his other grandfather, together with each of the patron saints of England, Wales, Scotland and Ireland: George, Andrew, Patrick and David. He was always known to his family as David and to the public as Edward.

Little exists to commemorate this important birth. A handsome loving cup (Plate 476) of art nouveau design commemorates the event. In the centre is the rose of England surrounded by the inscription 'Prince Edward of York' and the date, 1894, together with the quotation 'Bryght Be The Stars on the Eve of St John, Luckie the Babe That Is Born Thereon'. He was born on the eve of the feast of St John the Baptist.

A ribbon plate (Plate 477C), probably made in Germany, has in the centre the young Prince, about two years of age, in a blue sailor suit with the words above: 'Prince Edward of Wales', and below: 'Our Future King'. This is incorrect because he was not Edward, Prince of Wales, but Prince Edward of York.

He went to Osborne and then on to Dartmouth. A small parian bust of the head and shoulders of the Prince in naval uniform, mounted on a plinth, bears the arms of the City of London. It was published by Aldwych China for Samuels of the Strand in London. A small tin for pen-nibs has the Prince in naval cadet uniform in the central oval – the two small anchors would indicate that this was contemporaneous with his naval cadetship.

The Investiture

Prince Edward appears on several of the commemorative mugs which were made for the coronation of King George V. But it was his historic investiture at Caernarvon Castle which resulted in several commemoratives being made.

Caernarvon Castle was selected, as it was the castle where King Edward I first presented his eldest son to the people of Wales with ceremony. Largely at the instigation of David

Plate 476. *Art nouveau loving cup to commemorate the birth of Prince Edward of York.*

Plate 477A. *Plate for the investiture, by Trent Pottery.* **B.** *Kneeling figure of the Prince at his investiture.* **C.** *Ribbon plate – Prince Edward.*

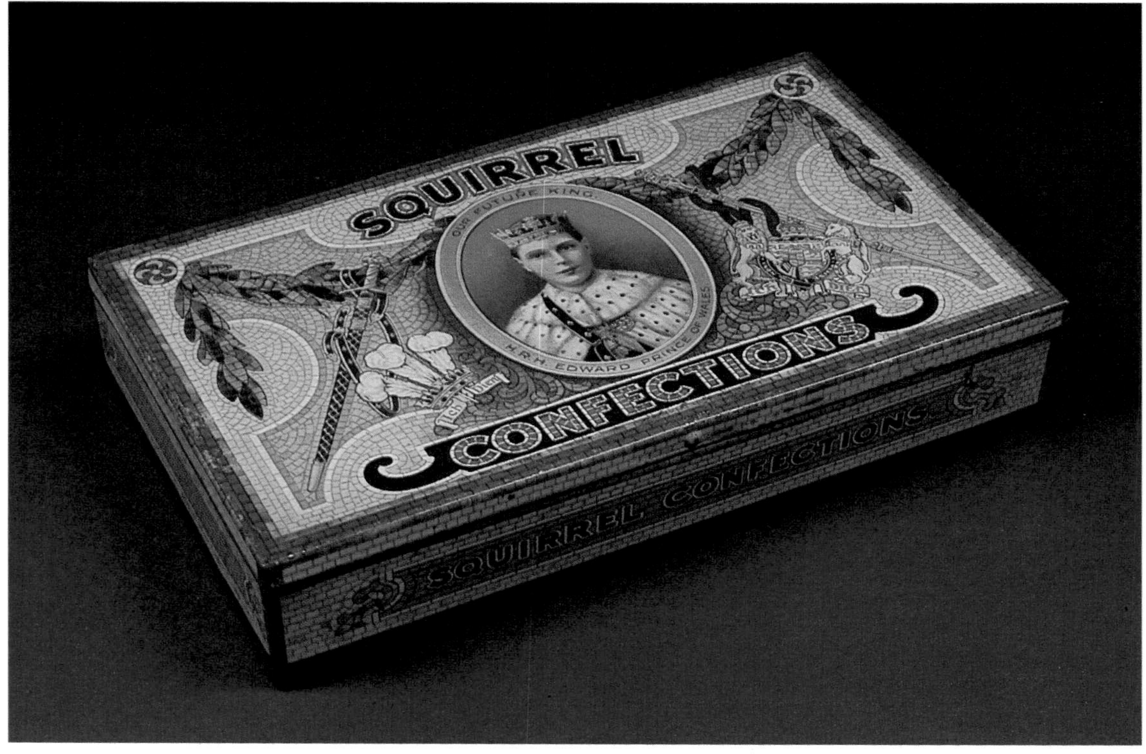

Plate 478. *Squirrel Confections tin for the investiture.*

Plate 479A. *Compact with head and shoulders of the Prince.* ***B.*** *Cardiff investiture mug.*

Plate 480A. *'Our Prince' parian figure, 1922.* ***B.*** *Crested figure of the Prince as a naval cadet.* ***C.*** *'Coming of Age' tin.* ***D.*** *Crested china figure of the Prince in Guards' uniform.*

Plate 481A. *Edmonstons toffee tin.* ***B.*** *Lovells toffee tin.*

Lloyd George, the King consented that an investiture should take place at this famous Welsh castle.

A colourful oblong tin was made by Squirrel Confections (Plate 478). The centre has a head and shoulders portrait of the Prince in an oval wearing his ermine mantle and his princely crown with the sash and the sword over his shoulder, headed 'Our Future King' and underneath, 'HRH Prince of Wales'. Within a swag of laurel, on the left, is the sword itself with the Prince of Wales' feathers and, on the right, the sceptre with the royal coat of arms bearing the heraldic label of the eldest son.

Other commemorative pieces include a plate from Trent Pottery of Staffordshire (Plate 477A). It has a bright blue border and within the centre the Prince of Wales as midshipman, surmounted by his feathers and recording his investiture by His Imperial Majesty, King George V. Below are the royal arms of Wales surmounted by the Prince's feathers and the Welsh motto 'Cymru am Byth'.

The same portrait is shown on a mug (Plate 479B) which was specially made for the City of Cardiff and commissioned by James Howells, the well-known Cardiff draper. It was published by Royal Wintonia and made at Grimwades, Stoke-on-Trent. The reverse shows the Cardiff coat of arms, with the words: 'City of Cardiff, Presented by the Lord Mayor to all the Children of the City'. This was a free gift and although these mugs can still be obtained because there are many families in Cardiff whose children received them, the price has soared from what would have been about six pence in 1911.

Caernarvon itself provided a small cream figure (Plate 477B) of the Prince of Wales in his robes with the Caernarvon coat of arms and the Welsh motto beneath it. It was published by Duchess China. A small needle tin was produced (Plate 504).

Victoria China produced a small ornament with the Prince of Wales in the centre, surmounted by two Welsh dragons and the Welsh motto and the date of the investiture. Investiture commemoratives are comparatively rare.

Plate 482A. *Pewter box – 'Prince of Sport'.* ***B.*** *Chocolate tin for the Wembley Exhibition, 1924.* ***C.*** *Plate for the Prince's visit to Canada, 1919.*

Plate 483. Tin for the Wembley Exhibition.

The War Years

At the outbreak of war he was desperately anxious to serve his country and was gazetted in the Grenadier Guards. But the government and, in particular, Lord Kitchener were not anxious for the heir to the throne to play any active part in the field. This caused the Prince much resentment. A full-length figure of the Prince of Wales in Guards uniform (Plate 480D) stands on a plinth, with the City of London coat of arms.

In 1915 the young Prince came of age and this event is commemorated, it would appear, only by a tea tin made by Lyons (Plate 480C). On the front is a portrait of the Prince within laurel leaves surmounted by the Welsh dragon and his dates: 1894-1915. On one side of the tin are the words 'Our Empire' comprising a list of the dominions and the colonies which formed the Empire. On the other side there are two Union Jacks surmounted by a crown and on the reverse is a large oval with a red background surrounded by a gold wreath surmounted by the words 'Lyons Tea'.

There is a later, very large tin by Edmonstons Toffee which, although it bears no date, is clearly meant to indicate the fact that he was Prince of Wales. On the front is a very large medallion of the Prince of Wales wearing a lounge suit surrounded by gold leaves surmounted by the crown and the words: 'Ich Dien – I Serve'. On one side there is an oval picture of a Pass at Aberglaskyn and below of Llangollen and Castle Dinas. On the other side, again in a large oval, is Caernarvon Castle surmounted by the Welsh dragon with the Welsh motto. On a further side the large oval of Aberystwyth shows the sea, the seafront and below that, Chester Cathedral from the southwest, probably included because the Prince was Earl of Chester.

After the war the Prince made frequent visits abroad, and was regarded as the best ambassador that Great Britain could possibly have. Debonair, young and boyish looking, everybody adored him. He had developed an interesting taste in clothes. He disliked formal wear and was anxious to show flair by the use of large patterns in bright colours. King George V did not wholly approve – thinking them rather vulgar. He liked flannel trousers, 'bags' as they were called, and wore turn-ups. He also liked sports coats and plus-fours. He is featured in an elegant, full-length parian figure (Plate 480A), entitled 'Our Prince', wearing a top hat and morning coat with a bow tie and a cane. It was sculpted by P. Brown Baker in 1922.

On the other side of the tin referred to in the reign of King George V (Plate 446A), bearing a portrait of the Princess Royal, Princess Mary, as a nurse, is a portrait of the young Prince of Wales wearing a top hat and headed with the words 'Prince and Comrade'. This was probably made either after or during the First World War.

An unmarked biscuit tin (Plate 504) shows the Prince in naval uniform on a red and gold background. This was the Prince the people loved. In the four panels are the Taj Mahal, the Parliament Buildings of Ottawa, Cape Town and Table Mountain and Sydney Harbour.

Exhibitions

The great Wembley Exhibition of 1924 was an event in which the Prince of Wales and his brother, the Duke of York, took an active interest. They were both joint presidents. Many commemorative items were issued for this exhibition featuring the Prince.

There is a small chocolate tin (Plate 482B) with, in the centre, a coloured portrait of the Prince of Wales in an informal suit, on the right hand side a colourful bridge and gondola with the words: 'Australia, India, West Indies, Palestine, Malaya and Burma'. On the other side is a large building which was constructed as one of the pavilions with the words: 'Canada, New Zealand, British Guinea, South Africa, Bermuda and Malta' and underneath the Prince of Wales' portrait is the motif of the exhibition, the British Lion. The base reads 'Souvenir of the British Exhibition, Wembley, London 1924. Manufactured by Rowntrees & Co of York'.

A cup and saucer (Plate 453D) depicts in oval medallions the Prince of Wales and the Duke of York headed 'Presidents of the British Empire Exhibition in 1924'. The handle of the mug is in the shape of the exhibition's lion and is black and white printed.

Another tin (Plate 483) shows seven scenes, The Imperial Stadium on the front and the Pavilions of South Africa, India, Australia, New Zealand and Canada. Each are in cartouches with their national emblems together with the oriental bridges. The lid carries, in an oval cartouche, the head and shoulders of the Prince with two sprigs of oak leaves. Though it is a registered design there is no indication as to who published it or what it contained, it was probably for tea, coffee or sweets.

The Prince opened the North East Coast Exhibition in Newcastle-upon-Tyne in 1929. A cup and saucer (Plate 484B) shows the Exhibition buildings which had been

Plate 484A. *Cremona tin.* **B.** *Cup and saucer for the Newcastle Exhibition, 1929.*

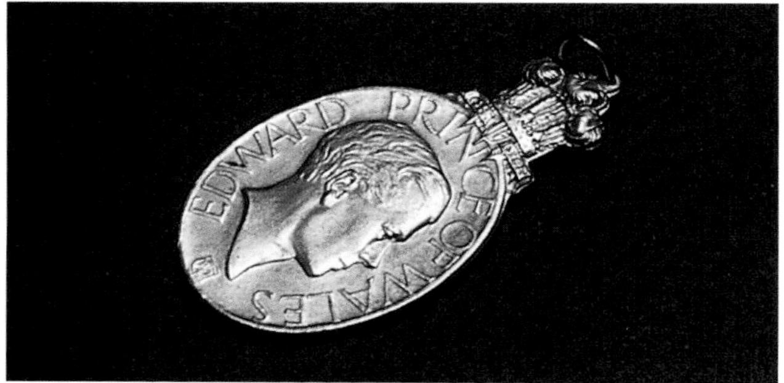

Plate 485. *Medallion for the visit to India, 1921.*

Plate 486A.(below) *Plate for the Royal Arsenal Exhibition at Woolwich.* **B.** *Mug for the visit to Egremont, 1927.* **C.** *Prince of Wales playing cards for the National Relief Fund.* **D.** *Plate for the visit to South Africa, 1924.*

***Plate 487.* (opposite centre right)** *Paper programme for visit to Hastings, 1927.*

Plate 488. *Radio personalites – cigarette cards produced by W.D. & H.O. Wills.*

Plate 489. *Film stars – Player's cigarette cards.*

Plate 490. *Motor cars – Player's cigarette cards.*

Plate 491. *Tin for Madeleine Carroll.*

Plate 492. *Tin for Gracie Fields.*

specially erected for the occasion; and on the cup the Prince smoking a cigarette in uniform. King George V thoroughly disapproved of the Prince's habit of smoking.

A tin (Plate 484A) for the same event was made by A.S. Wilkins for Cremona, Newcastle-upon-Tyne. On the front is a very colourful detailed drawing of the actual exhibition grounds and in the left hand corner the young Prince wearing a black top hat and a morning coat with a silk border, fashionable at that time.

Official Visits

His first official visit after the war was to Canada. He laid the corner stone of the Victory Tower of the Parliament Buildings, Ottawa, on 1st September 1919, the third 1st September on which such a ceremony was enacted. King Edward VII laid the original stone in 1860 and the Duke of Connaught again in 1916 after the Parliament Buildings had been burned. This day is also Labour Day in Canada. Later he inspected a parade of over 5,000 War Veterans. A plate (Plate 482C) has an engaging portrait of the young Prince wearing a trilby hat and a grey suit on a background of maple leaves in colour.

His visit to India in 1921 does not seem to have been ceramically recorded. However there is a silver pendant (Plate 485), struck for the visit. It bears on the front the head of the young Prince, surrounded by the words 'Edward, Prince of Wales', and 'The Visit of His Royal Highness, Bombay 1921'. Despite the boycott of Gandhi, this visit was a great success, the Prince charmed them all and made a triumphant entrance into Delhi.

The Prince visited the Royal Arsenal Exhibition at Woolwich under the auspices of the Co-operative Society. A plate (Plate 486A) has the head and shoulders of the Prince in Guards' uniform, beneath which is an inscription describing the event.

He also visited South Africa. A plate (Plate 486D) has the Prince in naval uniform within a laurel wreath surmounted by the Prince of Wales feathers and the date, 1925. The bottom of the plate has a much larger set of his feathers.

On 29th June, 1927 he visited Egremont, in Cumberland and a mug (Plate 486B) commemorates this event showing another portrait the Prince liked, in this case wearing his Welsh Guards' uniform. Many of the visits he made were commemorated by mugs or plates bearing either this portrait of him or the one in which he is smoking.

An unusual object is a commemorative powder compact (Plate 479A) which carries an attractive portrait of the boyish

Plate 493A. *Charlie Chaplin statuette.* ***B.*** *Laurel and Hardy pepper and salt.*

Prince of Wales in military uniform, but without a cap.

On Wednesday 6th April 1927, he visited Hastings. The commemorative programme for the visit (Plate 487), bearing the head and shoulders of the handsome Prince in a lounge suit, is surrounded by the anthem 'God Bless the Prince of Wales'. The programme is embellished with flags and the royal flowers.

In August 1932 he went over to France to unveil the memorial at Thiepval to the thousands of British troops who fell at the Battle of the Somme. The Prince had always taken a great deal of interest in military matters and it is a pity that there is no ceramic record of this important event.

An indication of the Prince's interest in ex-servicemen's organisations can be seen on a pack of cards (Plate 486C) entitled 'The Prince of Wales Relief Fund' set up at the beginning of the war. In the centre of the cards are the Prince of Wales' featheres and above them the crown surmounted by the British Lion and on each side, the Union Jack.

The Prince frequently visited Wales and, in particular, Cardiff. There are few ceramic records of these visits. Paper souvenir programmes exist which show his opening of the laboratories of the University College of Cardiff and also his unveiling of the national war memorial in Cathays Park. The Prince opened this memorial on 13th June 1928. There is a plate (Plate 403) portraying the actual memorial which now stands in Cathays Park. The designer of this great national memorial was Sir Ninian Comper, a well-known architect of the period.

Entertainment and Sport

This was the age of radio, the motor car and film stars, and thank heaven for cigarette cards (Plates 488, 489 and 490) which made most interesting ephemera and are a marvellous example and record of the events which took place during the period.

Madeleine Carroll, the Princess Flavia in *The Prisoner of Zenda*, is featured on a small tin (Plate 491) with a blue background. Gracie Fields ('Our Gracie' of *Sally, Sing as we Go* and *Queen of Hearts*) is featured on a tin (Plate 492) with a sepia portrait. Charlie Chaplin is featured on a plaster bust, with baggy trousers, bowler hat, moustache and cane. Those two great comedians Stan Laurel and Oliver Hardy are pepper and salt cellars on a tray, produced by Beswick Ware. Olly is the salt, Stan the pepper.

The Prince of Wales was properly described as the Prince of Sport. He took an interest in every sport and caused great consternation when he participated in steeplechasing and point to point.

England and Australia were prominent in cricket at this time, and John Player produced an album for cigarette cards 'The Cricketers'. Shown here (Plate 494) is one page with T.W. Goddard, A.R. Glover, Wally Hammond – the great Gloucester captain, Joseph Hardstaff Jnr., Len Hutton – the great Yorkshire captain subsequently knighted, and James Langridge. Signed cricket bags and scorecards are also sought after by cricket buffs.

Ceramic mugs recording cricketers are keenly collected. One shows George Hirst (Plate 495) – Yorkshire's celebrated all round cricketer, and on the reverse Wilfred Rhodes, Yorkshire's celebrated bowler. Another shows Lancashire's celebrated cricketers – Tydesley and R.H. Spooner. Herbert Sutcliffe, world record maker, is shown on a mug (Plate 496) published for Pudsey Corporation, with their coat of arms 'Be just and fear not', and indicates test records. The other side shows his father, W. Sutcliffe, who was 'the old Dacre Banks and Pudsey St. Lawrence Cricketer'.

Another mug (Plate 497A) is for Hedley Verity –

Plate 494. *Cricketers – Player's cigarette cards.*

Plate 495A. Mug – George Hirst. B. Plate – Wilfred Rhodes.

Plate 496. Mug for Sutcliffe, father and son.

Plate 497A. Mug for Hedley Verity. B. Salt and pepper set – Hobbs and Tate.

Plate 498A. Pair of plaques – Hobbs and Tate. B. Signed Australian team, 1930.

Plate 499. Paper programme for the visit of the Prince of Wales to Cardiff – Silver Jubilee, 1935.

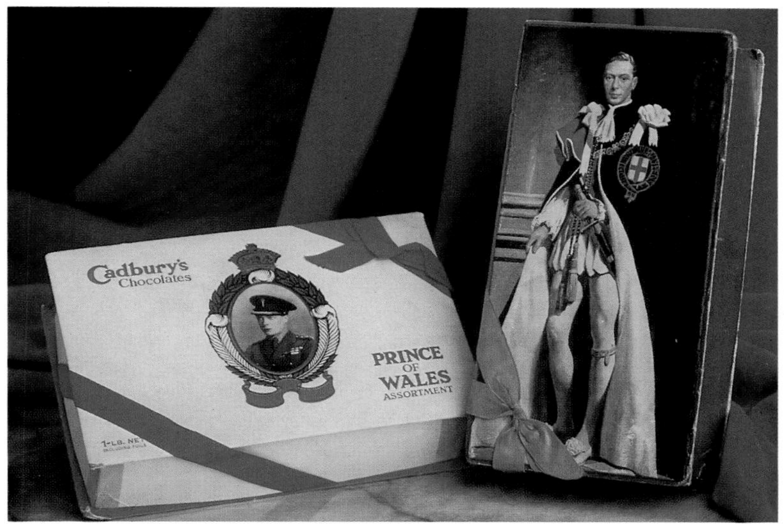

Plate 500. *Prince of Wales chocolate assortment.*

Plate 501. *Accession tin, 1936.*

Plate 502. *Paragon coronation plate and mug.*

England's famous spin bowler. On the reverse it reads: 'record bowling by Hedley Verity, against the Australians at (Lords) June 23rd and June 25th 1934. 15 wickets for 104, 7 wickets for 61, first innings. 8 wickets for 43 second innings. Other notable performances 17 wickets for 91 in one day against Essex at Leyton, July 14th 1933. 10 wickets for 36 at Leeds against Warwickshire, May 18th 1931 (including the 'Hat-trick'). 10 wickets for 10 at Leeds against Notts, July 12th 1932. The latter performance creating a world record 19.4 overs, 16 maidens, 10 runs and 10 wickets'.

There is a pair of fine plaques (Plate 498A) – one of Jack Hobbs coming out of Lords Pavilion, and one of Don Bradman in action. Both Hobbs and Bradman were subsequently knighted.

A salt and pepper set (Plate 497B) depicts Jack Hobbs in action (the salt) and Maurice Tate bowling (the pepper).

A pewter cigar box (Plate 482A) with a portrait of the Prince of Wales smoking his favourite cigarette is marked 'The Prince of Sport'.

The Silver Jubilee and the Accession

This handsome Prince, who was so interested in everything in his country, took part in so many activities, visited so many places, had such a keen sense of fashion and lived the life of the time, was still unmarried. He played a prominent part in the celebrations for the Jubilee of his father and his mother, the King and Queen, in 1935.

He represented the King for the Silver Jubilee celebrations in Cardiff on 11th May 1935. A programme for the visit (Plate 499) contains a three-quarter length portrait of the Prince in Welsh Guards' uniform and, in a wreath of laurel and oak leaves, portraits of the King and Queen. The programme is embellished with Union Jacks with silver motifs. It ends 'This Souvenir was compiled as briefly and as accurately as possible "God Save The King"'. Cadbury's produced a Prince of Wales assortment (Plate 500), featuring the Prince wearing Welsh Guards' uniform in a laurel wreath cartouche.

The Prince continued to carry out his duties until he learnt in January 1936 that his father lay dying in Sandringham.

On the death of his father he ascended the throne, though not as King David, but as King Edward VIII. His accession has been recorded in ceramic and on a tin (Plate 501) which shows, on the lid, Buckingham Palace, The Queen Victoria Memorial and one of the Guards Bands watched by members of the public with the Royal Standard flying over the Palace. There is a portrait of the new King's head and shoulders wearing military uniform with the ribbon of the garter, stars and medals, wearing a plumed hat, and on each side on a gold background, surmounted by a crown, the words 'Edward VIII Accession to the Throne 1936' and also his titles.

The nation was looking forward to a glorious coronation. The people were unaware of what had been going on behind the scenes, unless they happened to read the gossip papers from America. The Prince had formed an association with Mrs Simpson, a woman once divorced and about to be divorced for the second time.

Arrangements for the coronation proceeded and it was fixed for 12th May, 1937. A very large number of commemoratives was issued for this forthcoming event. Many of these are still available and should become, in the future, collectors' pieces because they were produced for a coronation which in fact never took place. At the moment they are in plentiful supply.

Paragon published a large plate (Plate 502), highly coloured as was their custom. The centre shows the lion and the unicorn, both holding the royal standard and the motto of the garter surmounted by a crown. The signature of the designer, J.A. Robinson, is shown and around the rim are the words 'Edward VIII, King and Emperor' and his Imperial cypher 'EIR Crowned May 12th, 1937'. The rim is in gold and on the reverse is the Paragon sign – 'A special souvenir in paragon china to celebrate the coronation'.

Paragon made a number of pieces in different sizes, including cups and saucers and mugs. They normally have gilt handles, sometimes in buff colour, are all highly decorative and carry the royal standard and various flags. It is noticeable that, as in the case of the Paragon plate of the Silver Jubilee of King George V, there is no portrait of the King.

Some of the commemoratives were in the art deco style. A jug (Plate 503) with a narrow neck made by Crown Devon and designed by Charlotte Rhead, had a geometrical design around the base and the rim in red, white and blue, with the inscription 'EVIIIR 1937'.

Coronet Ware published a biscuit barrel (Plate 503) in the shape of a caravan, showing on the lid underneath the caravan chimney a portrait of the King, above which is the date of the coronation.

A well-known artist of the period, Dame Laura Knight, published several mugs (Plate 503) with different designs for Woods Ivory Ware. They bear in the centre a portrait of the uncrowned King with royal flowers in colour and an elephant and other exotic beasts on either side. The royal coat of arms and lion and unicorn are also included in the design.

An interesting pink beaker (Plate 503) made by Johnson Bros. of England took a bit of a risk because this shows a white portrait of the King in relief actually wearing the crown, which he never did.

A tin (Plate 504), unmarked, goes even further. It portrays the King in full coronation robes and wearing the state crown. In colour, the King stands full length wearing the white silk stockings he so despised at his investiture. The background is bright red and is embellished with a design of gold, the crown being the central motif.

Cadbury's manufactured boxes of chocolates entitled 'King Edward VIII Chocolates', bearing his head surmounted by a crown (Plate 504).

Another tea tin (Plate 504), with no mark recorded, has the head and shoulders of the King, uncrowned, in military uniform on a petunia coloured background. Buckingham Palace and Windsor Castle are on each of the two sides, and the design includes the King's monogram and the national symbols.

Peak Freen and Co. produced a similar biscuit tin (Plate 505) for both Edward VIII and George VI, both manufactured by Hudson, Scott and Son. That for Edward VIII bears on its hinged lid a portrait of the King in garter

Plate 503. (Left to right). *Abdication green art deco jug; Johnson's pink beaker; caravan biscuit barrel; Laura Knight mug; Charlotte Rhead jug.*

Plate 504. *Three coronation tins: Cadbury's chocolate box; small plaster statuette and Investiture needle tin.*

Plate 505. *Peak Freen coronation tin.*

Plate 507. *Crown Devon abdication mug.*

Plate 506. (Left to right). *Windsor and Bovey beakers; Stanley plate; Empire china teapot.*

Plate 508. *Framed envelope for the wedding of the Duke and Duchess of Windsor.*

Plate 510. *'In Memoriam' plate for the Duke of Gloucester.*

Plate 509. *'In Memoriam' plate for the Duke of Windsor and tankard with a portrait of the Duchess.*

robes, the side portrays scenes from the four dominions – sheep from Australia, ostriches from South Africa, cattle from Canada, each showing horse riders in jodhpurs and trilby hats and a fine scene from India portraying elephants in a ceremonial procession. The tin for George VI bears on the hinged lid photographs of the King and Queen, attributed to Speaight Ltd. There are also, on this tin, portraits of the two princesses taken by Marcus Adams and pictures of ships of the Royal Navy.

Abdication

The King was never crowned because on 10th December, 1936, in the presence of his three brothers, he signed his abdication. This was taken to the House of Commons and read by the Prime Minister, Stanley Baldwin.

A plaster bust (Plate 504), modelled by G.N. Morowon features the Prince. An art deco teapot, produced by Empire in cream (Plate 506), has the King in a central cartouche with royal supporters and flags for the coronation. A gold rim is on the spout, lid and pot and around the handle.

Windsor China produced a beaker (Plate 506), the handle art deco with an orange decorated line, the rim with a blue band and the base with a blue and orange band. The portrait of the uncrowned King is surrounded by national flags and the royal flowers including the daffodil. Bovey Pottery had a similar beaker (Plate 506), with art deco handle, the portrait is different but one of those used for the Coronation. The King's uncrowned head faces left in profile and it is in a cartouche gold wreath. Added later on the reverse are the words 'Souvenir of his Abdication, December 10th 1936'. The base is in the form of a barrel.

For the abdication there are not many commemorative pieces, many of the commemorative items for the coronation were in fact altered. One such jug (Plate 503) is in a green art deco style, bearing the uncrowned portrait of the King surrounded by national flags, above which are the dates of the coronation and underneath, 'Abdicated December 11th 1936'. This date is an error.

Stanley China used one of their coronation souvenirs by adding 'Proclaimed January 23rd 1936 – Abdicated December 10th 1936', on the cup and plate. The cup has an interesting handle in the shape of the Union Jack.

Devon Pottery used their beaker with an art deco handle by adding 'Souvenir of his Abdication December 10th 1936'.

One mug was exclusively produced for the abdication by Crown Devon (Plate 507). It is a cream mug bearing in relief, also in cream and blended into the mug itself, the uncrowned portrait of the King and around the rim the dates of his accession and his abdication.

On 3rd June, 1937, at the Château de Conde, Prince Edward, now created Duke of Windsor, was married to Mrs Simpson. No member of the Royal Family was present and only a few of the King's friends, as well as those of Mrs Simpson, attended. There are two known ceramic pieces to record this event, although they are extremely difficult to find.

There is, however, an envelope (Plate 508) bearing portraits of the Duke of Windsor and Mrs Simpson, who had reverted to her original name of Warfield, in the clothes they wore at the wedding and described in French. The date marked is '3rd June 1937 at 12 heures'. The stamp for 1F 50c depicts the International Exhibition with the words 'Paris, 1937'.

Plate 511. *Coalport 'In Memoriam' plate.*

Death of the Duke of Windsor

The marriage was never recognised by the Royal Family and Queen Mary would never receive the Duchess of Windsor. The Duke lived the life of an exile, although for a short period as Governor of Bermuda he was given some authority. He received a visit from the Queen in 1972 and a week later, just short of his seventy-eighth birthday, he died. The Queen was anxious that his funeral should be in accordance with that expected of a former sovereign and arrangements were made for him to lie in State in St George's Chapel, Windsor, which he did for four days, and many thousands filed past his coffin.

The Duchess stayed with the Queen at Buckingham Palace. It is said that the funeral itself was planned in detail by the Duke. His wish to be buried at Frogmore was fulfilled. The plate on his coffin reads 'HRH Edward Albert Christian George Andrew Patrick David, Duke of Windsor born 1894 died 1972, King Edward VIII 20th January to 11th December, 1936'.

There are very few commemoratives for his death. A plate published by Panorama Studios (Plate 509) shows a portrait of the elderly Duke surrounded by laurel leaves surmounted by a crown with his titles and his dates and, in large gold letters, 'In Memoriam'. On the reverse are details of his life and a quotation from Shakespeare's *Richard II* which reads as follows:

'I give this heavy weight from off my head
And this unwieldy sceptre from my hand
The Pride of Kingley sway from out of my heart
With mine own tears I wash away my balm

Plate 512. *J. & J. May 'In Memoriam' mug for the Duchess of Windsor; Wilton of Dorincourt mug with portraits of the Duke and Duchess.*

With mine own hands I give away my crown
With mine own tongue deny my sacred state
With mine own breath release all duty's rights'.

This plate is a pair to a similar one produced in 1974 for the death of the Duke of Gloucester (Plate 510) who was the last surviving member of the House of Windsor of that generation. This plate contains a central portrait of the head of the Duke in the same design as that of the Duke of Windsor, giving his full names and titles. As far as is known this is one of the very few commemoratives ever issued for the Duke of Gloucester.

Coalport produced a fine quality porcelain plate (Plate 511) limited to one thousand with, on a purple border embellished with gold, three portraits of the head of the King in gold, and in the centre the Duke's arms surmounted by angels. In between is the crown which is surmounted by laurel leaves. At the base, his dates and his name and on the reverse there is the following quotation: 'In this Prince there will descend qualities of courage, of simplicity and sympathy, and above all sincerity, qualities rare and precious which might have made his reign glorious in the annals of this ancient monarchy'. Winston S. Churchill.

A memorial tankard by Mercian China shows, for the first time on any commemorative piece, both the Duke and the Duchess (Plate 509). It is in black and white and funereal in style. There follow details of his title and names and the date of his birth and death and the quotation from *Richard II*.

The Duchess of Windsor went into total seclusion after the death of the Duke and died at the age of 89 years on the 24th April, 1986. The Queen arranged for her to be buried next to her husband in Frogmore and the silver plate on her English oak coffin was inscribed simply, 'Wallis, Duchess of Windsor 1896-1986'.

Though hardly recorded ceramically in life, the death of the Duchess has been remembered. A mug (Plate 512) to remember her death has been published by J. & J. May, the commemorators. The mug is of bone china decorated in royal purple and black and the design is the authentic reconstruction of the art deco designs of 1936. The inscription reads 'Wallis, Duchess of Windsor' with the details of her dates of birth, marriage and death. Within the details of the cartouche, taken from the title of Duchess' own book, is the epitaph 'Her Heart Had Its Reasons'. The handle and the rim are suitably embellished with black enamel.

In death they have both been remembered. A permanent ceramic record was published by Wilton of Dorincourt (Plate 512), which is a charity for the mentally disabled. It bears a well-known photograph of the Duke and Duchess in a cartouche surmounted by the ducal coronet of strawberry leaves with the British and American flags swathed by a purple mourning symbol of scroll and honour. On the right of the Duke are his titles and dates. On the left are those of the Duchess indicating that she was born on 19th June, 1896 at Blue Ridge Summit, USA

CHAPTER 6

King George VI and Queen Elizabeth 1936-1952

No ceramic record appears to exist for the Duke of York before his marriage. Nothing for his birth, nothing for his childhood, and nothing, it appears, for the part he played in the Battle of Jutland.

His marriage to Lady Elizabeth Bowes Lyon, daughter of the Earl and Countess of Strathmore of Glamis Castle, took place on 26th April, 1923. A small chocolate tin (Plate 513) with contemporary photographs of the Duke and Duchess surrounded by national flags was made by Rowntree. In the centre, between the two portraits, are the arms of the City of Cardiff, and on the base an inscription: 'Presented by HRH the Duke of York'. It may well be that other cities and towns received similar tins of chocolate.

An unmarked tin (Plate 514) for the wedding is in purple and shows on one side the Duke, head and shoulders in naval uniform and on the other side the Duchess, wearing a necklace of pearls. On a third side is York Minster and on the fourth, Glamis Castle. York Minster was clearly chosen because, although the wedding took place at Westminster Abbey, the Duke held the title of Duke of York. The lid has a central motif of a wreath of roses in the middle of which are the letters 'A' and 'E' surmounted by the royal crown.

The national magazines covered this marriage and *The Illustrated London News* had a 'wedding number' (Plate 515).

On 21st April 1926 Princess Elizabeth was born and to commemorate this event there is a teaset by Paragon China made especially for HRH the Duchess of York to honour the birth (Plate 516). The decoration is of two magpies and sprigs of roses with the words 'Two for Joy' surrounded by a turquoise border. Princess Elizabeth was christened Elizabeth Alexandra Mary, Elizabeth after her mother, Alexandra after her great-grandmother, and Mary after her grandmother.

An octagonal plate published by Paragon China Co bears a portrait from a photograph by Marcus Adams of the Princess at about two years of age. This plate was probably manufactured later. An attractive porcelain figure (Plate 517) published by Tuscan China and potted by Plant entitled 'HRH Princess Elizabeth' shows the young Princess carrying a teddy bear.

Crown Devon published a teaset. The saucer has, in the centre, surrounded by a motif of gold foliage, the head of Princess Elizabeth. The same is shown on the side of the cup. It is in art deco style with snow glaze finish. Around the lip

Plate 513. *Chocolate tin for Cardiff for the marriage of the Duke of York to Lady Elizabeth Bowes Lyon, 1923.*

Plate 514. *Unmarked royal wedding tin.*

Plate 515.(left) *Front cover of* The Illustrated London News *wedding edition.*

Plate 516. *Paragon cup, saucer and plate for the birth of Princess Elizabeth, 1926.*

of the saucer and the cup are art deco designs of orange, black and gold check spots. The same head appears on a mug for Crown Ducal (Plate 517), the base bearing her date of birth. Similar mugs carry a portrait of Princess Margaret Rose from a photograph by Marcus Adams. Another mug has the small head of the Princess within a gold wreath surmounted by a coronet, a gold rim around the top, it has no maker's mark.

Cadbury's of Bourneville produced chocolates (Plate 518) in a box of pale blue, with the description 'Princess Elizabeth Chocolates'.

On 21st August, 1929 Princess Margaret Rose was born at

Plate 517. *Crown Devon cup and saucer; Tuscan china figure of Princess Elizabeth; Crown Ducal mug.*

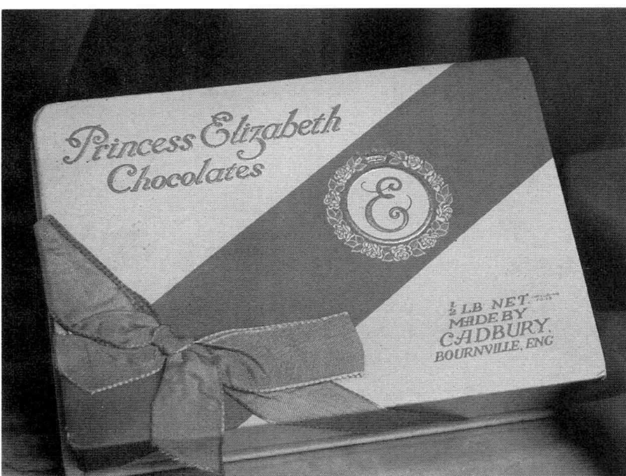

Plate 518. *Princess Elizabeth chocolates.*

Glamis Castle. Paragon produced a teaset (Plate 519) for this event. The theme here is budgerigars with flowers on a cream coloured background.

A small powder compact exists of Princess Margaret shown at the age of about six months holding a rattle and wearing a white bonnet and white dress from a photograph by Marcus Adams (Plate 520).

Official Visits

The Duke and Duchess of York carried out many public engagements. The first was their visit to Australia sailing in HMS *Renown* on 6th January, 1927. A tin entitled 'Halls Duchess Assortment' for Brothers Whitefield Ltd, of Manchester, is a souvenir of the visit (Plate 521). The very colourful lid shows portraits of the Duke in naval uniform and the Duchess wearing the tiara which was a wedding gift from her father, the Earl of Strathmore. Above the portrait is the coat of arms of Australia together with national flags. HMS *Renown* is pictured at sea.

Bushell's of Australia provided a tin of Blue Label Tea, one pound net. It bears three-quarter length portraits of the Duke in naval uniform and the Duchess, again wearing the Strathmore tiara, in a cartouche of gold surrounded by the Union Jack and the Australian flag. On one side is HMS *Renown* entering Sydney Harbour, on the other, the Federal Parliament House at Canberra and captioned 'Parliament House, Canberra, on 9th May 1927'. The lift-off lid carries the head of Mr Bushell holding a cup of his tea (Plate 522).

Aynsley of London produced a mug, within the centre a kangaroo, surrounded by laurel leaves and the Union Jack and the Australian flag, between which are the words 'Australia, a Nation', and below, 'May 1927. To commemorate the opening of the Federal Parliament House at Canberra'. On the rear is a likeness of the new parliament with the caption 'The Capital, Canberra opened by the Duke and Duchess of York, May 1927'.

A mug (Plate 523) commemorates their visit to Pudsey in Yorkshire on 24th April, 1928. It carries portraits of both the Duke and the Duchess with the flag and the crown and the words 'Presented by the Mayor, Councillor Simeon Miles and Mrs Miles'. The mug is published by Wellington China.

After the accession of his brother as King Edward VIII the Duke of York became heir apparent and following the abdication, on 10th December, 1936, he unexpectedly found himself King of England. He did not become King Albert, but King George VI and the Duchess became Queen Elizabeth.

Three Kings reigned in 1936. Bovey Pottery produced a three handled mug (Plate 524D), captioned around the inside

Plate 519. *Paragon cup and saucer for the birth of Princess Margaret Rose, with the marriage cup and saucer.*

Plate 520. *Powder compact for Princess Margaret.*

Plate 521. *Tin to commemorate visit to Australia, 1927.*

Plate 522. *Duke of York on Bushell's tea tin.*

rim 'The Three Reigns of Nineteen Thirty Six'. George V and Queen Mary are featured with their Silver Jubilee double cartouche, Edward VIII is uncrowned in the central cartouche with the coronation date and George VI and Queen Elizabeth appear in a double cartouche as in the one of the official coronation portraits.

The Coronation

A mug (Plate 525) records the actual proclamation at the Royal Exchange. The date of the coronation was that originally chosen for the coronation of Edward VIII. Many ceramic commemoratives which had been prepared for Edward VIII, were remodelled and renamed by the manufacturers for the coronation of King George VI.

The ceremony was masterminded by the Duke of Norfolk, the Earl Marshal. A beaker (Plate 526) was published by Doulton for this Duke on his twenty-first birthday on 30th May, 1929. On one side is a sepia head and shoulders portrait of the young Duke and on the other, Arundel Castle, the traditional and historic home of the Norfolk family. Despite his youth the Duke arranged the coronation with impeccable style.

Plate 523. *Mug to commemorate visit to Pudsey, 24th April 1928.*

Plate 524. A. *Unmarked pottery mug;* **B.** *Voronoff mug;* **C.** *Unmarked coronation plate;* **D.** *Bovey Pottery, Three Kings 1936 mug;* **E.** *Crown Devon beaker;* **F.** *Shelley dish.*

Plate 525. *Proclamation mug.*

Plate 526. *Duke of Norfolk's coming of age beaker, 1929*

A large number of commemoratives were produced, many of which are still obtainable. There is a similar caravan to that produced for Edward VIII and bowls, plates and tankards designed by Charlotte Rhead for Crown Devonware for the coronations of both George VI and Edward VIII (Plates 527 and 531F and G), depicting in either blue or orange and cream check design the monograms of the two kings upon each.

An unmarked plate (Plate 524C), the rim in various shades of blue, has in the centre one of the official coronation portraits of the King and Queen and the date. A Shelley dish (Plate 524F) in art deco style has a shell-like pattern carrying another of the official coronation double portraits in a central cartouche surmounted by a crown and a billowing design of the Union Jack with the date. Crown Devon produced a cream beaker (Plate 524E), with gold rimmed handle and rim, the base in gold, orange and blue. There are embossed heads of the King and Queen and in gold letters around the top rim are the coronation details and date. Another unmarked pottery mug, with art deco decoration (Plate 524A), has one of the official coronation double portraits in oval cartouches surrounded by flags with the same orange and blue rimmed border on the top and base. An interesting pottery mug, by Voronoff (Plate 524B), is tapered, on grey ground with deep blue bands carrying King George and Queen Elizabeth at the top and on the base band the Coronation date. A crown, sceptre and orb are featured on the main grey ground in the centre.

Paragon again produced the same commemorative pieces as they had done for Edward VIII with the simple difference of the initials. There were plates and teasets (Plate 528), loving cups with panther handles and cups and saucers. The more detailed cup has a panther handle and more colourful embellishments. This was designed by Dame Laura Knight and published by Burleigh Ware.

A pair of busts of the King and Queen (Plate 529B) were produced in plaster. They both contain the marks of the modeller, G.N. Morowon.

Typical examples of art deco commemorative items are two jugs (Plate 530A) published by Wadeheath Pottery with a bright orange base in both cases, the handles being different. In one case there are three circles and in the other an arc containing the coronation portraits of both the King and the Queen. On the reverse of both is a small portrait of Princess Elizabeth.

Doulton published a mug (Plate 531A) with classical portraits of the King and Queen in a medallion on a blue

Plate 527. *Charlotte Rhead plate.*

Plate 528. *Paragon plate, cup and saucer.*

Plate 529A. *Kilnhurst Co-operative tea tin;* **B.** *Pair of plaster busts of the King and Queen;* **C.** *Shipley tea tin;* **D.** *Craven A cigarette box;* **E.** *Small round sweet-tin;* **F.** *Chocolate tin.*

Plate 530A. *Two Wadeheath jugs;* **B.** *Ivory plate;* **C.** *Two mugs for George VI and Edward VIII with initialled handles.*

Plate 531A. *Doulton mug;* **B.** *Pewter cocktail shaker;* **C.** *Cup and saucer with flag handle for Edward VIII (with abdication details) by Stanley China;* **D.** *Coalport plaque;* **E.** *Podmore beaker for Whiston;* **F.** *Charlotte Rhead blue bowl;* **G.** *Charlotte Rhead orange tankard for Edward VIII. A similar tankard was produced for George VI.*

Plate 532. *Art deco plate.*

Plate 533. *Royal Staffordshire 'Biarritz' plaque.*

background, surrounded by the royal flowers and the national flags. Underneath are the State Crown, the orb and the sceptre on a cushion. The handle is a typical example of art deco.

Podmore of Hanley published an art deco style beaker (Plate 531E) specifically for the town of Whiston.

C.W.S. Windsor China published mugs for both the coronation of King George VI and Edward VIII with the interesting addition of the handles being in the shape of the initials of GR in the case of George and ER in the case of Edward VIII (Plate 530C).

A plate (Plate 532) with a border containing a design of

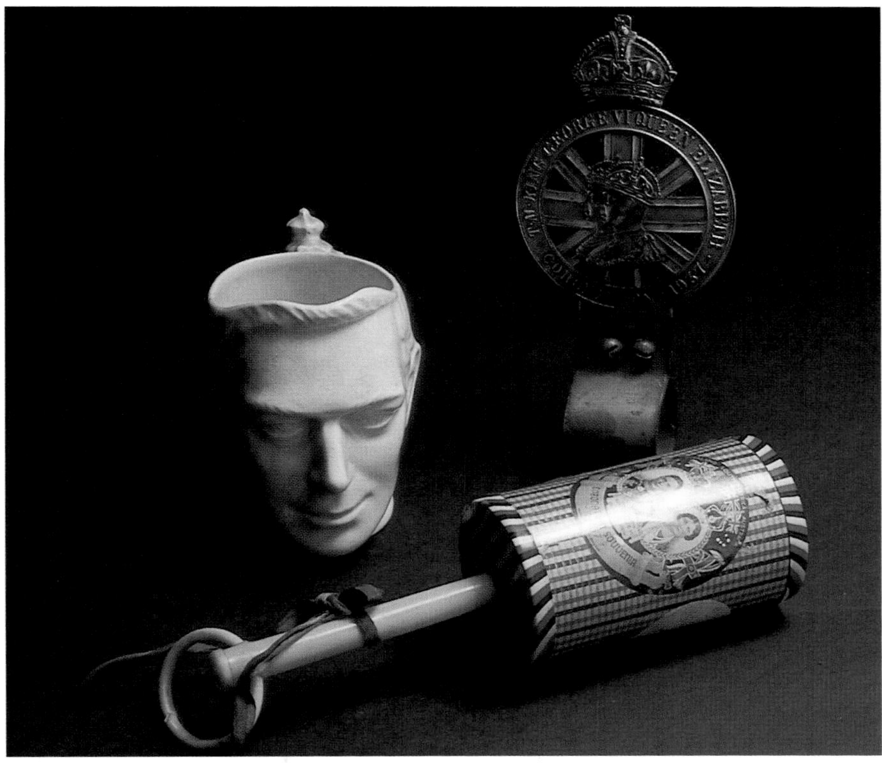

Plate 534A. *Portrait jug of the King;* **B.** *baby's rattle;* **C.** *RAC badge.*

Plate 535. *Coronation souvenir brooch.*

Plate 536. *Oxo money boxes for George VI and Edward VIII.*

Plate 537. *Coronation* Radio Times *and 'Cheerio' poster.*

trees and flowers in art deco style has in the centre the royal family, captioned 'The Royal Family Coronation Souvenir'. It is from the famous photograph of the Royal Family by Marcus Adams.

A splendid plaque by Coalport (Plate 531D), in art deco style, has a peach background. A circle contains a photograph of the two princesses and a corgi in the garden of the Royal Lodge, Windsor, taken in May as the tulips are in bloom. The circle is surmounted by an embossed crown. Another plaque (Plate 533), in cream, shows Marcus Adams' photograph surmounted by a crown, enclosed within a gold laurel leaf. Beneath is a shield with Royal supporters and the family details, entitled 'Coronation Souvenir'. It is produced by Royal Staffordshire and called 'Biarritz'. The same photograph appears on a tin (plate 529F). A round sweet tin (Plate 529E) pictures the two princesses in an embrace. Both are unmarked.

There were some unusual souvenirs – a baby's rattle (Plate 534B) which shows the King and Queen surrounded by crowns and flags; an RAC badge (Plate 534C) moulded in metal with the profile portraits of the King and Queen in the centre against the Union Jack and a brooch (Plate 535).

Oxo produced a tin moneybox (Plate 536) in the shape of a post box, in bright red, with the royal monogram surmounted by a crown on one side and the heads of the King and Queen on the other. They are surrounded by the four national emblems – the rose, thistle, shamrock and the daffodil. The base reads: 'Coronation Souvenir Moneybox containing six Oxo cubes, Oxo Limited, Thames House, London, England'. A similar moneybox was published for Edward VIII in several different shapes and sizes.

A colourful poster (Plate 537) shows head and shoulders portraits of the King and Queen in an oval cartouche surmounted by a crown in a bright red background. The poster is captioned:' Coronation Cheerio, a non-alcoholic champagne – a Kingly drink'. The *Radio Times* produced a special coronation number (Plate 537).

A model of the coronation coach marked 'Crescent' has eight horses and four postillions. The coach is gold, the horses are white with gold trimmings and the postillions have red jackets and black caps. A matchbox holder in silver metal has gold profile portraits of both the King and Queen wearing their crowns.

The Society of Miniature Rifle Clubs of Ludgate produced a cased set of nine Bravington EPNS spoons (Plate 537A). Each bears the head of the King and Queen, Queen Mary, Princess Elizabeth and Margaret Rose and the Dukes and Duchesses of Gloucester and Kent. Princess Alice of Gloucester is rarely seen in commemorative form.

Various calendars (Plate 538) were made with portraits of the King and Queen in oval cartouches surmounted by two crowns and surrounded by a design of the Union Jack and the flags of the dominions. The frame is decorated in red, white and blue and has a rear metal stand as a support.

Several chocolate, sweet, tea and biscuit companies provided tins for the coronation. One tin has a design in gold

Plate 537A. *Set of nine EPNS spoons produced by The Society of Miniature Rifle Clubs of Ludgate.*

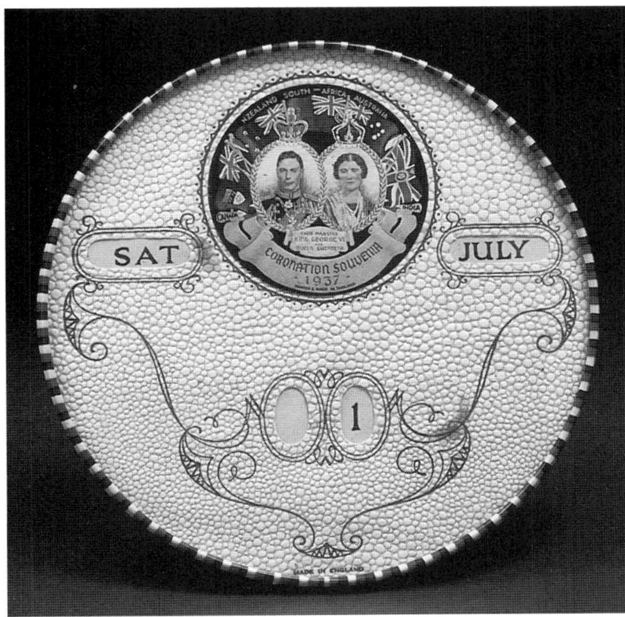

Plate 538. *Coronation calendar.*

of the royal flowers by Macfarlane and Lang (Plate 539). In the centre is the well-known family portrait by Marcus Adams, set in its own raised design of a cartouche surmounted by a crown. Beneath are the letters 'GR', the interesting feature being that this has been specially arranged to fit in the centre of the hinged lid, as a separate adornment.

Perhaps the finest tin is a splendid model of the state coach provided by W. & R. Jacob and Co. (Plate 540). The coach has a lift-off lid, surmounted by the crown. The four wheels revolve, and it must have been a great temptation after the biscuits had been consumed for the coach then to be used by children as a toy. The one shown here must have escaped this fate because it is in mint condition. When it comes to price and value it may well be that this coronation tin is worth considerably more than any ceramic record.

The Kilnhurst Co-operative Society produced a tea tin (Plate 529A) bearing on a golden background portraits of the head and shoulders of the King, informally dressed, captioned 'George VI, King Emperor'. There are views of Edinburgh Castle, Westminster Abbey and a collar formed by dominion and colonial shields. The hinged lid bears a view of Windsor Castle, all within a border of red and blue amid gold motifs.

E. & I. Shipley of Yorks. provided a tin (Plate 529C) wholly in sepia with a striking portrait of the King in admiral's uniform with medals and decorations and the Queen wearing a tiara, and a well-known photograph of Princess Elizabeth and Princess Margaret in dresses with puffed sleeves.

Craven A placed their well-known cigarette tin (Plate 529D) in a cardboard cover bearing the King, Queen and the two Princesses in a central design on a red background. The rear has a picture of the coronation, rays of sunlight shining through the Abbey on to the two sovereigns with Peers in their velvet and ermine robes observing. '50 Craven A, Coronation 1937' is on the side pieces. It is a colourful souvenir.

Carr and Co. produced a biscuit-coloured tin, probably manufactured by Hudson, Scott and Sons. The hinged lid bears the royal portrait accredited to Speaight Ltd. The portrait is in a cartouche surmounted by a crown with the initials 'C' and 'E' on either side, having the effect of a brooch.

A commemorative of interest is a tankard (Plate 541) published by Doulton which commemorates both the coronation and the Grand National. The front is in colour and shows the coronation procession with a coach and horse and two postillions walking alongside. The upper half shows the winner of the Grand National, Royal Mail, and on the reverse are the words 'Grand National Coronation Year 1937. Royal Mail – My Prince Flying May. Owner – Mr Hugh Lloyd-Thomas, Trainer, Mr Ivor Anthony, Jockey, E. Williams'.

An unusual pottery flask (Plate 542) was published for Emu by South Staffordshire Pottery, A.J. Wilkinson Ltd., with the words: 'To commemorate the Coronation' and the date. On either side are maps of the world in two parts, the new world and the old world showing the British possessions in the customary red.

Abbey Pewter produced a cocktail shaker (Plate 531B) in art deco design with a small medallion carrying the head and shoulders of the King and Queen and the date of the coronation.

Most cities and towns provided mugs to be presented by the Mayor to the schoolchildren. Cardiff's is a plain mug bearing the portraits of the King and Queen, published by Booths. The city's coat of arms is on one side.

Perhaps the most impressive and certainly the largest commemorative item for this coronation was a vase (Plate 543) published by Doulton. This stands about ten inches high, very colourful and detailed, mostly in relief, showing a portrait of the King and Queen in profile with trumpeters and

Plate 539. *MacFarlane and Lang coronation biscuit tin.*

Plate 540. *W. & R. Jacob & Co. biscuit tin coach.*

Plate 541. *Grand National tankard by Doulton.*

Plate 542. *Emu pottery flask.*

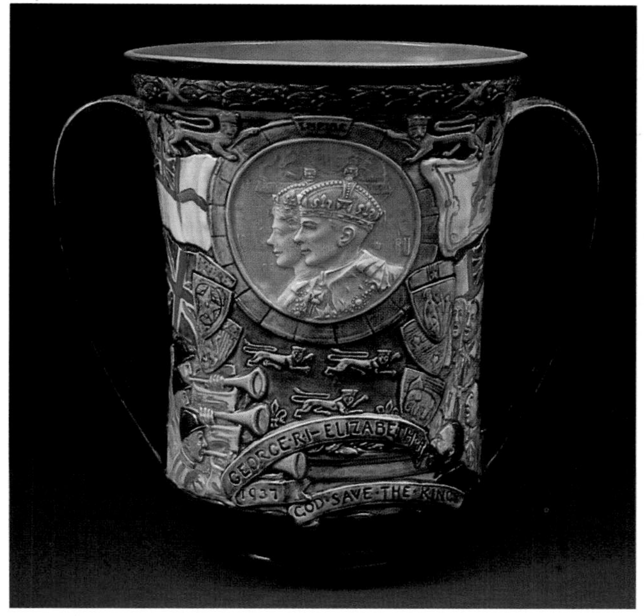

Plate 543. *Doulton coronation vase.*

Plate 544(left). Illustrated London News *cover for the State Visit of King Carol of Romania.*

Plate 545(below left). *Covers from* The Sphere *and* The Illustrated London News *for the State Visit of the French President.*

Plate 546. *Plate for the State Visit to Paris, 1938.*

members of the public, The Lord Chancellor and a Member of the Order of Chivalry are surrounded by national flags and various shields of the dominions. On the rear, again in relief, is a figure of St George on his horse, though without a dragon. In the background are Windsor Castle and royal flags and on the handles the names of the dominions and colonies. It was sculpted by Fenton, and the base reads: 'May 1937 – To Celebrate the Coronation of King George VI and Elizabeth, Loved and Honoured by Their Loyal People'. There was an edition of two thousand. This design comes in two sizes, the other being smaller. Both sizes were also published for the coronation of Edward VIII. These impressive commemorative pieces are occasionally to be found, though they tend to be expensive.

The King carried out many public engagements, opening Parliament and attending the Remembrance Day Service at the Cenotaph. He received state visits from King Leopold of the Belgians and King Carol of Romania (Plate 544), as well as the President of the French Republic (Plate 545). Unfortunately, no ceramic records were made for any of these events.

Official Visits and Exhibitions

In July 1938 the King and Queen made a state visit to Paris. This was a resounding success. The Queen completely captivated Paris. Norman Hartnell designed a series of magnificent creations for her, reviving the crinoline. The feathered hat she wore at the Bagatelle Gardens, and her 'lovely gown of lace', as described by the *Daily Sketch*, were a sensation. Her elegance and regal poise were captured by Cecil Beaton in a series of ravishing photographs.

A plate (Plate 546) commemorates this visit, manufactured in French porcelain. The plain white plate is edged with gold and circles of red and blue. In the centre are portraits of the King and Queen with the date of their visit to France in 1938.

In May and June, 1939 the King and Queen visited Canada and the United States of America. This triumphant tour, the first ever made by a British sovereign, has few commemoratives. A plate published by Wedgwood (Plate 547) in cream and the well-known Wedgwood blue has a relief portrait of Queen Elizabeth. Above are the American eagles with the date 1939, and beside: 'A Friendship makes Peace'. The border contains, again in relief, the royal flowers and the royal insignia. The reverse reads as follows: 'Commemorating the first visit of British reigning sovereigns to the United States in 1939 and made exclusively for W.H. Plummer and Co. Ltd., New York by Wedgwood Etruria, England and limited to 3,000'. A pair to this plate bears a portrait of the King.

A plate was published by Ducal Ware (Plate 548) on a cream background with a thick navy blue border. In the centre are portraits of the King and Queen surrounded by the national flags and surmounted by a crown and in the background is the Capitol of Washington and the Ottawa Building with maple leaves in a cartouche of laurel. The reverse records the visit to the United States and Canada and the date.

Royal Winton produced a teaset in bright yellow lustre with gold trim. The coronation portraits of the King and Queen are on the cup (Plate 549B), with the arms of Canada on the reverse – the saucer bears a caption to mark the visit to the U.S.A. and Canada in 1939 and the arms of the Dominion of Canada. The handle is in art deco style.

Another plate (Plate 550) commemorates the New York World Fair which the King and Queen visited. It is decorated in maroon panels, the centre depicts a rising sun and a scene from the exhibition buildings with the words 'New York Fair, 1798-1939'. Surrounding it, in ovals and rectangles, are scenes of the exhibition buildings. The reverse indicates that

Plate 547. *Wedgwood plate for the State Visit to USA, 1939.*

Plate 548. *Ducal ware plate for the USA visit.*

Plate 549A*. Paragon loving cup for Glasgow Exhibition.* ***B****. Royal Winton cup and saucer for the visit to Canada and the USA.*

it was published by J.C. Meakin, England.

The King and Queen visited Glasgow in 1938 to open the Empire Exhibition. Paragon published a plate very similar in design to that which was produced for the coronation, and also a loving cup (Plate 549A), again in typical Paragon design and colours, bearing on the front the arms of Scotland, the lion and the shield, surrounded by national flags. On the rear, surrounded by a cartouche of thistles, are the words: 'Opened by King George and Queen Elizabeth, 1938'. The loving cup has the traditional gold handles in the shape of a lion and the base contains the words: 'Souvenir to commemorate the Empire Exhibition, Scotland held at Bell Houston Park at Glasgow'. This is number one of a limited edition. It can only be presumed that number one must have been purchased or presented to the Lord Provost of Edinburgh. In 1960 records were destroyed and it is not

Plate 550*. Plate for visit to the New York World Fair, 1939.*

Plate 551*. Marlborough Crescent Glasgow Exhibition plate, 1938.*

Plate 552. *Two mugs for the visit to South Africa, 1947.*

possible to identify the donee of this particular piece.

Marlborough Crescent produced a fine octagonal plate (Plate 551), featuring the tall exhibition building and entitled 'The Clachan Empire Exhibition'. It is in colour and shows a village, farm buildings, pond, bridge and trees. The border is embellished with a design of encrusted foliage. It bears the Scottish Lion Exhibition emblem. There is a beaker of similar design, though less ornate, by Carlton Ware.

In 1947 South Africa was showing signs of unrest and it was felt that a visit by the King and Queen might cement relations between South Africa and Great Britain. It was a full tour and the two Princesses accompanied the King and Queen. In February 1947 the King opened the new session of the South African Parliament. He was president of all his Parliaments but until this date had never opened a dominion legislature in person.

Two mugs (Plate 552) commemorate this visit. One shows the King and Queen in a central medallion surrounded by oak leaves surmounted by a crown and the Union Jack and the South African flag. Above it are the words 'Visit to South Africa, 1947'. The second shows portraits in profile of the two Princesses within a central circle of green laurel leaves surrounded by a red circle surmounted by a crown with a similar caption, and the words 'Princess Margaret and Princess Elizabeth' below.

A visit to Australia was also planned in 1949 but never took place because of the King's state of health. However, some commemoratives were prepared. A mug (Plate 553) has sepia portraits of the King and Queen surmounted by the words, 'Souvenir of the Royal Tour, 1949'. The figures have a background of the map of Australia and New Zealand is

Plate 553. *Mug for the cancelled visit to Australia, 1949.*

BRIDE AND GROOM ON THE PALACE BALCONY

Plate 554. *Two pages from* The Sphere *showing pictures of the wedding of Princess Elizabeth.*

also shown. The handle is in the shape of a koala bear.

The Marriage of Princess Elizabeth

When Princess Elizabeth became engaged to Lieutenant Philip Mountbatten, the King and Queen were delighted. They were both great-great-grandchildren of Queen Victoria, Princess Elizabeth in direct line through King Edward VII,

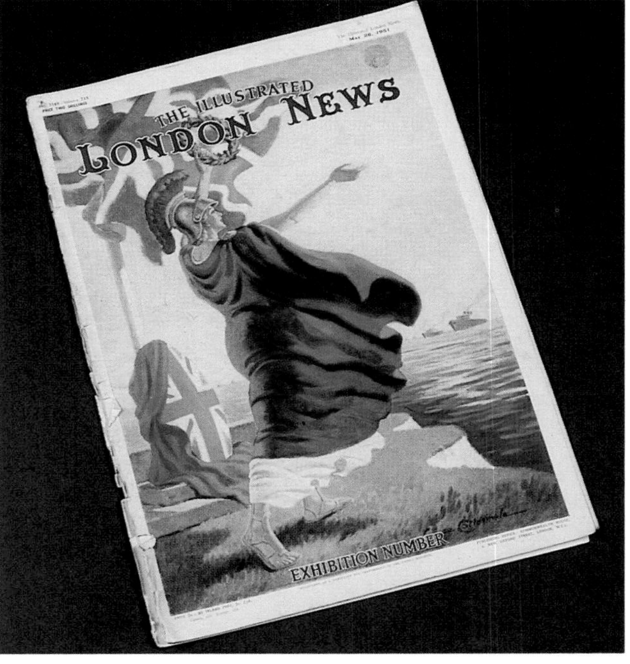

Plate 556. Illustrated London News *cover for the Festival of Britain, 1951.*

Plate 555. *Festival souvenirs: Wedgwood mug, metal teapot, horse brass.*

Plate 557A. *Brentleigh Festival of Britain tankard;* ***B.*** *Festival souvenir powder compact.*

the young naval lieutenant through the second daughter of Queen Victoria, Princess Alice of Hesse.

This almost fairytale wedding in 1947, attended by a host of foreign royalty at Westminster Abbey, has very little commemoration (Plate 554).

Minton, however, produced a two handled goblet vase. It is printed in colour and decorated in enamel and gilt and limited to one hundred. Minton also produced a porcelain vase, the edition in this case limited to five hundred.

Local potteries may have produced mugs – Ewenny Pottery, near Bridgend in Glamorgan published a yellow mug giving the date of the wedding. Popular souvenirs, however, were available on the streets of London. A card with a badge attached bears the arms of the City of London in enamel and the portrait of Elizabeth and Philip. A powder compact carried a photograph of the bride and groom and the acknowledgement of their marriage (Plate 642B).

The Festival of Britain

The last important event to take place during the reign of King George VI was the Festival of Britain in 1951. There are a number of commemoratives for this event but nothing records any part played by the King, who declared it open in St. Paul's Cathedral on 3rd May, 1951. All the national magazines carried details of the scope of this large exhibition which was staged to commemorate the centenary of the 1851 Exhibition at the Crystal Palace in Hyde Park.

Several commemorative pieces were commissioned for this Exhibition, most of which show its motif, the head of Britannia, in the form of a cross (Plate 555). Teapots, glasses, a horse brass and ashtrays were the most popular. The *Illustrated London News* exhibition number (Plate 556) features Britannia welcoming the world with outstretched arms.

Cardiff produced mugs (Plate 557A), having as a main feature, in colour, the City Hall. They were published by Brentleigh, Staffordshire, and the base reads: 'A fine view of the City Hall, the main frontage of which is 265 feet. Above the Council is the dome which is 50 feet in diameter and is surmounted by a huge Welsh Dragon, of special interest to visitors in the magnificent hall in the City Hall'. Above this is the Festival of Britain motif. The mugs are in cream and the handle has a design of green lines and rings. A powder compact has an enamelled view of the exhibition site and the Festival motif (Plate 557B).

The most attractive and original commemorative was the mug produced by Wedgwood. It has all the features of Eric Ravilious, though it is not suggested on the base that he was the designer. The design incorporates the skylon, the Festival motif, and the entrance to the 1851 Exhibition. It is a contemporary design of red, white and blue.

Death of the King

This gentle and devoted King died in February 1952, having carried out his duties during all of his reign with great dedication.

He saw his country enter into the Second World War with all its terrible consequences and emerge victorious six years later. He endeared himself to his people, to his own dominions and colonies and to France in particular. Yet despite the service he had devoted to his people, nothing of a ceramic nature exists to record the death of King George VI. This is a very great pity. National newspapers and magazines, however, gave full coverage (Plate 558).

Popes

During the early part of King George VI's reign, the Pope was

I'd rather have a Gin and VOTRIX

The Daily Telegraph and Morning Post

LONDON, THURSDAY, FEBRUARY 7, 1952

Printed in LONDON and MANCHESTER

DEATH OF KING GEORGE VI

PEACEFULLY IN SLEEP AT SANDRINGHAM

LAST WALK IN GROUNDS ON PREVIOUS EVENING

NEW QUEEN ON WAY HOME: PROCLAMATION TO-MORROW

PEERS AND M.P.s TAKE OATH : MR. CHURCHILL TO BROADCAST

HIS MAJESTY KING GEORGE VI DIED IN HIS SLEEP AT SANDRINGHAM HOUSE IN THE EARLY HOURS OF YESTERDAY MORNING. A SERVANT FOUND HIM DEAD IN BED AT 7.30 A.M. AN ANNOUNCEMENT FROM SANDRINGHAM, REPEATED IN A SPECIAL ISSUE OF THE LONDON GAZETTE LAST NIGHT, SAID:

The King, who retired last night in his usual health, passed peacefully away in his sleep early this morning.

Princess Elizabeth, who accedes to the Throne, was informed of her father's death while she was at the Royal hunting lodge near Nyeri in Kenya. A thunderstorm delayed for two hours the departure of the plane which is to bring her to London, where she was expected at 4.30 p.m. to-day.

The Accession Council, a larger body than the Privy Council, met at 5 p.m. yesterday to decide on the accession proclamation. This will be

The Last Pause Where The King, Who By Our Custom Belongs To The People, Would Remain Among

DAYS OF HOMAGE

Plate 558. Daily Telegraph *and* Picture Post *covering the death of the King.*

Pius XI, Achille Ratti who died in 1939. A plate (Plate 559) commemorates this Pope, published for the Eucharistic Congress held in Dublin in 1932. The words on this plate are written in Gaelic and published for Royal Ivory by John Maddox and Sons Limited of England. It is green and white with yellow embellishments. The portrait shows the Pope, head and shoulders, giving a blessing. Above his head are the Papal tiara and the keys of St. Peter's. On either side, in ovals, are two Irish scenes and underneath, the Parliament House, Dublin.

He was succeeded by Pius XII, Eugenio Pacelli, a highly cultivated and polished Diplomat in the Vatican Papal Curia, who was Secretary of State to the Holy See during the Pontificate of Pope Pius XI.

Though his part in the war has been criticised, he was a widely respected Pope and a very distinguished scholar. He died in 1958 and there is a plate (Plate 560) published by

Plate 559. *Plate for Pope Pius XI.*

Plate 560. *Plate for Pope Pius XII.*

Plate 562. *Portrait figure jug of Chamberlain, with umbrella handle.*

Plate 561(left). *Clarice Cliff portrait figure of Neville Chamberlain.*

Plate 563. *Paragon plate for Munich Agreement.*

Plate 564. *Copeland Spode plate for the three Chamberlains.*

Plate 565 (Left to Right) *Tall figure of Chamberlain; Bulldog; Doulton plate for Churchill; Clarice Cliff figure of Winston Churchill; woven 'Victory' pennant; three Gestapo 'potties' – Fieldings; two Matchbox holders – Roosevelt and the allies; Burleigh ware plate for Churchill; ATS dish; plaster bust of President Roosevelt; Kent plate – Churchill and Roosevelt.*

Crown Clarence of England which shows the Pope in a praying position wearing his white skull cap.

Prime Ministers

At the time of the King's accession the Prime Minister was Baldwin, but after the Coronation he retired, and was succeeded by Neville Chamberlain.

There are several commemorative records for him, but perhaps the most impressive is a character figure (Plate 561) with top hat, umbrella, black tail coat and grey striped trousers. He is seated, with the words 'Peace, Justice, Truth and Happiness' inscribed. Also shown is the plane to Munich and the scroll. This unusual model was designed by Clarice Cliff for Royal Staffordshire Potteries, A.J. Wilkinson. It is not in any way like Clarice Cliff's well known highly decorative contemporary art deco designs.

A character portrait jug of Chamberlain (Plate 562), published by Gibson's of England, has a handle in the shape of an umbrella.

Paragon China published a plate (Plate 563), in typical Paragon colours, to commemorate and record the Munich agreement. In the centre is a portrait in sepia of the Prime Minister, surrounded by laurel leaves and the national flags. Underneath are the words 'The Right Honourable Neville Chamberlain, The Prime Minister' and around the border the

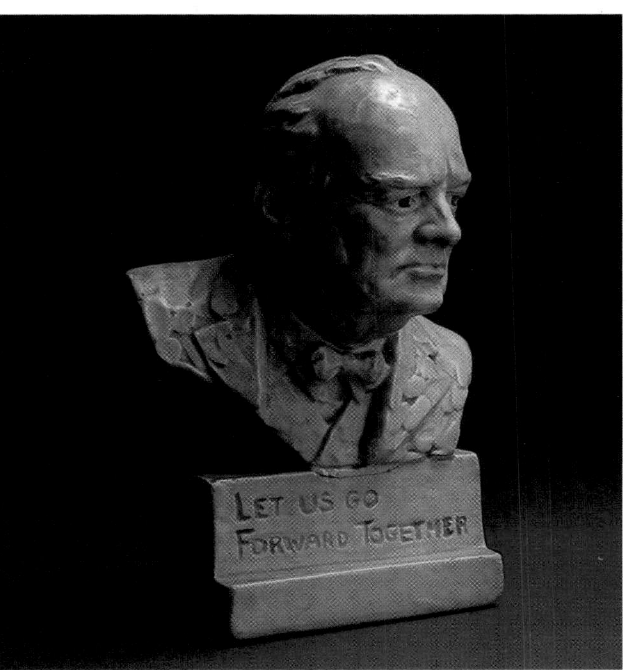

Plate 566. *'Let us go forward together' Churchill bust.*

words 'Chamberlain the Peacemaker'. Beneath the royal flowers, which include the daffodil, as well as the rose, the shamrock and the thistle are the words 'I am myself a man of peace to the depths of my soul'. The reverse has the following inscription: 'A perpetual souvenir to commemorate the Peace Conference at Munich, September 29th 1938. The four great powers represented by the Right Honourable Neville Chamberlain, Herr Hitler, Monsieur Daladier, Signor Mussolini', and the quotation 'out of this mortal danger we pluck this flower safely, produced by consent and approval of the Right Honourable Neville Chamberlain'. Paragon also published a loving cup, with the traditional gold lion handle.

Also to commemorate the Munich Agreement, Copeland Spode produced a plate (Plate 564), the front of which bears portraits in medallions of the three famous members of the Chamberlain family surrounded by laurel leaves and the national flowers printed in blue. The blue border also contains a wreath comprising the national flowers. The reverse of the plate reads 'A souvenir of Britain's most famous political family – the Right Honourable Sir Austen Chamberlain KG PC MP, the Right Honourable Neville Chamberlain securing peace for Europe during the crisis in September 1938'.

A tall plaster figure (Plate 565) of Neville Chamberlain, painted in gold, shows him carrying his umbrella, wearing his top hat and tail coat and winged collar, carrying a despatch box on a plinth with the words '1939 and 1918'. There is no indication as to who produced this figure, except that on the reverse of the base is the word 'England'.

The Second World War

Chamberlain was clearly not regarded by the House of Commons as the kind of man who could lead his country in war, and the rest of the King's reign was dominated by the most celebrated politician not only of the century but probably for all time since Chatham – Winston Churchill. Churchill, throughout the war, was the inspiration behind victory. He never faltered in his belief that his country would defeat Hitler.

He appears on a number of ceramic commemoratives. A plate published by Burleigh Ware (Plate 565) in blue on a white background shows the Prime Minister in a central oval of laurel leaves surrounded by flags with a warship and fighters of the RAF. Underneath it reads: 'Prime Minister of Great Britain the Right Honourable Winston Churchill' and

Plate 567. *Kent China handled beaker with quotation from Churchill; plaster head of Churchill; plate for Roosevelt – from the Allied Nations Commemorative Series; Churchill in garter robes; two Paragon cups and saucers of Churchill and Roosevelt from the Patriotic series; Wedgwood tankards for Churchill and Roosevelt; plaster plaque of Stalin; ashtray for Churchill.*

Plate 568. *Crown Devon Spitfire plaque; four Paragon cups and saucers from the 'Patriotic' series; cakestand recording bomb that fell on House of Commons; pair of dolls – British soldier and ATS woman soldier.*

around the border are the names of the Dominions, Australia, Canada, New Zealand, South Africa and India. Beneath the portrait of the Prime Minister are the royal flowers, the rose, the thistle and the shamrock, alas no leek or daffodil.

A tankard bears a portrait of Winston Churchill, smoking his famous cigar, and a bulldog, sitting on the flags of England, underneath which are the words 'Come On' and also, 'Britains Challenge'. This was published by Coronet Ware, Parrott and Company, Burslem.

A head and shoulders bust of Winston Churchill (Plate 566), bears the words 'Let us go forward together'. The face is tense and full of determination. There is a figure of the great British Bulldog (Plate 565) wearing a tin hat on which are the words 'Where's Hitler?'

Several items show Churchill wearing his black homburg hat, some with his cigar. Doulton produced one and Wedgwood published two mugs (Plate 567) in their blue bearing the embossed head and shoulders of Churchill with his cigar and a similar one for Roosevelt. These of course would have been produced after the entry of America into the War. The Churchill mug has the caption 'Give us the tools and we'll finish the job', and in the case of President Roosevelt: 'This can be done, it must be done, it will be done'.

Doulton produced a fine plate (Plate 565) showing the head of Churchill against a design of St. Paul's and Tower Bridge, surrounded by a wreath of acorn leaves with the caption: 'For a thousand years men will still say this was their finest hour'.

Taylor and Kent of Longton, England produced a handled beaker (Plate 567) with a silver rim bearing the wings of the RAF and the quotation: 'Never in the field of human conflict was so much owed by so many to so few'.

Perhaps the most exciting and interesting commemorative piece for the Royal Air Force was in the shape of a plaque published by Crown Devon (Plate 568). It has a Spitfire, in green, on a background of blue sky and clouds with the same famous quotation. The Spitfire has its wings raised.

The entry of America into the War following the Japanese attack on Pearl Harbour was a great tribute to Churchill who had kept up a dialogue since the start of the war between himself and President Roosevelt. The famous alliance is shown on a plate published by James Kent Limited, Fenton (Plate 565), showing the President and the Prime Minister in medallions against their national flags with, in between, a warship, and underneath the words 'For Democracy'. The plate is in white and has flowers in relief, around the rim, and an orange border.

A plaster bust of President Roosevelt (Plate 565), has underneath the words: 'I pledge allegiance to the flag of the United States of America and to the Republic for which it stands one nation indivisible with liberty and justice for all'. And in larger letters 'Remember Pearl Harbour'.

Plate 569. Left to right, rear of picture: *Plaster bust of Eisenhower; two plates from the Allied Nations Commemorative series, with portraits of General Eisenhower and Field Marshal Marshall; Dyson and Horsfall teapot; plaster bust of Field Marshal Montgomery.* ***Foreground:*** *Ashtray for Allied armies in Italy; Royal Stafford beaker for the outbreak of war; 'Allied Front for Freedom' beaker; war medals – Pacific Star, Normandy Star, Defence medal, War Service Star (awarded to Mr. A. W. Blyth).*

A matchbox cover (Plate 565) with a portrait of a smiling President Roosevelt bears the words 'Today the whole world is divided between human slavery and human freedom, between pagan brutality and the Christian Ideal. We choose human freedom which is the Christian Ideal' from a speech of 28th March 1941. In a specific reference to the part Britain was playing there appeared the words 'As President of the United Determined People, I repeat the word of the signers of the Declaration of Independence fighting long ago against overwhelming odds, but certain as we are of ultimate victory, we mutually pledge to each other our lives, our fortunes and our sacred honour. The delivery of needed supplies to Britain is imperative'.

Also shown is another matchbox containing the original matches, clearly prepared for the actual signing of the peace treaty, which bears, in medallions, Roosevelt, Churchill and Stalin, together with the three flags of those countries and the words: 'Our Deepest Gratitude and Admiration to the Allies who stood United in Defeating the Greatest Tyranny in History'. The matchbox is British made.

What could be regarded as a joke (Plate 565), is a series of 'potties' published by Fieldings in England. In the centre of one is Hitler and around him, the word 'Gest-a-po', underneath which is the German Iron Cross and on the other side 'Flip your ashes on old nasty – the violation of Poland'. Another contains in the centre the head of Benito Mussolini, with the caption, in this case 'We've got him on the run' and on the other side 'Wop No 1' with German swastikas and the Italian Eagle and underneath 'Albania – Taranto – Bardia'. The third has in the centre the head of Field Marshal Göring with the quotation around the side 'Gerry No 2' and the German cross and on the other side 'Flip your ashes on old piggy', again with the swastika and 'the violation of Poland'.

Ducal Ware produced an interesting teapot (Plate 569) which bears the two crossed flags of France and Britain surrounded by smaller flags of the British Dominions and French colonies. The flags on one side bear the bold caption 'WAR AGAINST HITLERISM'. This souvenir teapot was made for Dyson and Horsfall of Preston to replace aluminium stocks taken over for 'ALLIED ARMAMENTS 1939'. This teapot was an early war commemorative and must have been manufactured before the entry of the United States and Russia, since there are no national flags of those countries and subsequent allies.

Perhaps the most impressive piece of Churchilliana to commemorate his part in the war is a splendid and handsome portrait jug by Clarice Cliff, published by Wilkinson Limited of Burslem (Plate 565). This shows Churchill with a bulldog and the Union Jack, in cabinet uniform, wearing the cabinet hat, in his hand a cigar and also a model of a British warship.

Around the base is inscribed 'Going into action and may God defend the right'.

Paragon China produced teasets containing various aspects of the war and quotations (Plate 567). They are in varying colours and include Winston Churchill smoking his cigar, the rim of the saucer bearing 'Never was so much owed by so many to so few'. That for Roosevelt has the head and shoulders of the President in the bowl of the cup. Another has in the centre famous quotation in the cause of democracy 'We shall not fail or falter, we shall not weaken or tire, give us the tools and we'll finish the job'. This is in a central cartouche surrounded by a design of flags and embellishments. Around the rim are the English oak leaves. Another cup, this time in blue, has a spitfire in the centre and in the middle of the saucer the RAF motto 'per ardua ad astra' surmounted by the crown and the eagle. Another has in the centre, against the background of a wooden ship of the 18th century, a quotation from Longfellow sent from President Roosevelt to Churchill: 'Sail on O Ship of State, Sail on O Union Strong and Great, Humanity with all the hopes of future years, Hangs Breathless on thy fate'.

Around the inside of another cup is the quotation: 'Britain shall triumph, her ships plough the sea, her standard be justice, her watchword be free', and in the centre are three warships in full battle order sailing on the high seas. Another, in blue, has in the bowl of the cup the map of the United Kingdom with the caption 'There will always be an England'.

There is a dish which has in the centre the quotation '"Never has she been so truly Great Britain than today. When you write with the trail of our scars the greatest chapter in the history of freedom" – Dorothy Thompson'. This also forms part of the series. These cups and saucers are not easily found. They were part of an export drive to America.

The ATS, which formed such an important part of the war effort, is commemorated in the form of a very small dish published by Shelley (Plate 565), the centre of which has the motif 'ATS' surmounted by the crown on a blue background surmounted by a laurel wreath. A pair of dolls, a British soldier and an ATS girl (Plate 568), both wear wartime uniform – he battledress and forage cap, she skirt and jacket with the ATS cap.

During the war the King and Queen were a fine example to their people. They were frequently on hand to visit cities that had been bombed, touring large parts of London which had suffered so severely. Buckingham Palace itself was bombed and the Queen is reputed to have said that she was glad that this had occurred because, as she put it 'Now we can look the East End in the face'.

A pair of jigsaw puzzles (Plate 570) has the King presenting RAF officers with their wings and the Queen inspecting members of the WRAF.

They were very soon on the scene to witness the destruction of Coventry Cathedral during the so-called Baedeker Raids by the Luftwaffe. The King was anxious that there should be some medal struck for civilians who had shown extreme bravery to compare with those who received the Victoria Cross for Bravery in action. He instituted the George Cross and the George Medal, taking a great interest in the design.

The Worshipful Company of Playing Cards issued a special pack of cards to record the awarding of the George Cross to the island of Malta. The design comprises the island surmounted by the George Cross suspended over the harbour at Valetta. It bears the Company's coat of arms and one thousand packs were issued.

The King also initiated the idea of doing something for the bravery of the Russians at the Battle of Stalingrad. He suggested that there should be a special sword struck and the result was the Stalingrad Sword.

There is little to record the entry of Russia into the war. There appear to be no commemoratives, for example, of the meetings of President Roosevelt, Churchill and Stalin. There is however a plaster plaque of the head of Stalin (Plate 567) in cream on a black background.

The outbreak of The Second World War has been commemorated by a handled beaker published by Royal Stafford in bone china (Plate 569). The central design is of three uniformed figures of the Army, Navy and Air Force. The soldier is backed by the rising sun and on each side is the Union Jack and the caption: 'The French Empire'. Beneath are the words 'Freedom and Justice. The Fight for Freedom of All Nations, September 3rd 1939'. The reverse bears the words 'Peace with Honour' within a laurel wreath.

Another beaker records the outbreak of war (Plate 569). It has on the front a design of flags 'Allied Front for Freedom'. It was published by British Anchor.

Perugia Pottery produced an ashtray (Plate 569) with the words: 'Allied Armies in Italy 1944'.

The bombing of the Houses of Parliament is recorded on a cakestand (Plate 568). It has a metal base, the plate bears in sepia the House of Commons captioned 'Houses of Parliament – bombed during 1940'.

The bombing of the Guildhall in December 1940 is commemorated by the Worshipful Company of Playing Cards in a pack of cards showing the fire during the Blitz in London. Thirty thousand packs were issued to assist relief of hardship in the United Kingdom playing card industry because of the War.

The Normandy Landings were the theme of the 1944 packs of playing cards issued by the Worshipful Company. The design shows the dramatic scene on the beaches and the caption: 'D Day 6th June 1944'. The Union Jack and the Stars and Stripes are portrayed on each of the top corners and the base holds the Company's coat of arms.

It was considered inappropriate that members of the Royal Family should serve in any combative form in any of the armed services and rather like the Prince of Wales in 1914, the Duke of Kent had to content himself with a staff job.

In August 1942 he was scheduled to visit Iceland to inspect some American bases. He went there in a Sunderland flying boat, which at that time was a form of air transport in common use, but bad weather caused the plane to crash into a hillside in Northern Scotland. The Duke and all the crew were killed, and he was the first member of the Royal Family to die in action. Due to wartime economy, no ceramic record was produced to commemorate the Duke's death.

Like the music for the Boer War, this war had its songs. *Run Rabbit Run* and *We're Going to Hang Out the Washing on the Siegfried Line* were made famous by those great

Plate 570. *Pair of jigsaw puzzles, King and Queen visiting RAF and WAAF.*

Variety stars, Flanagan and Allen. There was a souvenir song of the Armed Forces in Germany dedicated to Major General Henry T. Allen commanding the Afling, price ten marks. It is entitled *On the Rhine*, with the words and music by Corporal Walter Woodward Trahern. It contains a full page front cover (Plate 571) of facsimile signatures of members of the forces with a central portrait of a British soldier wearing a tin helmet.

Benito Mussolini, the Italian fascist dictator, met an ignominious end. He was captured by Italian partisans and shot at Dongo on Lake Como, after which, together with his mistress, Clara Petacci, he was hung upside-down. A glass tumbler (Plate 572) portrays this miserable event with an engraved likeness of Mussolini hanging from a gibbet captioned: 'Musso's last drop', dated July 25th 1943. This is a clear mistake in the engraving as the actual year was 1945. It is a ghoulish commemorative object.

Victory in Europe

The Times of 9th May 1945 described the end of the War as follows:

'The Prime Minister officially proclaimed yesterday that the German War is at an end. In the broadcast message he announced that the act of unconditional surrender of the enemy was signed at 2.41 am on Monday, and was to be ratified in Berlin. Last night the King broadcast a victory salute to his people testifying to their faith and unity in the cause of World Freedom.'

Street parties were held throughout cities, towns and villages. Princes Street in Cardiff presented, in March 1946, a certificate of appreciation (Plate 571) to Mrs C.E. Thomas who organised the street party, signed by all the residents 'with sincere appreciation of services rendered through the War', flanked in the left corner by two Union Jacks.

Some of the War Commanders have been commemorated as figures. There is a pair of plaster busts (Plate 569) of General Eisenhower and Field Marshal Montgomery, shown head and shoulders, both wearing uniform, on a black base sculpted by T.A. Jones.

A portrait jug records General Sir Archibald Wavell (Plate 572). It was produced by Royal Winton. The General is wearing his Field Marshal's hat and the handle is in the form of a sword. There is a similar portrait jug for Lord Montgomery wearing his black beret and his two badges. A portrait figure of General Eisenhower (Plate 572) wearing his American cap and his General's stars is very severe looking. There is no indication as to who the potter was in this case.

The Americans were anxious to record their commanders and a series of plates entitled 'Allied Nations Commemorative Series' was produced by the Salem China Company, Ohio, made in the U.S.A. They carry in the centre most of the American Generals who took part in this war, around whom are the various flags of the Allies. The American Eagle is placed above on the rim among the flags against the United States' Stars and Stripes. Among those

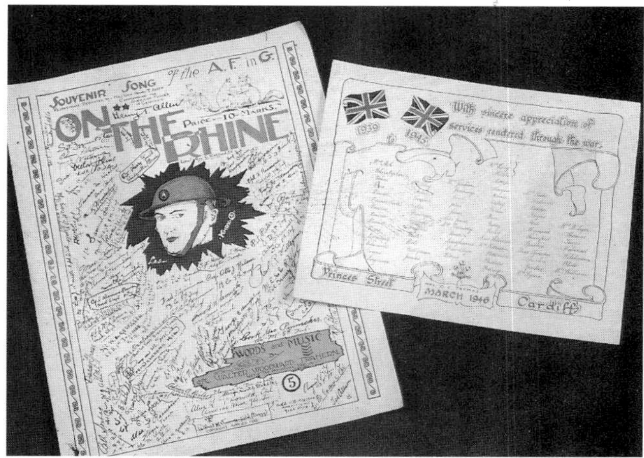

Plate 571. *Souvenir song, 'On the Rhine'; Princes Street, Cardiff victory street party certificate.*

Plate 572. *Portrait jugs of Field Marshals Wavell and Montgomery; portrait figure of Eisenhower; VE and VJ day plate – Mary Birtwhistle; three plastic VE day beakers; Shelley VE beaker; glass tumbler for the execution of Mussolini; Paragon cup and saucer – patriotic series; framed postcard.*

Plate 573. Left to Right: *Pottery figure of Churchill in Trinity House uniform; Churchill silver statuette; Churchill French medal; Ewenny and Cardiff VE and VJ mugs and a casket of Pol Roger champagne 'Cuvée Sir Winston Churchill'.*

included are General Marshall and General Eisenhower (Plate 567).

VE Day was not the subject of many commemoratives. Shelley produced one plain beaker (Plate 572) which has as the centre '8th May 1945' in the Victory 'V' and around it are the names of those who took part: Churchill, Truman, Alexander, Stalin, Eisenhower, Montgomery, M. Clark, Konier Zhukof and Tedder.

However, some towns produced plastic beakers (Plate 572). Luton's carries the Victory 'V' with the scroll '1945' and another for an unknown town, which may have been for general sale, shows a young girl carrying the Union Jack in one hand and in the other a scroll with the word 'Victory'. A dark brown nondescript beaker has, in the centre, in a scroll, 'Victory Celebrations' and the date, '6th June 1945'.

One of the few items which commemorate both the ending of the War in Europe and also in Japan is a plate by Mary Birtwistle (Plate 572). In the centre is the Union Jack within a blue circle and around it in bold lettering of a high quality are 'V.E.' and 'V.J.' and underneath each 'May 8th' and 'August 15th', in between the year, '1945'.

Ewenny Pottery produced a mottled ochre and green mug (Plate 573), for the VE and VJ celebrations in 1945. There is a similar mug for the Heath Park Cardiff celebrations. Churchill, in his Trinity House uniform waving his hat, with

Plate 574A. *Hitler in the Allied Group – matchbox cover;* ***B.*** *Royal Doulton Girl Evacuee.*

a tin helmet and gas mask slung over his shoulder and holding a walking stick is the subject of a pottery figure (Plate 573). Royal Doulton produced 'The Girl Evacuee' (Plate 574B), a porcelain figure modelled by Adrian Hughes. An appealing figure, it shows a sad young girl sitting on her suitcase carrying her teddy bear and a gas mask on a haversack, with two labels indicating she is an evacuee and her destination.

A matchbox cover (Plate 574A) has Hitler being strangled by a hand, denoting on each finger and thumb China, Britain, America, Russia and Free French. On the other side Mussolini's note to Hitler: 'Why o why must I die, all through you. Oh the pity of it all, with one sharp twist of that wrist we'll be through. I'm sure we're heading for a fall. Yours brokenheartedly, Mussolini'. The side has the caption: 'The greatest enemy in history against humanity is at last in the Allies' grip'. It is produced by Cartwright, British made.

A dark blue pennant (Plate 565) has a design, on the left, of the Dove of Peace over a globe with the flags of Great Britain, the USA, the USSR and the Blue Ensign with the caption: 'Peace in Europe'. As the pennant tapers it carries the word 'Victory' and, at its narrowest end, '1945'.

In 1945 the Worshipful Company of Playing Cards issued three thousand packs of cards to commemorate the victory in Europe and in the Far East. A winged goddess stands over the prostrated flags of Germany and Japan with, in the background, St. Paul's Cathedral in darkness and Big Ben in floodlight. The Company's coat of arms lies beneath the two flags of the defeated nations.

France struck a commemorative bronze medal (Plate 573) dated '10th November 1942', which shows the head of Winston Churchill wearing the Trinity House uniform. The reverse carries the Marlborough coat of arms and the inscription: 'Nous n'avons qu'un désir voir une France, forte et libre entourée de son Empire et réunie a L'Alsace Lorraine'. France's tribute to the great war leader.

The Evacuation from Dunkirk, which resulted in the miraculous rescue of the British Expeditionary Force, was not the subject of commemorative record. But fifty years later Sutherland China has come to the rescue. Although not strictly a commemorative it would seem unpatriotic not to make an exception. A mug (Plate 575) depicts the little ships taking British troops from the beaches. This memorial to British gallantry bears the inscription '50th Anniversary of Operation Dynamo, the Evacuation of 338,226 Allied troops from the beaches of Dunkirk, May 26th-June 4th 1940'.

The Occupation of France

The occupation of the German forces after the fall of France resulted in the 'Vichy Regime' headed by Marshal Pétain, who collaborated with Hitler. A white china plate (Plate 576) with brown sepia transfer print decoration, contains in the centre a fine litho portrait of Philippe Pétain, Marechal de France, captioned underneath the portrait. The Marshal is depicted in military uniform in the later years of his life when he was head of the French puppet government imposed upon France by Hitler and the German state. The rim of the plate is decorated with acorn leaves and top centre is the motto of France: 'Travail Famille Patrie'. It is marked on the reverse with a printed stamp 'Limoges GIF France' and the additional stamp 'Visa de Century'. The plate also bears an impressed stamp 'T & H'.

In 1941 Royal Worcester commissioned Eileen Soper, an artist particularly well-known for her etchings as a book illustrator for Enid Blyton, to model a series of war episodes connected with Air Raids (Plate 577). These included 'Salvage', showing a small boy rescuing house contents after

Plate 575. *Coalport evacuation from Dunkirk 50th anniversary mug.*

Plate 576. *Pétain plate.*

Plate 577. *Eileen Soper war figures.*

a raid. 'The Rescue' shows a small girl rescuing her cat. 'Spitfire' shows a boy and a girl looking up at the sky for a Spitfire and 'Take Cover' shows a girl evacuee. The 'Stowaways' model is of a boy and girl with a small dog cowering for shelter.

Post-war events – Labour elected

At the conclusion of the war in Europe the Labour party decided that they wished to break with the coalition government and a General Election took place in August 1945. Much to Churchill's dismay, the Labour party swept into office. Churchill's slogan 'Let him finish the job' was not enough.

Austerity may well be the reason for there being no commemoratives for this election and Attlee was hardly commemorated at all. However, a pair of plaster figures of Churchill and Attlee was published for this election (Plate 578). Attlee, smaller and almost dwarfed by Churchill, has his pipe. It is a rare record of a much under-rated Prime Minister.

The only other commemorative that seems to be available for Attlee is a badge in the form of a rat, which was published by the Conservative party after Aneurin Bevan, Minister of Health, had remarked that as far as he was concerned, 'The Conservative Party was lower than vermin'. This caused an outcry and these little badges were published and distributed as part of what might be regarded as anti-Bevan propaganda.

Plate 578. *Churchill and Attlee General Election plaster figures.*

CHAPTER 7

Queen Elizabeth II
1952-

During the reign of Queen Elizabeth II there has been a dramatic increase of interest in commemoratives. At the time of her accession there were still signs of some remnants of post-war austerity and no commemorative was issued.

It was not until the bicentenary of *The Times* that a commemorative mug appeared. This quoted a passage from *The Times* dated Saturday, 9th February, 1952 which reads: 'The accession of Queen Elizabeth II was publicly proclaimed with ancient pageantry yesterday throughout Britain in many parts of the Commonwealth. Earlier the Queen at her first Privy Council had made her accession declaration and had pledged herself to uphold constitutional government and to advance the happiness and prosperity of her people'. This is not a commemorative in the strictest sense because it was not made contemporaneously with the event. The death of Queen Mary in 1953 has unfortunately produced no ceramic record of a commemorative nature, although the national newspapers and magazines gave full coverage (Plate 579).

No doubt austerity also prevented any commemoratives for the births of Prince Charles in 1948 or Princess Anne in 1950, or indeed for the death of King George VI but the Queen's coronation started an interest which has continued and increased ever since.

Coronation Day started off with splendid news about the conquering of Everest by Sir John Hunt and Edmund Hilary together with Sherpa Tensing. A plaster hand-painted plaque (Plate 580) is inscribed: 'Conquest of Everest. Sir Edmund Hilary and Tensing Norkey G.M. 29th May 1953' incised under the central design, marked W. Bossons. This plaque depicts Hilary and Tensing wearing oxygen masks and special protective clothing on the top of Everest with a small Union Jack.

For the coronation itself there was a large number of commemoratives of various shapes, styles and sizes. All the well-known pottery and porcelain manufacturers contributed. These took the usual form of mugs, cups and saucers and plates, and various other interesting aspects were portrayed.

Paragon again produced one of their attractive plates (Plate 581), very similar to those for previous Kings and Queens, this time the border is in pale blue and has in the centre the royal coat of arms supported by the lion and the unicorn and surmounted by the crown. There are several other Paragon pieces in the shape of loving cups with gold

Plate 579. Illustrated London News *and* Sphere *covers for the death of Queen Mary.*

Plate 580. *Mount Everest plate.*

Plate 581. *Paragon coronation plate.*

Plate 582. *Burleigh Ware jug.*

lion handles, cups and saucers.

Burleigh Ware of England provided a very colourful jug (Plate 582) to commemorate the event. It shows, in relief, the Queen seated in St Edward's chair receiving the homage of the Duke of Edinburgh, around whom are various peers wearing their coronets, and the Bishops who took part. Underneath the lip is St Edward's chair itself, and on the reverse is Westminster Abbey in grey relief. The handle is shaped to hold the crown at the top with the Queen's monogram underneath. Burleigh Ware also produced a colourful plate (Plate 583), having in the centre the uncrowned Queen in a laurel wreath surmounted by the crown and the national flags, beneath which are the round tower of Windsor Castle and Westminster Abbey and around the border the national flowers in a wreath of acorns.

Royal Doulton produced a dark brown glazed jug (Plate 584) with a portrait of the Queen. In the centre are the flags and underneath the rim, in relief, are the shields of the dominions and colonies. On the reverse, also in relief, Windsor Castle.

Plate 583. *Burleigh Ware plate.*

Plate 584. *Royal Doulton coronation jug.*

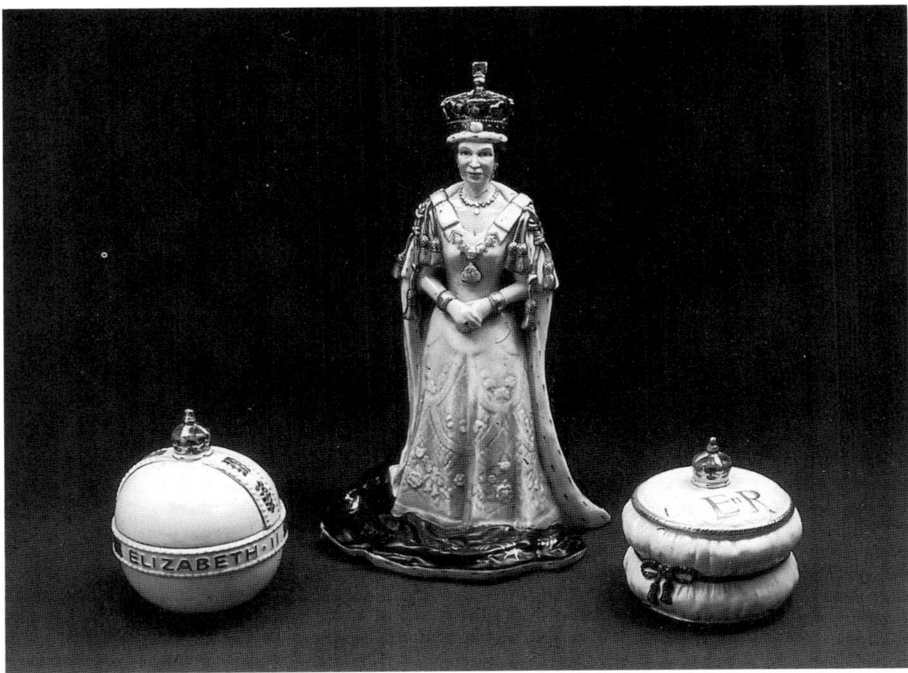

Plate 585. *Porcelain figure of the Queen. Unicorn orb and cushion souvenirs.*

Plate 586. *Pair of Aynsley cups and saucers.*

A fine full-length figure of the Queen (Plate 585), modelled and hand painted, was produced by Michael Sutty for the Porcelain Manufactory. The Queen wears her coronation robes and her purple and ermine mantle. Around her neck is the Garter Chain and on her head is the State Crown. Around her wrists are heavy gold bracelets.

Aynsley of England manufactured teasets in several colours – red, blue, turquoise and orange. The inside of the cup (Plate 586) bears the portrait of the Queen's head surmounted by a gold crown and around the side is the date of her coronation and her titles.

A pair of plaster busts (Plate 587) sculpted by G.H. Paulin RSA and approved by the Council of Industrial Design show the Queen and the Duke of Edinburgh.

Clarice Cliff, Newport Pottery, produced a teaset (Plate 588) on a cream base with a turquoise scalloped border, bearing the head of the Queen.

Royal Bradwell produced a coronation loving cup in

Plate 587. *Pair of plaster busts by G. H. Paulin.*

cream with lion handles with a half-portrait of the Queen on one side and Westminster Abbey on the other. Around the rim: 'Elizabeth II crowned at Westminster'. The base indicates that this was presented by the Directors to M.A. Gartlidge – in appreciation of long and loyal service.

Royal Doulton published a beaker (Plate 589) with the portrait of the Queen in the centre, surrounded by oak leaves, the handle being in the shape of an 'E'.

A musical tankard (Plate 589), designed in cream, with the embossed head of the Queen, with a gilt surround around the lip, the handle and on the base plays 'Here's a Health Unto Her Majesty'.

Unicorn of England produced souvenirs in the form of an orb and of a cushion (Plate 585). These are on a cream base, embellished with gold, either with the full name of the Queen or the monogram 'EIIR', both surmounted by the imperial crown.

Maylings of Newcastle upon Tyne published a teaset (Plate 589) of a pale green lustre bearing the head of the Queen surmounted by the Crown and surrounded by the royal flowers, including the daffodil.

Washington Pottery also produced a teaset. The head of the Queen is surrounded by flags and surmounted by the crown held by the two royal supporters and the date. The Queen is surrounded by two circles of blue and red, the design is on a cream base and there is a gold rim to both cup, saucer and plate.

Wedgwood published a large tankard (Plate 590) designed by Eric Ravilious. This is a contemporary design by a well-known designer of the period.

Austerity is still seen to have played a part. Whereas Cardiff normally presented mugs to the school children, this time they were confined to a pair of spoons (Plate 591).

Harvey's of Bristol provided a magnum of sherry (Plate 591) captioned 'Coronation Bottling Bristol Cream' around the Queen's monogram and the date, 1953. A bottle of claret was provided by Christopher's entitled, 'Coronation Reserve Special' and there were half pints of Websters Old Brown Coronation Ale, and Coronation Ale by Mitchison and Butlers of Birmingham. A glass decanter in the shape of the Queen wearing coronation robes, the stopper in the shape of a crown, contained Armagnac.

Various biscuit, tea and chocolate manufacturers also provided coronation souvenirs. A Dundee tin has a portrait of the Queen on the lift-off lid surrounded, in ovals, by portraits of all the Kings and Queens of England from Elizabeth I.

G.F. Lovell of Newport produced a rectangular tin with Buckingham Palace on the lid and in each corner, in oval

Plate 588. *Clarice Cliff cup, saucer and plate.*

Plate 589. (Left to Right) *Lion handled loving cup, Maylings cup, saucer and plate, musical tankard, Royal Doulton handled beaker*

cartouches, head and shoulders portraits of the Queen and the Duke of Edinburgh (Plate 592).

Bilsland Bros. provided a tea caddy (Plate 593) in bright red with a casket style lift-off lid bearing a portrait of the Queen in ovals and the Duke of Edinburgh and captioned 'Coronation Souvenir'. The Oxo coronation tin is red, the lid has a portrait of the Queen surrounded by the royal standard and the Union Jack. Inside the lid are details of the Queen's life.

W.D. & H.O. Wills provided a tin of Wild Woodbine Cigarettes for the coronation (Plate 594). It is turquoise and the hinged lid bears a portrait of the Queen and her monogram.

Plate 590. *Wedgwood tankard designed by Eric Ravilious.*

Wright's Biscuits Ltd., of South Shields, had a cake tin in blue (Plate 592) bearing on the lift-off lid oval portraits of the head and shoulders of the Queen and Prince Philip, held by the lion and unicorn. An unmarked tin for cakes (Plate 594) has on the lid the royal family, the Queen seated holding Princess Anne and Prince Charles, and seated behind them is the Duke of Edinburgh. It is in blue and around the side are flags and crowns.

Fox's Glacier Mints of Oxford Street, Leicester produced a gold tin with a portrait of the Queen (Plate 592).

Brooke Bond's tea tin (Plate 592) carries portraits of the Queen and the Duke of Edinburgh with the caption: 'A Souvenir of the Coronation'. An unmarked tea tin carries a full length portrait of the Queen in a blue evening dress with, in three ovals, Westminster Abbey, Buckingham Palace and Windsor Castle.

The Peak Frean red cake tin (Plate 594) carries on the lift-off lid the state crown surmounted by the British lion and the Queen's monogram surrounded by the national flowers, again no daffodil. Around the side are the state trumpet, the royal standard and the Queen's monogram.

Rowntree's of York provided six tins of chocolate, one for the present Queen and one each for the five previous Queens regnant, Elizabeth I, Mary I and Mary II, Anne and Victoria (Plate 593).

Prince Charles and Princess Anne are on part of a set of glass dishes for the coronation (Plate 595), captioned 'Royal Souvenir'. Another dish in the set (Plate 642D) shows the royal family.

The Royal Pageant on the Thames was the subject of packs of cards by the Worshipful Company showing the royal barge being escorted as part of the coronation

Plate 591. (Left to Right) *Christophers Claret; pair of Cardiff spoons; Coronation Bristol Cream; Coronation Ale; Websters Brown Ale and a Queen-shaped decanter of Armagnac.*

Plate 592. (Left to Right) *Wright's cake tin; G. F. Lovell rectangular tin; Fox's Glacier Mints tin and Brooke Bond tea tin.*

Plate 593. *Two Rowntree's tins – Queen Elizabeth II and Queen Anne. Bilsland tea caddy.*

Plate 594. (Left to Right) *Woodbine cigarette tin, Peak Frean cake tin, unmarked cake tin, Cadbury's Chocolate tin, cake tin.*

Plate 595. *Two glass dishes – Prince Charles and Princess Anne.*

Plate 596. *Magazine covers portraying the Queen's Commonwealth coronation tour.*

celebrations in July, 1953 (Plate 660).

The Queen and the Commonwealth

The Queen takes her position as head of the Commonwealth very seriously. After her coronation she embarked on a tour of the Commonwealth. The illustrated 'weeklies' gave full and colourful coverage (Plate 596).

Her visit to New Zealand is recorded on a plate by Ambassador Ware, Simpsons Potters Ltd. (Plate 597A) with a central sepia portrait of the head and shoulders of the Queen surrounded by a vivid cobalt blue border with a decoration of gold. The base is captioned:' To Commemorate the visit of Queen Elizabeth II to New Zealand 1953-1954'.

She visited Canada to open the St Lawrence Seaway with President Eisenhower. A Paragon cup and saucer records this event (Plate 598C). It has a pink border and in the centre of the saucer is the crown surrounded by maple leaves and roses captioned, 'The Royal Visit to Canada, 1959'. The cup has a different motif, at the base of the cup is the monogram, around which are the British lion and the unicorn holding the royal crown, captioned, 'Canada 1959'. The base of the saucer reads 'Their Visit to British Columbia 1959'. A beaker was also produced for the 1959 visit (Plate 598B). The Queen, as Princess Elizabeth, had made a previous visit to Canada with the Duke of Edinburgh in October 1951. Paragon produced a similar cup and saucer for that visit (Plate 598D) which has around the cup and around the saucer a design of maple leaves and roses, and in the centre of the base of the cup is the royal crown with initials 'E & P' surrounded by a laurel wreath.

A mug (Plate 598A) records the actual opening of the St Lawrence Seaway. It shows the Royal Yacht *Britannia* surmounted by the word 'Canada' with the heads of both the Queen and the Duke and on the other side, the great lakes of Canada indicating the position of the Seaway. Tuscan Fine English and Bone China produced a cup and saucer for the event (Plate 599). The Queen's head is surmounted by her title and a map of the Seaway is portrayed, with the maple leaf of Canada and the American eagle.

In addition to providing a coronation souvenir in their usual attractive design, Paragon produced a different cup each year to record anniversaries (Plate 600). They are all of the same design in pale blue with the monograms 'E & P' and have different motifs at the base of the cup and on the saucer, normally wreaths of flowers, some with and some without maple leaves or the Queen's monogram. The one for the coronation itself is slightly more decorative. There was a gap until the twenty-fifth Anniversary in 1978.

State Visits

When the Queen visited Japan in 1975 the Commemorative Collectors' Society commissioned a design from the well-

Plate 597A. *Plate – visit to New Zealand.* ***B.*** *Wedgwood plate – visit to Bermuda.* ***C.*** *Plate for visit to the Home Fleet 1957.*

Plate 598. *(Left to Right)* A. *Mug for visit to Canada.* ***B.*** *Beaker for visit to British Colombia, 1959.* ***C.*** *Paragon cup and saucer for visit to Canada and British Colombia.* ***D.*** *Paragon cup and saucer for visit to Canada 1951.*

Plate 599. *Tuscan cup and saucer for the opening of the St Lawrence Seaway.*

known designer, Clifford Richards. The plate (Plate 601B) is white porcelain with on glaze transfer print coloured decoration of red, blue and white with a gold rim. The design incorporates the red sun, national emblem of Japan, and the cross of the union flag, complementing each other against a background of sky and sea, representing the water which surrounds both islands. This was the first state visit ever made by a British sovereign to Japan.

In 1986 the Queen made a state visit to China, the first visit there by a British monarch, and carried out a tour including the Great Wall (Plate 601A). A fine bone china plate was published by Wilton, Dorincourt. It has in the centre colourful portraits of the Queen and the President of China surrounded by flowers and the Chinese flag and the Union Jack surmounted by a pagoda. Around the border are the royal arms and the arms of China, surrounded by swags of the royal flowers, including the daffodil. There was a limited edition of 250 plates.

In October 1988 the Queen and the Duke of Edinburgh visited Spain. A highly colourful plate was produced by Panorama studios (Plate 602B), having in the centre portraits of Queen Elizabeth, the King of Spain, the Duke of Edinburgh and the Queen of Spain. It is surrounded by the two national flags and the two national emblems and around the border, all in colour, are the various coats of arms and shields of Spanish Provinces.

An elegant folding fan (Plate 602A) with carved and pierced ivory sticks and guards was produced for this visit. The design is hand printed in full colour on hand-made paper. It consists of painted miniature portraits of the Queen and the Duke of Edinburgh and the King and Queen of Spain in the centre, with national flags of each country on either side. On each side of this central design are the royal arms of Spain on the left and the UK on the right. They are surrounded by a scroll containing an inscription which reads: 'To commemorate the first state visit of a British Reigning Sovereign to Spain; 17th to 21st October, 1988'. The top and bottom edges of the fan are decorated with the shields of the seventeen autonomous Spanish regions and in the left lower corner the badge of the Order of the Garter. The carved and pierced ivory sticks and guards are decorated with a design consisting of crossed and draped flags on the guards and the sticks are carved as columns with a pennant draped around them. It was manufactured by John Brooker of Kings Lynn in Norfolk.

Her visit to the United Arab Emirates in 1979 has been recorded by a mug (Plate 623C). It carries the portrait of the head of the Queen in a cartouche surmounted by a crown,

Plate 600. *Five Paragon cups and saucers for coronation anniversaries.*

Plate 601A. *Plate for visit to China.* **B.** *Plate for royal visit to Japan.*

Plate 602 A. *Fan for visit to Spain, 1988.* **B.** *Plate for the visit to Spain.* **C.** *Limited edition mug for the visit to Cyprus, 1993.*

Plate 602D. *Coronet Pottery plate for the visit to Russia, 1994.*

Plate 602E. *Coronet Pottery plate for the visit to South Africa, 1995.*

Plate 603. (Left to Right) A. *Visit to Aberfan beaker.* ***B.*** *Visit to Rye mug.* ***C.*** *Edinburgh Commonwealth Games mug.* ***D.*** *Rye mug – Queen's 60th birthday.* ***E.*** *Aynsley 60th birthday mug.* ***F.*** *Lledo model Rolls Royce – Ruby Wedding of the Queen.* ***G.*** *American Bicentenary visit beaker.* ***H.*** *Duke of Edinburgh – Presentation of Colours beaker.* ***I. (at the back)*** *The EEC plate.*

Plate 604. (Left to Right) A. *Coalport bonbonniere.* ***B.*** *Aynsley plate.* ***C.*** *Snowdon designed Wedgwood Silver Jubilee tankard.* ***D.*** *Wedgwood Guyatt mug.*

Plate 605. *Upton Pottery plaque for the Silver Wedding.*

Plate 606 . *Royal Worcester figurine.*

with a design of Arab buildings and palms and there are the flags of each of the states she visited: Oman, Qatar, United Arab Emirates, Kuwait, Bahrain and Saudi Arabia. The base has the caption: 'First woman to be accorded equal rights in a male dominated society'. The mug was published by Panorama Studios of Ashburton in Devon.

The Queen's visit to Bermuda is recorded on a Wedgwood plate (Plate 597B) in the usual blue and white, the centre carrying a profiled head of the Queen in relief surrounded by laurel leaves and the base is inscribed: 'Made especially for A.S. Cooper and Sons Ltd., to commemorate the visit February 1975'.

The Queen visited America as part of the Bicentennial celebrations in 1976 and a mug (Plate 603G) records this event, also published by Panorama Studios in the serigraphic medium. It carries a portrait of the Queen, above which are the Union Jack and the Stars and Stripes and a portrait of President Ford is on the other side.

The Queen visited Cyprus in 1993 and a mug (Plate 602C) was published to commemorate the event. Commissioned by Paul Wyton and Joe Spiteri in a limited edition of one hundred and produced by J & S Chown, Hayle, Cornwall, the mug has as its centrepiece the head of the Queen wearing a wide brimmed hat in a design of sun rays, underneath which is the island of Cyprus surrounded by two separate sets of Corinthian columns. On the reverse is an inscription which reads –

'Historical Royal visit to Cyprus 1993
H.M. The Queen accompanied by H.R.H. Prince Philip.
First visit of a ruling British Monarch since
King Richard the Lionheart on his way to the Crusades.'

In October 1994 the Queen became the first British reigning monarch to visit Russia, as a guest of President Yeltsin. She visited Moscow and St. Petersburg and attended a gala performance of the Bolshoi's 'Giselle'. She laid a wreath at the war cemetery in St. Petersburg. Aynsley China produced a mug, Sutherland China a lion head beaker and Caithness Glass a royal purple paperweight featuring St. Basil's, Moscow. Goss China produced a plate featuring photographic portraits of the Queen with President and Mrs. Yeltsin. Around the plate are four medallions of the Kremlin, St. Basil's Basilica in Moscow. The Winter Palace and St. Isaac's Basilica in St. Petersburg. At the top is the new Russian coat of arms. Coronet Pottery produced a prestigious plate with portraits of the Queen and President on the new coat of arms (Plate 602D). The plate has a red, white and blue border, the royal arms and the Russian arms at the top, with sprigs of oak leaves and flowers (the rose, thistle, shamrock and carnation) all around. On the left is St. George (patron saint of both England and Russia), on the right the arms of St. Petersburg and at the bottom the flags of the two countries. The Queen presented a number of these plates during her visit.

In March 1995 she visited the new South Africa and conferred the Order of Merit on President Mandela. Aynsley China produced a mug and Sutherland China a lion head beaker to commemorate the royal visit. Each displays a central portrait of the Queen in a wide-brimmed turquoise hat. Coronet Pottery produced a plate with portraits of the Queen and President Mandela in the centre, on a colour picture of the king protea flower (Plate 602E). The two countries' coats of arms are at the top of the plate and the border has the names of the main South African towns between sprigs of South African flowers.

Royal Visits

The Queen made several visits to towns and cities in her kingdom. Her visit to Aberfan after the terrible tragedy takes the form of an ordinary Welsh mug (Plate 603A) showing a cottage scene of a Welsh lady wearing a tall hat with a spinning wheel taking tea captioned: 'Souvenir of Wales' with the daffodil, and superimposed specially for the occasion are the words: 'Queen's visit to Aberfan, March 1973'.

The Queen visited the Home Fleet on 27th and 29th May 1957, and a plate published by Minton records this event (Plate 597C). It is of bone china, and carries around the border the royal emblems, this time including the leek. It is in a design of anchors and ship's ropes.

Her visit to Rye is recorded on a mug made by Rye Pottery (Plate 603B). This is in the usual Rye Pottery colours of cream and blue, with a viking ship above the word 'Rye' and the date of the visit, 'October 28th, 1966'.

Her visit to the Commonwealth Games held in Edinburgh is recorded on a mug by Weatherby (Plate 603C). It has a portrait of the head of the Queen surrounded in a cartouche by thistles, the royal standard and the flag of St Andrew, above which is the well-known Olympic figure of the discus thrower. It is captioned: 'Commonwealth Games, Edinburgh, 1970'.

The Duke of Edinburgh presented new colours to the 40th Command of the Royal Marines on Plymouth Hoe on 1st July 1976, and a mug (Plate 603H) records this event. It has a portrait of the head of the Duke surmounted by the Union Jack and the blue ensign featuring the badge of the Royal Marines.

The Queen's Birthdays

The Queen's fiftieth birthday is recorded on a mug by Rye Pottery (Plate 603D), again in their usual colours, having as its central motif the crown and the dates '21st April, 1926-1976'.

Her sixtieth birthday is recorded by Aynsley on a china mug (Plate 603E), showing the Queen at the Trooping of the Colour, riding her horse Burmese, in ceremonial uniform. The inscription reads: 'God Save Our Gracious Queen, Long Live Our Noble Queen'. Around the inside of the lip of the cup is the date of her sixtieth birthday – '21st April 1986'.

The Queen's Silver Wedding, 1972

Aynsley manufactured a quality plate (Plate 604B) which records this event. It has, in the centre, Westminster Abbey, on either side of which are the Queen's monogram and that of the Duke of Edinburgh, and underneath, a caption to say it was made for the Silver Wedding.

The Wedgwood mug (Plate 604D) was designed by Richard Guyatt. This is on a base of light cream with the head of the Queen in black silhouette surrounded by a garland of gold and black surmounted by a crown; a similar garland contains the silhouette of Prince Philip. The decoration involves wedding bells entwined around the top and it is clearly a highly desirable commemorative. The base records the purpose of the mug. The inside lip is in silver, as is the handle.

Coalport produced an attractive bonbon dish (Plate 604A) in gold and purple on a white background with the heads of the Queen and the Duke, in profile in gold. The base of the foot records the date of the wedding, 'November 20th, 1947'. This is a limited edition and was designed by D. Brindley. The lift-off lid has a gold knob in the centre of the basic design of purple and gold. The words 'Elizabeth and Philip' are around the lid.

Perhaps the most original and certainly the most handsome commemorative is a plaque by Groves and Beard of Upton Pottery (Plate 605). The centre has a bold oak tree in purple, in the branches of which there are twenty-five candles. The rays of the sun shine from a central silver rim into the tree and standing to the left of the tree is a large bull representing Taurus, the Queen's zodiac sign. There are the royal flowers, thistles and roses are separate and the leeks are placed in a planted position with Gemini, the Duke's zodiac sign represented by two boys in pastoral tunics. It is captioned: 'Royal Silver Wedding', but only six of these were produced, putting it well outside the reach of ordinary members of the public.

Among more reasonably priced commemoratives for the Silver Wedding were ashtrays, sweet dishes and candy jars, most of these were by Wedgwood in their well-known blue and white.

The Queen's Silver Jubilee, 1977

The Queen had, during her reign, shown herself to be readily available to the public and her Jubilee was looked forward to with enormous interest by the people. Factories of all kinds ensured that it was properly celebrated in a commemorative form.

An exhibition entitled 'Jubilee Royal' was promoted by the Commemorative Collectors' Society and opened at the Goldsmiths Hall by Princess Alice, Duchess of Gloucester. It travelled to Edinburgh, Cardiff and Sheffield, and comprised the most comprehensive list of royal memorabilia for the Jubilee that had ever been produced. Every aspect was covered, ceramics, glass, silver, printed ephemera, pewter and leather. The prices varied from the most expensive bowl, supplied by Garrard & Co, selling at £4,950 to an ordinary pencil, price 7p.

The most expensive ceramic was provided by Royal Worcester at £1,000. It was a porcelain figurine of the Queen (Plate 606), the third of the Queens Regnant series produced by the company. Modelled by Ronald Van Ruyckvelt, the Queen is depicted in full ceremonial dress of the Order of the Garter and mounted on a hexagonal walnut plinth. It stands 14¾in. high. The figure was limited to 250. There are six in the set and they are intended to join up to make one large centrepiece. The others already completed are Mary I 1553-58 and Elizabeth I 1558-1603. Mary II 1689-94, Anne 1702-14 and Victoria 1837-1901 are yet to be made.

A fine white earthenware Wedgwood tankard carries a portrait photograph of the Queen by Lord Snowdon (Plate 604C). The royal coat of arms is depicted on the reverse with a commemorative inscription. Lord Snowdon's name as designer is acknowledged on the back stamp.

At the lower end of the price scale is an earthenware mug with a handle which has a screen-printed design in silver on a cobalt blue background. On the front of the mug appears the Queen's Silver Jubilee emblem with a further decoration around the top and bottom of the mug, consisting of a continuous band of crowns. A similar mug has in it an Easter egg in silver paper (Plate 607E).

A mug by Carlton Ware (Plate 607A) has two legs with blue striped stockings and black shoes. The design inside is the royal cypher together with the inscription of the Queen's Silver Jubilee on a scroll surrounding it. It was designed by Roger Mitchell and Danka Napiorkowsk.

Mayfairs Pottery produced a teapot (Plate 608A) with a portrait of the Queen surrounded by the royal flowers and surmounted with a crown. The dates 1952-77 are on each side.

An exhibition was opened by the Duchess of Kent on 9th May, 1979 and featured the collection of royal memorabilia. A mug was produced for this occasion (Plate 608B) captioned: 'To commemorate your visit to Jubilation, Bethnal Green Museum, London'. It has a portrait of Charles II and of King George V. It was available to those who attended the exhibition.

A special mug entitled 'Operation Friendship. Britain Welcomes Old Friends in Silver Jubilee Year' is designed in blue with three crowns and the dates (Plate 608C).

The Queen reviewed the fleet on 28th June at Spithead. Both a plate and a mug were published for this occasion. The mug is earthenware, amber in colour and with a silver coloured handle decorated with transfer prints. The front shows contains colour portraits of the Queen surrounded by illustrations in part silhouette of the ships of the fleet. The reverse side is decorated with an illustration of the royal yacht *Britannia* dressed overall and captioned 'HMS Yacht Britannia, June 28th, Fleet Review at Spithead 1977' on a ribbon band underneath. The plate (Plate 609B) has a similar design on a white earthenware octagonal shaped background with embossed gilding.

The Queen reviewed her troops in Germany, and a fine earthenware cylindrical handled tankard (Plate 609C) was produced with enamelled coloured transfer decorations. On the front is a three quarter length portrait of the Queen by Gilroy. On the reverse are the combined flags of the United Kingdom, Germany and NATO with the inscription underneath, 'Army Silver Jubilee Review, Sennelheer, 7th July, 1977', the top rim of the tankard is decorated with three wine coloured bands. It was manufactured by Wedgwood and was on sale exclusively to members of HM forces in West Germany through the NAAFI. It was not available for sale in the UK.

Other well known manufacturers, Spode, Paragon, Coalport, Minton and Wedgwood, all produced a large number of commemorative pieces in their usual designs.

Battersea produced several enamelled boxes and beakers. Royal Brierley Crystal and Stuart and Sons Crystal were

Plate 607A. Carltonware 'two legs' kneeling mug. B. Aynsley plate. C. New Quay Cardiganshire mug. D. Llandaff Cathedral School – Rumney Pottery mug. E. Mug with Easter Egg.

***Plate 608. (left to right) A.** Mayfairs Pottery Jubilee teapot. **B.** 'Jubilation' mug for Bethnal Green Exhibition. **C.** 'Operation Friendship' mug.*

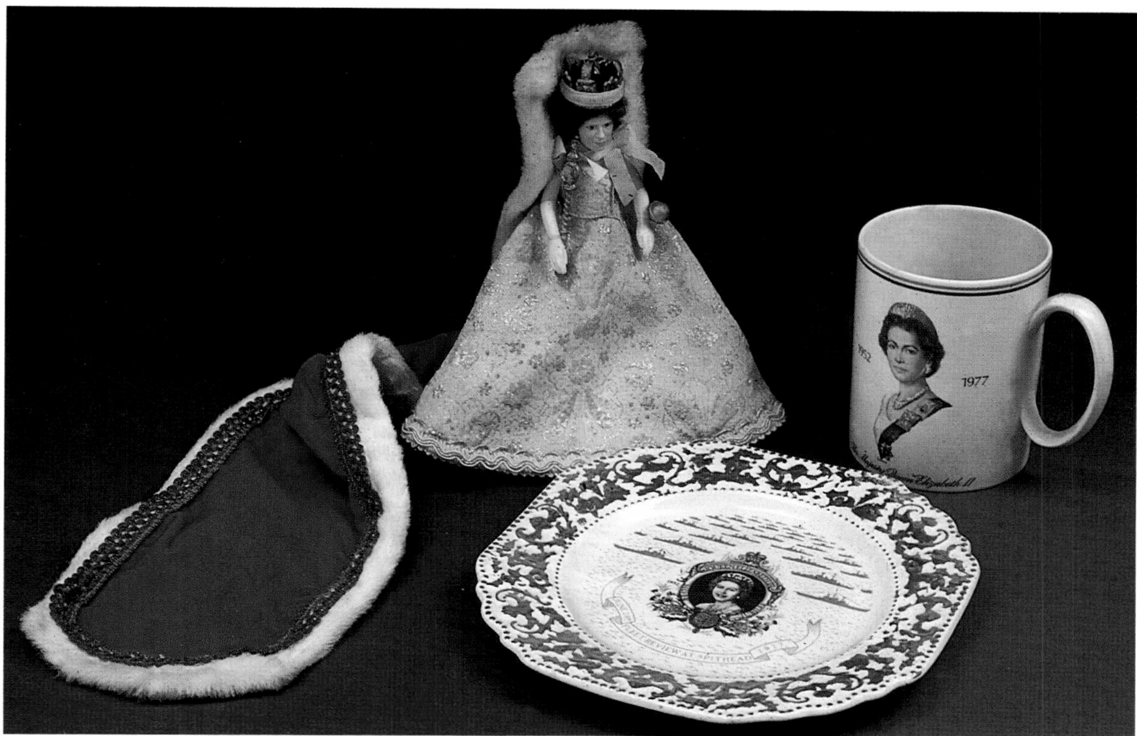

Plate 609A. *Peggy Nisbett doll.* ***B.*** *Spithead Review plate.* ***C.*** *Tankard for the Review of troops in Germany.*

Plate 610. (left to right) A. *Beaker for the Poets Laureate.* ***B.*** *Beaker for Masters of the Queen's Music.* ***C.*** *Whitbread's Jubilee Ale.* ***D.*** *Ansells Jubilee Ale.* ***E.*** *Mettoy state landau.*

among many firms which provided glass goblets and decanters, and various items of glassware.

Many cities and towns produced mugs for distribution to children or for sale. New Quay, Cardiganshire had a small tankard bearing portraits of the Queen and the Duke between bunches of the royal flowers, including the daffodil (Plate 607C). Many schools themselves produced mugs. The Cathedral School in Llandaff, Cardiff provided a mug by Rumney Pottery (Plate 607D). It has a blue design with a silver rim and base and an embossed crown and the Queen's titles and the date and on the reverse the mitre of the Bishop of Llandaff.

Crown Staffordshire published a mug commissioned by *The Observer*, entitled 'The Observer Silver Jubilee Mug'. In the centre is a portrait of the Queen beneath the crown supported on either side by lions rampant holding the royal parliamentary maces. Beneath the portrait of the Queen, in an oval frame containing his name and the year 1976, appears a portrait of the Prime Minister, James Callaghan. On either side of the mug set against a background design of roses and an elaborate scroll pattern are oval frames, three either side, containing portraits, years of office and names of the six previous Prime Ministers who held office during the Queen's reign: Winston Churchill, Anthony Eden, Harold Macmillan, Alec Douglas-Home, Harold Wilson and Edward Heath.

Aynsley China provided a white bone china plate (Plate 607B), the rim decorated with coloured enamel transfers and gilding to the outer and inner rim edge. In the centre of the plate appear the royal arms, above a decorative scroll panel edge with the national flowers and surmounted by a coronet containing the names and dates of reign of the Kings and Queens of England since 1042. The designer was R. Heath.

In addition to promoting the exhibition 'Jubilee Royal', the Commemorative Collectors' Society commissioned a set of plates and beakers to cover various aspects of the Queen's reign and her interest in the Commonwealth. A beaker (Plate 610A) carries the Queen in the centre and around are the three Poet Laureates of her reign, Sir John Masefield, C. Day Lewis and Sir John Betjeman. Around the base is the caption: 'Let The Bells From Every Steeple Ring Out Loud The Jubilee'. Another beaker (Plate 610B) has portraits of the Queen with the Masters of the Queen's Music, Sir Arnold Bax, Sir Arthur Bliss, and Malcolm Williamson. These portraits are framed in a design of musical instruments. A third beaker has the Archbishops of Canterbury in her reign.

Male members of the royal family are depicted on a plate (Plate 611B) with Prince Philip in the centre surrounded by Prince Charles, the Duke of Kent, Angus Ogilvy, Prince Andrew, Earl Mountbatten of Burma, Prince Edward, Captain Mark Phillips and Prince Richard, Duke of Gloucester. This particular plate shows several members of the royal family who had not previously been ceramically commemorated – the Duke of Kent, Angus Ogilvy, the Duke of Gloucester and Prince Edward.

The ladies of the Royal Family are depicted on a similar plate (Plate 611A), the Queen in the centre with portraits of the Queen Mother, Princess Margaret, Princess Alice, the Duchess of Gloucester, the Duchess of Kent, Princess Alexandra, Princess Anne and Princess Alice, Countess of Athlone. The same applies to this plate, neither the Duchess of Gloucester, the Duchess of Kent nor Princess Alexandra have been ceramically recorded on other pieces.

A coupe plate (Plate 612A) has the Queen in the centre surrounded by monarchs reigning at the time of her Jubilee. They include King Baudouin of the Belgians, the Shah of Persia, the King of Jordan, the Emperor of Japan, Prince Rainier of Monaco, Queen Juliana of the Netherlands, the Grand Duke of Luxembourg, King Rama XI of Thailand and King Sobhuza II of Swaziland.

Another coupe plate (Plate 613A) has, in the centre, the Queen as head of the Commonwealth surmounted by a crown and surrounded by the shields of the Commonwealth countries.

The Queen is shown on a plate (Plate 614A) with members of the judiciary, including the Lord Chancellor, Lord Elwyn Jones; the Lord Chief Justice, Lord Widgery; the Master of the Rolls, Lord Denning; the President of the Family Division, Sir George Baker; the Vice Chancellor of the Chancery Division, Sir Robert Megarry, Lord Wilberforce, the Senior Lord of Appeal in Ordinary and also shown are a recorder, a circuit judge and the chief metropolitan magistrate.

She is shown on another plate (Plate 614B) with all her Prime Ministers, carrying the same portraits as those on the *Observer* mug.

A special plate was commissioned for the Queen, as Queen Elizabeth I of Scotland (Plate 615A). It has, in the centre, the head of the Queen surrounded by a garland of thistles and held by the lion and unicorn as supporters. The caption reads: 'I can never forget that I was crowned Queen of the United Kingdom of Great Britain, Northern Ireland'. A further plate (Plate 615B) has the Queen in the centre surrounded by former sovereigns who had reached jubilees. Queen Victoria: sixty years; King Edward III, King Henry III and King George III: fifty years and King George V: twenty-five years.

A plate was published for the royal Silver Jubilee visit to Tonga on 14th February, 1977 (Plate 612B), with portraits of the Queen and the King of Tonga in the centre of the plate with the cross and the dove of peace from Tonga's royal arms in between. The royal arms of Tonga appear at the top centre of the plate and the royal arms of the Queen at the bottom centre. The rim of the plate is decorated with the national flower of Tonga.

For her visit to New Zealand in March a similar coupe china plate (Plate 616A) has coloured enamel transfer print decorations and fine litho portraits in sepia of the Queen, the Governor General and the Prime Minister of New Zealand. Top centre of the plate appear the royal arms on a shield surmounted by a crown and encircled by the garter belt. Bottom centre appear the arms of New Zealand with supporters. Illustrations of the duck-billed platypus and a kiwi bird decorate the rim together with a design of New Zealand national flowers.

The visit to Australia is recorded on a similar white coupe china plate (Plate 616B). In the centre of the plate is a portrait of the Queen flanked either side but slightly lower, by portraits of the Prime Minister, Mr Malcolm Frazer and the Governor General, Sir John Kerr. Top centre appear the royal arms on a shield surmounted by a crown and encircled

Plate 611A. *The Queen and ladies of the royal family.* **B.** *Prince Philip and male members of the royal family.*

Plate 612A. *Reigning Monarch's plate.* **B.** *Tonga plate.*

Plate 613A. *Commonwealth plate.* **B.** *Nottingham jubilee visit plate.*

Plate 614A. *Judiciary plate.* ***B.*** *Prime Ministers plate.*

Plate 615A. *Queen Elizabeth I of Scotland plate.* ***B.*** *Plate for former royal jubilees.*

Plate 616A. *New Zealand plate.* **B.** *Australia plate.*

Plate 617A. *Visit to Wales plate.* **B.** *Opening of Welsh College of Music and Drama plate.*

by a garter belt. Bottom centre are the arms of Australia with supporters. The rim of the plate contains illustrations of a merino sheep and koala bear together with sprays of the various national flowers of Australia. Very few of these plates were published but a similar one appears with, in the place of the Prime Minister and the Governor General, portraits of Prince Philip and the Prince of Wales.

The Queen's jubilee visit to Nottingham is recorded on a plate (Plate 613B) showing in the centre a portrait of the Queen surmounted by the royal arms and being held by two stags, and around the rim are decorations of oak leaves. At the base is the Nottingham Town Hall and another public building, between which are the County of Nottingham coat of arms and its motto, *Vivit post funera vertus*. The caption is: 'The Royal Visit to Nottingham, July 7th'.

The Queen's jubilee visit to Wales is recorded on a plate (Plate 617A), the Queen in the centre, beneath a smaller portrait of the Prince of Wales. Above him are the crown and two daffodils. Around the plate are places the Queen visited: Caerphilly Castle, Llandaff Cathedral where she attended a service, Harlech Castle, The Abbey at Neath, the City Hall of Cardiff, the Priory at Haverfordwest, and the Welsh College of Music and Drama, whose premises she officially opened.

A separate plate was published for the Queen's official opening of the Welsh College of Music and Drama (Plate 617B). It has in the centre a portrait of the Queen surmounted by the Cardiff coat of arms and around this are the portraits of the Lord Mayor and Lady Mayoress of Cardiff, the Speaker of the House of Commons, and the Prime Minister (both of whom were members of parliament for Cardiff), the Recorder of Cardiff, the Bishop of Llandaff, the Lord Lieutenant of the Counties of Glamorgan and the Principal of the Welsh College of Music and Drama.

There were several jubilee ales, champagnes and wines (Plate 618). A bottle of ale from Courage Ltd., bottles of champagne from various well known champagne houses, including Joseph Perrier Fils & Co., a bottle of Skol lager and a bottle of jubilee port from Delaforce and Sons Co. The bottle reads 'This very old tawny port has been specially bottled to commemorate the silver jubilee of the Queen which comprises a limited production of 5,000 bottles and 100 magnums all bottled in Oporto'. Whitbread and Ansell's also provided pint bottles of silver jubilee ale.

Jubilee Novelties were also produced. Sunarama produced a naughty bra and brief set. On the vital parts is the Queen's jubilee motto.

Peggy Nisbett manufactured several dolls in different shapes and sizes. A special large model was made of the Queen in state robes and crown and holding orb and sceptre with the cross (Plate 609A). The robe is trimmed with ermine and decorated at the hem with the royal cypher. The doll is produced from a composition material and is 18ins. high. Only ten of these models were manufactured and they were not available generally for sale. A smaller model of similar design was available to the public and was limited to five hundred dolls.

The Mettoy Co. Ltd., provided a model of the 1902 state landau (Plate 610E) manufactured from a combination of die-cast metal, plastic and decorative transfer labels. The landau is fixed to a display base and is pulled by four horses with outriders with two footmen seated on the back, behind the seated figures of the Queen and the Duke of Edinburgh. A model of a small corgi stands at the rear of the landau. The inscription along the front of the base plinth reads '1902 State Landau – Silver Jubilee 1977'. This edition was unlimited.

A jigsaw puzzle (Plate 619) shows the Queen seated on a tall, throne-like gold chair with her hand on the head of a lion which forms part of the arms of the chair.

Aristoc Ltd., a subsidiary of Courtaulds, sold nylon knee

Plate 618A. *Skol Jubilee lager.* **B.** *Courage Jubilee ale.* **C.** *Delaforce Jubilee port.*

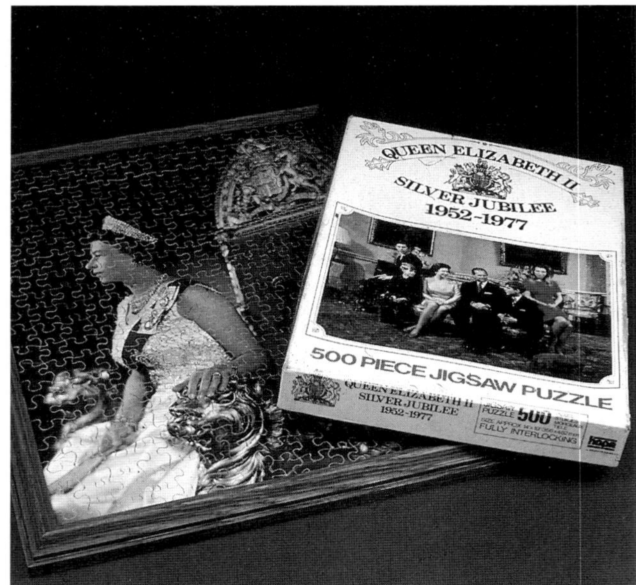

Plate 619. *Jubilee jigsaw puzzles.*

Plate 620 (left to right) A. *Courtaulds socks.* ***B.*** *Rowntree Macintosh toffee tin.* ***C.*** *Huntley and Palmer's rectangular biscuit tin.* ***D.*** *Meltis Fruits tin.* ***E.*** *Huntley and Palmer's cylindrical tin.*

high socks (Plate 620A) with red and white vertical stripes and a union jack. This was an unlimited edition and the price was only 90p per pair.

A model of a London routemaster silver jubilee bus (Plate 621A) was produced in die cast metal with transfer labels. Along the side of the bus are the words, 'Woolworth welcomes the World'.

Reeves of Lincoln Road, Enfield produced a small box containing four paints (Plate 621E), each in an enamel tin displaying different motifs: the Queen and the Duke of Edinburgh, the royal jubilee symbol, the Queen and the Duke on the balcony of Buckingham Palace with Prince Charles and Princess Anne after the coronation, and the royal flags and the royal standard.

Liberty produced a cottage entitled the 'Jubilee Arms' (Plate 622). It was a kind of pastiche model of the Rockingham cottages and pastille burners which were made in the early part of the nineteenth century.

Aidee's Home and Export Co. produced a clear plastic pack of two tablets of soap (Plate 621B), each carrying a portrait of the Queen in decorative frame acknowledging the jubilee, above the frame is St Edward's crown. Below is the royal coat of arms surrounded by the garter. Decorative sprays of national flowers are on either side. The same firm also had a round opaque cast glass bottle of perfume in a display carton which carries sprays of Devon violets (Plate 621D). The design is similar to the soap. Morny provided various products of soap, or bath oil in the shape of a bell.

A circular tin with the royal cypher in silver on a red background and circular bands in silver with red, white and blue on the lid contains matches and was a commemorative tin produced by the Cornish Match Co., St Ives, Cornwall.

Revlon Perfumers provided a special scent bottle in a silver box for the South Glamorgan silver jubilee gala held at Penllyn Castle, near Cowbridge.

Parker provided a big red, white and blue pen and Platignum a smaller pen. W.H. Smith provided a carton of four souvenir pencils. There were dusters, tea cloths, tray cloths, paper plates and one particular tea towel designed in the form of a telegram from Buckingham Palace which reads, 'Congratulations on the occasion of your Silver Jubilee. Your Loyal Subjects'.

All the main biscuit and chocolate firms produced jubilee commemoratives. Huntley and Palmer manufactured a biscuit tin, cylindrical in shape (Plate 620E) with a small knob on the lid, with portraits of the Queen and the Duke of Edinburgh together with the four heraldic symbols of the United Kingdom in full colour. Another tin from Huntley and Palmer was rectangular in shape (Plate 620C) with a portrait photograph of the Queen and the Duke taken in Windsor

Plate 621 (left to right) A. *London Routemaster bus.* **B.** *Aidee's soap pack.* **C.** *Cadbury's Milk Tray chocolate tin.* **D.** *Aidee's perfume bottle in display carton.* **E.** *Reeve's paint box, postcards, stamps and tea towel.*

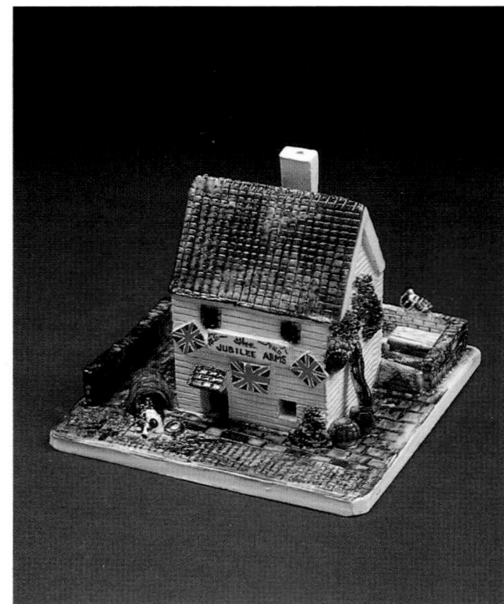

Plate 622. *Liberty's 'Jubilee Arms' cottage.*

Plate 623 (left to right) A. *Beaker for the 95th birthday of Princess Alice of Athlone.* **B.** *Caverswall mug for the assassination of Earl Mountbatten by the IRA.* **C.** *Mug for the visit to the Emirates.* **D.** *J & J May mug – death of Princess Alice.* **E.** *Paragon loving cup for the 25th anniversary of the coronation.*

Castle. The surround contains heraldic symbols of the United Kingdom.

Robert Jackson, the quality tea merchants of Piccadilly, had a tin bearing portraits of the Queen and the Duke in cartouches surrounded by silver laurel wreaths surmounted by crowns and the royal flags. On each side, in a wreath of the royal flowers, are Windsor Castle and Buckingham Palace.

Meltis Ltd. provided a circular printed tin (Plate 620D) with a loose lid in gold and blue and heavily embossed. In the centre of the domed lid inset in a gold frame is a colour portrait of the Queen. The portrait is encircled by a recurring decorative drape design embossed in gold relief against a blue background. The sides of the tin are decorated with a flat printed design of golden drapes in classical style. It contains approximately 9.2 ounces of Meltis Newberry Fruits.

Rowntree Macintosh produced a circular tin (Plate 620B) bearing on the lid a formal portrait of the Queen encircled by a red band. Below the portrait is the jubilee inscription and around the top of the rim of the lid is a simplified version of St Edward's crown. In an alternating design around the side of the tin are St Edward's crown and a floral motif incorporating the tudor rose. The Cadbury tin (Plate 621C) contains portraits of the Queen and the Duke on the lid within simple cartouche frames, with the royal arms appearing in the centre between the portraits and printed in colour. The decoration is white on a purple coloured background. They were produced for Cadbury by Huntley Bourne and Stevens of Reading. The tin contained one pound of Cadbury's Milk Tray assortment.

Old Holborn produced a tin of their well known tobacco, the lid of which is a design of tobacco leaves captioned: 'Royal Jubilee Celebration'.

The list is exhaustive. Cufflinks, necklaces, key rings, key fobs, paper knives, serviette rings, money clips, ashtrays and candles. There was something for everybody at prices all could afford if they wished to participate in this great national event. And they certainly did, it was a tremendous success.

The twenty-fifth anniversary of the coronation was separately recorded by Paragon on a loving cup with gold lion handles (Plate 623E). On one side are the dates 1953-1978' and Crowned in Westminster Abbey, June 2nd, 1952' within the wreath and the national flowers, including the daffodil. On the other side is the state coach, captioned: To commemorate the 25th Anniversary of the Coronation', and around the inside of the lip are the words: 'My Life Devoted to Your Service'.

Queen for Forty Years

The Queen's fortieth anniversary, 6th February 1992, has been the subject of several commemoratives.

Aynsley produced a garniture of three ruby vases (Plate 624) featuring a hand-painted view of Windsor Castle on a ruby background with 22 carat gold gilding on a pedestal foot. There is also a matching mug.

A lion's head beaker carries a half portrait of the Queen in

Plate 624(left). *Aynsley ruby vase.*

Plate 625. *Goss plate for the Queen's fortieth anniversary.*

a cartouche design in red and gold with the crown surmounting.

Caithness Glass made a paperweight with a ruby ground colour. A floral circle of the royal flowers is surrounded by a crown motif, the number '40' within the circle incorporating the dates 1952-1992.

Goss China produced an 8in. plate portraying a half portrait of the Queen surrounded by a design of cartouches within which are the royal residences: Windsor Castle, Buckingham Palace, Balmoral, Sandringham, and Holyrood House.

From Royal Worcester – a tea caddy showing a coach arriving at Buckingham Palace with uniformed guards. The coronation jewels and floral emblems are incorporated in the design.

Prince Charles, Prince of Wales

So far as is known little, if anything, has been recorded for the birth of Prince Charles. However, there is a small glass custard cup on a square base with a handle in the shape of roundels. An engraving carries the words: 'Our Royal Prince November 14th 1948'.

The Queen announced, at the conclusion of the Empire Games held in Cardiff in 1958, that she intended to create Prince Charles Prince of Wales. Nothing has been recorded ceramically for this proclamation as Prince of Wales, the nearest record is a cup and saucer for the Games themselves (Plate 626). This is by Windsor China and has the British Empire Commonwealth Games logo surmounted by the red dragon and captioned: 'British Empire Commonwealth Games Wales 1958'.

His investiture at Caernarvon Castle on 1st July 1969 followed the precedent set in 1911. Whereas on that occasion few commemoratives were commissioned, this time there were many more. However, although there had been an increase in the interest in commemoratives in 1969 the manufacturers had not really got to grips with the need for a popular souvenir, and those that were commissioned tended to be rather too expensive.

Cardiff presented a mug (Plate 627B) to school children and it is one of the only commemoratives which has a portrait of the Prince of Wales. He is shown in an oval cartouche surmounted by the crown and national flags and it was published by Coronet Pottery of Prestatyn. It bears on the other side the coat of arms of the City of Cardiff and the name of the Lord Mayor by whom it was presented. The cost of this mug initially cannot have been more than about 25p but prices have risen considerably. Those collectors who are fortunate enough to have both this and the 1911 investiture mug have two collectors' pieces.

The high quality porcelain manufacturers made the most of the commemoratives. Wedgwood made a large series of mugs and hexagonal moneyboxes. One of the mugs was designed by Richard Guyatt (Plate 628D). The bold design has a gold and black dragon and Prince of Wales feathers and an inscription in Welsh: 'Caernarfon 1969'.

A Wedgwood black basalt mug (Plate 628C), designed by Norman Wilson, is in the usual black and gold and has as its central motif the Prince of Wales feathers in the centre of a

Plate 626. *Cup and saucer, Commonwealth Games Cardiff, 1958.*

Plate 627A. *Plate of Prince receiving freedom of the City of Cardiff.* ***B.*** *Cardiff Investiture mug.*

laurel wreath on one side and the Welsh dragon on the other. It is captioned: 'July, 1969, Caernarvon. God Bless the Prince of Wales'. A third Wedgwood mug was designed by Carl Thomas (Plate 628A) from a nineteenth century view of Caernarvon Castle drawn by H. Gastineau and engraved by H. Lacey. The engraving is in black and white and carries around the top 'To commemorate the Investiture', the date and the place.

Aynsley produced a plate (Plate 629A) with, in the centre, the royal coat of arms bearing the eldest son's label. The border came in two colours, white embellished with gold and blue embellished with gold.

Royal Crown Derby had an attractive Welsh dragon (Plate 630B) in red and gold on a cushioned base with a limited number of 250, around the base is an inscription commemorating the investiture.

A rare Royal Worcester Prince of Wales investiture plate is printed in sepia and coloured with a view of Caernarvon Castle in the nineteenth century. It has a gilt rim. Only 150 were made (Plate 628B).

Coalport produced two goblets, one white (Plate 630A), the other blue, each with a gold design of Caernarvon Castle, the rim bearing festoons of pennants and standards of Wales and the leek, the lion and the daffodil.

Two less expensive mugs are both bottle green in colour, one by Holkham Pottery (Plate 629B) bearing the head of the Prince in relief and his feathers and the place and date. The other, a tall tankard by Rumney Pottery (Plate 629C) bears the Prince of Wales feathers and the investiture logo, 'Croeso 69'.

There were other less expensive pottery jugs and mugs. An interesting mug was published by *Private Eye* (Plate 642E), black printed with a grotesque portrait of Prince Charles surrounded by an elaborate cartouche of laurels, standards and the crown, with the caption, below the portrait, 'Good Luck' and a supposed royal cypher 'CR' contained within a laurel cartouche and with a bold inscription, 'King

Plate 628. The Investiture (left to right): A. *Carl Thomas Wedgwood mug.* ***B.*** *Worcester plate.* ***C.*** *Wedgwood black basalt mug.* ***D.*** *Richard Guyatt mug.*

Plate 629A. *Aynsley plate.* **B.** *Holkham Pottery mug.* **C.** *Rumney Pottery tankard.*

Plate 630A. *Coalport goblet.* **B.** *Royal Crown Derby dragon.*

Plate 630C. Beaker to record the 25th anniversary of the investiture of the Prince of Wales.

Charles III Coronation Mug' and a list of the Prince's former titles.

There were ales, claret, port and sherry in various bottles and decanters. Mundays, the Wine Merchants, of Swansea provided a special brew of their dessert sherry (Plate 631C) to honour the investiture of the Prince of Wales. The label indicates that there was a special shipment of sherry for this occasion. The corks are branded: 'Investiture 1969. This wine can be drunk now but will improve greatly over many years. Please decant if over 12 months old'. The label also bears an engraving of Caernarvon Castle.

Sandeman, not to be outdone, provided sherry bottled in the shape of their well known cloaked gentleman, the hat forming the stopper, and the base is captioned: 'Prince of Wales, Caernarvon July 1969'. It is made by Wedgwood, and includes the Prince of Wales feathers. On the back is a label which reads, 'This Wedgwood Don decanter contains Sandeman Armada Sherry, product of Spain'.

After his investiture, the Prince visited the Principality and on 5th July came to the capital where he received the Freedom of the City from the Lord Mayor. A plate (Plate 627A) records this event. In the centre is the Prince receiving the Freedom from the Lord Mayor and around this is a design of roses and daffodils. In other fields, Waterford Glass, Stuart Crystal and Brierley Glass made various goblets, brandy balloons and wine glasses (Plate 632).

Sutherland China produced a lion's head beaker to record the twenty-fifth anniversary of the investure in July 1994. The front shows the Prince in his investiture robes and the back has a picture of the Queen crowning him, with the caption 'To commemorate the 25th Anniversary of the Prince of Wales 1969-1994'.

***Plate 631A.** Sandeman's sherry in a Wedgwood don decanter. **B.** Investiture Ind Coope ale. **C.** Munday's dessert sherry.*

Plate 632A. *Brierley brandy balloon.* ***B.*** *Brierley Stuart crystal ale glass.* ***C.*** *Waterford goblet.*

The Marriage of the Prince of Wales

The Prince's betrothal to Lady Diana Spencer, daughter of the Earl of Spencer, is recorded on a mug by J. & J. May, the commemorators (Plate 633). The design has, in the shape of a heart, the official announcement from Buckingham Palace, held by the lion and the unicorn and surmounted by the Prince of Wales feathers and the date: '24th February, 1981'. A pair to this mug was made for the wedding itself. It also has, on a heart-shaped red background, details of the marriage, surmounted by the Prince of Wales feathers and supported by a griffin and the Welsh dragon, with the date '29th July, 1981'.

The success of the Queen's jubilee in 1977 indicated quite clearly that people were anxious to take part in this kind of royal celebration and commemoratives were produced in every medium and in every form. As in the case of the jubilee, they varied greatly in price but a very large number could be purchased inexpensively by anybody. At the upper end of the price range were those produced by Paragon, Royal Crown Derby, Coalport, and all the well known porcelain manufacturers. The Paragon loving cup (Plate 634B) has the usual gold lion handles and bears a design of the initials, 'C' and 'D', surmounted by a crown. On each side are the Welsh dragon and the Prince of Wales feathers and around are clusters of all the royal flowers, including the daffodil. It contains the details of the marriage, which took place in St Paul's Cathedral on 29th July 1981.

Royal Crown Derby provided several items including a small dish (Plate 634C), in the centre of which is a spray of flowers with the Prince of Wales feathers above, together with the names of the Prince of Wales and Lady Diana Spencer and in a golden scroll, 'St Paul's Cathedral, 29th July, 1981'.

An elegant bone china plate from Royal Doulton (Plate 633) bears an original work of art by the award winning artist, Mary Grierson. To celebrate the royal wedding, Miss Grierson used the language of flowers, so fashionable in Victoria's day, as a most appropriate theme. The bouquet's pink roses represent purity and loveliness, the delicate pinks speak of pure and ardent love, violets are a promise of faithfulness, forget-me-nots tell of love that is true, the fragrant cowslips express elegance and grace, and heartsease, the wild pansy, proclaims 'my thoughts are always with you'. The bouquet is framed with a border of royal blue daintily edged on both sides with 22 carat gold. A regal cartouche bears the monograms of the couple and the Prince of Wales feathers complete the design.

A fascinating wooden toy (Plate 635) was made by Peter de Witt of Faversham in Kent. The royal coach, with two postillions and a coach driver, is drawn by four horses, preceded and followed by a Lifeguard and a Horseguard with six Guardsmen presenting arms to the passing coach. The door of the coach has the royal arms and there is a caption:

Plate 633A. *J & J May betrothal and marriage mugs.* ***B.*** *Royal Doulton flower plate.* ***C.*** *Bell's Scotch whisky decanter.*

Plate 634A. *Pair of engraved wine glasses.* ***B.*** *Paragon loving cup.* ***C.*** *Royal Crown Derby dish.*

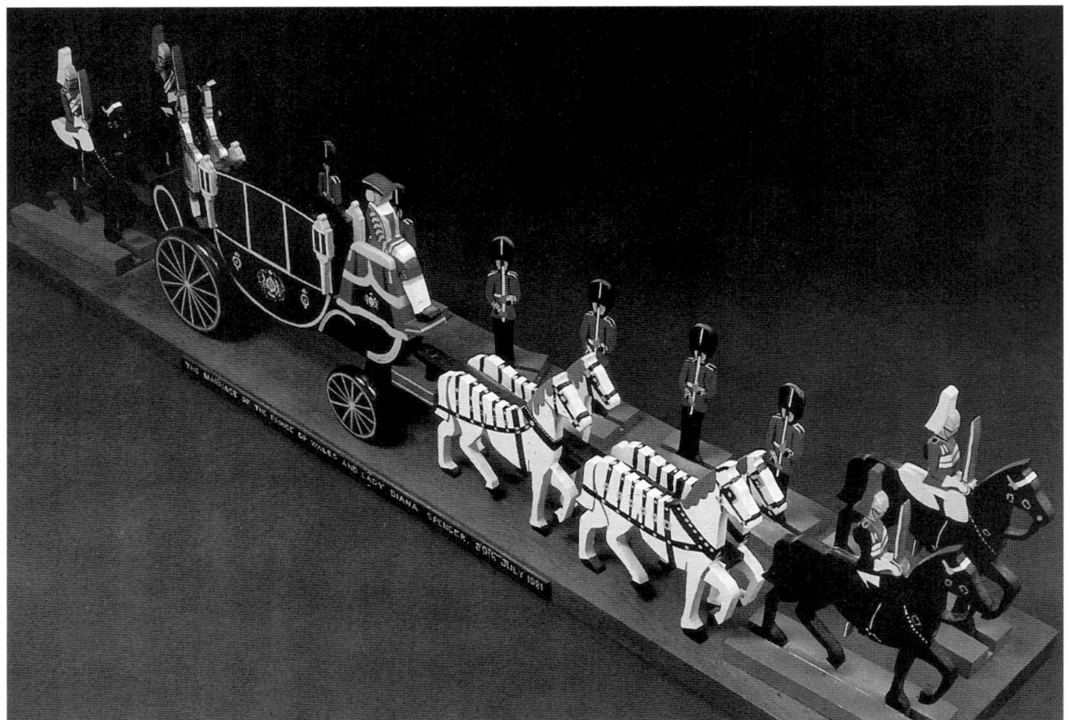

Plate 635. *Peter de Witt royal coach with outriders and guards.*

Plate 636. (left to right) A. *Courage's Prince's Ale.* **B.** *Harveys Sherry Bristol Cream Magnum.* **C.** *Brain's Prince's Ale.* **D.** *Jigsaw Puzzle.* **E.** *Whyte and Mackay whisky flask.* **F.** *Royalist Muscato Spumante.*

Plate 637. (left to right) A. *Hornsey Pottery black and gold mug.* ***B.*** *Rodda Cornish milk churn.* ***C.*** *Ewenny Pottery mug.* ***D.*** *Mrs Bridge's marmalade jar.* ***E.*** *New Quay Cardiganshire beaker.* ***F.*** *Chiswick ceramic teapot.* ***G.*** *Craven York toffee assortment in Hornsey Pottery mug.*

'Marriage of the Prince of Wales and Lady Diana Spencer, 29th July, 1981'.

At the lower end of the price scale are mugs, one for Cardiff and one for New Quay, Cardiganshire, both by Coronet Pottery of Prestatyn. Both carry, in different designs, the heads of Prince Charles and Lady Diana Spencer, in one case surmounted by the dragon and the royal flowers, the other, the Prince of Wales feathers without any flowers.

There were bottles of ale, champagne, port and sherry. A magnum of sherry (Plate 636B), similar to that produced for the coronation by John Harvey and Sons Ltd., has the inscription, 'Harvey's Bristol Cream Choicest of Old Full Pale Sherry Bottled in Bristol by John Harvey to commemorate the Wedding'. Muscato Spumante entitled 'Royalist', an Italian sparkling white wine made from muscat grapes, shipped by Victoria Wine Company, has around the neck a silver bell and the date in silver foil (Plate 636F).

Whyte and Mackay provided a glass flask of their whisky (Plate 636E) for the wedding, the front of the decanter has a metal label with the Prince of Wales feathers, the royal flowers and the caption: 'The Royal Wedding, Charles and Diana' and the date.

Courage produced a half pint bottle of their ceremonial ale with an inscription on the label commemorating the marriage (Plate 636A).

The independent brewery, Brain's of Cardiff, had a half pint bottle entitled 'Prince's Ale' (Plate 636C).

Sarcey, the well known champagne manufacturers, produced champagne, ranging from bottles to jeroboams.

A commemorative porcelain bell-shaped decanter from Bell's (Plate 633) has portraits of Prince Charles and Lady Diana in a heart-shaped cartouche surmounted by the royal crown and the royal supporters. The Prince of Wales feathers and the dragon also appear, together with the date of the wedding.

Ewenny Pottery made a mug (Plate 637C) which carries portraits of Prince Charles and Lady Diana surmounted by the Prince of Wales feathers and the date of the wedding.

An amusing teapot by Chiswick Ceramics (Plate 637F) has a blue and white transfer of royal flowers and the royal coat of arms, the handle is moulded in the shape of the royal flowers and the lid of the teapot is in the shape of a crown surmounted by the Prince of Wales feathers.

His title as Duke of Cornwall is recorded by A.E. Rodda, the Creamery, Scorier, Redruth, Cornwall in the shape of a milk churn (Plate 637B). It carries the silhouette portraits of Prince Charles and Lady Diana each side of the arms of the Duchy of Cornwall surmounted by the royal crown. The reverse of the churn carries the full arms of the Duchy with the jackdaws as supporters.

Novelties for the wedding took the same form as those for the silver jubilee. A large number of chocolate, biscuit and toffee manufacturers provided their goods in specially designed tins for the occasion (Plate 638); Meltis Newberry Fruits; a royal blend of fine tea carrying portraits of the Prince and Lady Diana and also of St Paul's Cathedral; a tea

Plate 638. (left to right) *A. Morny's soap. B. Callard and Bowser round toffee tin. C. Travel sweets – Smith and Kendon. D. Cadbury's Milk Tray Chocolates tin. E. Tea caddy from Bath. F. Austin Mini Metro. G. Aidee's soap. H. Matchbox London bus. I. Meltis Newberry Fruits tin.*

Plate 638J. *Mug to record the separation of the Prince and Princess of Wales.*

Plate 638K. *J & S Chown mug for the Queen's 'Annus Horribilus'.*

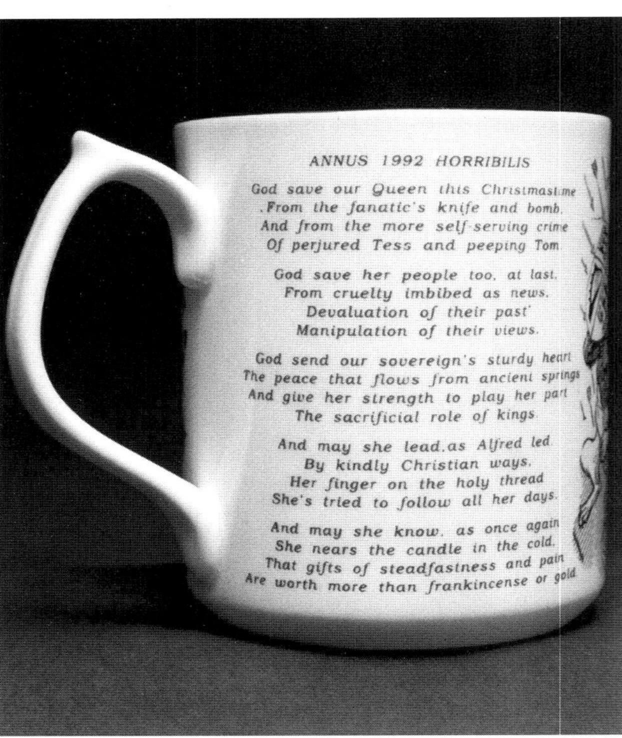

ANNUS 1992 HORRIBILIS
God save our Queen this Christmastime
From the fanatic's knife and bomb,
And from the more self-serving crime
Of perjured Tess and peeping Tom.
God save her people too, at last,
From cruelty imbibed as news,
Devaluation of their past
Manipulation of their views.
God send our sovereign's sturdy heart
The peace that flows from ancient springs
And give her strength to play her part
The sacrificial role of kings
And may she lead as Alfred led
By kindly Christian ways,
Her finger on the holy thread
She's tried to follow all her days.
And may she know, as once again
She nears the candle in the cold,
That gifts of steadfastness and pain
Are worth more than frankincense or gold.

Plate 639 (left to right) A. *Portmeirion loving cup.* ***B.*** *Royal blend of tea.* ***C.*** *Rye Pottery loving cup.* ***D.*** *Royal wedding holdall.* ***E.*** *Pack of cards.* ***F.*** *Petticoat shortbread tin.*

caddy captioned, 'Fine Quality Tea from the Jubilee Coffee Roasting Co., Bath' and a Cadbury's tin similar to that for the jubilee on a purple background bearing portraits, containing a selection of Milk Tray Chocolates. Thornton's provided a tin of Royal Wedding rock. Travel sweets in a round tin were manufactured by Smith Kendon Ltd. Waterton, Bridgend, Glamorgan. Petticoat Tails Shortbread by Crawford's of Liverpool and Callard and Bowser's Toffee Selection came in round tins.

Rye Pottery produced a two-handled loving-cup (Plate 639C) in their usual blue and grey colours with the Prince of Wales feathers on one side and Charles and Diana on the other.

Hornsey Pottery manufactured a mug in black with gold portraits and a gold inscription containing toffees with a label, 'Craven York Toffee Assortment of Candyland, York' (Plate 637G).

A jar of marmalade (Plate 637D) captioned, 'Mrs Bridges presents 1981 limited edition from Hudson's Pantry', carries on one side the inscription, 'A Royal Taste' 'Marmalade with Lochnagar Malt Whisky', including the Prince of Wales feathers, the initials 'C' and 'D' and the date of the wedding.

A jigsaw puzzle (Plate 636D) entitled 'A Royal Occasion' by Hestair Puzzles came in 500 pieces.

Matchbox provided a limited edition of the famous London bus specially produced to commemorate the marriage (Plate 638H). The bus is in silver and contains the wording 'The Royal Wedding' and the date and two small portraits of the heads of the bridal pair.

Portmeirion Pottery produced one of their well-known black and gold double handled mugs (Plate 639A) for the occasion.

There was a special purple Austin Mini Metro by Mettoy (Plate 638F) in a purple box, the door with the royal arms and initials 'C' and 'D'.

There were soaps and scent from Aidee's (Plate 638G) similar to those for the jubilee, fine English soap from Morny in a white plastic bowl and cover with the date of the wedding and the Prince of Wales feathers (Plate 638A), and a pack of cards (Plate 639E).

The couple paid a visit to Cardiff after their marriage and the Princess of Wales became a Freeman of the City. A plate records this event (Plate 640B), showing the Prince and the Princess in the Lord Mayor's parlour in a coloured photograph in the centre of the plate.

The marriage of the Prince and Princess of Wales ended in a formal separation announced to the House of Commons by the Prime Minister on 12 December 1992. A mug to record this sad occasion was published by Lady Grace China, Staffordshire (Plate 638J). It carries two separate head and shoulders portraits of the Prince and Princess, together and apart, within a fleurs-de-lis border with an inscription between them: 'Commiserations to the Prince and Princess of Wales on their separation. Buckingham Palace.... "Will no longer live together"' and the date. 1992 was a troubled period for the House of Windsor, culminating in a disastrous fire at Windsor Castle. In a speech at the Guildhall the Queen referred to 1992 as the 'Annus Horribilis' and a mug was issued by J & S Chown of Hayle, Cornwall, carrying a portrait of the Queen surrounded by a garland of holly leaves. The lion and unicorn being bombarded by arrows and a doggerel verse also appear on the mug (Plate 638K).

The Prince and Princess of Wales

At 9.03 p.m. on 21st June, 1982 their first child, Prince William was born and he now stands second in line to the throne. Some commemoratives were issued for this important birth, perhaps the most handsome being a loving cup painted by Michael Minoprio with a limited edition of fifty by J. & J. May, the commemorators (Plate 641F). It has gilt handles and portrays, in colour, Highgrove, the home of the Prince and Princess of Wales in Gloucestershire, in front of which is a perambulator in maroon with a black hood bearing the Prince of Wales feathers surrounded by stags, rabbits and flowers and trees. The inspiration for this may have perhaps come from a very rare cup which was published for the christening of Queen Victoria's eldest daughter, the Princess Royal.

Plate 640A. *Mug to commemorate the birth of Prince William.* ***B.*** *Plate, Princess of Wales in Cardiff to receive Freedom of the City.*

Royal Worcester produced an attractive coffee cup and saucer (Plate 641E) with a decoration of blue flowers, captioned: 'The Royal Baby, 1982', it carries the inscription,

Plate 641. (left to right) A. *Fluck and Law eggcups.* ***B.*** *Honiton plate for birth of Prince Harry.* ***C.*** *Coronet Pottery mug for christening of Prince Harry.* ***D.*** *Caverswall plate for birth of Prince Harry.* ***E.*** *Worcester cup and saucer for birth of Prince William.* ***F.*** *J & J May loving cup for birth of Prince William.*

***Plate 642.** (left to right)* **A.** *Mug for 40th birthday of Prince Charles.* **B.** *Powder compact for wedding of the Queen.* **C.** *Plate for the christening of Prince Harry.* **D.** *Glass dish for coronation, royal family.* **E.** Private Eye *mug for the Investiture.*

'A First Child for Their Royal Highnesses'.

Those naughty cartoonists Fluck and Law, well known for *Spitting Image*, provided three egg cups in caricature form (Plate 641A) – The Prince of Wales with a long nose and drooping ears, the Princess of Wales and a crying baby.

The birth of their second child, Prince Harry, has also been commemorated. Honiton Pottery made a plate (Plate 641B) captioned 'HRH Prince Harry' with the date, '15th September, 1984' and the full names of the Prince, 'Henry Charles Albert David' with a design of the royal flowers.

Coronet Pottery produced a bone china mug (Plate 641C) showing the Princess of Wales holding Prince Harry, and captioned, 'To Celebrate the Birth and also the Christening on 21st December, 1984 at St George's Chapel, Windsor'.

Caverswall provided an exclusive plate for the Peter Jones collection of Wakefield for the birth of Prince Harry (Plate 641D). The front of the plate shows a coloured portrait of Prince Charles and the Princess of Wales holding Prince Harry. Around this, in a design of crowns, are the next in line of accession, Prince William, Prince Henry, Prince Andrew, Prince Edward, Princess Anne, Master Peter Phillips and Miss Zara Phillips. The photograph is surmounted by the royal dragon and the royal supporters against the Union Jack and around the portraits is a wreath of all the royal flowers, including the daffodil. A large unmarked plate (Plate 642C) has a coloured photograph of the Princess of Wales holding the infant in his christening robe, captioned 'Princess of Wales with Prince Henry'. The interest lies in the dress and hat worn by the Princess.

To record their visit to Australia and New Zealand in March and April, 1983, Caverswall produced a mug which has a portrait of the Prince and Princess of Wales and the young Prince William in a cartouche and a design of blue and white scrolls with the caption 'Australia and New Zealand, Royal Visit, 1983', showing the Union Jack holding the Prince of Wales feathers on either side of which are the Australian and New Zealand flags. There is also the kangaroo and the emu together with a design of the royal flowers.

Prince Charles' fortieth birthday has been commemorated in a mug (Plate 642A) carrying a rather dour head and shoulders portrait of the Prince, on a red background – 'To celebrate the 40th birthday of HRH The Prince of Wales', which is also on the base. It was designed by Stephen Barnsley for Peter Jones China Limited of Wakefield and manufactured by Caverswall.

Princess Anne, Princess Royal

The title of Princess Royal is usually bestowed on the eldest daughter of the sovereign and it was not until 1987 that the Queen created Princess Anne the Princess Royal. She deserved this honour as a result of the great amount of work

Plate 643. (left to right) A. *Princess Anne Bethrothal beaker.* **B.** *Beaker for birth of Zara Phillips.* **C.** *J & J May marriage mug with assissination attempt on base.* **D.** *Beaker for birth of Master Phillips* **E.** *Princess Royal mug.*

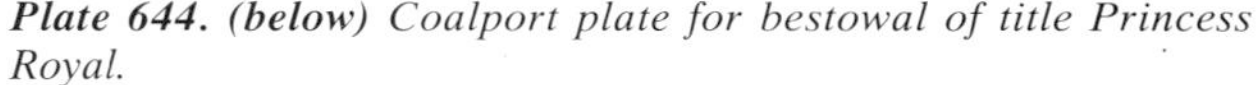

Plate 644. (below) *Coalport plate for bestowal of title Princess Royal.*

Plate 645A. and B. *Paragon loving cup to commemorate her marriage to Mark Phillips.*

Plate 646. Heritage Collection plaque and plate for the marriage of Princess Anne.

Plate 647. D. Beech sculptured head of Princess Anne.

she had done in the field of charity – in particular involved with children. This bestowal was commemorated by a china mug from J. & J. May (Plate 643E), carrying in gold letters the official wording from Buckingham Palace and dated 13th June 1987. It has a gold rim.

Coalport used a portrait of Princess Anne by Norman Parkinson as the central feature for a plate (Plate 644) to record the bestowal of the title Princess Royal. Above the portrait is her royal monogram held by the royal supporters. A design of blue and purple flowers is woven between her coat of arms. Designed by John Ball, with the date – June 13th 1987.

Princess Anne was the first of the Queen's children to enter the royal marriage stakes. In these days, with few foreign princes left in Europe, it has become the custom for members of the royal family to marry outside royalty and

Plate 647A. Caverswall mug to commemorate the marriage of the Princess Royal to Commander Timothy Lawrence.

***Plate 648 (left to right) A.** 21st birthday Caverswall mug for Prince Andrew. **B.** Wedgwood mug for creation of Prince Andrew as Duke of York. **C.** J & J May naval design marriage mug. **D.** Coalport marriage mug. **E.** Fluck and Law caricature egg cups.*

Princess Anne married Captain Mark Phillips. They both shared a common interest in horse racing and riding. Their betrothal on 29th May, 1973 was commemorated by an English bone china mug from Wilsons (Plate 643A) which has in the centre two joined hands above which is a horseshoe and around are the names of the Princess and, as he then was, Lieutenant Mark Phillips, and their birth dates.

Commemoratives for Princess Anne's wedding were considerable but again they tended to be in the higher price bracket. Ordinary people were however able to obtain the novelty type of commemorative souvenir such as tea towels and pennants, and a rather amusing revolving plastic lamp which has in the centre the engagement photograph of the Princess and Mark Phillips with a background of Westminster Abbey, the Horseguards and the Irish State Coach. It bears the date, '14th November, 1973'.

Paragon produced several of their loving cups in various sizes, the large one being very handsome (Plate 645) with gold lion handles and containing in the centre the entwined initials 'A' and 'M' surmounted by a crown and the year, 1973. Five hundred were issued. The inside of the rim on a blue background on a narrow band surrounded by gold contains both their names and underneath each of the handles in a purple heart are details of the marriage ceremony carried out by the Lord Archbishop of Canterbury at Westminster Abbey. The back shows a representation of the arms of the Abbey.

Portmeirion Pottery produced a mug, black with gold portraits of the Princess and Mark Phillips, in their well-known design.

The Heritage Collection provided a dish and a plaque described as a portrait medallion, rose manufactured by Hutschenreuther. It contains, in rose with a gold band, a relief portrait of the heads of the Princess and Mark Phillips in profile with their names in gold letters around the rim (Plate 646).

The same collection also had a sculpture portrait manufactured by D. Beech (Plate 647). This is the head of the Princess sculpted to include the long hairstyle she favoured at the time, on a mahogany stand.

The births of the two children of this marriage were commemorated by beakers published by Panorama Studios (Plate 643B and D). That for the eldest reads: 'Master Phillips, born 15th November, 1977' and bears a blue stork. In the case of their second child: 'Zara Anne Elizabeth Phillips, born 15th May, 1981', with a green stork.

These commemoratives, being limited editions, were not easily available to members of the public except at some cost. J. & J. May, the commemorators, published a mug especially designed by Clifford Richards for the marriage (Plate 643C). It has, in a heart shaped cartouche, the profile heads of the Princess and Mark Phillips and in another heart cartouche, in red, details of the marriage. The design includes Westminster Abbey and Big Ben and around the base are a series of galloping horses in between trees. The base has an interesting record. It reads, '20th March 1974 preserved from assassination' this is a reference to the attempt made to assassinate both the Princess and Mark Phillips as they were driving along the Mall one night after a function.

This marriage ended in divorce. A white china mug was published by Mayfair Ceramics to commemorate this. In the centre are portraits of Princess Anne and her husband facing in opposite directions, to the right, portraits of them on horseback in happier days. The mug also carries a reproduction of the submission of the court asking for a divorce decree, signed by the Princess and dated 21st April 1992.

On 12 December 1992 the Princess Royal married Commander Timothy Lawrence. A mug published by Caverswall records the event (Plate 647A). It shows the bride and bridegroom within a cartouche comprising blue and pink flowers and wedding bells, surmounted by a crown with the Princess Royal's heraldic label. The base states that the marriage took place at Crathie Church, Balmoral, Scotland.

Prince Andrew

The Queen's second son was born on 19th February, 1960, but there seems to be nothing ceramic to record this event .

Caverswall published a mug to record his twenty-first birthday (Plate 648A). It bears, in an oval, a sepia portrait of the head and shoulders of the Prince surrounded by the gold decoration of anchors indicating his naval career. Around the lip and base is a design of yellow and purple.

The Prince served in the Falklands War and became engaged to Miss Sarah Ferguson – popularly known as Fergie – who could claim descent from the Duke of Monmouth, the eldest natural son of Charles II. The engagement and marriage produced several commemorative items featuring their engagement photograph outside Buckingham Palace and their leaving Westminster Abbey after the marriage service.

These took the usual form of mugs and plates. Sutherland Bone China produced a miniature cup and saucer showing the bridal couple with a wreath of the royal flowers, including the daffodil. A silver plated spoon carried their portraits on the oval shaped handle.

An original mug came from J. & J. May, the commemorators, based on Prince Andrew's naval rank. The main part of the mug features his naval lieutenant's gold rings on a blue sleeve. Around the top are the names and date of marriage (Plate 648C).

Coalport produced an unusual mug for this occasion (Plate 648D). It shows, in colour, the procession from Buckingham Palace to Westminster Abbey, depicting, in their various carriages, the Queen and members of the royal family. It takes the form of three rows, interspersed with the Household Cavalry. The base records that it is to celebrate the marriage of the Duke and Duchess of York, 23rd July, 1986.

A similar mug was produced for the Queen's Ruby Wedding in 1987 with the same theme. The Ruby Wedding was itself commemorated in ceramic form, including a miniature cup and saucer, but also by a model in ruby of a miniature vintage Rolls Royce of about 1920, bearing on the passenger's door that it is to celebrate the Ruby Wedding of the Queen and was made for the *Radio Times* (Plate 603F). It

Plate 649. (left to right) A. *Hestair jigsaw puzzle.* ***B.*** *Cadburys heart-shaped Milk Tray chocolates tin.* ***C.*** *Waddingtons jigsaw in tin.* ***D.*** *Herb Farm tea caddy.* ***E.*** *Bell's Scotch Whisky decanter.*

Plate 650A. *Sutherland china mug for 50th Anniversary of the crowning of Queen Elizabeth, the Queen Mother.* ***B.*** *J & J May birth mug for Princess Beatrice of York with a design of eights.*

reads: 'Royal Celebration Collection', by Lledo.

Prince Andrew was created Duke of York on the day of his marriage and to record this conferment, Wedgwood produced a handsome mug (Plate 648B). Around it in a design of blue and gold is the head of the Duke of York wearing his naval hat in silhouette and a similar one of the Duchess of York. In the centre, being held by the royal supporters in black and gold are the royal arms surmounted by a royal coronet. The whole is based on a design of the sea. This was limited to one thousand.

Fluck and Law again produced cartoon egg cups in caricature of Prince Andrew and Sarah Ferguson (Plate 648E). Prince Andrew has a prominent nose and Sarah Ferguson has a determined chin. These 'Spitting Images' are rather cruel.

Cadbury's introduced a commemorative heart-shaped tin for their Milk Tray chocolates (Plate 649B).

A 500 piece jigsaw puzzle entitled 'A Royal Occasion' was produced by Hestair (Plate 649A) and Waddington's produced a limited edition of a jigsaw puzzle, in a tin, with a design of pearls, entitled 'Royal Wedding' (Plate 649A).

A Bell's Scotch whisky decanter similar to that for Prince

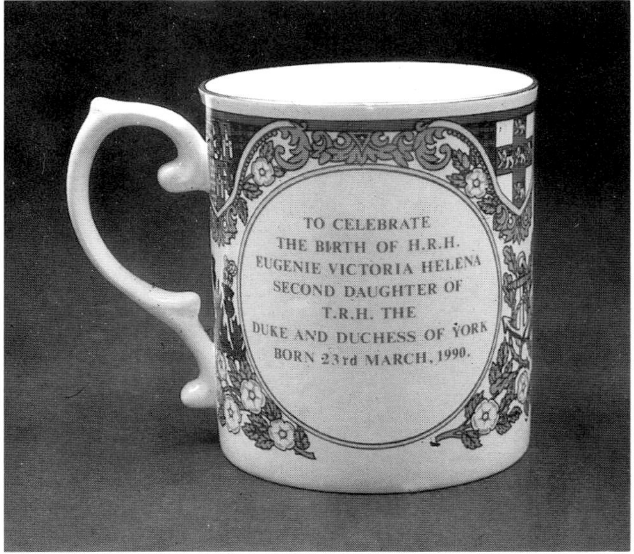

Plate 651. *Princess Eugenie birth mug.*

Charles has a design incorporating the Prince and Sarah Ferguson (Plate 649E).

A maroon and silver tea caddy (Plate 649D) entitled 'Royal Souvenir English Afternoon Tea Blend' by Herb Farm of Canterbury, hexagonal in shape, has portraits of Prince Andrew and Miss Ferguson with anchors and initials surmounted by a crown and 'Commemorating Their Wedding 23rd July 1986'. The lid has the royal coat of arms.

The Duchess of York gave birth to a daughter on 8th August 1988. She was christened Beatrice Elizabeth Mary. J. & J. May, the commemorators, published a mug to record this event (Plate 650B). The design is a series of eights to represent her date of birth, 8/8/88. The figures are designed in pink.

The birth of Princess Eugenie Victoria Helena – a delightful and historic selection of Royal names – to the Duke and Duchess of York is commemorated on a plate and a beaker by Caverswall. The centre of the plate carries a photographic reproduction of the York Family – the Duke, the Duchess holding the infant Princess Eugenie, and Princess Beatrice. Intertwined are the thistle and the bee for the Duchess, and the anchor and oak leaves for the Duke. The plate and beaker bear an inscription recording the birth and the backstamp exclusive to Peter Jones China of Wakefield who published the two items. A mug with a scroll handle and coloured enamel transfer print decoration with gilding to the rim commemorates the birth of Princess Eugenie Victoria Helena of York – 23rd March 1990 (Plate 651). On one side is a photograph surmounted by a ducal coronet flanked by thistles, oak leaves, anchor and white roses of York. To each side at the top are the arms of the 1st Duke of York and the City of York.

The Duke and Duchess of York agreed to separate but there is no commemorative record.

Princess Margaret

The second daughter of King George VI and younger sister to the Queen, Princess Margaret has been the subject of several commemoratives.

Her visit to Canada in 1956 is commemorated by Aynsley on an attractively shaped dish (Plate 652B), it has in the centre the head and shoulders of the Princess, wearing a diamond collared necklace, with a gold floral design around the border, which is pale green.

The Princess herself decided, probably for constitutional reasons, not to marry one of King George VI's equerries, Group Captain Townsend. She married Antony Armstrong-Jones, a highly skilled photographer and the son of a North Wales barrister, on 6th May 1960.

Rye Pottery, in their usual colours of green and blue, has a mug for the occasion (Plate 652D) bearing the initials 'M & A' in a cartouche surmounted by the design of a crown, wedding bells are on the other side.

The *Daily Mail* published an issue in silver to record the betrothal of Princess Margaret. The cover carries a studio portrait (Plate 653).

Paragon produced a tea set for the marriage (Plate 519). It is turquoise blue with royal flowers and the initials 'M' surmounted by a coronet and 'A' form a decoration around the rim.

A black and white mug (Plate 652A) records the official announcement from Kensington Palace, on 10th May 1978, which reads 'Royal Divorce, Her Royal Highness Princess Margaret, Countess of Snowdon and the Earl of Snowdon, after two years of separation have now agreed that their marriage should be formally ended. Accordingly Her Royal Highness will start the necessary legal proceedings'. The Princess has not remarried.

***Plate 652. (left to right) A.** Mug recording divorce of Princess Margaret. **B.** Aynsley dish – visit by Princess Margaret to Canada in 1956. **C.** Wedgwood plaque for chancellorship of Keele University. **D.** Rye Pottery marriage mug.*

***Plate 653.** Daily Mail 'Royal Romance' publication for betrothal of Princess Margaret.*

Plate 654. (left to right) ***A.*** *80th birthday Coalport plate – Queen Elizabeth the Queen Mother.* ***B.*** *Paragon 80th birthday loving cup.* ***C.*** *Panorama Studios 75th birthday plate.* ***D.*** *Crown Derby 80th birthday loving cup.*

Her appointment as Chancellor of the University of Keele in Staffordshire is recorded on a Wedgwood plaque in the well-known blue and white (Plate 652C), which bears in relief the head and shoulders portrait of the Princess, and on the rear is the inscription: 'HRH The Princess Margaret, Countess of Snowdon' indicating her Chancellorship. This was a limited edition of one thousand.

Queen Elizabeth, The Queen Mother

From the moment she became the Duchess of York, throughout the whole of her life as Queen of England and subsequently as Queen Mother, Queen Elizabeth has been held in the highest affection by the people. Indefatigable in her public duties, she has given great support to the Queen in many ways.

Her seventy-fifth birthday in 1975 was recorded on a plate by Panorama Studios (Plate 654C) in serigraphic medium. The centre has a smiling portrait of the Queen Mother wearing a feathered hat, surrounded by a design of yellow roses and forget-me-nots, with the caption '1900-1975', and at the base, the figure '75'.

For her eightieth birthday, Coalport made a quality plate, limited to an edition of one thousand (Plate 654A). It has, in the centre, the head and shoulders of the Queen Mother

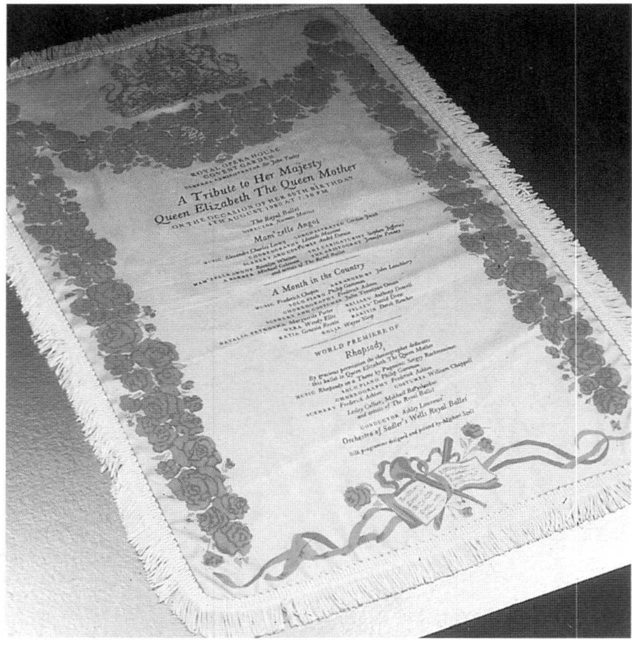

Plate 655. *Covent Garden silk programme for the 80th birthday.*

wearing the Ribbon of the Garter, and a tiara, surrounded by the royal flowers, including the daffodil, and around the rim are the various castles with which she has been associated: Glamis, where she was born, Clarence House where she now lives, Buckingham Palace, where she was in residence as Queen, Sandringham, which is one of her favourite homes, and the Castle of Mey in the north of Scotland, which she rescued from decay. There is a pink Queen Elizabeth rose in between each of the castles.

Royal Crown Derby produced a small loving cup (Plate 654D) in cobalt blue and gold with profile head in gold.

A silken programme for a Gala Performance by the Royal Ballet at the Royal Opera House, Covent Garden on 4th August 1980 is framed with a garland of pink roses (Plate 655).

Paragon produced a loving cup for her eightieth birthday, in their usual design, with lion handles (Plate 654C). In the centre is the head of the Queen Mother in gold in a cartouche formed by the garter and surmounted by a crown, held by the royal supporters, with a design of the royal flowers including the daffodil. The other side has the Queen Mother's initials 'ER' surrounded by a design of blue ribbons and red roses.

An intriguing pottery plaque was specially designed by Wharf Pottery (Plate 656). It has in the centre, in slipware, the Queen Mother with a hat made of roses, giving her

Plate 656. *Mary Wandrausch slipware plaque.*

Plate 657. (left to right) A. *Loving cup – opening Cardiff Magistrate's Court.* ***B.*** *Miniature cup and saucer.* ***C.*** *Royal Crown Derby plate.* ***D.*** *Lledo Rolls Royce.* ***E.*** *Miniature shoe.* ***F.*** *Walkers shortbread tin.*

customary wave and holding a rose, behind her is the head of a horse indicating her great interest in horse racing. It was modelled by Mary Wandrausch.

For her eighty-fifth birthday, Royal Crown Derby provided a loving cup bearing the Queen's monogram 'ER' surmounted by a crown with a cartouche of blue and gold and on the other side, the head of the Queen Mother in gold in a silhouette form. This was limited to five hundred.

A special mug from Sutherland China, produced for the Peter Jones Collection and limited to two thousand, records the Queen Mother reaching the fiftieth anniversary of her coronation (Plate 650A). The centre of the mug shows the Queen Mother's head and shoulders. She is wearing a pink coat, and the pink halo hat which she has favoured of recent years. Just as the toque was Queen Mary's hallmark, the halo hat is associated with the Queen Mother. The portrait is surmounted by the crown surrounded by the thistle and the rose. On the other side is the St Edward's chair within a cartouche around a similar design.

The nation rejoiced when the Queen Mother celebrated her ninetieth birthday on 4th August, 1990. Several events took place and many commemorative pieces were manufactured.

A review on Horse Guards Parade was a spectacular occasion. The programme for this event is printed with a design based on a marquee supported by decorated tent poles. The inscription reads 'A Birthday Tribute to H M Queen Elizabeth the Queen Mother – 90th Birthday – Horse Guards Parade – 27th June 1990'.

On 26th April, 1990, as part of her series of visits to various cities and towns, the Queen Mother officially opened the New Magistrates Courthouse in Cardiff. Coronet Pottery, Prestatyn, Clwyd published a loving cup limited to one hundred to record the event (Plate 657A). It bears the head and shoulders portrait of the Queen Mother wearing a yellow embroidered evening dress and a tiara. On the reverse is a photograph in sepia of the Stipendiary Magistrate for Cardiff.

Govier's of Sidmouth commissioned the Derby Factory to publish a plate and loving cup. The plate (Plate 657C) is fluted with a rich burnished gold decoration on a cobalt blue background. Designed by June Branscombe, it features a silhouette portrait of the Queen Mother wearing the sash of the Order of the Garter surmounted by a tiara. Below is a monogram 'E' entwined with '90'. The surround is richly embellished with thistles and roses.

The loving cup is similar to those produced for her eightieth and eighty-fifth birthdays and is part of a series which comprises the sixtieth birthdays of the Queen and the Duke of Edinburgh, the marriage of the Prince and Princess of Wales, the births of Prince William and Prince Harry and the wedding of the Duke and Duchess of York.

Aynsley published several items – a two-handled loving cup, a bon-bon dish, a beaker and a ten inch plate with a cobalt rimmed border and a bell. Each carries the coat of arms of the Queen Mother and they are similar in design to those produced by Aynsley for previous royal occasions.

The 'Glamis Castle Vase' is a handsome item, also produced by Aynsley, limited to ninety pieces. In rich cobalt blue and embellished with twenty-two carat gold gilding, the centre carries a hand-painted scene of Glamis Castle, the Queen Mother's ancestral home. The vase has a covered lid, two handles and stands on a round wooden plinth.

Plate 658. *Four Franklin Mint 'houses' plates.*

The same firm published a lion-headed beaker and also a plate which contains a design of flowers – rosemary, lavender, lilies of the valley, sweet pea, forget-me-not, lemon scented verbena, pansy, freesia, camellia, primrose and the Elizabeth of Glamis rose. At the base of the plate is a scene of Glamis Castle. Both carry the same official birthday portrait as the Cardiff loving cup.

Franklin Mint published a series of four plates in porcelain and gold (Plate 658). Each carries a different drawing of the Queen Mother's houses – Clarence House, Birkhall, Royal Lodge Windsor and the Castle of Mey. Designed by Rosanna Sanders, each plate is decorated with flowers in sixteen different colours.

Among the many other items is a fan manufactured by Fans Limited and designed by Peter Kent (Plate 659). Each leaf is hand-coloured by various members of the Fan Museum Trust. It features the Queen Mother against a background depicting castles and palaces with which she has been associated. The sticks and guards are hand made in Cumbria from fine horn with natural variations in colouring. The semi-precious stone rivets give an additional touch of distinction.

Glass crystal goblets from Stuart and Royal Doulton Crystal, enamel boxes from Crummles and Company, Poole, Halcyon Days and Staffordshire Enamels, Stoke-on-Trent have also been produced.

Coalport published a mug depicting the Castle of Mey.

Plates were produced by Rye Pottery, Royal Doulton,

Fenton China and Royal Albert China.

A shoe in blue china with gold transfer print bears the profile silhouette head of the Queen Mother (Plate 657E). It was originally intended to include a thimble, but this idea was abandoned. There are spoons from Watson of Solihull and tea towels from Ulster Weavers, Belfast.

Walkers Shortbread produced a tin-plate box carrying a photographic portrait of the Queen Mother – 'product of Scotland' (Plate 557F).

A paperweight from Swarovski, a small Tyrolean factory, bears the Queen Mother's coat of arms and an inscription amongst its pure and clear-cut facets.

The *Illustrated London News* published a special birthday edition entitled 'The 20th Century Queen' depicting the life of the Queen Mother and the cover is a colour reproduction of a portrait of the Queen Mother painted by Savely Sorina in 1923.

Two figurines – one from Royal Worcester, the other from Royal Doulton, both portray the Queen Mother in formal evening dress wearing the Sash of the Order of the Garter and the Royal Family Orders. That for Royal Doulton was modelled by Eric Griffiths and there is a difference in that the Queen is wearing an ermine cape stole.

Prinknash Abbey – a community of Benedictine monks, well known for their pottery works – produced an earthenware goblet.

Finally, a miniature Rolls Royce from Lledo – a replica of a 1925 Silver Ghost – bears on each side of the body an inscription to record her ninetieth birthday. The car is in rich royal purple and is contained in a cardboard box headed '90 Glorious Years'. For £4.95 this was a little jewel of a commemorative item (Plate 657D).

August is a special month for the present royal family and a plate has been published to record the birthdays of the Queen Mother, Princess Margaret and the Princess Royal – all of whom were born in August. The latest August royal birth, Princess Beatrice of York, is not included. Entitled the 'Royal Ladies Plate' it is published by Coronet Pottery and contains in the centre three oval photographic portraits of the three ladies – the Queen Mother in colour and the other two in sepia. Above is an elongated bunch of lilies of the valley tied in a ribbon bow. The rim consists of flowers – marguerites and the Elizabeth of Glamis Rose – with individual designs featuring the interests of the three ladies – bows and a lion for the Bowes-Lyon coat of arms of the Queen Mother; saddles, riding hat and crop for the Princess Royal; artist's brush and palette and two theatre masks for Princess Margaret, because of her interest in the Arts.

There is also a mug bearing only the heads of the three ladies.

Separate plates and mugs were produced for Princess Margaret and the Princess Royal by Peter Jones of Wakefield, designed by John Ball. That for Princess Margaret has a central portrait of the Princess wearing a tiara and pearls with a border of flowers surmounted by her coat of arms. Underneath is Kensington Palace. That for the Princess Royal is similar with a different design of flowers with a Princess' coronet, beneath is Gatcombe Park.

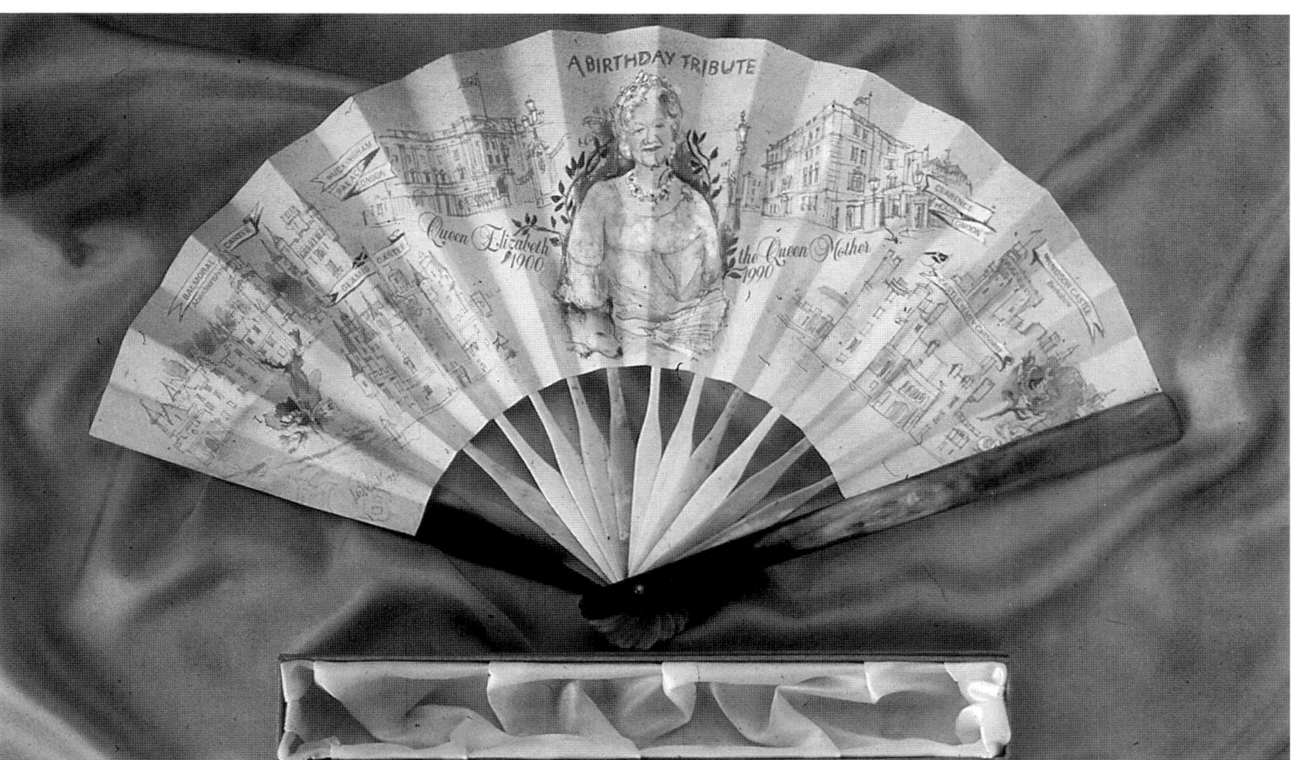

Plate 659. *Fan by Peter Kent for the Queen Mother's 90th birthday.*

Other British Royalty

The murder of Earl Mountbatten of Burma by Irish terrorists off the Irish coast in 1979 was recorded by a plate and a mug by Caverswall. The mug (Plate 623B) has a portrait of the head of the Earl within a cartouche, a wreath of purple and gold on one side, and his family coat of arms 'In Honour Bound' upon the other. On the base it reads: 'In Memoriam', the date of his birth – 25th June 1900, and the date of his marriage, 27th August, 1929, and the inscription 'His life ran like a golden thread of inspiration and service throughout the history of Britain this century'. The Earl was a great-grandson of Queen Victoria.

The last surviving grand-daughter of Queen Victoria was Princess Alice, Countess of Athlone. She married the Earl of Athlone, a brother of Queen Mary. A mug, limited to five hundred, by Panorama ceragraphics, records her ninety-fifth birthday (Plate 623A). A portrait of the head of Princess Alice is surrounded by a garland of yellow roses surmounted by the figure '95' and on the other side is the date of her birth, 25th February 1883, at Windsor Castle, daughter of Prince Leopold, Duke of Albany and grand-daughter of HM Queen Victoria. A photograph of the Princess was taken by Lord Snowdon for her ninety-fifth birthday. Her death on 3rd January 1981 has been recorded on a mug by J. & J. May the commemorators (Plate 623D). This shows in a funereal purple cartouche the caption 'In Memoriam' and her full names and the dates of her birth and death and on the base the fact that she was the last surviving grandchild of Queen Victoria.

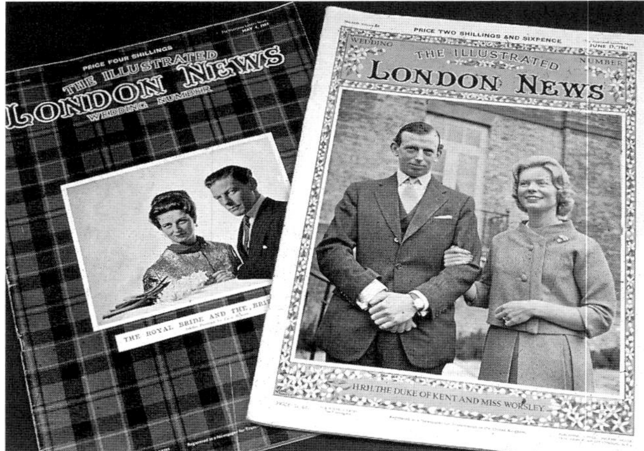

Plate 661. Illustrated London News *covers for the weddings of the Duke of Kent and of Princess Alexandra.*

The marriages of the Duke of Kent and his sister Princess Alexandra, have not been ceramically recorded, but the Worshipful Company of Cardmakers produced packs of cards for the two occasions (Plate 660). Each shows the

***Plate 660. Packs of cards for: A.** Marriage of the Duke of Kent and Princess Alexandra. **B.** Visit of the Queen to Copenhagen. **C.** The Investiture of the Prince of Wales. **D.** The Coronation Royal Pageant.*

Plate 662A. *Goss plate to commemorate the tenth wedding anniversary of the Prince and Princess of Wales.* ***B.*** *War-time plate for Queen Wilhelmina of the Netherlands.*

bridal pair leaving, in the case of the Duke, York Minister, and in the case of Princess Alexandra, Westminster Abbey.

The *Illustrated London News* published wedding numbers for both marriages (Plate 661). The front covers carry photographs. That for Princess Alexandra is on the Airlie (Ogilvie) tartan background recording Angus Ogilvie's Scottish ancestry.

Royal birthdays were not the subject of a commemorative record before 1900. In recent times they have gathered momentum and there is a danger that they may be overdone. The age of seventy-five would seem to be an event worthy of a commemorative piece and when eighty and ninety are reached these are such a landmark that they merit a mention.

Apart from reaching the age of majority for the heir to the throne the celebration of every decade seems rather extravagant. The next commemorative birthday should wait until the Queen is seventy-five, though ninety-five for Queen Elizabeth the Queen Mother ought not to go unrecorded in the commemorative field.

The same comment might apply to wedding anniversaries below twenty-five years. Perhaps because of the interest taken in the heir to the throne an exception might be made for the tenth anniversary of the marriage of the Prince and Princess of Wales. Aynsley China produced a vase to record this event. It is in turquoise and embellished in 22 carat gilding. The centre panel carries a hand painted scene of Highgrove House. It has a raised relief lid with a flute finial. The shoulder of the vase has finely lettered 'The Prince and Princess of Wales'.

Goss have a fine bone china plate which carries a family portrait. The floral border is made up of bouquets. Within the floral border are the two coats of arms and an illustration of Highgrove House completes the design. This plate has historical interest because it includes the two children (Plate 662A).

The Queen and Members of Foreign Royal Families

Most of the European royal families were descended from either Queen Victoria or further back to Princess Anne, Princess Royal, daughter of George II. Very few now remain.

Queen Wilhelmina of the Netherlands, directly descended from that Princess Royal, came to London during the last war, in exile. A plate recording this (Plate 662B) has, in the centre, the head of the Queen wearing a tiara, surrounded by a design of oranges and surmounted by the House of Orange coat of arms. Beneath are the flags of the House of Orange and the Dutch national flag, intertwined with the initial 'W' and around the rim of the plate are the words, 'Nederland Zal Herrijzen' (the Netherlands will rise again) in a scroll and beneath, in a similar scroll, 'London 1941'. This plate was published by the London Committee of the Netherlands Red Cross, Prince Bernhard Welfare Committee for the Netherland Fighting Forces and the Netherlands Emergency Committee. Prince Bernhard was the husband of Queen Juliana.

Queen Wilhelmina was succeeded by her daughter, Queen Juliana, who abdicated in favour of her eldest daughter Princess Beatrix on 30th April, 1980. A small tile records this event (Plate 663D). Within a circle surmounted by a crown are portraits of the heads in profile of Queen Juliana and Princess Beatrix.

The Grand Duke of Luxembourg is also directly descended through the same line and a plate recording the silver wedding of the Grand Duke and the Duchess, who was a daughter of King Leopold of the Belgians, was published by Panorama Studio (Plate 663A). It has, in the centre, within a cartouche in the shape of the crown, sepia portraits of the Grand Duke and Duchess surrounded by a border of sprays of lily of the valley and other flowers and surmounted by the Luxembourg twin coat of arms and beneath, wedding bells, with the figure '25'. The dates are 1953-1978, the inscription in French.

Prince Rainier of Monaco is also directly descended in a sideways direction from the same line and a mug was published (Plate 664B) showing the royal family of Monaco which includes Princess Grace, formerly Grace Kelly, the Irish American actress, and their children. The mug is designed in a chequer form, red and white checks.

King Juan Carlos I is directly descended from Queen Victoria through her youngest daughter, Princess Beatrice. Her daughter, Princess Ena, became Queen of Spain. Juan Carlos married a sister of King Constantine of Greece and they made a state visit to London on 22nd November, 1975. There is little doubt that since the death of Franco, when the King was restored to the throne, he has done a great deal to bring democratic rule to Spain, and he was accorded the honour of being able to address both Houses of Parliament at Westminster Hall upon this state visit. A plate records this event (Plate 663C). It has, in the centre, portraits of the head of the King and Queen and around, in ovals, the heads of former Kings and Queens of Spain, nine in all, the last being King Alfonso, who married Princess Ena and who was the grandfather of the present King. In a claim to the succession to the throne, the Prince's father was excluded and the throne descended to the grandson, the present King.

King Olav of Norway is directly descended from Queen Victoria through King Edward whose daughter, Maud, became Queen of Norway. King Olav is her son, and on 21st September, 1982 a plate commemorated the twenty-fifth anniversary of his accession to the Kingdom of Norway (Plate 663B). It is of Norwegian porcelain and the base indicates that the makers were Erling Kraje of Bergen, Norway. It is described as a 'samplatte' which translated means collector's plate. The plate has in the centre a coloured portrait of the head of the King in full uniform, displaying his medals.

King Carl XVI of Sweden made a state visit to London in July 1975. He is directly descended through the marriage of Princess Margaret of Connaught to the Crown Prince of Sweden. A mug recording this event has portraits of the King and Queen Elizabeth, both held by the royal supporters and in between are the crossed Union Jack and the Swedish flag (Plate 663E). The base records the visit in Swedish.

The Queen's visit to Denmark in May, 1957 is not ceramically recorded. However the Worshipful Company of

***Plate 663. (left to right) A.** Plate for the Silver Wedding of the Grand Duke of Luxembourg. **B.** Plaque for King Olav of Norway. **C.** Plate to record the Visit of King Juan Carlos of Spain. **D.** Small tile – Queen Juliana and Princess Beatrix of the Netherlands. **E.** Mug recording the visit of King Carl XVI of Sweden.*

Plate 664A. *Spode two-handled loving cup for entry to EEC.* ***B.*** *Mug of Prince Rainier of Monaco and his family.*

Cardmakers have come to the rescue providing two packs of cards, one red and one blue, showing the arrival of the Queen and the Duke of Edinburgh in Copenhagen (Plate 660B). Queen Margrethe of Denmark is directly descended from Queen Victoria through the Swedish line. Her mother was Queen Ingrid, a daughter of the Crown Prince of Sweden, who subsequently became King of Sweden.

The EEC

A fine plate was published by Mercian China for the entry of Great Britain into the Common Market in 1973 (Plate 603I). This has portraits of all the sovereigns of the EEC countries, the Queen, the King of the Belgians, the Queen of Denmark, the Queen of the Netherlands and the Grand Duke of Luxembourg. There are also portraits of the Presidents of France, West Germany, Ireland and Italy. The plate has the national flags of each of the countries concerned which form the ECC.

A very handsome two-handled loving cup was produced by Spode for the British entry into the EEC (Plate 664A). The design is a rich dark blue, with gold features. The centre has the Queen's monogram 'E' surrounded by the date 1973 and the shields of Belgium, Denmark, Eire, France and Germany. On the other side, Great Britain, Italy and the Netherlands. On the base in the language of each member country is the following sentence: By Order of the European Movement this piece has been produced in a limited edition to commemorate the enlargement of the European Community on 1st January 1973.

The Queen and the Papacy

In 1958, following the death of Pius XII, John XXIII was elected. Pope Angelo Guiseppe Roncalli was of peasant origin, and a fresh wind blew through the establishment-minded Vatican. The Vatican Council completely reorganised attitudes although there was – and still remains – some opposition to the abolition of the Tridentine Mass.

Crown Clarence published a plate to record the Pontificate of this humble and saintly Pope (Plate 665A). The centre carries the head and shoulders of the Pope wearing his white Papal skull cap and the highly embroidered Papal Stole.

Following his death in 1963 he was succeeded by Paul VI, Giovanni Battista Montini, the son of the editor of the *Catholic Daily Paper.* He entered the Vatican Diplomatic Service and was appointed Archbishop of Milan, during which time he became interested in social reform and was of liberal views. The Holy Year of 1975 took place during his Pontificate. Two plates, amongst other commemoratives, were published. A very fine porcelain plate (Plate 665C) by Di Doccia has in the centre and in relief the white head and shoulders of the Pope around which is a fluted blue patterned border. Richard Ginori's Panorama Studios produced a smaller plate (Plate 665D) having in the centre a design of the Papal Tiara and the Keys of St Peter with the head and shoulders of the Pope wearing his white Papal robe and skull cap and captioned 'Paul VI Pontifex Maximus'. Around the border in gold letters are the words 'Reconciliatio – Renovatio'. 'Annus MCMLXXV Sanctus' surmounts the central design.

Following his death he was succeeded by Albino Luciani, John Paul I – described as 'God's Candidate' and the 'Smiling Pope'. He refused the Tiara and the Sede Gestatoria. He reigned for only thirty-three days and was called 'The September Pope'. His death has been the subject of much controversy. Various theories have emerged, including murder by the Mafia because he was anxious to investigate the alleged corruption of the Vatican Bank. Despite his short reign, Sheldon of Nottingham published a

Plate 665. Plates for Popes: A. *John XXIII.* ***B.*** *John Paul I's visit to Great Britain.* ***C.*** *Paul VI.* ***D.*** *Italian plate for Holy Year.* ***E.*** *John Paul I.*

plate which fortunately commemorates this short pontificate (Plate 665E). The centre holds the head of the 'Smiling Pope' with his name and the date. The design of the plate includes, in maroon and gold, angels, the Papal Arms and the Dove of Peace.

His successor was the Polish Archbishop of Cracow who took the name of John Paul II. He is a highly charismatic Pope who followed the example of Paul VI in visiting foreign countries and has become the most widely travelled Pope. His custom is to kiss the ground of the country of his visit on arrival – Ireland being the first. His visit to Great Britain was highly acclaimed and the Queen received him at Buckingham Palace – a gesture which will have given enormous pride to her Catholic subjects, thereby cementing the cordial relations the Crown now has with the Vatican.

Several plates have been published to commemorate this Pope.

The plate commemorating his visit to Cardiff has the head and shoulders of the Pope wearing a mitre and carrying the Cross which, in the form of a staff, has become an important part of his pastoral function. The Pope stands outside the walls of Cardiff Castle where he had received the Freedom of the City. Published by K. Beavis of Cardiff, the caption reads: 'To commemorate the Visit of His Holiness Pope John Paul II to Wales, Cardiff 1982'. On the reverse are the details of the Pope's career from his birth on 20th May 1920 to his election as Pope in 1978.

Caverswall produced the Papal plate to commemorate the Pope's visit to Great Britain (Plate 665B). Designed by Holmes Gray, the plate has a central portrait of the head and shoulders of the Pope wearing his white Papal skull cap and the ornamental stole over his purple rochet. Around the border, between a design of crosses and keys, are the places he visited: Canterbury Cathedral, where he prayed in silence with the Archbishop of Canterbury; York Minster; Liverpool Cathedral and Glasgow Cathedral. Cardiff is represented by the City Hall.

Queen Elizabeth and Parliament

The Queen has been served by nine Prime Ministers. At her Accession the Prime Minister was Winston Churchill. It is understood that, at her special request, Churchill accepted the Knighthood of the Garter. A doll wearing the garter mantle of blue velvet, carying the hat, commemorates his acceptance. He had always refused a peerage and even the prospects of becoming a Duke did not attract him. His death on 24th January 1965 produced several commemorative items. Spode produced 'The Churchill Plate' (Plate 666), on the rear of which is the quotation 'He expressed the unconquerable spirit of the nation', setting out his full name and titles and the dates of his two periods as Prime Minister, 1940-45 and 1951-55. Also mentioned is that he was a British subject and an honorary citizen of the United States of America. The centre of the plate has, within a border of a central cartouche, the head of Churchill, held by supporters and a laurel wreath, above which are his coats of arms. The thick maroon border has a decoration of gilded acorns and oak leaves.

Wedgwood published a tankard entitled 'The Chartwell

Plate 666. *Spode plate for the death of Churchill.*

Plate 667. *'Chartwell Tankard' by Wedgwood.*

Tankard' (Plate 667). On the base are his full names and he is described as 'Soldier, Statesman, Man of Letters, Artist, Leader of a hard-pressed Nation in the finest hour'. It reads: 'here in the rolling downs of Kent, Churchill made his home from 1927 until his death in 1965. Behind his rise to political fame, Chartwell provided a constant background for his family, his literary works and his artistic and other pursuits'. The design of the tankard has, against a blue background, the forceful face of the great statesman and in two shades of blue and green 'Chartwell'.

All the national newspapers and magazines covered both his death and his state funeral at St Paul's Cathedral. A special edition of the *Illustrated London News*, in hard cover, was published to commemorate the death of Churchill, portraying various scenes of his life (Plate 668).

Huntley & Palmer's made a biscuit tin entitled 'World Famous Biscuits' (Plate 669). On the hinged lid is a three-quarter length portrait of Churchill wearing a morning coat, a

Plate 668. *Special editions of national magazines to commemorate the death of Churchill.*

Plate 669. *Death of Winston Churchill: two biscuit tins.*

Plate 670. *Sir Alec Douglas Home and Idi Amin mug by Mercian China.*

blue silk spotted bow tie and a heavy gold watch chain. Around the side are various motifs expressing his life: a paintbrush and a palette to indicate his interest in painting, a trowel to indicate his interest in bricklaying, a poodle for his fondness for dogs, and of course his famous cigar.

Another tin has on the lift-off lid a three-quarters portrait of Churchill seated, wearing the Ribbon of the Garter. Around his neck is the insignia of the Order of the Merit and the Star of the Garter is on his chest, and also his many medals. On each side are various quotations for which he was famous; 'We shall fight on the beaches, we shall fight on the landing grounds, we shall fight in the fields and in the streets, we shall fight in the hills, we will never surrender'. On another side 'I have nothing to offer but blood, toil, tears and sweat'. On another one 'Let us therefore brace ourselves to our duties and so bear ourselves that if the British Empire and its Commonwealth lasts for a thousand years, men will still say "this was their finest hour"', and the famous quotation about the Royal Airforce: 'never in the field of human conflict was so much owed by so many to so few'.

In more recent years Pol Roger have produced a special champagne entitled 'Cuvée Sir Winston Churchill' (Plate 573). The letters are in gold and the head of Churchill is shown in a circle surrounded by a laurel wreath.

Churchill was succeeded as Prime Minister on his resignation in 1955 by Sir Anthony Eden. Eden was not regarded as a great Prime Minister. This may be because he suffered from ill health during most of this period and his Premiership was overshadowed by the Suez Crisis.

There is very little known to record Sir Anthony Eden in either ceramic or in any other commemorative form. It is fortunate that the Commemorative Collectors' Society, on one of the plates published for the Queen's Jubilee, was able to include Sir Anthony Eden (Plate 614B).

Eden was succeeded, somewhat surprisingly, by Harold Macmillan. It was generally expected that R.A. Butler would succeed, but this never happened, and Butler has often been described as 'the Best Prime Minister We Never Had'.

Harold Macmillan, on succeeding Eden following the Suez Crisis, had some difficulty in getting the Conservative Party back on course. He represented Stockton-on-Tees, which brought him into contact with the problem of unemployment in the 1930s.

He called an election in 1959 and increased the Conservative majority considerably. He resigned as Prime Minister in 1963 and the Queen visited him in hospital in order to receive this resignation.

Once again it was thought that R.A. Butler would succeed, but eventually, after a great deal of internal fighting, the Earl of Home emerged as Prime Minister. He had renounced his peerage under the Life Peerages Act which Macmillan had himself engineered becoming, as a Knight of the Thistle, Sir Alec Douglas Home. Sir Alec also appears on the Prime Minister's plate of 1977 (Plate 614B).

A tankard published by Mercian China bears the head and shoulders of Sir Alec and also of Idi Amin, the President of Uganda. It commemorates the argument over two thousand Ugandan immigrants. Quotations from Sir Alec and the President are recorded. Sir Alec: 'I am sure that the British people as a whole will see the clear duty that rests upon us and will meet the problem pressed upon our Nation with our traditional calm and resolve'. Beneath is John Bull seated before a customs desk with a Ugandan holding the sign 'Uganda England'. Idi Amin is recorded as saying 'Those who remain be warned they will be sitting on the fire and they will find it very uncomfortable'. This appears to be the only other ceramic record for Sir Alec apart from his inclusion on the Prime Minsters plate (Plate 614B).

Harold Wilson succeeded Home in 1964 with a very small majority which was increased in 1966.

I'm Backing Britain was started in 1968 by five patriotic young typists working in the offices of Colt Heating and Ventilation Limited of Surbiton. The ladies decided to work an extra half-an-hour a day to help Britain out of economic crisis. An MP took up the cause and issued a slogan which included 'O.K. Enoch Powell, Quintin Hogg, Michael Foot, *Morning Star*, *Private Eye*, George Gale, Angus Maude and the critics of Help Britain Help Yourself – What would you do?' The campaign attracted a great deal of attention and support. The mug (Plate 675B) is earthenware with colour transfer print decoration in the form of a Union Jack.

At the General Election in 1970 Wilson was defeated by Edward Heath and these two Prime Ministers have been commemorated in some ceramic forms. They are both the subject of 'gurgling jugs'. These are portrait jugs. In the case of the Wilson jug, the handle is formed by a pipe (Plate 675G) and the handle of the Heath jug is in the shape of a boat (Plate 671B). Wilson is also recorded on a special plate to commemorate his being made a Knight of the Garter.

Edward Heath was defeated by Wilson in 1974. Heath was recorded on a Wedgwood Royal Tuscan bone china plate and also a jug to record his Premiership between 1970 and 1974. A rather cruel wooden figure shows Heath with flashing teeth wearing yachtsman's clothing (Plate 675A).

In 1976 Wilson resigned and James Callaghan became Prime Minister. There are a few commemoratives for Callaghan. An English bone china plate has, in the centre, a photographic portrait of Callaghan, showing details of his political career. A similar one was also produced for Harold Wilson.

Plate 671A. *Edward Heath jug.* ***B.*** *Edward Heath gurgling jug.*

Both Callaghan and George Thomas, while Members of Parliament for Cardiff, received the Freedom of the City in 1975. Two plates show in the centre photographic heads of the two statesmen, around which are laurel wreaths. The plates are in English and Welsh and contain the biblical quotation 'Euge Serve Bone et Fidelis'. They were published by Panorama Studios (Plate 672A and B).

A pair of Honiton pottery jugs in the Liverpool swollen cylindrical form are printed with photographic portraits of

Plate 672A and B. *George Thomas and James Callaghan – Freedom of Cardiff Plates.* ***C.*** *George Thomas, Speaker of the House of Commons plate.*

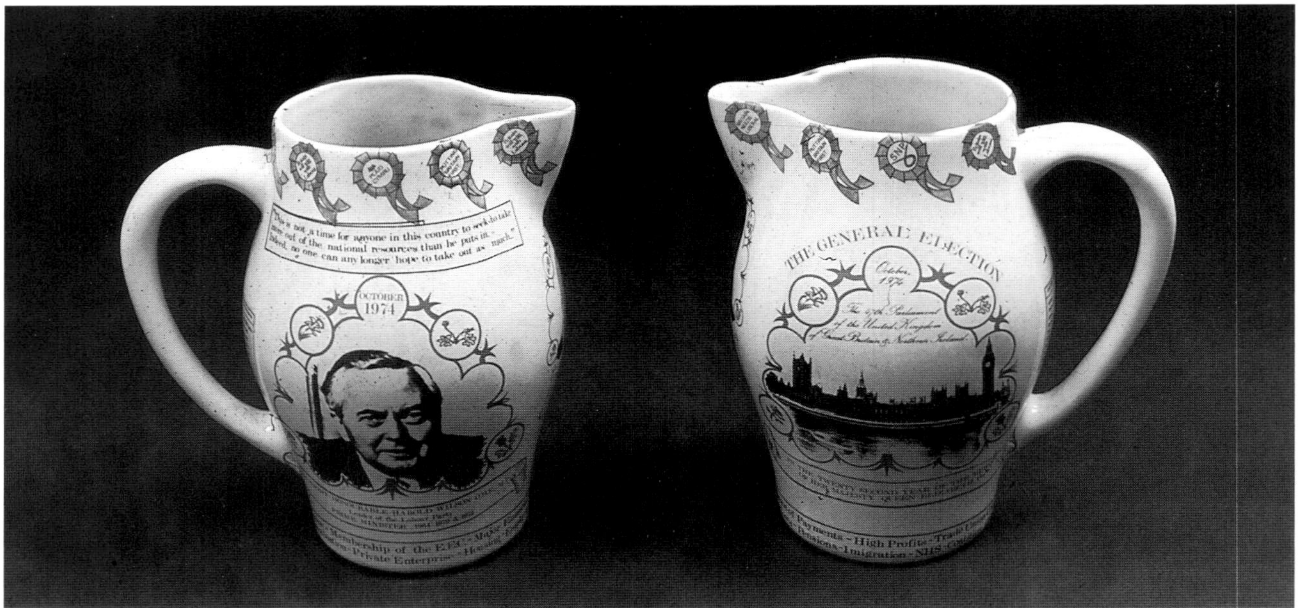

Plate 673. *Pair of Honiton jugs for Harold Wilson and Edward Heath, 1974 Election.*

Edward Heath and Harold Wilson (Plate 673). Under the lip is the Speaker of the House of Commons, Selwyn Lloyd, and the reverse has a view of the Houses of Parliament, commemorating the General Election of 1974. It is interesting that this seems to be the first occasion upon which a Speaker has been ceramically recorded.

In May 1979 the Labour Party was defeated and Mrs Margaret Thatcher became Prime Minister. For this unique historical event a Staffordshire bone china plate (Plate 674) was published, within the centre a photographic portrait of Mrs Thatcher, commemorating her election victory, making her the first woman Prime Minister of the United Kingdom. A mug also records the election result with portraits of Mrs Thatcher, James Callaghan and David Steel, giving the number of seats won by each party.

An amusing set of glass tumblers (Plate 676B) by Ravenhead Glass for the 1979 General Election shows a cartoon by Cummings on each glass: Enoch Powell is

Plate 674. *Mrs Thatcher as Prime Minister plate, 1979.*

Plate 675. (left to right:) A. *Wooden model of Edward Heath.* ***B.*** *'I'm Backing Britain' mug.* ***C.*** *Mug – Wapping newspaper dispute.* ***D.*** *Decimal currency mug.* ***E.*** *Mug for Kent miners on strike.* ***F.*** *Mug for 1974 general election – Thatcher, Callaghan and Steel, with result.* ***G.*** *Wilson gurgling jug.*

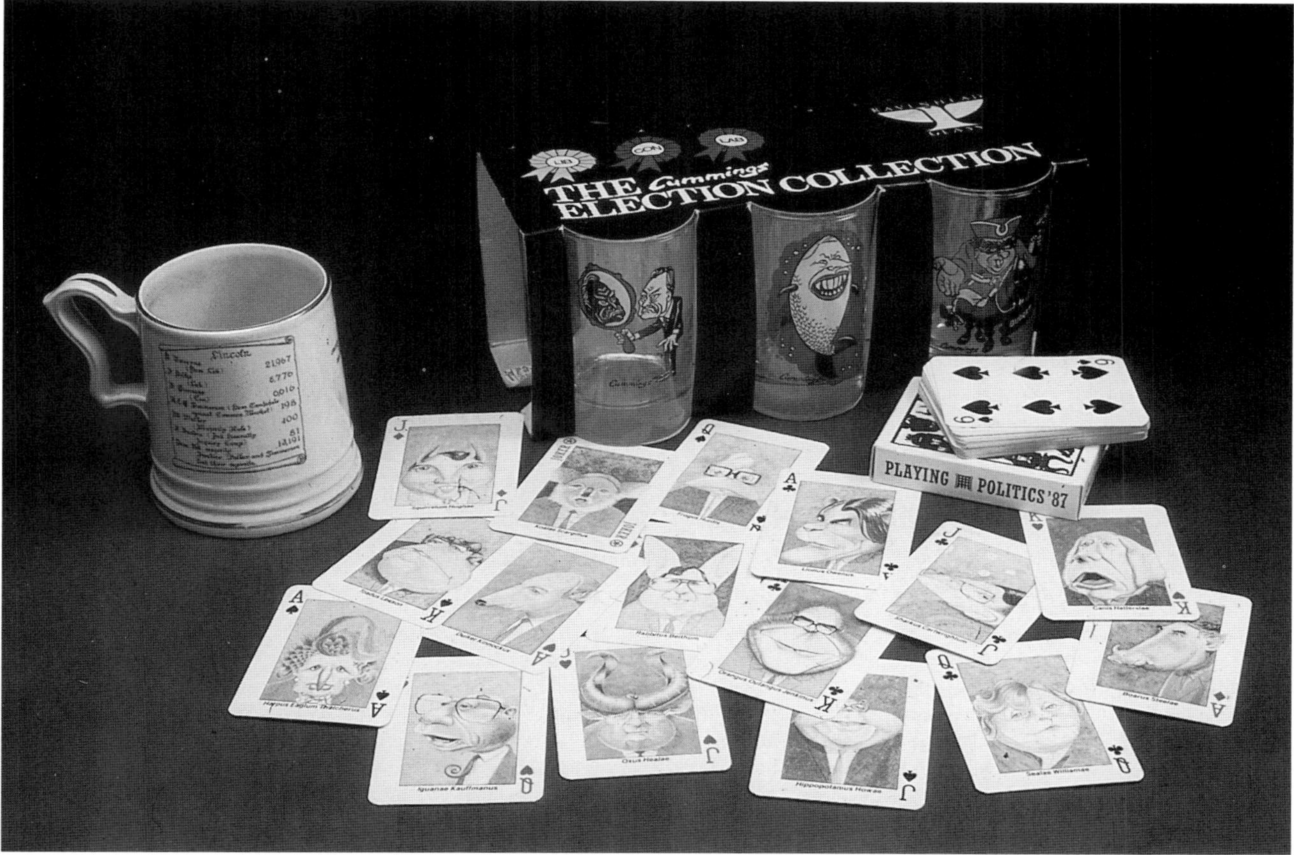

Plate 676 (left to right) A. *Dick Taverne mug for Lincoln.* ***B.*** *Cummings cartoon tumblers.* ***C.*** *Pack of political cards.*

looking into a green hand-mirror to see his reflection as a black face – a reference to his 'Rivers of Blood' speech which caused Prime Minister Edward Heath to sack him from the Government.

Edward Heath is featured as a grinning whale, Denis Healey as a highwayman on a horse carrying a bag marked 'Budget' and James Callaghan is lampooned as Moses carrying a tablet entitled 'The 10 Commandments – Follow me to the Promised Land'. Mrs Thatcher is pushing a pram captioned 'The Tory Party with 7 bowler-hatted men' and David Steel sits on a fence pondering the future of the Liberal Party. The three Party labels – yellow, red and blue – are on the top of the cardboard case. The whole set is entitled 'The Cummings Election Collection'.

Portmeirion published a black mug (Plate 680A) to record the Liberal 6,063,470 votes gained in the 1974 Election with facsimile signatures of the fourteen Liberal Members elected.

In 1973 Dick Taverne, the Labour Member for Lincoln, was becoming disenchanted with the trend of the Labour Party. He resigned his seat and stood as a Democratic Labour candidate. This was the beginning of the Social Democrat Movement which later became strong but unsuccessful in terms of General Election seats. Dick Taverne romped home with a majority of 13,191. A mug by Mercian China records this by-election (Plate 676A). It depicts the result and the votes cast for each candidate. A transfer shows the bicycle which Dick Taverne used to travel through the constituency. It carries a laurel wreath for victory. His success was short-lived. The seat has since returned to a Conservative Member.

There is an amusing set of playing cards entitled 'Playing Politics'. Each of the aces and court cards has a cartoon in animal form of a prominent politician (Plate 676C).

In the 1983 election, when Mrs Thatcher was again returned, Fluck and Law published a series of caricature egg cups; one for Mrs Thatcher with a shape portraying her long nose, and the other for Michael Foot wearing glasses (Plate 677). They are white glazed.

In 1988 Margaret Thatcher broke the record for the longest serving Prime Minister this century, formerly held by Herbert Asquith. Several commemorative items were produced for this event, perhaps the most attractive being a two-handled loving cup by Royal Crown Derby with a silhouette gold portrait of the head and shoulders of the Prime Minister against a blue background (Plate 678).

In May 1989 she had served a period of ten years as Prime Minister, having won three successive General Elections, a unique historical event. For this several commemorative pieces were commissioned.

Crown Derby manufactured a plate very similar in design to their loving cup (Plate 678). This was commissioned by

Plate 677. *Fluck and Law portrait jugs for Mrs Thatcher and Michael Foot and an egg cup for Neil Kinnock.*

Goviers of Sidmouth and has in the centre the head and shoulders of the Prime Minister in gold, around which are the words 'The Right Honourable Margaret Thatcher, Prime Minister 1979-89'. The main design is in cobalt blue, with the design of the national flowers, rose, thistle, shamrock and leek, and in an oval rondal on the base '10 years'. On the reverse, in addition to the reference of the ten years, is recorded that she has been a Member of Parliament for Finchley for thirty years.

The Commemorative Collectors' Society commissioned Panorama Studios to produce a plate for this event (Plate 679B). It portrays the Prime Minister in a central cartouche surrounded by the names of all those who had served in her cabinet since 1979. Portraits are shown of Sir Geoffrey Howe, Foreign Secretary; Douglas Hurd, Home Secretary; Nigel Lawson, Chancellor of the Exchequer; Lord MacKay

Plate 678. *Royal Crown Derby plate to commemorate Mrs Thatcher's ten years as Prime Minister and loving cup for the longest serving Prime Minister.*

Plate 679A. *Channel Tunnel plate.* ***B.*** *Panorama Studios plate to commemorate Mrs Thatcher's ten years as Prime Minister.*

of Clashfern, Lord Chancellor and the Secretaries of State for Wales, Scotland and Northern Ireland, namely Peter Walker, Malcolm Rifkind and Tom King. Surmounting the central rim are the House of Commons portcullis, two maces and the 'Dux Femina Facti' from Virgil's *Aeneid* Book I. During the production of this plate the potter died and only eight were completed. This caused the closure of Panorama Studios, a loss to the commemorative collector, since they produced many items for events which have not otherwise been recorded. Apart from Prime Ministers, not many well-known politicians have been recorded. This is probably the only plate which bears portraits of Cabinet Ministers in recent years.

There is little to record anything of the recent leaders of the Liberal Party. Nothing for Clement Davies and nothing it would appear for Jo Grimond. However, Jeremy Thorpe does

Plate 680A. *Portmeirion mug for Liberal Party in the 1974 election.* ***B.*** *Plate for the formation of the SDP, 1981.* ***C.*** *EEC referendum plate.*

Plate 681. *Decease of Liberal Party plate.*

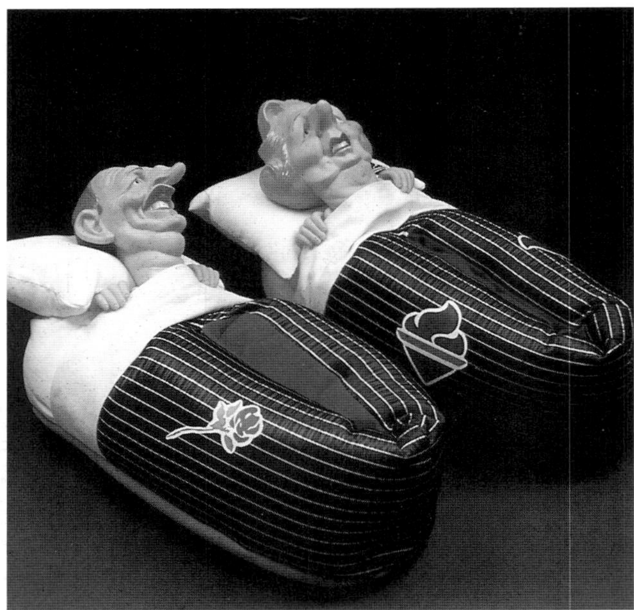

Plate 682. *Mrs Thatcher and Neil Kinnock in pair of bed slippers.*

appear on a plate which was produced to commemorate the United Kingdom's continuing membership of the EEC in 1975 following a referendum which was called by Harold Wilson. It has portraits of Margaret Thatcher, Harold Wilson and Jeremy Thorpe. It was produced by Royal Tuscan Bone China (Plate 680C).

Roy Jenkins, a member of Wilson's Cabinet, holding the Offices of Chancellor of the Exchequer, and also Home Secretary, resigned his seat to become President of the EEC in 1977 and a Mercian China plate records the event. It has, in the centre, a portrait of Roy Jenkins. As far as is known, this is the only ceramic record of Jenkins other than on a plate (Plate 680B) for the formation of the Social Democratic Party in 1981. He appears together with the other three founders, David Owen, Shirley Williams, and William Rodgers.

The failure of the Social Democratic Party to win through in either the 1983 or 1987 Elections caused a re-think to take place. There was a merger between certain members of the SDP and the Liberal Party and after a great deal of internal battling, the Liberal Party ceased to exist and the new Party became the Social and Liberal Democrats. To record the decease of the Liberal Party, a plate was produced (Plate 681). The centre has, on an orange background, the portraits of William Gladstone, Henry Campbell-Bannerman, Herbert Asquith and David Lloyd George, and around them the names of Herbert Samuel 1931, Archibald Sinclair 1935, Clement Davies 1945, Jo Grimond 1946, Jeremy Thorpe 1967, and David Steel 1976. Around the rim of the plate in large orange letters, are the words 'The Liberal Party' and its dates '1839-1988'. The reverse indicates that it was supplied by Silurian Ceramic Crafts Wales with the following inscription: 'Lord John Russell was using the term Liberal Party in 1839 and his administration of 1846 is sometimes regarded as the first Liberal Government; others reserve the distinction for Lord Palmerstone's 1855 administration. The first unequivocably Liberal Government was that formed in 1868 by Gladstone, under whose leadership these various elements became a cohesive Parliamentary Party. By 1989 the Liberal Party would have been 150 years old. This plate was commissioned by the Lloyd George Society on the occasion of the creation of the Social and Liberal Democratic Party 1988'.

Few Speakers of the House of Commons have been ceramically recorded. However, the appointment of George Thomas, Member of Parliament for Cardiff West, as Speaker on 3rd February 1976 has been recorded on a plate (Plate 627C), by a photographic portrait of his head and shoulders, wearing his full wig, and around the rim are the Welsh dragon, in between the portcullis and at the top, the maces of the House of Commons. On the rear is the following inscription:
'A tribute to the Rt Hon George Thomas MP upon his selection as Speaker of the House of Commons, February 3rd 1976 from Sir Charles Hallinan CBE and Sir Lincoln Hallinan DL, a father and son to whom he should forever be grateful for allowing him to defeat them', and around 'He who has no foe has no friend. They seemed like old comrades in adversity'.

Two very naughty Fluck and Law dolls show Margaret Thatcher and Neil Kinnock in bed (Plate 682). They are in fact a pair of slippers. Neil Kinnock is in a bed with the newly acquired red rose, whereas Margaret Thatcher's bed shows the Conservative symbol of the torch.

The one hundredth birthday of Mr Emmanuel Shinwell, MP, better known as Manny Shinwell, on 18th October 1984 was recorded on a Staffordshire bone china plate carrying in the centre a photographic portrait bust of Mr Shinwell (Plate 683).

Of the various controversial and political issues that have

taken place during the Queen's reign, some have been recorded. The miners' strike in which Arthur Scargill and the Government fought it out is recorded by a mug for the Kent Miners (Plate 675E). It is a bone china mug on a spreading foot printed in black with a call for support for the miners. A candle holder of tapering rectangular section is printed in black with face to face profile portraits of Mrs Thatcher and Arthur Scargill. 'King Arthur', as he was dubbed by the media, features on a plate, which carries his caricature head wearing as a crown, NUM, rather jauntily placed on his head, captioned 'Arthur Scargill – Old King Coal – January 1988' (Plate 684).

The miners from the Nottinghamshire coalfield who refused to strike and formed the breakaway union, UDM, are featured on two plates. The Thoresby area plate (Plate 685) features the head of a miner wearing his miner's hat and lamp, giving the names of the miners, captioned 'Loyal to the last – NUM 80 men 1984-85 strike'. Ollerton has a similar plate (Plate 686), with the names of 117 members. The miner is shown against the colliery shaft and it carries the additional words 'Ollerton Miners, Unity is Strength, Endure or Perish, Fight Oppression with Solidarity'.

For the dockers' strike, in which five dockers went to prison, a Mercian China plate with fluted rim commemorates the imprisonment of the 'Pentonville Five' (Plate 687). The centre of the plate carries the entrance to Pentonville Prison with the words 'The Law is an Ass' and around are the heads of the five imprisoned dockers and the TUC leader, Vic Feather, at the top.

The Wapping newspaper dispute of 1986 is recorded in a mug carrying the slogan 'Boycott' and the names of the papers, the *Sun*, the *Times* and the *Sunday Times* (Plate 675).

The conversion to decimal currency was recorded on a mug, black and red, showing the changes (Plate 675D).

Lord Hailsham, bell ringer and Brighton bather, appears on a Silver Jubilee 1977 mug for the St Marylebone Conservation Association (Plate 688). As Quintin Hogg he fought the by-election in the City of Oxford in 1938 at a critical time for the Conservative Party but he won and held it until succeeding his father as the Second Viscount. He was Lord Chancellor 1970-73 and from 1979-87.

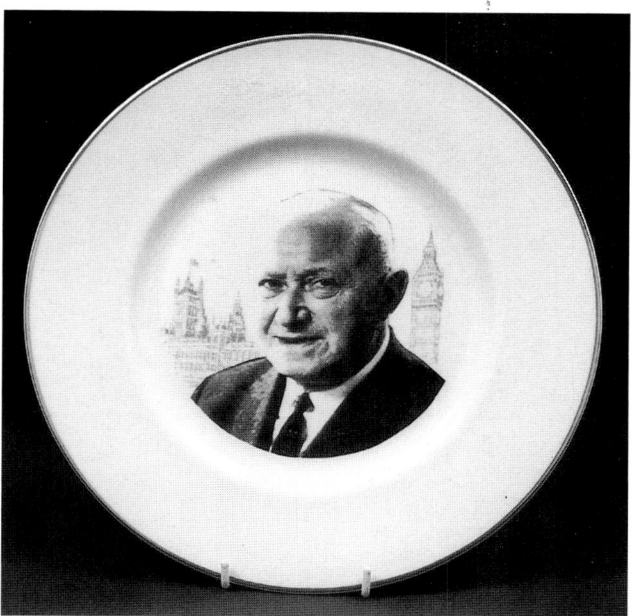

Plate 683. *100th birthday plate for Emmanuel Shinwell.*

This mug shows Lord Hailsham wearing his Lord Chancellor's robe and in addition there are portraits of the heads of Sir Wavell Wakefield who also represented that Constituency and also Kenneth Baker. It was specially

Plate 684. *Arthur Scargill 'Old King Coal' plate.*

Plate 685. *Thoresby miners plate.*

Plate 686. *Ollerton miners plate.*

Plate 687. *Dockers' strike, 'Pentonville Five' plate.*

designed by John Ward RA for the St Marylebone Conservative Association to commemorate the Silver Jubilee of the Queen in 1977.

The inauguration of the Channel Tunnel has been recorded on a plate by Panorama Studios (Plate 679A). The centre of the plate has in oval cartouches the Prime Minister, Mrs Thatcher, and President Mitterand of France, each on their national flags, and the caption to 'commemorate the commencement of the building of the Channel Tunnel 1987-1988' in English and French. Around the border are various historical aspects. 'Channel Tunnel Treaty signed at Canterbury on 12th February 1986', 'French Government Approval Granted 15th June 1987', 'Channel Tunnel Treaty ratified in Paris 29th July 1987', 'Royal Assent given in the United Kingdom, 23rd July 1987' in both English and in French. Interspersed are the royal arms and the French arms and beneath the portraits in circles, coming out of the tunnels, are trains. On the reverse is the inscription 'Work commences to dig the Channel Tunnel a) United Kingdom at Shakespeare Cliff Dover 1st December 1987, b) France at Sangatte near Calais, 1st March 1988' in both English and French. This plate was published by the Channel Tunnel Association in its Silver Jubilee year.

The Fall of Mrs Thatcher

Rumblings among Conservative back-benchers over the Poll Tax, culminating in the resignation of the mild-mannered Sir Geoffrey Howe, Deputy Prime Minister, led to a challenge to Mrs Thatcher and her subsequent fall. Her long term as Prime Minister came to an end when she resigned following a ballot by Conservative MPs in November 1990. This major

Plate 688. *St Marylebone Silver Jubilee 1977 mug.*

Plate 689. *Loving cup – Lady Thatcher with Sir Denis Thatcher.*

Plate 690. *Commemorative Collectors' Society plate and mug for John Major and his Cabinet.*

Plate 690A. *Kevin Francis Ceramics pre-election caricature jugs.*

Plate 690B.(left). *Election campaign mug for John Major.*

Plate 690C. *Potters Warehouse John Major Mug.*

Plate 690D. *'Playing Politics 92' pack of playing cards.*

political event has been recorded in permanent form. Goviers of Sidmouth produced a vase by Royal Crown Derby in the same cobalt blue as for her tenth anniversary.

The Commemorative Collectors' Society commissioned a loving cup and felt that included in the design should be mention of Denis Thatcher who was always in the background and ready to help his distinguished wife. A photograph of Mrs Thatcher, created a member of the Order of Merit, and Sir Denis is the centrepiece of the mug (Plate 689). The quotation chosen is her famous comment 'The Lady's Not for Turning'.

The Commemorative Collectors' Society felt that the election of John Major as Prime Minister should be recorded and a plate was commissioned (Plate 690). It shows the Prime Minister in the centre and around the rim are his biographical details and some members of his Cabinet:

Douglas Hurd – Foreign Secretary, Norman Lamont – Chancellor of the Exchequer, Kenneth Clarke – Secretary of State for Education, Michael Heseltine – Environment, William Waldegrave – Secretary for Health, Kenneth Baker – Home Secretary and Christopher Patten – Lord Privy Seal. A quotation from William Wordsworth's poem, 'The Excursion Book VII' is included in the design – 'A man of hope and forward looking mind'. A mug carries the same portrait.

John Major called a General Election on 9th April 1992. With the country in the depths of recession, with rising unemployment, businesses collapsing and high interest rates the Labour Party felt confident of victory, or at least a 'hung' Parliament. However, the Conservatives won an historic fourth term.

Kevin Francis Ceramics (on license from Spitting Image) produced pre-election caricature jugs (Plate 690A) of a smiling Neil Kinnock, a glum John Major and a cruel one for Margaret Thatcher with a knife plunged into her back.

A set of three campaign mugs was produced for the election itself, each bearing the head of Neil Kinnock, Paddy Ashdown and John Major, 'The Winner' (Plate 690B).

Another mug, manufactured by Potters Warehouse, Stoke-on-Trent, shows John Major, with the caption 'Fighting for the 4th Term' (Plate 690C).

Inter Col produced sets of playing cards in blue and red, with the main figures in each party in caricature. The Aces are John Major, Michael Heseltine, Paddy Ashdown and Neil Kinnock. The pack is entitled 'Playing Politics 92' and carries the House of Commons symbol (Plate 690D).

Sport

Horseracing is the sport of kings. The Queen enjoys it. She frequently visits race meetings, as does the Queen Mother, and the Princess Royal is a skilled equestrian. It is therefore a pity that not much has been done in the commemorative line.

However, there is a plate for champion jockey, Lester Piggott (Plate 691). The head of the famous jockey is in the centre wearing his jockey's cap with 'born 5th November 1935' and around the maroon and gold embellished rim are the names of his winning horses and, in another rim, 'The Derby, The Oaks, 2000 and 1000 Guineas and St Leger.

For the horse itself and to reflect the royal interest, Spode published a splendid plate to commemorate the 1970 St Leger, designed by Harold Holdway. Nijinsky is in the centre of the plate in sepia with Lester Piggott in the saddle with a gold laurel wreath surround (Plate 692). The border has a gold leaf and rose design between three shields bearing the arms of Lt General Anthony Firbeck, the race's originator (to the left). The arms of Charles Wentworth, Marquis of Rockingham, who in 1778 gave the race the name of his friend St Leger, are on the right. On the top are the arms of Doncaster where the race has always taken place. Joining the three coats of arms is a design of the white rose of Yorkshire

Plate 691. *Lester Piggott plate.*

Plate 692. *Spode plate for 'Nijinsky'.*

Plate 693A. *Plate for Colin Cowdrey, 'century of centuries'.* **B.** *Geoffrey Boycott, 'one hundred centuries for Yorkshire'.*

Plate 694 A. *Australia v England test match plate.* **B.** *Worcestershire championship plate.* **C.** *Brian Close ashtray.*

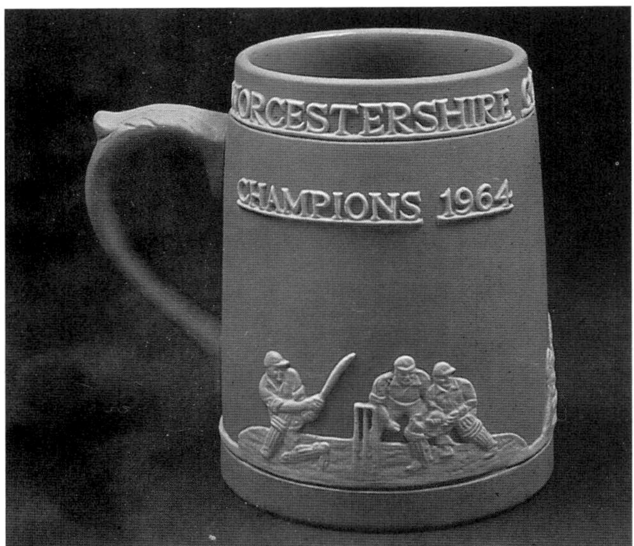

Plate 695. *Worcestershire Championship tankard.*

Plate 696A. *Ted Dexter tankard.* ***B.*** *Statuette of Freddie Truman.*

among plane tree leaves, signifying the avenue of trees which stretched from the town centre to the race course. This was the first of what was intended as an annual plate, but only two more were produced: 1971 Athens War and 1972 Boucher. On the reverse is an inscription to commemorate the 1970 St Leger: 'England's Oldest Classic run on the 12th September over 1 mile 6 furlongs and 127 yards at Doncaster Racecourse. Winner by one length in 3 minutes 6.4 seconds Nijinsky, owner: Charles W. Engelhard, jockey: Lester Piggott, trainer: Vincent O'Brien'. Published by Francis Sinclair Ltd of Doncaster.

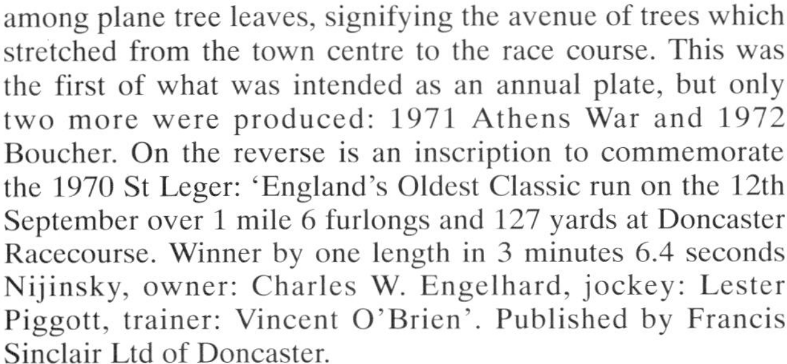

Cricket commemoratives are plentiful. Coalport has published several plates for those who have scored one hundred centuries. The design is based on the original W.G. Grace plate showing the individual cricketer in the centre, surrounded by a circle of bats, each of which carries the county played. Around the central portrait are the years during which they scored. One of those shown (Plate 693B) is for Geoffrey Boycott. The border has a design of cricket balls in red. The reverse carries an inscription: 'Geoffrey Boycott OBE, 100 centuries for Yorkshire 1963-85. X signifies not out', with a facsimile signature. A similar plate shown is for Colin Cowdrey for Kent (Plate 693A). The reverse inscription reads: 'M.C. Cowdrey CBE, century of centuries 1951-73'. The plate has a gold rimmed border and the design is all in blue. Other county cricketers are the subject of similar plates; John Edrich and Denis Amiss being among them. These are contemporary with the event during the lifetime of the cricketer and are therefore true commemoratives. Those produced for Hobbs, Ames and others no longer alive, do not fall into the commemorative category.

Coalport also published a series of plates for the Champion County. That shown (Plate 694B) is for Worcestershire in 1974. The centre carries a sepia drawing of Worcester Cathedral which overlooks the ground. The border consists of a series of seventeen county shields in colour with a yellow bat carrying a blue ribbon rosette with a sprig of laurel and a red cricket ball. The reverse has the club coat of arms: 'Worcestershire County Cricket Club established 1865. County Champions 1964, 1965 and 1974'.

Jasperware's tankard also records Worcestershire as Champions in 1964 (Plate 695). Based on the Wedgwood pattern in Wedgwood green, it carries in relief the Cathedral, a scene at the wicket, a bowler, the coat of arms and the club's name and date in relief.

A pottery figure of Freddie Truman depicts him on a

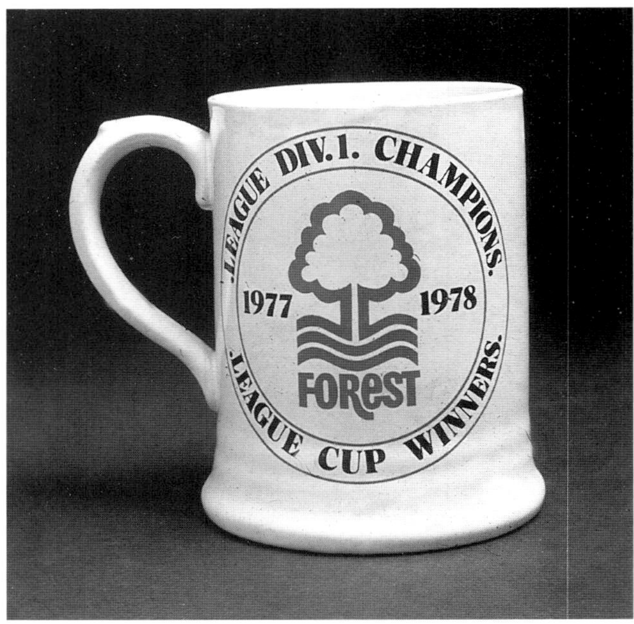

Plate 697. *Nottingham Forest League Cup winners tankard.*

Plate 698A. *Bobby Charlton plate.* **B.** *Torvill and Dean, skating champions – mug, thimble and dish.*

green base in bowling action (Plate 696B). The incised inscription reads: 'Freddie Truman, Yorkshire', by R. Underwood.

Ted Dexter appears on a tankard by Sandland Ware, Staffordshire (Plate 696A). An oval photogravure shows Dexter in action at the wicket captioned 'Australian Tour 1963'. The mug carries the occasion as 'Endon and District Club 13th Annual Dinner Friday 29th March 1963'.

A small ashtray by Sandland carries a black and white drawing of the Yorkshire Cricket Club, the Pavilion, Headingley, Leeds (Plate 694C). Facsimile signature Brian Close, Benefit Year 1961.

Royal Worcester published a series of Test Matches with gold etching and team signatures, and Royal Albert China covered the England and Australian Match at Headingley in July 1981. The scoreboard is printed in the centre of a plate (Plate 694A) showing Botham scoring 149 in the second innings. The decoration is in gold and the bottom of the plate has 'Howzat!' in gold letters.

The Football League may produce commemoratives for their clubs if the sovereign or a member of the Royal Family attends a cup final. Art Ceramico published a large white tankard (Plate 697) for Nottingham Forest who were League Cup winners 1977 and 1978. The centre carries the Forest logo and the reverse has facsimile signatures of the team.

Bobby Charlton's 100th cap is recorded on a Crown Staffordshire plate decorated with coloured enamel transfer print with gold rim (Plate 698A). The centre contains a

Plate 699A & B. *Whitbread Round the World Yacht Race tankard.*

Plate 700. *Formation of Malaya dish.*

Plate 701. *Rhodesia UDI mug.*

portrait head of Bobby Charlton with the inscription 'Well played Bobby'. The rim contains names of countries England played in which Bobby Charlton was a member of the English team with, top centre, an English cap and below the inscription '19th April 1958 to 21st April 1970'. The reverse has a facsimile signature: 'Bobby Charlton OBE of Manchester United and England'.

Despite the popularity of Wimbledon there seems to exist little of a commemorative nature. Golf, with names such as Tony Jacklin, Nick Faldo and Ian Woosnam has fared little better.

Torvill and Dean, world-famous skaters and winners of the 1984 World Championships have been commemorated on a beaker, a miniature plaque and a thimble, both competitors wearing their ribboned medals (Plate 698B).

Yachting interests are covered by the official Whitbread Commemorative Tankard for the Whitbread Round the World Race 1985/6 (Plate 699). Produced by Royal

Plate 702A. *Copper plaque of Bishop Muzorewa.* ***B.*** *Mug for creation of Zimbabwe with Robert Mugabe.*

Plate 703. *Death of De Gaulle plate.*

Plate 704. *Concorde plate.*

Plate 705. *Death of Laurence Olivier plate.*

Worcester, it has a design round the tankard of the world with the flags of competing countries around the rim and in the centre a compass with the zodiac signs. The base has mention of the Whitbread and Long John Trophies and states that this was the fourth race.

Overseas Events

The ill-fated Suez Campaign is recorded on an earthenware plate with a portrait of President Nasser of Egypt looking out over the Suez Canal which he nationalised, thereby causing Sir Anthony Eden, as Prime Minister, to launch an attack with disastrous results. No maker or manufacturer appears on the plate and it carries the name 'Gamal Abdel Nasser'. The President died of a heart attack on 28th September 1970 aged fifty-two, shortly after signing an agreement with Jordan to bring the ten day Civil War to an end.

Several countries in the Commonwealth obtained independence during Queen Elizabeth II's reign. A member of the Royal Family usually attended the ceremonial lowering of the Union Jack and the raising of the Independent State Flag. A shallow white dish with no mark or manufacturer, signifies the independence and formation of Malaya (Plate 700). The centre consists of the Federation coat of arms with the Malayan flag above and the date, 31st August 1957'. The rim of the dish is decorated with the arms of eleven states which made up the Federation.

When Rhodesia declared its independence in 1965 a mug was made for the Friends of Rhodesia by Drostdy Ware, earthenware with purple and brown transfer-print decoration (Plate 701). On one side is a full face portrait of Ian Smith surrounded by decorations of laurel leaves and the inscription above: '11th November 1965'. Below: 'Ian Douglas Smith'. On the other side: 'Rhodesian Independence. We have struck a blow for the preservation of justice, civilisation and Christianity and in the spirit of this believe we have this day assumed our Sovereign Independence. God Bless You All'. This is set in a decorative panel frame.

UDI was not popular with the Commonwealth – efforts to resolve the problem resulted in an attempt by Bishop Muzorewa to reach some agreement. But he was never recognised by Nkomo or Mugabe. A copper plaque was produced for the Bishop (Plate 702A). Zimbabwe became independent following the Lord Soames Commission, and a mug records this event. It has a full-face sepia portrait of Robert Mugabe inscribed 'Prime Minister'. The reverse carries the Zimbabwe flag inscribed 'Independence 18th April 1980' (Plate 702B).

The death of General de Gaulle in 1970 was recorded on a white porcelain plate with a coloured enamel transfer-print portrait in the centre (Plate 703). Produced by Royal Tettau, Bavaria, Germany, it has the inscription 'En souvenir de Charles de Gaulle'. This great Frenchman and war-time ally had differences with Great Britain over British entry to the Common Market. 'Non, non', was his approach. During his presidency he forbade any popular souvenirs but his death was widely commemorated.

The Church

For Church events little was produced. The Archbishops of Canterbury are featured on one of the Silver Jubilee beakers, and the Holy Year by a plate, both of which are mentioned in this chapter. But no known commemoratives seem to have been made for other Church leaders. This is a pity since the Church, in its different denominations, plays a vital part in the life of the nation.

The death of Cardinal Heenan, Archbishop, is an exception. A white porcelain plate by Panorama Studios has a coloured enamel transfer-print decoration. The rim has a

***Plate 706A**. 'Last of the Summer Wine' mug. **B.** 'Coronation Street' mug. **C.** 'Last of the Summer Wine' mug.*

design comprising the Cardinal's hat which is never worn, alternating with a stylised design of a pectoral cross. The top of the rim carries the arms of the See of Westminster. The centre contains a portrait of the late Cardinal with the inscription 'In Memoriam Cardinal John Heenan DD PhD, Archbishop of Westminster, died 7th November 1971. Requiescat in pace'.

People and Events

The first Concorde Transatlantic Service, London–Washington, is recorded on a plate (Plate 704) and a beaker. The design consists of two oval pictures, one depicting the Houses of Parliament and the other the Capitol Building in Washington. They are linked by a large Concorde showing its beak head rising majestically after take-off. The inscription reads: 'Concorde crosses the Atlantic' and the date, 'May 24th 1976'.

The death of Viscount Montgomery of El Alamein is recorded on a tankard by Panorama Studios. On one side is a portrait of the late Field Marshal wearing his beret in one frame and a later portrait in a second frame. An inscription contains his full title and decorations with his date of birth, November 17th 1894, and his death, March 24th 1976. The reverse reads 'Monty the hero of El Alamein'.

In the field of the arts and variety there is not much in the commemorative field. The death of Lord Olivier is recorded on a white china coupe-shaped plate with decorated

***Plate 707.** Beatles tin tray.*

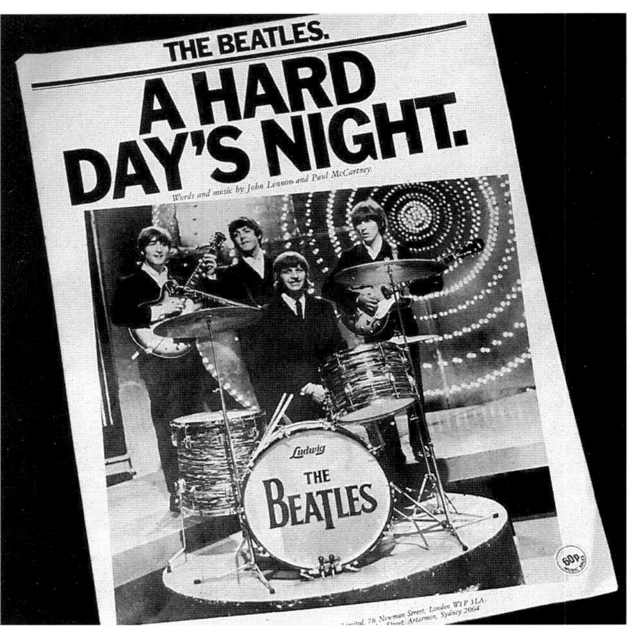

***Plate 708.** Beatles music sheet – 'A Hard Day's Night'.*

Plate 709A & B. *Lord Edmund Davies jug.*

escalloped rim and coloured enamel print (Plate 705). In the centre is a full-face portrait with an inscription 'Laurence Olivier 1907-84'. Above is the family motto: 'I rejoice in the house of the Lord even as the olive tree flourishes'. Around the rim are illustrations of various flowers mentioned in the plays of Shakespeare, identified on the reverse, together with fourteen quotations from Shakespeare. At the top are the mask symbols for drama and comedy. It was manufactured by Goss Bone China of the Royal Doulton Group.

Commemoratives are also recorded for television serials and soap-operas. Prince William Pottery produced a mug for 'Coronation Street' (Plate 706B). The design indicates that it must have been made during the time of Ena Sharples as her hairnet is visible. There is a coloured picture of the Rover's Return with doggerel verse: 'Life is so sweet in this little street, where everyone loves a good chat, nearly all that they earns aids the Rover's Return, and there's no greater cause than that'. The base carries the words 'Warranted 22 Carat Gold'.

Those three Yorkshire characters – Compo, Foggy and Clegg, from 'Last of the Summer Wine', feature on a set of mugs designed in Yorkshire. Nora Batty, with her untidy

Plate 710. *Queen's visit to Port Talbot mug.*

Plate 711. *Spode plate for the tenth anniversary of Coventry Cathedral.*

stockings, appears on a mug described as 'Nora Batty's Pin-Up Mug'. On another the three characters are easily distinguishable walking through the town, entitled 'Holmfirth Summer Wine town' (Plate 706A and C).

The Beatles are commemorated on a tin tray containing portraits and facsimile signatures of the four members of the pop group, John Lennon, Ringo Starr, Paul McCartney and George Harrison (Plate 707). This was manufactured by the Metal Box Co. Limited, Mansfield, Notts. A music sheet cover entitled 'A Hard Day's Night' shows the group playing (Plate 708). Published by Northern Songs Ltd, Music Sales Ltd, 78 Newman Street, London and Music Sales Australia Pty Limited, 27 Clarendon Street, Artarmon, Sydney. Price 60p.

The Law has not been well looked after in the commemorative field. A Liverpool style jug was produced by Panorama Studios to record the creation of Lord Edmund Davies as a Lord of Appeal in Ordinary (Plate 709). This was presented to him at a dinner in his honour given by the Cardiff City Council and reflects his long association with Wales and Cardiff, of which he was Recorder. It displays a transfer print taken from a photograph signed and presented to the author when he officially opened the Cardiff College of Commerce and Food Technology, in which premises he presided at the Inquiry into the Aberfan Disaster. The reverse has a transfer photograph of the Cardiff Law Courts, opened in 1904 and underneath the lip are details of his career.

Industry has seldom been recorded, although there have been many visits to factories and plant sites. 'A Mug for the Queen's Visit to Port Talbot' was produced for British Steel as part of her Jubilee Celebrations (Plate 710). Manufactured by Sadler, it has on the front the British Steel logo with the Welsh Dragon and Union Jack. There is a drawing in blue of the Works Deepwater Tidal Harbour which the Queen opened in May 1970. On the reverse, in a label on a grey background: 'Presented to the Children of Port Talbot Works Employees to commemorate the Silver Jubilee of H.M. The Queen and the Works 1977 Gala Day'.

Plate 712. *Falklands War mug.*

The building of Coventry Cathedral to replace what was bombed by the Luftwaffe during the Second World War was a major architectural achievement. There is no known commemorative for the consecration but Spode issued a fine plate to record the tenth anniversary (Plate 711). Although not within the parameters of a contemporary event, this plate at least recognises this important ecclesiastical achievement. The Coventry Cathedral plate has in its centre a representation of the angel which dominates the Chapel of Christ in Gethsemene. The angel is part of the mosaic back

Plate 713.*Gulf war garniture.*

Plate 714A and B. *Gulf war – invasion of Kuwait plate and mug.*

Plate 715. *President Gorbachov toby jug.*

Plate 716. *Margaret Thatcher toby jug.*

wall of the chapel designed by Stephen Sykes. The text surrounding the angel has been selected from among those inscribed on the great stone tables in the window recesses of the nave. The crown of thorns at the border of the plate reproduces the iron screen of the Gethsemene Chapel. The four figures, representative of the four evangelists, contained within the border are based upon those which appear on the Cathedral's processional cross.

Wars

The Falklands War in 1982 was recorded on a tankard by St George's Fine Bone China Company (Plate 712). It carries the Union Jack on which is superimposed a map of the the Falkland Islands and on the other side is the inscription 'to commemorate the liberation of the Falkland Islands from Argentine Occupation by Her Majesty's Forces operating from a Royal Navy Task Force 1982'. The blue and the white ensign of the Navy is superimposed on this inscription.

The coalition of forces which took part in the liberation of Kuwait resulted in a set of thimbles produced by the Thistle Guild.

More commemorative pieces have been produced for the War in the Gulf than for the Falklands. Aynsley China provided a garniture of three, five or seven vases (Plate 713). The largest and the centrepiece records victory in the Gulf. All are in cobalt blue with two handles and a lid embellished with gold. Each has a theme of land, sea or air. The centre depicts a tank with a battleship and three Tornado aircraft. Each stands on a mahogany stand.

Royal Worcester produced a plate and a tankard and a garniture of three vases specially commissioned for Saudi Arabia. The plate (Plate 714A) carries the Kuwait flag and the Union Jack surrounding the United Nations world motif and the centre carries a tank, a Tornado, a helicopter, a battleship and a British soldier in desert combat uniform. The back has quotations from the Queen, the Prime Minister, John Major, President Bush and Britain's Gulf Commander.

The Freedom of Eastern Europe, culminating in the demolition of the Berlin Wall, is commemorated on a fine portrait jug in the shape of President Gorbachov (Plate 715). The jug has the Russian Bear in red as the handle. The head of Stalin has been cracked and the President holds the word Perestroika'. Incorporated is a genuine piece of the Berlin Wall which was extracted on February 18th, 1990. It was modelled by sculptor Andrew Moss for Kevin Francis Ceramics who also produced a portrait jug for Mrs Thatcher (Plate 716), modelled to a design by Peggy Davies. It shows Mrs Thatcher, seated, wearing a string of pearls, holding in her left hand *The Wealth of the Nation* by Adam Smith. Her handbag is at her feet over the American Eagle and United Nations symbol on each side of the chair. The handle is embellished with a design of the Union Jack.

Hints for Collectors

Commemoratives are of historical interest and should be displayed, not kept in boxes or trunks in the attic or cellar.

The problem is always one of space, as they need to be seen to advantage. A collector must use discipline and perhaps specialise. The field is vast and collections can easily get out of hand.

Collectors of militaria may find it easier to select a subject – Nelsoniana, Wellingtoniana, or Napoleana can be the subjects of a compact display since they are rare and less easily available. When it comes to the Boer War the problem increases because much more was produced. The Great War would be a good subject to choose as commemoratives are cheaper and within living memory of some.

The same can be said of political pieces – this is a large subject and comprises not only actual ceramic records but figurines and busts in various forms. The Reform Bill of 1832 could itself form a special collection. Staffordshire figures are perhaps in a separate field as are medallions and medals. Some collectors have specialised in Gladstone and Lloyd George, for both of whom a large number of commemoratives were produced.

Royal memorabilia presents the problem of sheer volume and careful discipline is required; there are several methods.

If an overall picture is required, starting perhaps with George III, when items were produced in more quantity, even though they are still rare, one piece could be selected for each event known to have been ceramically recorded. To continue to our present Queen would entail collecting just one item for a coronation, marriage, birth, death, or any other event known to have been commemorated at the time. Where an event is not the subject of a ceramic, another medium could be used to 'cover' the event – a Staffordshire figure, a pack of playing cards, a medallion or medal. This may be too extensive for some collectors, in which case a selection of individual monarchs could be made. Some collectors have specialised in Caroline, the unhappy queen of George IV. Victoria or Edward VIII would also be a good subject for special selection.

Some collectors confine their interest to plates only - but this needs rather more space. Beware of wire hangers which do damage to plates – use plastic covered products. A combination of plates, mugs, cups and saucers make a more attractive display and if interspersed with figurines and tins can form a very pleasing effect.

Miniature cups and saucers and thimbles could be the answer for future collectors, as they are small and easily displayed.

As for the best method of display, this will vary according to the choice of subject, size of room, and display area. For those who cannot afford a George III breakfront bookcase or an Edwardian credenza, a stripped pine kitchen dresser can do marvels for a commemorative collector.

Royal memorabilia in tin form did not appear until around the Diamond Jubilee of Queen Victoria. Biscuit, tea, chocolate and mustard manufacturers produced fine examples of royal subjects in fascinating shapes. A collector of tins must be careful in making a selection. Scratches and marks of use are inevitable in old tins, and in many ways these add to the interest. But avoid those that are rusty. However, even a rusty tin is better than no tin at all and sometimes it is not a bad thing to purchase a rusty tin in the hope that in the future a better example will be forthcoming.

Although some Victorian tins are nearly one hundred years old, many can be found in almost mint condition. In some cases a tin is the only item which commemorates a particular royal event. A collection of tins of royal occasions discerningly displayed and carefully polished can, provided space permits, provide a most attractive example of history.

Index